DEMOCRATIC BLUEPRINTS

DEMOCRATIC BLUEPRINTS

40 NATIONAL LEADERS
CHART AMERICA'S FUTURE

EDITED BY
Robert E. Levin

INTRODUCTION BY
Governor Mario M. Cuomo

HIPPOCRENE BOOKS
New York

For information, address
Hippocrene Books
171 Madison Avenue
New York, NY 10016

ISBN 0-87052-466-6

Printed in the United States of America.

Contents

Acknowledgments   xiii

Preface by Robert E. Levin   xvii

Introduction by Governor Mario M. Cuomo
of New York   xxv

PART ONE
Toward a Better Future—Where the Democrats Stand   1

CHAPTER 1:
Governor Bruce Babbitt of Arizona
The Democratic Workplace   3

CHAPTER 2:
Senator Joseph R. Biden, Jr., of Delaware
Prescription for Economic Excellence   13

CHAPTER 3:
Governor Michael S. Dukakis of Massachusetts
*Innovation and Opportunity: Toward a
Competitive America*   31

CHAPTER 4:
Congressman Richard A. Gephardt of Missouri
*Making America First Again: A Plan for
Jobs and Growth for the Twenty-First Century*   52

CHAPTER 5:
Senator Al Gore, of Tennessee
Taking Control of America's Economic Destiny   64

CHAPTER 6:
Senator Gary Hart of Colorado
Facing the Challenges of Economic Leadership   75

CHAPTER 7:
Reverend Jesse Jackson of Illinois
New Directions for the American Economy   89

CHAPTER 8:
Congresswoman Patricia Schroeder of Colorado
A Rendezvous with Reality:
The New Global Economy   106

CHAPTER 9:
Senator Paul Simon of Illinois
Let's Put America Back to Work   118

PART TWO
The Goals and Principles of the Democratic Party   137

CHAPTER 10:
Governor Charles S. Robb of Virginia
Chairman, Democratic Leadership Council
Democratic Capitalism: A New Response
to Economic Change   139

CHAPTER 11:
Stuart E. Eizenstat, Former Chief of
Domestic Policy, Advisor to President Carter
The Crucial Dilemma and the
Democratic Response   149

CHAPTER 12:
Governor Richard D. Lamm of Colorado
The New, Painful World of Public Policy   157

CHAPTER 13:
Robert B. Reich, Professor, John F. Kennedy
School of Government, Harvard University
The Democrat's Promise of Prosperity   165

CHAPTER 14:
Alice M. Rivlin, Senior Fellow,
The Brookings Institution
Growth, Productivity, and the Federal Budget:
Advice for a Presidential Candidate   175

CHAPTER 15:
Congressman Thomas J. Downey of New York
Toward a Pragmatic Federalism   181

PART THREE
America's Agenda for the 1990s   187

A. Budget and Fiscal Policy

CHAPTER 16:
Congressman William H. Gray III of
Pennsylvania, Chairman, House Budget
Committee
A Time of Decision   189

CHAPTER 17:
Senator Ernest F. Hollings of South Carolina
The Borrow-and-Spend Economy: Just Say No   198

B. International Debt and Trade

CHAPTER 18:
Senator Bill Bradley of New Jersey
A Marshall Plan for the Nineties?   209

CHAPTER 19:
Congressman Charles E. Schumer of New York
Lessons of the Third World Debt Crisis:
Building a Sound Policy   218

CHAPTER 20:
Pat Choate and Juyne Linger of TRW, Inc.
Market Wars: Regaining Competitiveness
in the Global Economy   226

C. National Security and Defense Spending

CHAPTER 21:
Congresswoman Patricia Schroeder of Colorado
Stretching the Flag Too Thin   240

CHAPTER 22:
Congressman Ted Weiss of New York
President, Americans for Democratic Action
Revitalizing America's Economy Through
Economic Conversion   248

CHAPTER 23:
Gordon Adams, Founder and Director of
the Defense Budget Project, Center on
Budget and Policy Priorities
*Toward Real National Security:
The Reagan Legacy and Defense
Requirements for the 1990s*   256

D. The View From the State Capitol:
Leading Democratic Governors and the
Nation's Economic Future

CHAPTER 24:
Governor Bill Clinton of Arkansas
Making America Work: A New Social Contract   269

CHAPTER 25:
Governor Richard F. Celeste of Ohio
*National Economic Competitiveness:
Ohio's Response*   275

E. National Urban Strategies for the Future by
Leading Democratic Mayors

CHAPTER 26:
Mayor Dianne Feinstein of San Francisco,
California
When Education Fails, Democracy Fails   281

CHAPTER 27:
Mayor Raymond L. Flynn of Boston,
Massachusetts
*A Housing Agenda for America:
A Federal-City Partnership*   289

CHAPTER 28:
Mayor Edward I. Koch of New York City,
New York
*Compassion and Common Sense:
The Urban Agenda in 1988*   305

Chapter 29:
  Mayor Joseph P. Riley, Jr., of Charleston,
    South Carolina; Immediate Past President,
    U.S. Conference of Mayors
  Time for a National Urban Investment Policy   313

Chapter 30:
  Mayor Henry Cisneros of San Antonio, Texas
  Openings to the New Texas   333

F. The Crisis in American Agriculture

Chapter 31:
  Senator Tom Harkin of Iowa
  Why We Must Save the Family Farm   347

Chapter 32:
  Jim Hightower, Texas Agriculture Commissioner
  Grass-Roots Economic Development:
    From the Ground Up   359

G. Poverty, Hunger, Crime, and Pay Equity

Chapter 33:
  Mary Jo Bane, Professor of Public Policy at the
    JFK School of Government at Harvard
    University and Paul A. Jargowsky, former
    Project Director for the New York State
    Task Force on Poverty and Welfare
  A Democratic Framework for Poverty Policy   368

Chapter 34:
  Congressman Mickey Leland of Texas,
    Chairman, Select Committee on Hunger
  Hunger and Poverty at Home and Abroad   380

Chapter 35:
  The Honorable Elizabeth Holtzman,
    District Attorney, Kings County, New York
  Rethinking the Approach to Criminal Justice   389

Chapter 36:
  Congressman Geraldine A. Ferraro,
    Former Democratic Candidate for

Vice-President of the United States
*Bridging the Wage Gap: Pay Equity
and Job Evaluations*   396

PART FOUR
Nonpartisan Agendas for America   407

A. Full Employment: A National Priority

CHAPTER 37:
Coretta Scott King with Murray H. Finley
and Calvin H. George, National Committee
on Full Employment
*On the Road Again . . . A Six-Point Agenda
Toward a Full-Employment Economy*   409

CHAPTER 38:
Lane Kirkland, President, American Federation
of Labor and Congress of Industrial
Organizations
Jobs for a Healthy Economy   423

B. American Values and Economic Progress

CHAPTER 39:
Norman Lear, Television Producer and Founder,
People for the American Way
*Cashing in the Commonweal for the
Commonwheel of Fortune*   433

CHAPTER 40:
Robert Redford, Actor, Environmental Activist
Search for the Common Ground   445

C. National Space Goals

CHAPTER 41:
Dr. Sally K. Ride, Former Astronaut
Leadership and America's Future in Space: 451

D. National AIDS Policy and a National
Education Agenda

CHAPTER 42:
   Michael Zimmerman, Senior Associate Director,
   Human Resources Division, United States
   General Accounting Office
   AIDS Prevention: Views on the Administration's
   Proposed Budget for 1988   461

CHAPTER 43:
   The Carnegie Commission on Excellence in
   Education
   Education and Economic Progress Toward a
   National Education Policy: The Federal Role   471

E. Macro-economic Perspectives on the American
   Economy

CHAPTER 44:
   Raymond Dalio, President, Bridgewater
   Associates
   The Decline of the American Empire   477

CHAPTER 45:
   Dr. Henry Kaufman, Economist, Former
   Managing Director and Member of the
   Executive Committee at
   Salomon Brothers, Inc.
   The Need for a Better-Regulated
   Financial System   486

F. A Business-like Approach to
   Building Trust in the Democratic Party

CHAPTER 46:
   Michael W. Sonnenfeldt,
   Oh, to Be a Glad-to-Be-Back Democrat   498

Conclusion
   by Wilbur J. Cohen, Former Secretary
   of Health, Education and Welfare
   Needed: A New Political Agenda for the 1990s   507

Appendix

Biographies of Democratic Leaders   511
Index   535

Acknowledgments

OVER THE COURSE OF several months, many friends gave me valuable advice, encouragement and suggestions including Tom Byrne, Jr., Jeff Sachs, Ken Jacobson, Robert Schulman, Gary Gailes, Jim Barkas, Leslie Mann, Michael Manning, Frank Piuck, Julie Frank, Rabbi Leonard Guttman, Jennifer Lebsack, Todd Chanko, Steve Foley, Joe Rose, Richard Neustadt, Kristin Mannion, Jonathan Newhouse, Carolyn Harris, Fred Knoll, Matt Adell, Martin Varsavsky, Betsy Blumenthal, Morton Mintz, Simon Chilewich, Edward Newman, and Carol Levy. Brenda Goodman, Tom McVey, Kevin Greene, Robert Ware each spent several hours working on the concept for this book or editorial work or both. Their ideas and support made a significant difference in the content and quality of this book.

I also want to thank a friend who encouraged me with the right words at the right moment when I almost gave up on the book. I needed someone who believed I could do it.

Many of the contributors of essays to this book, besides producing great work, also offered excellent ideas and support for the book.

Finally, I appreciate the steadfastness and hard work of my staff, including Dore Hollander, who read and assisted in careful editing of various drafts for hundreds of hours. My secretary and administrative assistant, Kathy Cody, managed thousands of important details. I also thank Betty Marks, my literary agent, who worked hard to get the contract in the first place. Robert Schaeffer of Public Policy Communications helped considerably with national media relations.

These people were instrumental in the success of this project. They deserve recognition for seeing its potential when this book was only an idea.

You are a generation which is coming of age at one of the rarest moments of history—a time when all around us is crumbling. You have the challenge to lighten and enrich the lives of all those around you. In your hands—not with the current leaders—is the future of your world and the fulfillment of the best qualities of your own spirit.

—Senator Robert F. Kennedy,
speaking before students at Berkeley, 1968

Preface
Turning Point: America's Agenda for the 1990s

THERE ARE TURNING POINTS in each of our lives; there are turning points in the life of a nation. Each one signals change, new beginnings, new potential. Turning points have marked the advance of history and each defines the threshold to the future.

The presidential election of 1988 represents a turning point for the United States. We must make a choice among proposed public philosophies and governing principles. The result of our choice in leadership will determine our national course as we approach the twenty-first century. Either we can turn to a new national strategy and correct our economic problems or hold to our current laissez faire attitude and continue toward an economic decline.

Political labels like "liberal" or "conservative" do not accurately describe the choice we face in 1988. The choice is more fundamental: It is between the idea that government should not take major initiatives to help solve social and economic problems, and the idea that government can be a creative and dynamic catalyst for progress.

This is a book about the future of America. In order to define a new direction beyond our own economic turning point, Democratic presidential candidates, senior members of Congress, governors, mayors and other nationally recognized leaders throughout America have here articulated their vision and have charted a clear course for America in the post-Reagan era. Together, they have shaped a new political agenda for the 1990s. This book is a harvest of ideas—old ones, tried and tested, and new innovative blueprints that add substance to leadership style.

Our goals in this volume are to present a responsible and realistic vision of America's future, to offer several serious policy proposals for recouping our international economic leadership, and to focus public attention on our highest national economic priorities. One of the authors of this book will most likely be the Democratic nominee for president in 1988. Likely another will become the vice-presidential running mate of that nominee. Certainly, all of the authors represented here will continue to be engaged in the national debate about the direction of our country in the next decade.

The first essays are from the Democratic presidential candidates. They have made a serious effort to examine and discuss issues facing the nation. Although as you read this book, some already have dropped from contention, the viability of their ideas has not diminished and they continue to deserve an equal opportunity for national attention. Naturally, the media will focus more on the successful candidates' ideas, but I urge the reader to consider the merit in each non-candidate's essay as well. The mayors and governors, for example, make serious proposals for the national agenda that many of the presidential candidates do not address or gloss over.

In 1987, the media following the presidential campaign focused heavily on issues of character while generally overlooking the candidates' policies and ideas. We are fortunate that the press has the capacity—and, at times, the willingness—to elevate the level of public debate in this country. We generally expect presidential candidates to uphold high standards of honesty and integrity. We demand that our president be someone with principles and strength of character. We also need a president who has a clear sense of what this country's goals must be and how he or she can help the nation achieve those goals. It is this leadership quality, more than any other, that can shape the America we build in the 1990s and the early twenty-first century.

On one key issue discussed here, a bi-partisan consensus has emerged that the federal government has been fiscally irresponsible and that we must, at long last, find the political courage to balance the budget. Indeed, we must eventually run a surplus in order to start paying off the principal on the national debt. The federal debt ceiling will grow to about $2.5 trillion by the end of fiscal year 1988, according to the Congressional Budget Office (CBO); that debt was $914 billion when President Reagan took office. A CBO study shows that the bulk of this increase was a direct result of tax cuts in 1981 and defense spending increases initiated by the Reagan administration. Advocates of "supply-side" economics claimed that at least this portion of the shortfall between federal tax revenues and spending would be eliminated by the economic growth arising from tax cuts. Recent history has proved them wrong: the budget deficit widened between 1982 and 1986 primarily due to tax reductions, defense spending increases and nondefense spending cuts. This fiscal policy was President Reagan's initiative and his dream of balancing the budget with this policy turned out to be a fantasy. This is what Vice-President Bush implied when he referred to Reagan's economic policy as "voodoo economics."

The next president must find a way to educate the American people about the gravity of the debt problem so that they will be able to accept the politically difficult solutions that must be crafted and implemented. By 1992, the Congressional Budget Office projects that the cumulative federal debt will stand at $3.4 trillion. This forecast assumes that the next President and Congress in the early 1990s will make progress on cutting the federal budget deficit, which was $220.7 billion in fiscal year 1986 and $148 billion in fiscal year 1987. Payments of interest and principal on this growing mountain of debt must come out of our nation's future earnings. Realistically, these payments will have an adverse impact upon our future standard of living.

Finally, there is the annual trade deficit which was about $170 billion in 1987. This deficit was caused in part by an overvalued dollar, which peaked in 1985; that, in turn, was caused in large part by the budget deficit. The nation's current account deficit, which represents the difference between what we owe the world and what the world owes us, was about $400 billion at the end of 1987. It will continue to grow to over $1 trillion in the next decade. The net inflows of capital into the United States are primarily foreign investments in our bond, equity and real estate markets. Significant liquidation of these investments could lead to net capital outflows in a way that destabilizes our financial markets. Thus, the next President may inherit an economic time bomb.

The shock waves from the Great Stock Market Crash of 1987 are still being felt. The crash jolted the nation into an awareness of our economic problems and the fragility of the global financial system. While the 1987 crash led to a serious debate about our nation's economic future, fundamental changes in our economic game plan and fiscal policy have yet to be achieved. The next president should, with a sense of urgency, present an immediate plan for restoring our nation's fiscal health. That president should also articulate a far-sighted economic strategy in order to secure the American dream for the next generation.

This strategy must guide America through a historic economic transition as it exits the post-war period and enters a new and different era of information and technology. The nation has explored many frontiers since the Great Depression, in science, medicine, social progress, and space. The next frontier in which we must succeed in order to secure our future is the global economy. The Information Age has accelerated the trend toward globalization of markets, and the world that we dominated after World War II now challenges our nation's competitive position in our own domestic markets as well as overseas. But to survive and prosper in the international economic frontier, we must first repair and shore up our own economic foundations.

In spite of these enormous challenges, the ideas offered by the authors of this book give us many reasons to take heart. Dozens of new ideas are presented here: Ideas for continuing the exploration of space and ideas for making America more competitive. Ideas for efficiently fighting poverty and hunger and ideas for housing the homeless. Ideas for creating new economic growth so that all Americans who want to work can do so and ideas for educating our children for jobs that have yet to be invented. Ideas for balancing our national budget and ideas for setting higher goals; goals that focus our nation's energy on becoming economically secure while fulfilling as yet unmet human needs. The contributors articulate a national strategy that focuses on problem solving and engages the best values in the American spirit.

These essays collectively urge the next generation of leaders to put their best ideas into action. They call for all Americans to fairly share the burden of responsibility and discipline that will be required if our nation is to be successful in reaching its highest goals in the next quarter century.

In the 1960s and early 1970s the prevailing values emphasized activism for social goals reflected in the anti-war, civil rights, and environmental movements. In the late 1970s and early 1980s, society became introverted. Personal goals obscured our national purpose. The social pendulum swung to the right. Now it is heading back to a less cynical, more compassionate center. There is a renewed awareness about the needs of the handicapped, the homeless, the hungry and the poor—nationally and globally. Polls indicate that Americans are worried about their economic future and that they want a government that cares and knows what to do about it. Unbridled personal greed is not among the best of American values—the time has come to care again—about each other and the quality of life in our own communities.

The United States is fortunate to have the highest standard of living of all nations in the history of the world. Yet, amid great wealth there is also great poverty: Over 33 million Americans live below the poverty line, and about 40 percent of the poor are children. About 20 million Americans are malnourished. So one goal of our society must be the inclusion of all able citizens in the economic mainstream. Investments in children, including poor, hungry children, are investments in the future of our society. The welfare system, particularly the Aid to Families with Dependent Children (AFDC) program, must be reformed to induce self-sufficiency, not greater dependency. Work-oriented welfare and other programs should be viewed as a social investment with economic significance. Increasing the access of all citizens to education, training and opportunities to work productively will enable our nation to reach its highest economic potential.

Looking into the economic future of a nation in debt requires a special kind of vision. Given the magnitude of the national debt, fiscal constraints will create serious political dilemmas for the next few presidents. With regard to expenditures on national defense, we must broaden our definition of national security to reflect the importance of investing in education, infrastructure and our nation's cities. Without economic strength, military strength cannot long sustain our national safety and security. Republicans and Democrats, men and women, young and old, whether from the North or from the South—all Americans must understand and agree that our national economic strength must be the first priority, upon which all others depend.

Consider the essays here. They can help guide us to select the kind of America we want as a new century begins. The Reagan experiment was the next-to-last change in our national direction before the end of this century. We now have one last opportunity to reshape our national agenda, reorder our priorities and undergo the type of national economic course correction essential to sustain American leadership in the world economy. The goals, values, and blueprints we choose to incorporate into our national vision can directly determine the results we achieve in the mid-to-late 1990s.

Democrats believe government can play a productive and successful role to help foster economic growth when and where the private sector stagnates. The New Deal did not eliminate the Great Depression but strategic investments made by the US government in the thirties laid the foundation for much of the economic growth of later years. In 1961, President John F. Kennedy challenged NASA to land an American on the moon before the end of that decade. Under such a challenge we became united in the pursuit of that national goal. The result bolstered our national pride and achieved thousands of technological spin-off benefits. Democrats have always recognized that government can and should be a catalyst for economic growth.

The America of the early twenty-first century will be built in the 1990s based on ideas and blueprints being conceived in the late 1980s. Within these essays are specifications for some of the more significant goals and proposals that the next president, Republican or Democrat, can use to formulate an economic agenda.

The Democratic leader that emerges in these essays may help forge a new coalition for economic progress in the 1990s. These leaders are pragmatic and focused on promoting economic growth and opportunity. These new Democratic leaders do not stop at asking what goals are best for the nation. They also ask what investments in our future we can afford and what we can not. They are aware that in only four years we moved from being the largest creditor nation to having become the largest debtor nation on earth. Reversing this dangerous trend will require America to somehow start running budget and trade surpluses, whenever feasible, and continue that pattern for many years with the goal of eventually paying back what we borrowed from our children and grandchildren in the eighties. The United States has been living beyond its means.

In the months and years immediately ahead, there is a real risk that a major recession in the United States could trigger an economic crisis with global consequences. We need leadership that can reduce and manage this risk. Leadership that understands the urgency of the situation and that can make the necessary economic trade offs. The energy crisis and gas lines of the late 1970s jarred us to the realization that America was vulnerable to events in the world economy. The events of the mid-eighties have brought the jolting realization that we can no longer take American dominance in the world economy for granted. We must not wait this time for a full-blown crisis to convince us that we need to address our national economic problems as passionately and intelligently as we have addressed other issues at other points in our history.

Perhaps only once in a generation is our national consciousness challenged by leaders who ask us to take bold new risks for positive change. The leaders presented here ask us to get involved and to develop our potential to become leaders ourselves. They offer innovative ideas for creating economic growth at home and abroad. Several have defined specific goals and techniques to help American firms compete in world markets. Others suggest innovative strategies for promoting economic growth that they have successfully developed in their cities or states that can be applied with similar results on a national level.

Today we are at a new turning point, another time in history when words like those of President Kennedy in January 1961 could hopefully ring true again:

> Let the word go forth from this time and place, to friend and foe alike, that the torch has been passed to a new generation of Americans . . . .

This book is for those who care about our country's future and who believe deeply in our ability to carry that torch of high ideals farther than anyone ever thought we could or would dare try. It is for all who seek to realize a vision of a brighter future and the means for realizing our great expectations in its opportunity. For us, this can become a time for a new and vigorous involvement in which we can take part in the creation of another national turning point—the momentous turning point to the twenty-first century.

Robert E. Levin
New York City
November, 1987

Introduction

by Governor Mario M. Cuomo

AMERICA'S HISTORY IS NOT a long one, as world chronology goes, but it records the longest-running, most successful experiment in democracy the world has known.

At the heart of this experiment even today lies the struggle to demonstrate in practical, everyday reality the proposition that the original architects of this nation affirmed—the equal, unalienable rights of all to live, to be free, and to pursue happiness.

For more than 200 years, through periods of calm and periods of extreme turmoil, the American people have proven themselves strong enough, wise enough, good enough to open the circle of opportunity ever wider so that it embraced those once legally excluded—women and blacks—as well as all those who came to America as outsiders and found here the chance to succeed that no other place in the world offered.

But that work is now, even as it was in Lincoln's day, an unfinished one.

Millions remain outside the circle of opportunity, denied the dignity of honest, meaningful work. Their number includes poor people, especially women and children; blacks, Hispanics, Native Americans, whites; dispossessed farmers and displaced factory workers fallen from the middle class; the disabled; the unemployed; and the new immigrants.

Now, in 1988, the challenge is renewed. The exquisitely simple blueprint of purpose the founders left us must be applied in a world much different from theirs, much different even from the world in which most of grew up.

The current campaign will require all of us to deal with issues never dealt with before on such a complex scale. The list includes questions about global interdependence, arms control and defense, economic competitiveness, trade, Third World development and debt, the national deficit, a fragile environment, and yet another generation of poor children growing up in America malnourished, uneducated, and homeless.

It is a long, hard list.

The American people will demand that our next president understand these issues and have the competence to deal with them.

But understanding and competence will not be enough. The next president will not be selected solely upon the basis of a volume of clever position papers and impressive credentials. The American people will demand something more basic—a leader who views the world broadly and who understands our people deeply. A leader who will offer us something to believe in: principles, aspirations, and values. Someone with a clear vision of the future of America. Americans will demand a leadership and wisdom true to Jefferson, Madison, and Lincoln. A strength of character to make us proud.

As we seek insight into the critical questions of our day, we are fortunate to have available a valuable book such as this. *Democratic Blueprints* provides intelligent contributions from all of our party's presidential contenders and some of our foremost party leaders, policy experts, mayors, and legislators. In its varying viewpoints, it offers the first steps toward a realistic and practical vision of our economic future.

Editor Robert E. Levin has gathered a series of splendid and provocative essays ranging over the major issues of our time and their relationship to economic policy—employment, economic growth, debt, housing, homelessness, urban policy, agricultural policy, family policy, poverty, welfare reform, international trade, and national security.

These essays display the diverse opinions and keen insights that characterize our party. Yet they do more than that.

They reflect many of the values and principles upon which our party is built.

These values are critical, for times change and the needs and desires of our citizens change. What was good for Franklin Roosevelt's America, or John F. Kennedy's America, may inspire us but may not be precisely what we need today. Policies are altered to fit a new and different era. But the constant values, the principles, and the beliefs that make us Democrats need not change. These values are elegantly simple, and they have served us well.

We Democrats have always believed in hard work, personal accomplishment, and an abiding sense of responsibility. We believe that government should encourage the talented and nurture free enterprise, in order to foster the personal growth and honest rewards of imagination, ambition, and hard work that enabled this country to grow so strong.

The Democratic Party has always recognized as well that even at its best, the free enterprise system won't be able to include everyone, that some will always be left out—the frail, the poor, the old, and those without skills or hope. While we believe that the survival of the fittest may be a good working description of the scientific process of evolution, a government of human beings should elevate itself to a higher order, one that serves to fill the gaps left by chance or a wisdom we don't understand. Our history teaches us that government can have an affirmative role in people's lives, that it can act progressively and pragmatically to help those who can't help themselves, and that it can do so without suffocating the initiative of the strong.

We remain the only party working to open the circle of American opportunity ever wider, as these essays show. We stand for providing the best possible public education available, regardless of a person's wealth. We stand for job training and economic redevelopment. We stand for health care and help for the elderly, so our people may live lives of dignity and security. As Democrats, we know that these investments of the government's time, money, and effort are necessary to build the kind of future all of us, especially our children, deserve.

Democrats believe, too, that we must be strong enough to deter any enemy and to defeat any enemy who is not deterred. Democrats have guarded this nation for decades in the past, and we are committed to ensuring a strong defense well into the next century, through a level of preparedness and competence that is lacking today. But we also believe that the greater strength is in living together with our neighbors in mutual respect and cooperation.

The Democratic Party understands that the nations of the world are now more interdependent than ever. We know that our future prosperity depends on our ability to work meaningfully and productively with the rest of the world.

The years ahead will call for strength and a new realism to correct the enormous problems created by the arms race, the federal deficit, the international trade imbalance, and a growing gap between the richest among us and the most disadvantaged. The coming years will require difficult, sometimes politically unpopular decisions, but this book shows that Democrats are ready to speak the truth.

If we were to sum all this up, we might say the Democratic Party believes in a single, fundamental idea that describes better than any speech or paper what a good, proper government should be—the idea of family. Family embodies the notion of mutuality, of sharing the benefits and burdens for the good of all, reasonably and fairly, without respect to race, sex, geography, or political affiliation. This idea of family continues the legacy of our Founders. It is the very essence of our American nation, individual states bound together as collective federation under the great gift of our Constitution.

Democratic Blueprints offers us a guide to Democratic tradition and vision. It reminds us in 1988 that our party has the ability, indeed the obligation, to reshape and revive our society. The ideas and programs offered here will work, because at their core they spring from the passionate values and beliefs that have characterized our Democratic Party's history—a profound dedication to improving the lives of all of our people, to widen the circle of opportunity for the whole American family.

They are the ideas that Franklin Roosevelt used when he lifted himself from his wheelchair to lift this country from its knees. They are the principles that inspired Harry Truman to create the Fair Deal. They were the driving ideas behind John Kennedy's greatness, and they lent an exhilarating power to the words and vision of Lyndon Johnson. They gave us the great integrity and commitment to peace of Jimmy Carter.

As Democrats in 1988 we can remember for ourselves, and we can remind the American people, what one of our finest leaders, Robert Kennedy, told us over 20 years ago—that it is always within our power to choose the kind of America we want.

Toward a Better Future—Where the Democrats Stand

This country needs and, unless I mistake its temper, the country demands bold, persistent experimentation. It is common sense to take a method and try it. If it fails, admit it frankly and try another.

—President Franklin Delano Roosevelt

CHAPTER 1

The Democratic Workplace

Governor Bruce Babbitt

AMERICA TODAY IS AT the threshold of remarkable economic change. The causes are global, the consequences dramatic.

I believe the changes now in progress will bring enormous opportunities—opportunities that we can seize and prosper from, or opportunities that we can squander.

We have reached, in my judgment, one of those rare turning points in our history: the end of an economic era, and the beginning—still unformed—of its successor.

It happened here at home between the two world wars, when Franklin Delano Roosevelt first put capitalism into harness. Government, he said—and what a radical notion at the time!—would take the reins of the economy and guide its progress.

It happened abroad in the 1940s, at Bretton Woods and after, when America and its allies launched a true global economy with a new set of rules for trade.

The foundations we built then, in the 1930s and 1940s, have served us long and well. They supported half a century of American global leadership and decades of growth and prosperity.

Even today, there are encouraging signs. Yet, beneath the surface, many Americans sense that our prosperity is insecure. We all know that we are living on borrowed money, from budget deficit to trade deficit, and that one day we'll

have to pay that money back. We fear that something is out of
kilter in a recovery that leaves whole regions and industries
in distress. And we see as clear as day that we are falling
behind our competitors—in the quality of our products, in
our efficiency at producing them, and in the share we hold
of markets around the world.

In short, the institutions and habits of 50 years are beginning to fail us. They are not responding as they should be to
the challenges of change.

We are a great and a powerful nation, but we are not immune to history. And great and powerful nations have come
and gone before.

If we cling too fast to the old ways, we risk becoming a
more divided and less generous society. And a more vulnerable one, too—because with the erosion of our economic
might comes a progressive loss of control over the sources of
our security. None of this will happen tomorrow, or all at
once. The wages of inaction are paid slowly.

But we are left, as a society, with a choice. We can turn
inward, away from our new global challenges—shut out the
world, look back to the past, and settle slowly into a period
of decline. Or we can turn our economy outward—embrace
change, build new habits and new institutions, and lead the
world again.

That is what the nation must decide in 1988. And that is
the reason I am running for president of the United States. I
want to lead a dynamic America that meets and conquers
the challenges of change—that builds an economy of unlimited opportunity for our children.

I deeply believe that the next president must guide us
through a transformation in the way we do business, both at
home and abroad.

The American people are ready for that kind of change.
They deserve leaders who know how to make it happen.

In my judgment, we must be guided by three consider-
ations. First, how do we earn, rather than borrow, a higher
standard of living? Second, how do we ensure that all Americans share in the benefits of economic change? Finally,
how does this generation build an economy that makes life
better for the next generation? My answer—and the program

I will offer through the course of this campaign—rests on two powerful ideas.

One idea is the "global growth economy." Our economic future depends on the prosperity of the whole world economy, and we must recognize that the world is going our way. Political freedom and market economics are on the rise—from South Korea to South America—and they must have American leadership so that we all may flourish together. The next president must say no to protectionism and forge a new trade agreement that expands trade instead of contracting it. And the next president must lead the way to restructuring of the crushing burden of debt, with full participation by Japan and other emerging economic powers.

The second idea, and my subject for this essay, is called the "Democratic Workplace." It aims to create an explosion of productivity by giving every American worker a stake in our economic success and the means to keep pace with a changing world.

These ideas represent a new economic vision for the United States. They can improve work and life for all Americans. They can make a better world.

The starting point for all this change is the federal budget, because an economic policy is not what you say, it's what you do.

What we've done, in the last six years, is this: We've created the first, second, third, fourth, fifth, and sixth biggest federal budget deficits in American history.

I won't try to speak of trillions. Those are numbers that no one can really understand. But I will say this. We cannot possibly build a growing and dynamic economy when our government is spending more than 12 months' income every year. We are investing in deficits, when we should be investing in education and science to modernize our economy. We are raising real interest rates for farmers and small businesses, when we should be lowering them to compete in world markets. And worst of all, we are stealing from the future—placing a burden of obligations on our children, when we should be assuring them the opportunity for a better life.

A lot of people have grown cynical about budget deficits, because all they see is politicians pointing fingers.

The president blames Congress, and Congress blames the president. Both blame something called "the budget process." I don't think the process is to blame. I think our leaders are.

Let's be honest. Does anyone really believe we can balance our budget with a sin tax or an oil fee? Is there one serious economist who thinks we'll find a tenth of the answer in "enforcement"?

It is time to end the conspiracy of evasion by our candidates for national leadership. We've been dancing around the truth, nickel-and-diming the deficit with proposals that don't scratch the surface of the problem.

The plain fact is that we need answers. We need to live in the real world of causes and consequences, and we have an obligation to take responsibility for our views.

As governor of Arizona, I balanced the budget nine times in nine years. The choices were sometimes difficult, but the arithmetic was not.

If we want to get the federal budget under control, we'll have to do it the old-fashioned way: We'll have to cut spending and raise taxes. Why don't we just come out and say so? The first budget of my presidency will cut spending and raise taxes. And it will do them both at once, because I will refuse to sign one bill without the other.

To discipline government spending, I have called for a Universal Needs Test: Every government expenditure—from farm programs to defense—should be targeted on some measure of need.

I don't think we need to pay subsidies to corporate megafarms. I don't think we need grants to finance parking lots for big-city hotels. I don't think we need three new kinds of nuclear missiles all at once. And I don't think the Vanderbilts and the Mellons need exactly the same tax-free Social Security benefits as a widow in a cold-water flat. This is what I mean by a needs test. I believe it will cut government spending and cut it fairly.

To raise revenue, I have considered, even spoken of, several options. But I have concluded it would be wrong to break faith with last year's tax reform, and I would not raise the income tax as president. A recent General Accounting Office study concluded that a national consumption tax offers the only alternative capable of making a dent in the federal deficit. I agree.

As president, I would propose a Progressive National Consumption Tax. It should be broadly based, so that the rate of taxation is held low. And it should be structured progressively, so that it is paid by those who can best afford it. There are many ways to make this tax progressive—from income tax relief for working people to exemptions for food, medicine, and housing—and I am committed to working with Congress to do so.

A consumption tax, even a very progressive one, would raise the revenue we need for deficit reduction. A five percent tax, for example, would generate $40-$60 billion a year, depending on how it was structured. It would be simple and fair, with no loopholes and no special breaks: Everyone pays it, and every transaction is taxed the same way. It would be more progressive than the taxes we pay today— because the rich could not dodge it, and the poor would be shielded from its impact. And it would help us make the shift from a debtor to an investor economy—an economy that leaves a legacy of opportunity, and not old debt, for our children.

THE DEMOCRATIC WORKPLACE

Coming to grips with the federal budget is an essential first step in creating the conditions for economic growth. But it is only a first step. The really big changes will have to come in the way we are organized to do business.

After World War II, our productivity grew fast enough to double America's standard of living every 24 years. Today, we've slowed down. Productivity gains, at their current rate, will not double our standard of living again until well into the next century.

We can't wait that long. America needs to compete for

world markets, and there are only two ways to compete: by lowering wages or increasing productivity.

We must never accept low wages as the predicate of competition. America was built on a high-wage, high-value economy, and an American standard of living requires no less. The right alternative is to build the most productive economy in the world.

We must start where the economy starts, with the backbone of our economic strength: the individual American worker. For America to prosper, we need workers who are motivated, knowledgeable, and versatile. Yet, today three out of four American workers say that they don't do their best on the job, either in quality or in effort, and that if they did do their best, the company would do nothing to reward them. That attitude reflects an elemental fact about the old American workplace. Managers feel valued. Workers do not.

American capitalism has too often regarded workers as disposable drones—as "costs" to be minimized—and their managers as the creators of value. Somehow, we got the idea that innovation and company performance depend on a tiny, elite corps of highly paid executives, and that their workers are interchangeable units of labor.

It's an absurd and pernicious idea, but we see it in industry after industry—with executives asking for give-backs on the shop floor while awarding themselves bonuses in the boardroom. We see it more cynically yet in the widespread adoption of "golden parachutes" for top management. These are nothing more than cushy arrangements to pay enormous sums for failure, and they symbolize everything that's wrong with the aristocracy of capitalism.

The next president must lead us away from these practices and toward new ways of doing business.

We must move to new models that emphasize things like teamwork, shared goals and values, and company loyalty.

We must turn away from hierarchical and highly centralized models of management, and toward models that disperse decision-making power much more widely.

We must turn away from a concept of employees as mere costs, and toward an understanding that they are among a company's most important assets.

We must turn away, most of all, from an adversarial notion of management-versus-labor, and toward the idea that joint planning for mutual benefit works better.

In this quest for a new democratic workplace, the next president must seek allies in forward-looking sectors of both labor and management.

Consider this example: The Herman Miller Company in Michigan makes office furniture. The company asks workers to take part in management and pays them 50 percent of its productivity gains.

What are the results? Between 1983 and 1986, Herman Miller had a 26 percent compounded net sales gain, one of the best in the industry. Its cost savings exceeded $27 million. Its stock appreciated more than 46 percent. Workers have a stake in Herman Miller's success, and they show it. Absenteeism is about a third of the national average. Morale is high. Turnover is low. *Fortune* magazine rates Herman Miller as one of the 10 most admired companies in the United States.

Or consider this: In the spring of 1987, for the first time since the early 1920s, the Ford Motor Company earned more profits than General Motors. Both the union and management attribute that success to the company's Employee Involvement Program—in which workers have more say in, and more profit from, the way the company operates. Ford guarantees workers' job security. Workers have the right to stop an assembly line whenever anything is wrong. Managers and workers meet together each week to discuss matters such as equipment changes, production flows, scheduling, and quality control.

The results have been spectacular. Productivity in some Ford plants has increased by eight percent a year since 1980. Quality has soared. Defects have been cut from an average of 16 per car to one.

What's happening at Herman Miller and Ford is not unique. It is possible throughout the American workplace. And if America is to adapt successfully to a rapidly changing global economy, the democratic workplace must become the rule and not the exception.

We must have an economic environment in which labor

and management can jointly pursue competitive success—sharing risks, responsibilities, and rewards. We must say to every worker: If you make first-rate efforts—if you pay attention to detail, if you improve the quality of your product, if you find a better way to do the job—you will have first-rate rewards.

The democratic workplace will not be handed down from on high. The American people must create it for themselves. It must evolve locally and autonomously, after careful thought and bargaining between the workers and management of individual enterprises. The way it works in practice will vary from company to company and from industry to industry.

One possibility is gain sharing, which rewards managers and workers alike by sharing increases in overall productivity or performance. Another is profit sharing, which cuts workers directly into a portion of company profits. Still another is equity sharing, which enables every worker to earn an ownership stake in the company.

Workers and management must negotiate for themselves about what kind of performance should be measured, and whose performance should be measured. The company's? The plant's? The work group's? The individual's?

No one should legislate these decisions. But legislation can begin to establish the right environment. As president, I would sponsor legislation for a democratic workplace, aimed at several broad goals.

First, pay for performance. By 1996, after two terms of the next Democratic administration, at least two-thirds of all American workers should earn part of their wage in performance-based pay.

Second, employee ownership. What capitalism needs is more capitalists, and government should find ways to encourage more American workers to take an equity stake in their companies.

Third, strategic investments in people. The democratic workplace depends on the collective ingenuity and performance of all American workers, and we must empower our workers with education and training and the means to contribute their best.

I would advance these goals through the following proposals:

- *Bonuses for all or for none.* No American company should be permitted to deduct an executive bonus as a business expense unless it offers some kind of performance pay for all its employees.
- *Golden parachutes.* I would propose to prohibit severance packages of this kind—or restrict them to companies that are prepared to offer equivalent multiples of salary to every departing employee.
- *Government loans and guarantees.* Any direct government loan or guarantee to an individual company should be conditioned on a restructuring that creates partial ownership, and partial control, by the company's employees.
- *Performance pay in federal contracts.* The federal government should experiment with direct performance bonuses for the employees of federal contractors who fulfill their contracts on time and under budget.
- *Financing federal contracts.* Where federal contracts call for asset financing, some proportion of that financing should be required to be undertaken through an Employee Stock Ownership Plan—one that puts meaningful control of employee shares in the hands of employees themselves.
- *Individual Equity Accounts.* Workers who elect to take a fraction of their salary in company stock should be entitled to create a tax-deferred account with that stock until they sell it. The longer they hold the stock, the lower the rate of tax they should pay at the time of sale.
- *Worker training tax credits.* The federal government creates tax incentives to invest in machinery and research, but not in employee training and education. We should value investment in people at least as much as investment in technology—with a tax credit for training that exceeds a company's three-year historical average.
- *Child care vouchers.* Most industrial nations have recognized child care as critical to a productive workplace. Ours has not. The lack of decent options is sharply reducing the employment, working hours,

flexibility, and performance of at least half of all American workers. We should create a uniform national child care voucher, scaled to income and funded jointly by the federal government and the states.

- *Portable pensions.* Members of a flexible work force must be able to change jobs, occupations, or employers without losing pension security. We should require any employer without a retirement plan approved by the Employee Retirement Income Security Act, or ERISA, to withhold two percent of each employee's wages, match that with an additional two percent contribution, and create a fully funded and portable pension that could be cashed out or moved whenever the worker changed jobs.

This, then, is the new democratic workplace. Bringing it about will be one of the central goals of my presidency.

Performance pay, employee ownership, and strategic investments in our work force would bring profound changes in the way we work and live in America. They would help create better-motivated, more flexible, and more productive workers. And they would do much to ensure that America's success is shared equitably among those who create it.

This is the work force we need. This is the workplace of the future. And this is a model we can proudly display for other nations, because this is capitalism at its best.

America today faces a historic opportunity to take on the mantle of world economic leadership—for the second time in this century. It is an opportunity, but it is also a test. A test of whether our democracy is bold enough and flexible enough to change with changing times.

We still have, as we always have, a choice. We can opt for the known and the secure, ignoring the changes all around us and rejecting the opportunities that they offer. Or we can plunge ahead into the future—enlisting every American citizen for the journey. We can come to terms, after all these years of recklessness, with our national budget. We can build a democratic workplace that creates an explosion of productivity and growth. And we can become the engine, once again, of a prosperity that makes the world a better place.

CHAPTER 2

Prescription for Economic Excellence

Senator Joseph R. Biden, Jr.

A MERICA HAS ALWAYS BEEN a land of opportunity, where through hard work, people can advance themselves and build a better future for their children. Throughout most of our history, each generation has found itself better off than the one that came before. Most recently, in the 1950s and 1960s, workers in the prime years of their lives saw their incomes rise substantially. Their rising standard of living was no fluke: Workers earned higher wages by increasing their productivity at the impressive rate of three percent a year. The American postwar economy was the most powerful, dynamic, and innovative the world had ever seen.

Today, Americans find themselves in a very different situation. Despite the recent economic recovery, the standard of living for the average American has hardly budged. Workers in their thirties and forties have seen their wages actually fall during the 1970s and 1980s, after accounting for inflation. National productivity growth has slowed to less than one percent a year. Even with better economic times since 1982, total national output has grown at a slower annual rate in this decade than in either of the previous two.

These trends are especially disturbing in light of the current administration's "credit card" approach to economic policy. Instead of paying for what government has consumed, the administration has run up the largest budget

13

deficits in history. At current projected rates, America will add almost two trillion dollars to the national debt in this decade alone.

Enormous and unprecedented trade deficits are the mirror image of this fiscal policy. Government has been able to spend so much more than it takes in only because foreigners have provided the difference. But foreign interests have only loaned us the money so that we can buy their goods. As a result, last year, the U.S. trade deficit hit a record $170 billion. As recently as 1980, the United States remained the world's largest creditor. Today, we are the world's largest debtor, and by the end of this decade, we will owe more than $500 billion—far more than Mexico, Brazil, and Argentina combined—to banks and investors overseas.

While the facts are now widely recognized, many leaders of both political parties believe that the challenges they pose can be met by tinkering with trade laws—as if to shrink the trade deficit by fiat. Such thinking is misguided. Adjusting trade laws will have, at best, only a modest impact on the trade balance. More fundamentally, our trade deficit is only a symptom of far deeper economic challenges. Indeed, if we embraced the calls for protection heard in some parts of this country, we would only compound our problem, by increasing the cost of materials U.S. firms use to make goods that they sell abroad.

The hard fact is that during the four decades since the end of World War II, the rest of the world has caught up with us. Our lead in many key economic areas is quickly narrowing; in some, it is already lost. Other nations educate their people as well as, if not better than, we do. Some countries manufacture better products at lower prices than do American firms.

Our economic future—our destiny—is in our hands. Certain key elements of our economic life must change: the way we produce goods, the way we educate our youth, the way we adapt to technological innovations. In short, our nation's economy must start to do better at many of the things it has historically done well at—but with which our rivals are now catching up.

If we allow much of the world to surpass us economically, we will create an America for the twenty-first century that is completely unacceptable. We must not bequeath to our children a country stripped of its basic industries, whose land and factories are owned by foreigners, a country that has lost the ability to produce what it invents and to create high-paying jobs for its citizens. Current trends, if allowed to continue, will lead to exactly such a future for our people. Our challenge is to reverse these trends.

America can rise to these challenges—but only with presidential leadership committed to making it happen. The next president must lead our entire society in a period of sweeping economic reform.

What are the goals of these efforts?

Economic revitalization requires this nation to achieve four great goals. To ensure economic success into the next millennium, there are four challenges we must meet as a people.

- America can and must have the most productive industry in the world.
- America can and must have the best education system in the world.
- America can and must product the best products and deliver the highest-quality services in the world.
- America can and must have the most dynamic and innovative economy in the world.

Our next president should be committed to achieving nothing less. But he cannot do it alone. Achieving each of these objectives requires the active involvement of all Americans. The president can help all of us meet these goals. He can stimulate, prod, and encourage the American people to move forward in the right direction. And he can implement policies that make the government a catalyst for effective private-sector actions.

It is time that we regained our economic might, dynamism, and excellence. Time we sought not merely to become "competitive," but to win the new world economic contest. Time we ended the games played in Washington and on Wall Street and got down to the business of rebuilding our economy.

This will require the American people to do several things simultaneously. We must acknowledge new realities, and at the same time, we must forge new attitudes that will serve as the basis for implementing new policies.

First, both this country and our trading partners must acknowledge that America's economy remains the largest, most productive, and most diversified in the world. It is still the engine of global economic growth, and the fortunes of other nations' economies are intimately tied up with ours. The international economy is not a zero-sum game. We all talk of "competing" and "winning" the global economic contest, but such talk should not obscure the reality that when America wins, the rest of the world wins. Indeed, as the global recessions of the 1970s proved, only when America wins can the rest of the world win.

Second, even as we acknowledge that the economy of the twenty-first century will be more transnational in nature and feature a relatively larger service sector, we must not be fooled into believing that we can remain a great economic and military power if we let basic industries disappear. Once our steel, auto, and machine tool sectors shrink and weaken, we will not be able to revive them at will in the event of a national crisis. We lose more than thousands of well-paying jobs when our manufacturing capability declines. We lose our very industrial memory—the knowledge, skills, and processes that make up a vibrant and productive manufacturing sector.

Finally, the institutions of American society—business, labor, government, the education system, and others—must be prepared to adapt to the demands of a changing economy and a changing society.

FOUR GOALS FOR AN AMERICAN ECONOMIC RENAISSANCE

A. We Must Make Our Industry the Most Productive in the World.

Americans have enjoyed the highest living standard in the world because our industries have been the world's most productive.

But to achieve new growth in our standard of living, we must do better. We must build an economic environment in which it is more attractive for our brightest young people to become entrepreneurs, engineers, and scientists, rather than lawyers and investment bankers.

America's productivity is in the hands of its workers and managers. Their efforts are the ultimate dictator of our economic performance—not any law passed in Washington. But a president, if he chooses to be a leader of the society, can do much to raise the productive performance of American industry.

- We must insist that management and labor in major industries improve their productive performance.

Americans should not sit idly by while major industries—steel, autos, and now semiconductors—get battered in the international marketplace. But at the same time, permanently protecting firms in these industries from import competition is not the answer. The American economy has been strong precisely because we have encouraged competition.

A president committed to revitalizing our economy can make a real difference by bringing together management and labor in these industries, and working with them to save our businesses and our jobs. Labor can be told to abandon outdated and unproductive work rules—rules that limit the use of new production techniques. Management can be told to streamline, cut its waste, and stop worrying about golden parachutes and other perks.

- We must increase our rate of productive investment and finance it with our own savings.

New technology, new equipment, and new facilities will be needed if the economy is to be revitalized. These goods cost money—and that means business will need a flood of new investment to fund its drive to be more productive.

We cannot make our industry the most productive in the world without increasing the share of our capital resources that is devoted to investment in the private sector. And we should be disturbed that despite the vast tax breaks given to encourage investment in 1981, U.S. net investment is lower now than it was during earlier economic expansions.

Even worse, much private investment has been unproductive, partly because of tax breaks that have rewarded the construction of office buildings that remain empty and the proliferation of socially wasteful tax shelters. The 1986 Tax Reform Act repealed many of these provisions, but there is still much to be done.

We must reverse the high interest rate and high budget deficit policies pursued under the current administration, which limit the potential for increased private investment. The president must support actions by the Federal Reserve to offset the economic effects of deficit reduction with monetary policies that will lead to lower interest rates. Under no circumstance should the Federal Reserve Board allow the money supply to expand at a rate that will rekindle the disastrous inflation of the 1970s.

Deficit reduction will have another important benefit: It will permit us to finance our investment with domestic, rather than foreign, funds. The enormous deficits amassed in recent years have absorbed so much of our own savings that we have had to borrow from foreigners in order to finance our spending. This must be stopped.

We need to attack the deficit with such sound economic initiatives as the following:

- Continue with a disciplined program of gradual deficit reduction that achieves a balanced budget by 1993.
- Trim the defense budget by cutting wasteful weapons systems.
- Convert import quotas into tariffs, raising as much as $10 billion dollars a year.
- Impose a fee on oil imports sufficient to ensure a domestic price of $19–$22 per barrel.
- Finally, to hold the line on the deficit, new spending for programs needed to meet urgent national priorities should be funded with specific revenue increases related to the spending programs. For example, taxes on tobacco and alcohol should be used to pay for drug abuse and health care programs.

A Biden administration would employ three principles in evaluating fiscal policy changes necessary to reduce the deficit: First, no cuts should be made in programs that are vital to maintaining America's competitive position in the world economy. Second, revenue increases, which should be considered only as a last resort, must not make the tax system less progressive or burden lower-income Americans disproportionately. Finally, any proposed new spending programs must specify a source of funding.

- The federal government—and the president—must encourage firms to increase worker participation in management and profit sharing.

It is striking that while government has long encouraged home ownership—believing that ownership gives individuals a stronger stake in keeping up their residences—we have only recently begun to encourage employee ownership of the companies they work for (through Employee Stock Ownership Plans, or ESOPs). It is time to do more. Firms are also now developing production pay plans, where workers get paid more if their firm does better.

Common sense tells us, and many studies have confirmed, that workers develop greater pride in the products they make and the services they deliver if they share in the benefits of success and the price of failure.

- We must stop the raiding of corporate treasuries by fast-buck artists.

Economic historians will look back at the 1980s as the decade of the corporate takeover. To many Americans, Wall Street looks like a vast carnival where fast-buck artists play shady games with the nation's largest corporations. Often, the well-being of millions of shareholders, and the jobs of thousands of workers, hang in the balance.

In particular, one takeover practice—"greenmail"— should be stopped. By buying large blocks of stock and then holding out for greenmail before agreeing to drop a takeover bid, corporate raiders pocket for themselves vast, quick profits, draining resources that companies need to make their operations more productive.

Since the revenues earned from greenmail belong to the corporation, its shareholders, and its workers, they should be returned to them. Securities laws should be amended to require that large shareholders—those holding more than five percent of a corporation's stock—return to the corporation any profits made from the sale of that stock, if it has been held for less than two years.

- Private firms must be encouraged to provide on-site child care for employees who are parents.

One consequence of the increasing participation by women in the work force is significantly greater need for child care services. Given the importance of family in our society, government should encourage employers to provide child care at the job site.

Many companies throughout the United States have already recognized that providing on-site child care can increase productivity. A Biden administration would encourage the private sector to do more by supporting a tax credit of 10 percent of the amount currently deductible for corporations that provide child care facilities at work sites.

B. We Must Give Ourselves and Our Children the Best Lifetime Education System in the World.

The link between national excellence in education and national economic success has always been clear. In the Information Age already embarked upon, quality education will be even more essential for individual and national economic success. Indeed, America has been the most productive nation on earth largely because our entrepreneurs, managers, and workers have been among the most educated people on the planet.

But we have slipped—and other nations have caught up. In educational attainment and in international tests, many of our children are outranked by their peers in Japan, Germany, Sweden, and even the Soviet Union. The problem hits adults, too. Millions of workers, displaced by rapid advances in technology, have found they lack the skills to find new jobs. Perhaps the most tragic fact is that 13 percent of all Americans cannot even read or write.

This can and must change. America must implement and make available to its citizens the best lifetime education system in the world. To accomplish this objective, we must take a number of steps.

- We must fundamentally reform elementary and secondary education.

Basic education in America must be overhauled in an unprecedented way. Among the reforms needed are longer schooldays and longer school years, tougher curriculum requirements, and increased homework.

New performance standards should require students to learn the material and to prove it on tests that fairly measure their achievement.

There must be new standards and new recognition for the teaching profession, as well as greater professional rewards in line with greater responsibilities, for teachers.

Without sweeping and deep reforms of the American elementary and secondary education system, our children will not be able to compete in the world economy of the year 2000.

- We must provide new support for higher education.

We should expand the student loan program, and tie repayment to the borrower's future income. Total lifetime borrowing would be limited to $50,000, and annual loan repayment would be limited to 15 percent of annual income. Higher-income borrowers would repay at a faster rate than lower-income borrowers.

Our current loan programs are restricted to families with incomes no higher than $30,000. This limit should be raised substantially. By shrinking opportunities for middle-class youths to obtain the best education available, we discourage competition among educational institutions to get the best students, and we deprive our nation of thousands of trained people we need to succeed in tomorrow's world economy.

Loans should be made available to working adults who wish to gain additional education. Each person should be able to borrow a set amount for educational purposes, again with repayments tied to future income levels. In a constantly changing world, no one can afford to stand still. The best time for retraining is while we are still working.

An effective, far-reaching loan program need not be a drain on the federal budget. If individual loans are packaged and sold off in the secondary market to investors, the only cost to the federal government would be the cost of repayment fees (as is the case for federal housing programs).

- We must concentrate federal support for job training and retraining on people with the fewest skills.

Job training assistance should be available to everyone. But we must go a step further, and also help the millions of Americans who have the fewest job skills—many of whom cannot even read or write.

The next Democratic administration should concentrate federal support for job training on upgrading the skills of those in greatest need. Unfortunately, many current job training programs tend to skin like cream, enrolling individuals who already have basic work skills. We must change our priorities, by funding training programs that seek to improve the reading, math, and other job-related skills of the most disadvantaged. At the same time, we should aggressively seek out and encourage all Americans who need help to enroll in these programs.

Job training programs for those most easily retrained should continue. But the best retraining for unemployed and displaced workers with good skills and long job histo ries occurs on the job at new jobs.

C. We Can and We Must Make the Best Products in the World.

Americans cannot expect their living standard to improve unless "Made in the U.S.A." stands for the highest-quality goods and services in the world. Government cannot make this happen. Responsibility for making the best products and delivering the best services lies with American workers, managers, and owners.

But here, too, the next president can help create an environment conducive to quality.

- We should avoid sheltering American firms from fair competition. But if our trading partners or rivals use unfair practices to gain an advantage, we should respond swiftly and strongly.

Competition provides the best guarantee that American firms will produce the highest-quality goods and deliver the very best services. Thus, we must resist trying to eliminate the trade deficit with protectionist remedies that, in the long run, will cost more jobs than are saved.

Our response to unfair practices must be swift and strong. American firms should be granted import relief if they can show they have been hurt by unfair practices or if their industries have been seriously injured by import competition. Import relief should be temporary, and should be granted in the form of tariffs or duties, not quotas.

- We must put our best and brightest to work building the best products in the world.

America cannot be the home of the world's best products unless our top graduates are producing them. Today, many are siphoned off to occupations that manipulate wealth instead of creating it.

Presidential leadership is paramount in encouraging young Americans to seek careers in important, productive areas. By recognizing outstanding achievement in the sciences, computers, math, and engineering, the president can add to the prestige and importance all of us accord to these professions—and draw more and more young people to them.

D. We Must Continue to Be the Most Dynamic and Innovative Economy in the World.

A key strength of the American economy is that it is both dynamic and flexible.

American dynamism is reflected in our extraordinary number of innovations and inventions, which keep us ahead of the competition in technology and thus keep our workers in high-paying jobs.

We are also a highly flexible society, capable of adapting to rapid change. This flexibility has allowed total employment in this country to increase by over 10 million since 1981, even though productivity has been flat. We will need this flexibility in the years ahead in order to move people and resources into activities at the technological frontier.

The next president must be committed to preserving and enhancing our economic dynamism and flexibility in several ways.

- We must reallocate part of the federal support for military research and development (R&D) toward civilian R&D.

Innovation will not occur without research and development. Although the U.S. ranks well in resources devoted to all R&D projects, since the mid-1960s the share of gross national product devoted to civilian R&D in the United States has been lower than that in Germany, Japan, or the United Kingdom.

We cannot expect to win any competition among our trading partners unless this pattern is reversed.

Too great a share of our R&D spending is allocated to the military. Defense-related R&D spending as a percentage of total federal R&D expenditures rose from 61 percent in 1982 to 69 percent in 1985.

We must reallocate part of the federal resources now devoted to military projects to civilian purposes. Economic studies have consistently demonstrated that society reaps substantial gains from research and development. It is time to put more of our scarce research dollars into activities that will help American companies stay ahead and will yield new products for all of us to enjoy.

- We must adapt our antitrust policy to the new global competition.

Federal antitrust laws, enacted in an era when the nation's economy was relatively isolated, are still needed to preserve competition. Today, however, the world is increasingly a single global market. Our companies must compete not only with other domestic businesses, but also with companies around the globe.

Moreover, many new product and technologies—particularly computers and semiconductors—require vast R&D expenditures. These investments are often beyond the means of any one firm, requiring a joint effort to succeed. So we must ensure that our antitrust policy is well suited to meet the challenge of global competition. Joint ventures and mergers should be examined in a new light to develop new products.

- We must assure that private pensions belong to the individual, not to corporations.

Our dynamic economy requires that managers and workers be flexible and capable of moving to new opportunities where they arise. Yet, workers often hesitate to switch careers because they may lose their pension savings when they leave their jobs. This must be changed.

The federal government should allow pension benefits to be portable—that is, to be carried by workers from one career to another, throughout their working lives.

- We must redesign our unemployment benefit programs to provide stronger job-seeking incentives.

As a nation, we have a strong interest in seeing that workers who lose their jobs promptly locate and accept alternative employment. Such prompt reemployment is the key to adaptation to economic change. Furthermore, as noted above, the most effective retraining for experienced workers occurs on the job in the new jobs, not in government training programs. Overall, the faster unemployed workers return to work, the higher our national income, the less we spend on unemployment insurance, and the lower our federal budget deficit. Equally important, speedy reemployment is the key to restoring the pride and confidence of unemployed workers themselves.

Government can speed the difficult transition between old and new jobs by adding a "wage insurance" component to the Unemployment Insurance (UI) and Trade Adjustment Assistance (TAA) programs. This would mean that an unemployed worker who finds and accepts a new job after losing his old one, but who must take a cut in pay, would receive a portion of the wage cut for the next year.

A wage insurance plan would have several benefits. It would give unemployed workers who go back to work right away at a lower-paying job while looking for more permanent, higher-paying work some supplemental income while pursuing their job search. In addition, wage insurance would make it easier for unemployed workers to start over in new careers where initial wages may be lower than their previous wages. In both cases, wage insurance can put unemployed workers back to work more quickly, reducing costs of unemployment insurance and generating income tax revenues for federal and state governments.

- We must require firms permanently closing major plants to give advance notice to their workers and communities.

It is widely recognized that the sooner displaced workers learn they are going to be laid off or fired, the sooner they are placed into new jobs. In fact, the current administration is proposing that federal "SWAT" teams be sent to the sites of major plant closings to assist the affected workers in finding new jobs.

This proposal does not go far enough. Firms deciding to close large plants permanently should be required to give at least some advance notice to the workers and communities that the closings will affect.

- The federal government should encourage private insurance companies to develop programs to protect communities against sudden, significant losses of their tax base, and should stand as a guarantor for those programs.

Communities that, through no fault of their own, suffer severe economic misfortunes—plant closings, agricultural crop failures or price collapses, or oil price declines—find themselves facing a difficult choice: They can either slash needed public services or increase the per capita tax burden on their residents at a time when they can least afford it. In either event, the communities stand to lose even more businesses.

We can help these cities and towns better adapt to change. The federal government, in partnership with private insurance companies, should offer to local governments insurance policies that compensate localities for some portion of any sudden and sharp loss in their tax base. The program would entail minimal cost to the federal government; it would be largely self-financing through the premiums paid by communities for the insurance.

DEALING WITH THE FOREIGN CHALLENGES TO ECONOMIC REVITALIZATION THROUGH EFFECTIVE PRESIDENTIAL LEADERSHIP

Achieving the four goals described above will revitalize the American economy from within, but the job of the next president does not stop there. He must lead our renaissance by coping with the economic challenges not found on our own shores.

- We must employ America's full range of political and economic leverage in trade negotiations.

America has traditionally pursued its trade negotiations in isolated fashion. When other countries' unfair trade practices hurt us, we threatened to retaliate by closing our markets to their goods. This is a shortsighted policy that risks triggering a destructive round of protectionist retaliation. It reinforces the myth that our choice in trade policies is limited to free trade or protectionism.

Today's world is more complicated than this simple

choice. Accordingly, the United States should broaden the negotiating agenda with its trading partners. For example, we can insist that countries such as Japan and West Germany, which have healthy domestic economies, pick up a greater share of their own defense. We can tell countries like Taiwan, which subsidize exports by preventing their currencies from appreciating against the dollar, that they must open up their markets to American goods if we are to address their concerns about the dollar's decline.

In short, America has wide-ranging political and economic negotiating leverage that could be used to gain broader access to foreign markets. Unfortunately, we have failed to use much of that leverage so far. In a Biden administration, this would change.

- We must bring together major debtor countries and their creditors to reduce debt burdens, thereby freeing resources for the purchase of American exports.

Recent economic difficulties in Brazil and Ecuador dramatized the fact that the worldwide debt problem will not be solved by wishful thinking or by increasing the debt burden, as proposed by the administration's so-called Baker Plan. The continuing failure to address the world debt problem poses severe risks to newly established democratic governments in many of these countries.

Foreign debt also significantly reduces the demand for American exports, particularly machinery and capital goods, that these countries need to help themselves grow out of their debt miseries. The fact is that countries with high debts cannot afford to buy the American-made goods they would otherwise purchase.

Our president must make foreign debt one of his highest priorities. He must tell the banks what the financial markets have already indicated: Some of their loans are not collectible at market interest rates, and attempts to do so will only drive indebted nations deeper into despair.

In return for debt relief, foreign countries must do two things. First, to qualify for relief, debtor countries must agree to increase their purchases of American goods. Second, those countries must relax current restrictions on foreign investment.

The current administration has failed to use its regulatory and foreign policy leverage to bring banks and debtor countries to the bargaining table. A Biden administration would display the presidential leadership required to reverse the current course.

Finally, America must enlist the cooperation of other industrialized countries in expanding the role of the World Bank by buying up debt and facilitating negotiations between the banks and the debtor countries. Because the less developed countries' debt problem affects all creditor nations, the latter should all participate in the solution.

CHAPTER 3

Innovation and Opportunity: Toward a Competitive America

Governor Michael S. Dukakis

MORE THAN AT ANY other time in this century, Americans now are preoccupied with the competitive stance of this nation's economy in the much larger economy of the world. As American industries lose market share to overseas rivals, as American workers lose good jobs, as American communities suffer the effects of economic dislocation and disinvestment, much of our national economic debate—too much, in my view—has become a one-dimensional argument about trade.

To be sure, trade policy is one of the three or four most significant economic challenges our nation confronts today. But much that is usually said about the subject misses the main point. Politicians especially tend to divide everyone who speaks about trade policy, and everything that is proposed, into two camps—protectionism and free trade—and to suggest that one approach will always work, the other always fail. Unfortunately, our preoccupation with labels and our penchant for choosing sides obscure a mosaic of policy choices that is far more complex and subtle.

31

Is it protectionism or free trade when Massachusetts tries to help her machine tool and wood products industries consolidate, retool, and grow?

Is it a level playing field when we invest public funds to help our state's fledgling photovoltaic industry penetrate world markets?

Are we providing unfair subsidies when we reinvest massively in our older cities as centers of service-sector growth, or when we train the people who live there to work in knowledge-intensive jobs?

The questions and the labels hardly fit. All of these policies, and many more undertaken by Massachusetts and other states over the last several years, represent the hard work of economic development. And they are examples of what we must do here at home to build a stronger and more competitive America.

Our task centers on two strategic necessities: innovation and opportunity. And behind each lies a myth.

Innovation—the key to the modernization and growth of this nation's economy—is often viewed as merely the domain of businesses engaged in mysterious new technologies. But innovation usually reaches the marketplace through a partnership of entrepreneurs, inventors, financiers, workers, universities, and, yes, government. And innovative means far more than making new things. It means making old things in new, more efficient, and more creative ways. It means developing new ways of delivering goods and services to market.

Opportunity—for every person and family in every corner of America—is often viewed as merely the social goal of a caring society. It is that, but it is also an economic necessity. The Massachusetts experience has taught us that when we include everyone in the mainstream of economic opportunity, we expand the overall capacity of the economy to grow and compete.

As important as sound macroeconomic policies are, they are merely the foundation on which innovation and opportunity must be built. A true national economic strategy must reach into America's shop floors and research labs, her downtowns and neighborhoods. And the creation of innovation and opportunity across America will require Washington not only to care and to invest, but to reach out to successful state, local, and regional partnerships that are already under way.

ONE STATE'S EXPERIENCE

Ten years ago, states were barely involved in economic development. At best, they had traditional commerce departments and traditionally narrow economic agendas—promote, recruit, and cut taxes for new business, a sort of state-level equivalent to the erection of trade barriers. But in the last decade, most states have taken a much broader view of economic development and assumed a catalytic lead role in the process.

In 1975, Massachusetts was in the worst economic condition she had faced since the Great Depression. Our commonwealth was being called the "New Appalachia," with a frightening ring of truth. As the national recession of the early seventies bottomed out in June of 1975, statewide unemployment in Massachusetts hit a high of 12 percent, and 332,000 working men and women were without jobs. In many of our older cities, unemployment rates were closer to 20 percent, and the outlook was very bleak.

But Massachusetts was determined to recover and rebuild. By the fall of 1978, we had created 253,000 new jobs—110,000 in 1978 alone—and the state's unemployment rate had dipped below the nation's for the first time in years. A boom period of growth and diversification was under way, bringing with it a surge that lasted into 1980 and allowed Massachusetts to ride out the national recession of 1981 and 1982 with greater resilience than virtually any of her sister states.

We did not escape that recession without pain. In the spring of 1983, over 100 Massachusetts communities were suffering double-digit unemployment. However, in the years since, Massachusetts has not only bounced back a second time, but achieved a level of economic success that is the envy of America. Statewide unemployment, which stood near eight percent in January of 1983, was at or below four percent throughout 1987. September 1987 was the forty-fourth month out of forty-six in which Massachusetts enjoyed the lowest unemployment rate among America's eleven major industrial states. In July and September of 1987, state unemployment fell to 2.5 percent—its lowest in 17 years. From 1983 through September 1987, our resurgent economy created over 400,000 new jobs and over 100,000 new businesses. Reinvestment in our communities and our industrial base is strong and gaining. And in the 1980s, real per capita income in Massachusetts has risen a phenomenal 75 percent. The "New Appalachia" has given way to the "Massachusetts Miracle."

What happened? How did a state that was an economic basket case become an economic showcase? Massachusetts surely benefited from the two partial national recoveries; but

TABLE I

Job Growth in Massachusetts, 1975–1986

Year	Total jobs	Change from prior years
1975	2,273,000	————
1976	2,324,000	+ 51,000
1977	2,416,000	+ 92,000
1978	2,526,000	+110,000
1979	2,604,000	+ 78,000
1980	2,652,000	+ 48,000
1981	2,668,000	+ 16,000
1982	2,638,000	− 30,000
1983	2,692,000	+ 54,000
1984	2,852,000	+160,000
1985	2,926,000	+ 74,000
1986	2,981,000	+ 55,000
1987 (through September)	3,049,000	+ 68,000
Total gain, 1975–1986	703,000	776,000
1982–1986	343,000	411,000

national trends cannot explain our surge from way behind the national curve to way ahead of it.

Nor can any one factor, like defense spending. While Massachusetts ranks fourth in the nation in prime defense contract awards, defense spending employs only 150,000–180,000 Bay Staters—just five percent of our work force. Moreover, our share of Pentagon spending and the share of our total job base that defense employment represents have remained virtually constant throughout the 1980s.

The first thing we did was to put our fiscal house in order. In 1975, Massachusetts was a financial disaster. Our state budget deficit of nearly $600 million was proportionately the largest in America and our property taxes were the highest anywhere. Between 1975 and 1979, we did what we had to do—we cut spending, we raised taxes, and we managed much better. Along with a first wave of economic recovery came a first giant step toward fiscal strength and stability. In 1979, Massachusetts enjoyed a $200 million surplus.

Between 1983 and 1987, we faced a new round of fiscal challenges, beginning with the very real possibility of a new state budget deficit in 1983. We managed our way out of that, and in the four years that followed, Massachusetts was able to cut its general taxes five times. We were also able to direct massive new aid to our cities and towns, guaranteeing them in the process a generous and predictable share of the state's annual revenue growth. It was this initiative by the state that made Proposition 2½, the 1980 referendum that cut and stabilized property taxes, an economic plus rather than a major blow to the stability of local governments.

Although good management and economic growth have accounted for much of our new fiscal strength, they do not account for all of it. Another key factor was REAP—our nationally recognized effort to enforce our tax laws and make everyone pay their fair share. In its first three years of full operation, REAP produced nearly $1 billion in increased revenue and became an important part of our economic strategy.

Most of that strategy, though, revolves around investment—specifically, how we invested, and continue to invest, in the three basic building blocks of economic growth:

- Public infrastructure
- Affordable capital for business and development
- Education and training for people

Not only have we greatly expanded the state's involvement in all of these areas, but we have undertaken from the start to blend and target our investments to fill needs and seize opportunities, and to use public dollars to leverage as much private investment as possible. In short, Massachusetts since 1976 has been more than activist when it comes to economic development—it has been entrepreneurial.

Infrastructure

In 1975, we began rebuilding a neglected and crumbling economic infrastructure. In an era when every major construction project poses legitimate environmental and community concerns, we have planned and built interstate highway segments that have been critical to the economic revitalization of western, central, and southeastern Massachusetts. We have all but completed a $2 billion modernization and expansion of the metropolitan Boston transit system. We have substantially rebuilt the Port of Boston and the rail freight network in the state. And we have helped local and regional governments build nearly $400 million in sewage treatment works.

The job of creating an infrastructure for the twenty-first century is far from over. More than a dozen new transportation projects of great regional significance are in the planning or early construction stage, from the long-awaited Pittsfield Bypass and Airport Connector in the Berkshires to the restoration of an extensive commuter rail network south of Boston. Our legislature has committed another $400 million for local sewage treatment facilities.

And two projects that hold the key to economic progress in all of metropolitan Boston, and therefore in all of New England itself, are now on a firm timetable for completion in the late 1990s—the $3.3 billion Third Harbor Tunnel, Seaport Access Road, and reconstruction of the Central Artery; and the $2.5 billion cleanup of Boston Harbor.

Capital

It was clear a decade ago that if entrepreneurs were to invest in our industries and developers were to invest in our cities, Massachusetts had to help. And help we did, with a series of capital formation initiatives that have paid off handsomely. The Massachusetts Industrial Finance Agency, created in 1078, has now financed $4 billion in growth and 76,000 new jobs through the issuance of industrial revenue bonds, and it is already packaging taxable issues and direct loans to keep the ball rolling after tax reform.

The Massachusetts Technology Development Corporation, also created in 1978, was America's first—and has been its most successful—state venture capital company; it has helped 40 of this state's most creative entrepreneurs get to market.

Today, these two agencies head an extraordinary array of more than a dozen public financing tools designed to stimulate the kinds of private investment Massachusetts needs—in old and new industries, in strategic land and buildings, in commercial centers and housing.

People

Massachusetts invests in her people. Even a decade ago, while concentrating on the infrastructure and capital needs of an aging economy, we began new initiatives in education and training. Today, our commitment to education and training is paramount. Alongside a solid implementation of the Job Training Partnership Act, we have placed perhaps the nation's best customized training program, the Bay State Skills Corporation, and the first of a series of regional partnerships to match private-sector expansion commitments with the necessary work force, MassJobs Southeast.

ET, our program for recipients of Aid to Families with Dependent Children, has become a national model by bringing over 40,000 welfare families into the economic mainstream, in jobs with more than 8,000 Massachusetts employers that pay, on average, more than double the yearly welfare grant. And in 1986, ET meant $120 million for Massachusetts in welfare savings and increased revenues—an important fiscal benefit of helping people find opportunity.

Our Reemployment Assistance Program has helped over 20,000 workers displaced by plant closings and layoffs face the economic challenge of their lives. Three-quarters of them have found jobs, at salaries averaging over 85 percent of their old wages.

The foundation on which any training effort must be built is education. In 1985, the Massachusetts legislature enacted the comprehensive Education Reform Act. This bill strengthens our entire K–12 system through special state aid to poorer districts, teacher development, and a stronger curriculum.

Finally, we are making Massachusetts's 27 public colleges and universities into the intellectual resource they must be for this state's economic future. We quadrupled state scholarship assistance between 1983 and 1987. We have increased state support for public higher education by a percentage greater than any other industrial state in the country has. Now, we are ready to undertake a $954 million, 10-year modernization and expansion of the system and a prepaid College Opportunity Fund that will keep tuitions affordable for tomorrow's students.

Even these investments, and the private commitments they help produce, would amount to less than the sum of their parts if we did not have a clear sense of where we want the Massachusetts economy to go. For while most decisions about which investments to make, which technologies to try, and which communities to build in are private and are made for business reasons, the public role in shaping some of those decisions at the margin can be profoundly important. Massachusetts has set her sights on innovation and opportunity.

Innovation

Since 1982, Massachusetts has made a conscious effort to help both her mature manufacturing industries and her promising new technology producers gain a solid footing in the state, national, and world economies.

On the basis of findings and recommendations of the Commission on the Future of Mature Industries, which I appointed in 1983, we are now able to focus a full battery of resources and analytical talent on companies that have a legitimate chance to change and grow. We have had some widely reported successes—contributing infrastructure and training support to the new world headquarters of Ocean Spray cranberries in Lakeville; providing low-interest, subordinated financing through two buyouts to keep Morse Twist Drill, one of our oldest and proudest tool makers, in New Bedford; and finding Cabot Stain a new headquarters and plant site in Newburyport, and making the loan that closed the deal.

We have helped General Electric launch new, technology-intensive ventures in Pittsfield and Lynn in the face of severe contractions in its natural transformer, jet engine, and turbine businesses, and we helped GE to expand as well as modernize its plant in Fitchburg.

There are many more examples, deeply significant to Massachusetts, if less widely known. Our objective is not to deny economic change. On the contrary, our objective is to help ensure that change in the form of technological, capital, and managerial innovation, reaches into our older industries and fashions a competitive future for them.

At the same time, we have actively joined with businesses, educators, and venture capitalists to promote the most promising of this state's leading-edge technologies. At our Massachusetts Microelectronics Center, our engineering schools and computer companies are training the next generation of VLSI engineers. In four other Centers of Excellence, creative partnerships are advancing our capabilities in biotechnology, marine sciences, photovoltaics and polymer plastics and bringing new ideas to market.

In 1987 we began a new agenda of initiatives to speed the process of technological innovation. We are planning a new Center of Excellence in applied technology and productivity—actually, a network of "greenhouses" to help companies and workers find the solutions to more modern, efficient manufacturing capabilities. We intend to build a series of small business incubators across Massachusetts. And our already successful Office of International Trade and Investment will step up its efforts to help key Massachusetts industries—from machine tools to software—find targeted overseas markets for their goods.

The fruit of our efforts can be seen in two examples. One is Interleaf, a new company that makes integrated desktop publishing systems for textbooks and manuals—a stunning combination of applied computer hardware and software. Interleaf's new headquarters is located in East Cambridge, one of this nation's true beehives of innovation and entrepreneurship. Interleaf's emergence is owed chiefly, of course, to the vision and daring of its two creators. But the Massachusetts Technology Development Corporation was there, too, when private sources could not finance the entire start-up. And Interleaf's building was developed with the help of a low-cost state mortgage—part of a Lechmere Canal revitalization project in which the commonwealth has financed comprehensive public improvements as a necessary prelude to developer investment.

A second example is the Taunton-based Kopin Corporation, a photovoltaics company that was the brainchild of a Chinese immigrant named Dr. John Fan. Photovoltaics is one of our Centers of Excellence technologies, and Taunton, an old industrial city in southeastern Massachusetts, is a distressed community on the way back. In 1986, these two state priorities converged when a package of city, state, and private financing enabled Kopin to establish its headquarters in Taunton's Myles Standish Industrial Park. There, Kopin will make the transition from research and development (R&D) to commercialization.

It is precisely this convergence of economic innovation and regional revitalization that brings us to the second of our strategic priorities, economic opportunity and good jobs for every region of Massachusetts.

Opportunity

In 1975 the cities of Massachusetts bore testimony to everything that had gone wrong with urban America. Our historic downtowns were economic ghost towns; the infrastructure and housing of our cities were in disrepair; and urban unemployment was far in excess of an already distressing statewide average.

But we rejected the conventional wisdom that our cities were dead, and we undertook a state urban policy unlike any in America. Starting in Lowell—the city my father came to from Greece 75 years ago—we created an urban heritage park program; today, 13 heritage parks are open, being built, or being planned. These are not parks in the traditional sense—they are careful, loving restorations of buildings and canals and mills and waterfronts that celebrate the industrial and ethnic histories of our cities and help pave the way for downtown revitalization.

We required state agencies to locate their offices and facilities in older downtowns whenever possible. We used housing subsidies to rehabilitate landmark buildings. We made commercial development projects eligible for industrial revenue bonds—but only in established downtown and neighborhood business districts.

We invested in regional transit systems that focus on downtown centers, and we provided the funds to help our cities build convention centers, auditoriums, and parking garages, streets, sidewalks, and access roads, to nail down private investment and create good jobs for their people.

Today, Lowell is a national success story. Her unemployment rate has dropped from over 15 percent to five percent. She has 25,000 new jobs, and has spearheaded the creation of many thousands more throughout the Merrimack Valley. Wang Labs and Prince Spaghetti have deepened their roots in this, their headquarters city. And in 1986, 800,000 tourists visited Lowell, Massachusetts, the city all but given up for dead 11 years earlier.

We are now within sight of a goal I set over a decade ago—the revitalization of every downtown in Massachusetts. Some, like Springfield, are very far along. Others have farther to go. But virtually all have put in place a critical mass of public and private investment and an all-important sense of self-renewal. That has enabled us to broaden our view, to look beyond downtowns—to neighborhoods, on one hand, and to entire regions, on the other.

One negative consequence of our economic resurgence is a serious shortage of affordable housing. The average single-family home in Greater Boston now costs $170,000, and for several years, housing production fell some 20,000 units per year short of demand. With the federal government's withdrawal from the affordable housing business, Massachusetts has a major challenge on its hands.

Our response has been the Massachusetts Housing Partnership—a state-led family some 111 local alliances of cities and towns, developers, builders, nonprofits, banks, union pension funds, and neighborhood leaders. Through public contributions of land and innovative new financing programs, the partnership has provided for over 6,000 new units of public housing and over 8,000 units of mixed-income rental housing. We have found a way to produce affordable homes for middle-income families, and the partnership will produce thousands of such units in the next few years.

The partnership not only ensures that affordable housing—an indispensable part of genuine economic opportunity—is available to the people of Massachusetts. It also is a prime ingredient in the effort to revitalize neighborhoods and villages throughout Massachusetts.

Our other strategy for area development is called Targets for Opportunity. However strong the state's overall economic performance, and however powerful the economic momentum of downtown Boston and Route 128, Massachusetts still has communities and entire regions that are not sharing fully in our booming economy.

In Merrimack Valley, an area brimming with prosperity, Lawrence is a poor city with a large and needy immigrant population. In the shadow of downtown Boston's high-rise resurgence, neighborhoods like Roxbury and Dorchester need new investment and new economic vitality. And in northern Berkshire County, the Northern Tier, northern Worcester County, the Blackstone Valley, and southeastern Massachusetts, entire regional economies need special help to move into the mainstream. Their unemployment rates—in double digits and far in excess of the statewide average in the winter of 1983—have come down substantially. But we have more work to do if we are going to build diversified, innovative, and durable area economies throughout Massachusetts.

In each of these target areas, the commonwealth has reached out to leaders of local government, business, labor, and education to help them fashion a revitalization strategy that they and we believe can work. The initiative and the insight come from the people of the region—but essential support and encouragement come from the state.

Taunton is a prime example. One of five proud old industrial cities in southeastern Massachusetts, Taunton in early 1983 had an unemployment rate of 14 percent. But there was a plan. In 1977, the commonwealth had transferred 400 acres of surplus state land to the city to create the Myles Standish Industrial Park—a badly needed regional magnet for industrial growth. That same year, construction began on a long-delayed piece of the state's interstate highway system, the so-called missing link of I-495. Where that highway passes through Taunton, the state designed an interchange that would ensure good access to the planned industrial park.

In 1983, the highway was opened and 200 acres of Myles Standish were made available for industrial use. But there were only two plants—and early that year, one of them closed.

The commonwealth went to work with the people of Taunton. We invested heavily in the park's streets, sidewalks, and sewers. We promoted Myles Standish as a gateway to the abundant land and high-quality work force of southeastern Massachusetts. And when a resurgent Massachusetts economy needed a new direction to grow, Myles Standish Industrial Park was ready.

Today, 50 new plants are open or under construction in Myles Standish. They will employ more than 3,500 men and women. They range from Kopin Industries to a new GTE plant with 800 employees. These two and many others came to Taunton with the assistance and encouragement of state government. In May of 1987, unemployment in Taunton was down to 4.6 percent.

The success at Myles Standish is only part of the story. In my second week in office, in January of 1983, I brought my entire Development Cabinet to Southeastern Massachusetts University for an economic summit conference with leaders of the region. From that day to this, state government has worked with the region's leaders to recruit a diversified industrial base, revitalize historic downtowns, produce affordable housing, and rebuild the working waterfronts of New Bedford and Fall River.

A NATIONAL CHALLENGE

The lesson of Massachusetts is not that everything we did will work for other states or for the nation. The lesson lies in how we saw the job of economic development:

- We set our sights on innovation and opportunity as fundamental strategic goals.
- We played the role of an entrepreneurial investor in a wide array of public-private partnerships.
- We understood that the work of economic development is done—and its benefits are enjoyed—in regions and communities, not in overall economic statistics.

National economic policy can and must embrace these same principles—not as a substitute for sound macroeconomic policies, but as an essential complement to them.

The trailblazing efforts of Massachusetts and other states can find expression in federal policy if the next president and the Congress take a number of key initiatives.

Get the nation's fiscal house in order. Our economy simply cannot sustain innovation or provide opportunity for all Americans if it is choking on an annual deficit of $150–$200 billion. There is a direct relationship between our budget deficit and our inability to compete in the international economy. According to the Commerce Department, "the critical element [in producing the trade imbalance] was the uninterrupted expansion of the federal budget deficit from about $60 billion in 1980 to over $200 billion in 1985."

The debt service that carries that deficit not only drives up interest rates and depletes American savings, but balloons the deficit even more, sapping the national government's ability to invest in the makings of economic innovation and growth.

There are three ways to reduce the budget deficit—control spending; improve our economic performance; and increase revenues. We must do all three. But before we rush to impose new taxes, it's about time we collected those taxes we are already due.

Tax compliance in America is now down to 81 percent. One out of every five American taxpayers or businesses have failed to pay some or all of the taxes they owe. At that rate, $110 billion in annual revenues that are legitimately owed the United States of America will not be collected.

In Massachusetts, the REAP program has shown that tax compliance can be increased dramatically and permanently. Seventeen other states, from New York to North Dakota, California to Illinois, have used aggressive and creative tax compliance programs to change their fiscal conditions. Tax enforcement and compliance should be the nation's first weapon in the war against the deficit.

Invest in infrastructure. Greater Boston is a world center of finance, technology, education, medicine, and communications. It is a labor market of some two million workers, the economic center of New England, a major exporter of some of America's most innovative products, and a global destination for travelers. Without the Central Artery, Third Harbor

Tunnel, and Seaport Access Road, the region's movement of goods and services would grind to a crawl. Without the cleanup of Boston Harbor, the law of the land would require a halt to new sewer hookups. Either way, economic growth would stop, and that would clearly be bad for the national economy.

Yet, early in 1987, both the Highway Bill and the Clean Water Act had to be passed over the president's veto. What kind of economic strategy is that? In the last decade, every state has shown that public infrastructure is indispensable to durable economic growth, and infrastructure is never cheap. Federal assistance is both essential and appropriate—what higher national economic priority could we have?

Invest in people. If the concrete, asphalt, earthworks, and piping of public infrastructure is one basic underpinning of growth and competitiveness, the other is surely the skill, knowledge, and commitment of the American work force. The challenges facing that work force are legion:

- Between now and the year 2000, literally millions of jobs in manufacturing and traditional services will change radically or become obsolete.
- In the year 2000, new jobs coming on-line will require higher skill levels from workers, more than 75 percent of whom are already working today.
- Smaller companies, which produce most new jobs and most of our innovations, find it hardest to provide training.
- Between now and the year 2000, one out of every four ninth-graders will drop out of high school, and teenage pregnancy rates will continue to rise.
- Nearly 14 million young Americans are growing up in poverty, with dependency rather than work as a model for later life.

In the face of these challenges, the nation's principal employment and training program—the Job Training Partnership Act (JTPA)—needs to be strengthened, deepened, and broadened, not cut repeatedly. JTPA is a good model. It revolves around area partnerships rather than centralized bureaucracy; it reaches out to key populations, like disadvantaged youth and dislocated workers; it responds to the needs of regional economies; and it has encouraged the beginnings of real collaboration among the states' training systems, employment services, and vocational schools.

Yet JTPA must do more. It must be linked even more tightly to the employment security system, so that every displaced worker receives a package of training, counseling, and placement services as well as unemployment insurance. At the Quincy shipyard in Massachusetts and the San José auto assembly plant in California, well-planned and caring reemployment programs found decent jobs for most of the victims of two massive closings. These are models for national action. By helping the hundreds of thousands of experienced American workers each year who are caught in the winds of change, we can advance the progress of innovation and keep the promise of opportunity.

JTPA must be given the resources and the flexibility to help build training and recruitment programs for innovative companies that are ready to take root in distressed urban and rural areas.

And JTPA must be given the task, alongside effective national welfare reform, of providing a full range of training and support services for welfare recipients taking the giant step into the world of work.

Build strong area economies. Today, 31 states are in recession, and even prosperous ones have cities, counties, and entire regions, both metropolitan and rural, in deep economic trouble. That is simply unacceptable if we are serious about a stronger national economy.

Change will not happen by accident. Innovation and opportunity did not simply trickle into southeastern Massachusetts or Greater Springfield, and they will not simply trickle into the Iron Range of Minnesota, Greater Waterloo, Iowa, or the Rio Grande Valley of Texas. Just as Massachusetts has helped to rebuild her Targets for Opportunity, America must help her state and local leaders build sustained economic recovery in every region of the nation.

One way to do that is to cut through the bureaucracy, fragmentation, and lack of regional focus that so often characterize the implementation of federal development programs. A small group of regional specialists—working with governors, mayors, and county officials; building partnerships of business, labor, and education; and fashioning individual projects into coordinated regional agendas—could make an enormous difference in this country's economic future.

But we also need a new centerpiece for area development, an initiative that embodies our belief in local and regional partnerships, and for that I propose a Strategic Investment Fund. This program would build on the best features of our existing economic development programs. It would direct the most assistance to states in the greatest distress, but it would give all states the opportunity to invest in those regions within their borders that need help to rebuild their economies.

The fund would help both to build public infrastructure and to finance private industrial and commercial expansion. The secret, of course, is not for Washington to pick the projects, do the work, or discourage state financial participation. The secret is for Washington to call forth from every state and community in the land the kind of strategic initiatives that many governors and mayors have already undertaken—and to support those initiatives as an essential part of national economic policy.

The Strategic Investment Fund would play a pivotal role in the reconstruction of area economies. But two other national investment priorities—new technologies and decent, affordable housing—would broaden and deepen the participation of every state, community, and region in the growth of the American economy.

Invest in technology. Every American knows that technological innovation is at the heart of the global economic race. And we must do more to promote innovation by investing heavily in civilian R&D rather than cutting back, by maintaining favorable tax treatment for private R&D investment, and by reducing the budget deficit—one of the principal impediments to entrepreneurship and innovation.

But increased investment alone will fall short of the mark without a national strategy that makes full use of our people's creativity. In Japan and Western Europe, large-scale partnerships of business, universities, and governments are moving exciting new technologies, both basic and applied, from the research lab to the marketplace. And here in America, efforts like New York's seven Centers of Advanced Technology and Ohio's Thomas Edison Program are proving that states have an important role to play.

America needs a national network of Centers of Excellence, focused wherever possible on our state universities— the onetime land grant colleges, where innovations in agriculture helped build the strong national economy of another era. Each center would be a partnership of academic, entrepreneurial, and government commitment, and centers would work together in networks.

The mission would be twofold: to advance America's competitive position in technologies of world importance, and to make sure that the economic benefits of this bold enterprise are diffused to all parts of the country. Like the Michigan and Massachusetts programs, national Centers of Excellence should address not only new products and services, but the application of new process technologies to America's mature industrial base.

The National Science Foundation's fledgling network of Engineering Research Centers represents one important part of the effort we need. The proposed National Center for Manufacturing Sciences—a nationwide network of applied technology R&D partnerships—is another. But these and other proposals must be pulled together into a concerted national campaign for technological innovation.

Invest in affordable housing. The strength of America's economy cannot be separated from the fabric of her communities. From big-city neighborhoods to rural towns, from the national disgrace of homelessness to the slow, steady deterioration of places where families have lived, we are not keeping our national commitment to provide decent, affordable housing for low- and moderate-income families. And communities that are ready to grow and create jobs cannot bring housing on-line at prices that workers can afford.

Until 1981, the commitment to affordable housing had been a bipartisan one for nearly half a century. As recently as the Ford and Carter Administrations, we were producing more than 200,000 units of federally assisted housing for families of low and moderate income every year. About 25,000 were projected for 1987.

A National Partnership for Affordable Housing is the answer—not a massive new federal construction program that repeats old mistakes, but a creative alliance of state and local partnerships supported by a federal government that cares.

The partnership would have three goals: to build and rehabilitate good housing at affordable cost; to protect our existing investment in low- and moderate-income housing from expiring contract restrictions and wholesale disinvestment; and to expand home ownership opportunities for young families and other first-time potential buyers, who, for the first time since World War II, are finding the American dream of home ownership beyond their reach.

From Boston to Chattanooga, from Cleveland to San Francisco, communities are marshaling public and private resources to produce affordable housing in new and exciting ways. It is time to make this a truly national effort.

CONCLUSION

This essay began with the widespread concern of Americans about the ability of our economy to compete in the world market. Yet much of the discussion was directed not outward, to other nations, but inward, to the workings of our own economy. And most of the ideas presented here deal not with traditional macroeconomic policies but with the ability of America's economy to sustain innovation and to provide opportunity across the rich tapestry of our regions and communities.

None of this means that a thoughtful, fair, and effective foreign trade policy is less than essential, or that America no longer needs to manage its fiscal and monetary systems successfully. But if the Massachusetts experience teaches us anything, it is that economic development is largely local and regional in nature; that it requires strategic investments by government and the private sector alike; that it can combine the goals of innovation and opportunity; and that it works.

If America is to compete, it is time for us to elevate the successful development initiatives of our states and cities into a great national idea. And it is time to act.

CHAPTER 4

Making America First Again: A Plan for Jobs and Growth for the Twenty-First Century

Congressman Richard A. Gephardt

AS AMERICA PREPARES TO enter the twenty-first century, there is one fundamental requirement for preserving our political stability, reaching the social goals of a just society, and restoring our international security. This requirement is economic growth with job creation. A growing economy means new opportunities for our young people, new resources to solve our pressing problems, and new chances for all groups to join the parade of prosperity. By contrast, a stagnant economy allows our social ills to fester, widens the gaps between the haves and have-nots, and erodes our standing in the world.

Since 1980 America has tried to purchase short-term economic growth by running up "twin towers" of budgetary and trade deficits. President Reagan's supply-side revolution has meant that foreigners supply our products and our capital. If current trends continue, our net foreign debt will top $1 trillion by early next decade. Unless strong action is taken, we and our children many have to repay this debt through economic decline in the future. It is disturbing to consider that ours may be the first generation of Americans to knowingly leave the next generation with a lower standard of living and fewer opportunities than we ourselves enjoyed.

This specter cuts to the heart of the American psyche. Can we still compete as a world economic power? Or, in a fundamental sense, have we passed our golden age? Are we like an aging athlete, who should retire from the economic arena and leave the competition to younger and more vibrant societies?

It need not be that way; indeed, it must not be that way. America's finest days are still ahead of us. But we must begin today to take the tough steps required to restore our international competitiveness. In this essay, I propose a serious of measures to guide us through the task of making America first again. There are four broad types of steps: (1) trade reforms to create an international environment where American workers and business have a fair chance to compete; (2) education and training programs to prepare the American people for foreign competition; (3) fundamental changes in policies to deal with taxation, federal budget deficits, and Third World debt; and (4) changes in management practices, business practices, and research and development priorities. In essence, these measures will use the federal government as a catalyst for a new partnership among business, labor, farmers, academia, and state and local governments to lead America forward.

STANDING UP FOR AMERICA'S TRADE INTERESTS

The most pressing threat to our future prosperity is our yawning trade deficit. Under the Reagan administration, our trade deficit soared from near equality to $167 billion in 1986. Even the prospect of modest improvement in this deficit still leaves us with an unacceptable flood of red ink. We are racing against time: The additional $500 million net debt we incur each day can be serviced only through the sale of major American firms or physical resources, the

transfer of huge amounts of federal securities to foreign financiers, or the devaluation of the U.S. dollar to the debased
status of a developing country's currency.

About 1.4 million well-paying jobs in the export sector
have been lost in the process. When President Reagan boasts
of job creation, he neglects to note that more than half the
jobs created in the American economy since 1980 pay below
the poverty line. We are exporting our industries and our
jobs.

Hardship is reaching beyond our traditional "Rustbelt"
industries. Even growth sectors like high technology, services, and agriculture, which will be keys to our long-term
economic prosperity, are suffering unprecedented declines
as the world's greatest economic power has been transformed from the largest foreign lender to the largest debtor
in just four years. In 1980, America led the world in the
high-tech wave of the future with a $26 billion trade sur-
plus. Today, this surplus has totally vanished. A similar dis-
appearing act has hit our agricultural trade balance.

But as disturbing as these trends are, even more poignant
are the human tragedies they reflect. Traveling around our
country, I speak every day with disheartened steelworkers,
farmers, and high-tech entrepreneurs. The work ethic runs
deep in these people; they are proud of their self-reliance.
But they have lost their livelihoods for reasons beyond their
control.

Can the president explain to these people why his administration refused for years to bring the dollar down to a competitive level while they lost their foreign markets? Or why
his administration placed a low priority on the elimination
of foreign protectionist practices that stole their jobs? Or
why his administration insists on fiscal policies that drove
the federal budget deficit to a record high and sacrificed
their exports?

We must begin to take trade seriously, raising it to the top
of our national agenda. Trade must be on our minds when
we debate our federal budget, negotiate with our strategic
allies, and adopt an exchange rate policy. We must come out
from behind a dogmatic, unilateral "free trade" stance and
recognize that, as Benjamin Disraeli noted, "Free trade is

not a principle, it is an expedient." To replace this administration's record of what has been called malign neglect, I propose new policies to exploit foreign trade to our national economic advantage. We must insist on equal access to foreign markets, assert our trading rights in a consistent yet forceful fashion, foster high-growth sectors key to our economic future, and ease the transition process for workers, entrepreneurs, and communities hurt by foreign competition.

Specifically, I have sponsored legislation to pry open protected markets in foreign countries that build up huge surpluses with the United States. At present, the concept of free trade means that Americans are free to buy, but not to sell. Foreign trading partners must be forced to abandon such practices as Japanese dumping in the American market; massive subsidization of agriculture in the European community; worldwide protectionism in telecommunications equipment; restrictions on American service and construction firms; tariff and nontariff barriers to our exports to Japan, Taiwan, Brazil, and Korea; abuses of our intellectual property rights; and violations of workers' rights. Even the most conservative estimates acknowledge that up to one million Americans are deprived of jobs because of these practices.

We cannot be afraid to threaten market sanctions in the United States in order to force foreign countries to provide us reciprocal access to their markets. This technique is not protectionist, nor does it tie the president's hands. It simply puts a tool in the president's hands and asks him to use it to dismantle protectionist barriers abroad in support of the world's free trade system. We cannot ask the American people to take the tough steps necessary to become competitive if every time they try to get their foot in the door, the door is slammed shut. American entrepreneurs need to know that if they develop new technologies and make good products, their government will make sure there is a market for them overseas. This isn't protectionism: It's fair play.

But gaining access to foreign markets is only the first step. Once these markets are opened, American producers have to broaden their perspectives and enter the new world of international commerce. Many of our largest firms are experts in the export game, but most small and medium-sized firms are still on the sidelines, neglecting the opportunities offered by foreign markets. It has been said that for a firm in Texas, exporting means sending goods to California or New York, and vice versa. It takes a substantial financial and managerial commitment for a firm to decide to start exporting. Government has a role to play in supporting firms making this commitment. I sponsored legislation to create systems to collect and disseminate information on export opportunities, to promote aggressive use of the Export-Import Bank to combat predatory financing by competitors abroad, to expand export credit and loan guarantee programs under the Commodity Credit Corporation to boost farm exports and offset foreign subsidies, and to expand the role of American embassies abroad in identifying trade opportunities and promoting exports.

To ease the transition process for trade-impacted communities, we also need an innovative program to help communities adjust to the sudden displacements that result from foreign trade and other shocks. The Tax Base Insurance Program, similar to the federal flood insurance program, would allow a community to insure itself against the reduction in its tax base as a result of the decline of industries hurt by trade. It would allow these communities breathing space to attract new industries and to retrain workers. After a start-up period in which government efforts would serve as a catalyst, the program would be turned over to the private sector.

INVESTING IN OUR GREATEST NATURAL RESOURCE: PEOPLE

But are Americans up to the challenge of foreign competition? A level playing field is of no use unless your team can compete. The first step on the road to reclaiming our international excellence is investing in people. At a time when President Reagan calls for slashed funds for higher education, experts predict that by the next decade, half of all Americans will be virtually unemployable because they will lack the reading skills necessary to compete in the job market. Sixty million Americans are illiterate. They cannot read a book, a lease, the American Constitution, or the names on a ballot.

A commitment to education and training is required for the sake of our national economy and our participatory democracy. We must set a national goal of wiping out illiteracy by the end of this century, and we must be willing to pay to do it. Our schools must no longer be made the first victims of budgetary stringency. What sense is there in spending our scarce resources on an additional aircraft carrier or some half-baked space-based defense system if such expenditures force us to sacrifice the educational fabric of the very nation we are seeking to defend? Edmund Burke was right in pointing out, "Education is the cheapest defense of nations."

To this end, I have formulated a National Literacy Project to assist educational development at all levels. We must have students who are prepared, right from the start, to enter the work force with the newest technologies and information at their fingertips. At the elementary and secondary school levels, federal subsidies should help poorer districts construct good schools, hire the best teachers, and purchase advanced educational equipment. Incentives should be available to support private contributions of new equipment to such schools. We should also bring the marketplace into the schoolroom to enhance the partnership between private industry and public education. We should promote job training linked to job opportunities, team teaching using teachers and industry specialists, on-site instruction at factories and offices, training of teachers and students in the use of new technologies, and business-sponsored recognition for outstanding teachers. American high school students must have the skills in trade-related disciplines. The President's Commission on Industrial Competitiveness proposed stipends to encourage students to pursue graduate-level degrees in engineering. We must take the next step to expand this to programs at all levels in mathematics, sciences, and foreign languages.

No qualified student should be barred from attending college because of the inability to pay. I support a two-track system of support for college-bound students. First, there should be a mix of federal loans, grants, and work-study programs. And second, I propose creating a new Individual Development and Education Account (IDEA). The IDEA program would enable parents to set up an educational savings account for their children. The federal government would provide matching funds for family contributions based on a formula tied to income level. For families with incomes so low that they could not afford to contribute to the account, the federal government would make the contributions for them.

To combat adult illiteracy, stipends would be available to retired teachers and other qualified individuals to go into their communities and teach adults to read and write.

In the related field of worker retraining, experts tell us that the average person entering the work force today will have to change professions at least five times during his or her lifetime. We must facilitate this professional mobility by involving the federal government in activities such as job search banks, counseling, training, and limited relocation assistance. We should also consider a new federal program to promote pension portability. To encourage the development of small business, we should allow individuals to use their unemployment insurance money to start their own businesses. I have proposed legislation to do this.

GETTING THE BASICS RIGHT: REFORMING OUR NATIONAL ECONOMY

American trade and competitiveness issues do not occur in a vacuum. To set a proper environment for American firms to exploit their natural comparative advantage, we must attend to the basic parameters of our national economy. Congress took a major step in that direction when it passed the Tax Reform Act of 1986. This was not an easy task. Bill Bradley and I faced stiff odds when we introduced the Bradley-Gephardt Fair Tax Bill, which formed the basis of the 1986 reform. The president opposed us. The special interests tried to preserve their privileges. The politicians were afraid of anything likely to upset so many applecarts.

But we had a clear vision of where we wanted to go. Our goal was to create a tax system we could be proud of, a system that imposed an equivalent burden on all Americans, a system that no longer allowed loopholes to skew investment into unproductive sectors. When the lobbyists came, we were able to mobilize public opinion to resist narrow, sectarian interests. Eventually, even the president came on board, and we saw the triumph of fairness reach its conclusion in October 1986.

This reform enhances our competitiveness by creating a more rational investment climate. It lets capital flow to productive sectors able to offer the best rates of return rather than investments that offer the best tax breaks. It rewards individuals for their own hard work: Workers know that for each extra hour they work, they'll get to keep more.

A second economic reform to enhance our competitiveness is the reduction of our federal budget deficit. The Reagan administration's unwillingness to face up to the tough decisions regarding taxes and spending digs us into a deeper and deeper hole. To finance this deficit, we soak up most of the investment capital in our economy. We borrow at home and abroad to finance today's consumption, selling off government securities, major American corporations, and large chunks of our real estate. We also watch the impact of these deficits on our exchange rate, pricing American producers out of their rightful markets and bidding up interest rates that squeeze out productive investment. We already use almost one-fifth of our budget for interest payments, money that should be invested in people, machines, infrastructure, and research. The real impact of these deficits will be felt by our children. As Jonathan Swift once noted, "How free the present age is in laying taxes on the next."

We need to balance our books in a rational and considered fashion. We must reject the mechanistic approaches or draconic hatchets that imply that all federal programs are of equal worth and should meet equal fates. We need so-called sunset legislation, which insists on periodic reevaluation of programs to determine whether they still are effective and fulfilling their stated purposes. We need to make selected cuts in our defense spending. We need to enhance federal revenues, in part through an oil import fee. This fee would also be a vital step in reestablishing our energy security, ensuring that we will never again be vulnerable to the energy blackmail of foreign suppliers.

We also need to deal with the problem of Third World debt. Farmers and manufacturers watch markets dry up as countries use scarce foreign exchange not to buy U.S. goods but to repay foreign bankers; investors wonder about the security of banks whose solvency depends on repayment of $100 billion in shaky loans to Third World governments; stability in Latin America, Africa, and Asia is threatened by austerity measures that may bring stagnation, massive unemployment, emigration, and, paradoxically, expanding debt. As developing countries try to service their $1 trillion debt through quick-fix exports and by squeezing imports, the United States has played more than its fair role. Since 1979, our imports of manufactured goods from developing countries have increased 150 percent; those of Japan and Western Europe dropped. Since 1981, our $4 billion trade surplus with the leading countries of Latin America has been transformed into a $16 billion deficit.

For all the complexity of the debt crisis, the solution boils down to the questions of who is responsible and who should pay. There is enough blame to go around: Third World countries refused to cut consumption in the face of large oil debts in the late 1970s; banks gambled for quick profits in dubious loans; creditor countries encouraged bank lending to recycle petrodollars; and our nation allowed budgetary deficits to bid up the dollar's value, raising service payments on debts denominated in U.S. dollars, and soaking up capital vital to Third World development.

Developing countries, creditor banks, the International Monetary Fund/World Bank, and industrial countries should all play a role in solving the problem. Several approaches should be considered: (1) Cap annual debt service payment from debtor nations on the basis of ability to pay; (2) begin selective bank write-downs of the worst debts, encouraged by changes in tax and banking laws; (3) expand structural adjustment loans for Third World debtors through a new World Bank subsidiary; (4) encourage special aid from large surplus countries, including Japan; and (5) require Third World countries to adopt growth-enhancing policies that are likely to loosen import restrictions. This program may be costly, but delaying the day of reckoning for massive default throughout the Third World would be even more expensive for the world economy.

INVESTING IN INNOVATION AND REFORMING MANAGEMENT PRACTICES

Finally, we must reform our marketplaces and our management practices. Most important is the stimulation of research and development (R&D). We must seek a national commitment to invest up to three percent of our gross national product in R&D each year. We must help our universities and R&D centers improve and modernize their facilities.

In federal research, we cannot maintain an environment in which three-fourths of federal funds going to R&D are dedicated to defense-related activities. In 1986, more than $4.3 billion was devoted to Star Wars research alone, while private-sector commercial R&D was squeezed out. Beyond the financial burden, many of our best minds are being diverted to investing in new instruments of terror in space rather than solving our pressing social, environmental, and commercial problems here on earth. We must reorder our priorities by establishing an Advanced Technology Institute to foster applied research aimed at developing new products and discovering cost-saving production techniques. This institute would fund regional technology centers, encourage government-industry projects in applied research, and develop curricula for programs in manufacturing engineering across the country. It would be sponsored through a partnership between the government and the private sector. Further, military R&D now taking place has provided little benefit for commercial development. We must create a review office in the federal government to determine whether currently classified research can be made available to American producers.

Reordering the priorities of our financial and business communities is a process in which government has a limited direct role. But our leaders need to speak out for a new corporate culture that emphasizes long-term thinking over short-term profits, that stresses human values of honesty, integrity, and community spirit over the prospect of a quick buck. It is a travesty that the best-known businessman of 1986 was not the chief executive officer of a major corporation or an innovative producer—it was inside trader Ivan Boesky. Many of our business executives are more interested in creating junk bonds than quality products. Our financial institutions were created to raise capital for corporations, to provide a conveyance for corporate growth and increased productivity. But the corporations have become chips in a giant poker game played for high stakes by people who produce nothing, invent nothing, grow nothing, and service nothing. What social needs did the top 10 Wall Street financiers fulfill in 1986 to justify their average earnings of $68 million apiece?

In the workplace, too, management must look to foster human values of self-pride and responsibility. We need to manage for quality, rather than mere cost cutting. A recent survey noted that up to one-fourth of American workers are assigned full-time to repairing the errors of their coworkers. We need to listen to our own management gurus, such as J.M. Juran and W. Edwards Deming, as closely as the Japanese have. A new work ethic must emerge on the shop floor, one that emphasizes shared duties, fosters cooperative working relations between labor and management, and gives labor a stake in the success of its enterprise. We should encourage management to make use of incentives such as stock options and employee stock ownership plans to link pay and performance by rewarding the efforts of employees to boost productivity. We must support foster institutions such as the Quality and Productivity Improvement Center at the University of Wisconsin, as well as similar institutes that exist in North Carolina, Pennsylvania, and Southern California.

In this crucial period in the history of our country, too many of America's elected officials are trying to substitute idle criticism for leadership. But it is not enough to find fault with American management patterns, the state of American education, our massive budget deficit, the militarization of research and development, and our low national savings rate. We must adopt measures to help give Americans a fair shake in world markets, empower people with the capacity to compete, and set a proper economic environment for American business and labor. And most importantly, we must provide leadership: leadership that inspires and motivates, leadership that asks us to transcend narrow interests, leadership that renews our belief and commitment to sacrifice for excellence.

If we fail to act, we risk the continued loss of jobs, reduced industrial and agricultural capacities, a debased self-image, and a lower standard of living for ourselves and future generations. This is a legacy we must refuse to pass on to our children.

CHAPTER 5

Taking Control of America's Economic Destiny

Senator Al Gore

ONE OF THE IRONIES of our present situation is that several states on both coasts are doing very well for various specialized reasons, while people in the Farm Belt, in my home region of the South, and in the Rust Belt are not doing very well. We are a nation seriously divided by the failed trade and economic policies of the Reagan administration. After seven years, the Republican administration has not only failed to strengthen our economy, it has also undermined our industrial competitiveness, threatened our family farms, and weakened our chances for progress in the future.

The chaos inflicted by Reaganomics can be seen in a federal budget that is massive and still growing at a rate of $500 million every day. It can be seen in a trade deficit which, every two days, is fueled by imports that are almost $1 billion in excess of the goods and services we export. And it can be seen in an international debt that increases by $1 billion every three days.

But even numbers of this magnitude do not convey the full human dimension of economic neglect and wrong-headed policies. The real tragedy is families whose farms have been foreclosed. It is workers who have lost their jobs and young people who do not have decent job prospects. It is small businesses forced to close their doors, and whole communities that are powerless in stemming the movement of manufacturing jobs to operations overseas.

As a nation, we can do far better. For all communities and all Americans, we must do better. The solutions are not to be found in a collection of narrow-interest agendas, nor can they be readily drawn from the unique experiences of a few coastal states that enjoy a wealth of special resources. The challenges we face are far more complex and the opportunities of each community are far more diverse than can be solved by promises of quick fixes or miracle formulas.

Despite growing challenges, our economy has retained its basic strength. We still have vast natural and technological resources, and we certainly have the most talented workforce in the world. But we have come to a critical juncture. From every direction we are being challenged—in world trade, international leadership, technological prowess, and our very capacity to govern. The Reagan administration has chosen to ignore these challenges, passively watching as foreign competition has put thousands of Americans out of work, uncontrolled federal spending has robbed from our future, and the farm crisis has devastated our small towns and rural communities.

It is time to reverse this pattern of neglect. We need leadership that is up to the tremendous challenges we face. We have been challenged before, and we have responded to those challenges with a determination no other nation could hope to match. We can rise to the challenge again, and we can succeed again to build a bright future.

BUILDING ON OUR STRENGTHS, DEVELOPING NEW ONES

We are in the midst of a fundamental restructuring of our economic and industrial base, with far-reaching implications for farms and business, individuals and communities. Dramatic shifts are changing the way we work, what we produce, and how we compete in an increasingly global economy.

Retaining our economic leadership has been increasingly difficult over the past decade, as the United States has lost its competitive edge in one key industry after another. We first saw signs of trouble in our traditional manufacturing industries—textiles, cars, steel, and industrial chemicals. Many companies responded to the challenge by making extensive investments in new plants and equipment, but still more is needed to restore their strength in international markets. And now our leadership is being just as seriously challenged in agriculture and high technology areas—advanced computers, semiconductors, plastics, synthetics, and scientific instrumentation—as well as in services, such as insurance and banking.

There are no easy answers to the trade deficit or other economic problems. Nor will any single approach work forever or in every situation. We must find many ways to create full employment, to stabilize prices, and to build a future of opportunity for all citizens.

All of us—elected officials, business owners and managers, workers and educators, community leaders and concerned citizens alike—have a role to play in revitalizing our economy and creating new jobs. Reestablishing American economic leadership will take nothing less than an ambitious, concerted national effort—a commitment to think imaginatively, to choose wisely, and to act decisively.

The challenge of rebuilding and strengthening our economy is among the greatest challenges we have ever faced. But this nation has many unique strengths and opportunities, and I am an unwavering optimist about our prospects for success. Our opportunities are everywhere. They can be found in our vast natural resources. They are in our stock of advanced technologies. They are in our pool of skilled and hardworking people. Most importantly, our opportunities flow from this nation's spirit of initiative and drive—the desire and wherewithal to try and to succeed.

FREE, FAIR, AND EXPANDING TRADE

Our national strategy for progress and prosperity must have among its first priorities free, fair and expanding trade. The global economy currently faces tensions greater than at any time since the trade wars of the 1930s. Our $165 billion trade deficit is the largest in our history, having increased fourfold since 1980.

Yet we have a president who thinks the best trade policy is no policy at all. What we need, instead, is a president prepared to take the kinds of actions, domestically and internationally, that will both improve the American trade position and the management of the global economic system.

Our trade problems have been decades in the making. Yet trade has made the top of the national agenda only relatively recently. The next president of the United States must make trade a permanent national priority—he or she must articulate our trade policy and then implement it with a strong, single voice. This will entail, among other measures, the streamlining and reorganization of jurisdiction over trade matters that is currently splintered among over a dozen different departments and agencies. Improved coordination—coupled with a president who understands the critical importance of greatly expanded trade—would do much to clear up international confusion about U.S. trade policy.

Our trade policy must have four basic objectives: the effective enforcement of existing trade agreements, the expansion of products and services covered under GATT and other treaties that come up for negotiation, the stabilization of international currencies, and greatly expanded export opportunities for U.S. industry and agriculture.

Unfair trade practices must be eliminated, and systematic violations of trade agreements must be stopped. Japan, in particular, must be required to end its dumping in U.S. markets, to open up its domestic markets to U.S. products, and to practice greater reciprocity in general.

In seeking to end unfair trade practices, however, we must be careful to avoid counterproductive protectionism. Fixed, inflexible, and arbitrary targets forcing reductions in bilateral trade surpluses are likely to do more harm than good. Unilateral punitive actions would only invite retaliation against American exports. We must see the world as it is— complex, highly interdependent, and already under great strain from recent recessions and ongoing international economic competition. Trade wars are in no one's best interest.

We must look to creative ways for dealing with Third World debt and for promoting economic growth in developing countries as well as our own.

THE TOOLS TO COMPETE: FISCAL RESPONSIBILITY, TECHNOLOGY, AND TALENT

Improvements in trade relations and the stabilization of international currencies will help level the playing field and set the stage for revitalization of our economic base.

But efforts in these areas alone will not suffice as a long-term strategy for prosperity and progress. For this, we need an offensive strategy that goes beyond the bargaining tables to the real battlegrounds of our economic future—America's schoolrooms and boardrooms, our universities and factories, the Congress and the White House. The next president must not only look for solutions to our economic challenges in international trade practices but also in factors here at home that will improve our ability to compete and grow.

America still has the most advanced technologies, the finest universities, the most flexible political system, and the most dedicated and talented workforce of any nation in the world. These are our strengths. What we have lacked is the leaders with the foresight to steer those strengths to our advantage—to increase access to capital, to expand and utilize our scientific and technological expertise, and to make the most of the vast talents of the American people.

BUDGETS THAT BUILD FOR THE FUTURE

Ronald Reagan was elected president in 1980 on a promise of balancing the budget by 1984. Through two terms of such promises, this administration has amassed deficits that are greater than the debt of all previous administrations combined. The Reagan administration has led an unprecedented spree of borrow and spend at a time when we desperately need to grow and save.

These fiscal policies have changed the international landscape of wealth and financial power. At the outset of the Reagan administration, we were the world's largest creditor, with a net international balance of $140 billion. We now owe the rest of the world more than $330 billion, more than the foreign debts of Mexico, Brazil, and Argentina combined.

As we sink deeper and deeper into debt, other countries have capitalized on our fiscal disarray. Today, Japan is the world's largest creditor, with overseas assets of $180 billion. Even Britain, with all its economic troubles, maintains net external holdings of $163 billion.

Our economy cannot grow if we go on borrowing at a rate of $500 million each and every day. As a consequence of the Administration's fiscal irresponsibility, the cost of capital is twice as high here in the United States as in Japan. We need to rebuild a national consensus in favor of reasonable and responsible budgets that build for the future, instead of deficits that burden future generations.

The president must have the courage and conviction to submit to Congress a budget that is fiscally responsible, not one that steadily adds to the budget deficit. This document should be more than the sum total of individual line items representing the wishes of powerful special interests. Instead, the president's budget should be a plan for the future that outlines the federal role and commitment to investments in America's future.

In developing a reasonable and responsible budget, our central goal must be a full employment economy through growth and stable prices. An essential means to this goal is steady progress on deficit reduction, with the target of a balanced budget.

No item in the budget, whether defense or nondefense related, should be immune from careful scrutiny. The necessary sacrifices must be shared equitably by all, and not fall disproportionately on those who lack the power and resources to effectively make their case on Capitol Hill.

INVESTMENTS FOR THE FUTURE

Technology and Innovation

Ultimately, the competitiveness of American business—whether factories or farms, large corporation or small firms—depends on the people who manage and work in these enterprises. Only business can decide to make the necessary investments in new technologies, plants, and equipment. Only business can experiment with new processes, management techniques, and other innovations.

What government can do is create a dynamic and supportive climate in which businesses and working Americans can prosper.

Change has always been a central component of economic growth in the United States. Entire new industries have been created and older ones revitalized, through technologies that have enabled the development of new goods and services and improved the productivity and efficiency of our workers and factories. In a competitive global economy, technological advances will be the key to creating new and better jobs and a higher standard of living.

Historically, the federal government has played a key role in funding research leading to some of the nation's most impressive scientific and technological advances. But too many of our finest scientists and engineers are being drawn into weapons research when they could be involved with searching for promising new products, cures for our most dreaded diseases, new sources of energy, and ways to reduce the deterioration of our environment.

We must get the federal research agenda back on track. In the past our government helped produce some of this nation's most impressive technological advances. Now, other countries have far surpassed us in civilian R&D. Without new ideas and new products, we cannot create new business opportunities and new jobs.

In addition to basic and applied research, our public policies should also support more rapid application of new technologies. The historic focus of post-World War II science and technology policy in the United States has been on the generation rather than on the rapid utilization of new technologies. Foreign firms have made significant strides in accessing and utilizing new technologies developed in academic and laboratory settings. A similar emphasis on technology transfer initiatives should be promoted here in the United States.

Many states have already responded to this challenge by establishing a variety of high-technology initiatives and by funding collaborative research centers in areas such as microelectronics, biotechnology, advanced materials, and industrial technology. Deliberate efforts to explore and exploit special scientific and technological strengths have led to the development of economically dynamic centers from Austin to Albany, from the Silicon Valley in California to the Research Triangle in North Carolina.

States and localities are in the best position to identify their unique strengths and special opportunities. The role of the federal government in this endeavor must be one of supporter and collaborator, serving as a partner in funding research and training and in providing greater access to special resources such as federal laboratories.

Education and Training

The foundation for our strategy for progress and prosperity is education and training—a key investment that will enable America to compete for decades to come. Our goal must be to give our children the best public elementary and secondary education system in the world—second to none.

Our schools are our future. If we want to give our children hope, we should give them schools that are worth attending. Significant progress has already been made in improving curricula, teacher training, and student graduation requirements. We must also pay teachers salaries that better reflect the tremendous contribution they make to our children and our society. And we must do more to attract our best and brightest young people to the teaching profession.

At the same time we must grapple with the crippling

problem of illiteracy. The Department of Education estimates that 27 to 30 million Americans are wholly illiterate—in stark contrast to Japan's literacy rate of 99 percent. I have proposed a simple but important step toward the goal of 100 percent literacy by the year 2000. I call it "Readfare"—a program to set up literacy programs for welfare and food stamp recipients. Readfare will give thousands of Americans the basic tools they need to control and shape their own destiny. It will also help those whom illiteracy hurts most—children whose parents cannot read.

Today's investment in education will pay high returns tomorrow. A 20-year study by the High/Scope Education Research Foundation determined that every dollar spent on preschool programs saves seven dollars in future educational and welfare benefits. A study of high school dropouts by the National Center for Research in Vocational Education concluded that the price of neglect is even higher: in the long run, the current dropout rate will lead to $6 billion in expenditures on crime, welfare, and unemployment benefits.

Our public education system must provide our young people with the basic education and skills they need to secure a job or attend a college or university. At the same time we must also focus on the training and retraining needs of workers that are already in the labor force.

Technology and innovation represent tremendous opportunities and advantages for our efforts to recapture international markets and rebuild our economy. But, like any other change, these advancements require adjustments as well.

Our economy is clearly in the midst of dramatic transformations that threaten to leave many Americans behind. In the first half of this decade, technological change and rising foreign imports put more than five million experienced employees out of work, a third of whom could not find new jobs.

A substantial portion—from 20 to 30 percent—of displaced workers lack basic skills. At the same time, industry demand for special skills and training will continue to grow. Yet, our government is spending enough to train only five percent of the Americans who need it. Sweden devotes 90 percent of its unemployment assistance to job creation and training; by contrast, we spend less than 20 percent. We offer unemployed workers a only few months of subsistence, and then we fail to help them develop new skills.

We must require corporations to give workers at least sixty days advance notice of plant closings. A 1987 study by the National Academy of Sciences suggests that displaced workers who receive substantial advance notice of permanent job loss find another job more quickly than workers who do not receive such warning.

During the first half of this decade, federal spending on employment and training programs declined by 80 percent in real terms. Because of budget cutbacks and a tight job market, two-thirds of the unemployed in this country go without a job for such a long time that they exhaust all their benefits.

To prepare for the future, we must offer vocational education and opportunities for lifelong learning. We need programs that make it easier for workers to keep pace with the rapidly changing world economy—from young people just entering the work force and skilled workers who want to learn more to keep their jobs secure, to workers who have lost their old jobs and need retraining to start anew.

Now and in the future, everyone needs to share in the challenge of educating and retraining our work force. The Ford Motor Company and the United Auto Workers (UAW) have earmarked a nickel of each worker's hourly wages to establish the National Development and Training Center in Dearborn, Michigan. The UAW has signed another landmark agreement with General Motors to guarantee lifetime job security for workers at the new Saturn plant in my home state of Tennessee.

For its own part, the federal government needs to restructure Title IV of the Job Training Partnership Act (JTPA)—the primary federal program for displaced workers. This program needs to be improved to provide training for the substantial number of workers who need better basic skills, so that they can find new jobs faster and not suffer a large cut in wages when they are re-employed. JTPA should also place greater emphasis on providing extended training in job-related skills for non-displaced workers.

Another important federal program is Trade Adjustment Assistance (TAA)—a program that has been targeted repeatedly by the Reagan Administration for unjustifiable funding cuts. Instead of being gutted, this program may need to be modified to provide assistance under circumstances that are not necessarily directly related to foreign competition—situations such as the introduction of new technologies and other workplace changes. When someone plays by the rules and then suffers when the rules are changed, they deserve help.

CONCLUSION

One of the highest priorities of a Democratic administration will be the development and implementation of trade and economic policies that have as their goal full employment and stable prices. This means new jobs and better wages for Americans throughout the country. It means new business opportunities and strong local economies in rural communities as well as urban areas. It means opportunities in the South as well as the northeastern states, in the Farmbelt and the Rustbelt as well as the West Coast.

I am convinced we can grow and have everyone share in the progress and prosperity if we draw on our great strengths and commit ourselves to moving forward. We must ensure that our future remains with our traditional strengths—family farms, small businesses, and manufacturing industries. But our future also lies with new technologies and whole new industries, with diverse corporations, and with innovative financial institutions.

It will take vision and hard work, but there is no excuse for keeping America from being a leader in today's dynamic global economy.

CHAPTER 6

Facing the Challenges of Economic Leadership

Senator Gary Hart

WHEN AMERICA FACED COLLAPSE in the 1930s, we rebuilt the very foundations of our economy. We marshaled our strength behind national investments and institutional change—creating a renewed infrastructure and manufacturing base, a reformed financial system, and a restored commitment to the prosperity and productivity of America's working men and women. Enlightened leadership made our recovery possible, overcoming the forces of inertia and despair—and the old voices that called only for marginal change.

With our democratic allies a decade later, we created out of the ruins of war a remarkable engine of world economic growth that offered hope and opportunity to the Western world. Together, we created the International Monetary Fund, the World Bank, and a Magna Carta of international trade, the General Agreement On Tariffs and Trade. These new institutions permitted us and our allies to enjoy three full decades of prosperity, helped secure a durable peace, and insulated Western Europe against communist threats.

While the challenges of the current era are, on the surface, less daunting, the old conventions and old arrangements are again breaking down. We have yet to acknowledge the fundamental and structural reasons for our economic problems: persistent high unemployment, a rusting industrial base, a deteriorating public infrastructure, an inadequate system of public education, an astounding accumulation of public and private debt, and the threat of economic collapse of struggling Third World nations that fear a slide back into dictatorship.

Economic change stands between many of our families and their realization of the American dream. Personal incomes stagnate as personal debt soars. Families whose hard work once produced their dreams must now rely on second jobs just to stay even. Millions of workers displaced by changes in the global economy are unemployed, underemployed, or seeking new jobs with old skills.

When these workers do find employment, they are often absorbed into the work force at lower salaries, and without health benefits, pension protection, and, all too often, their dignity. Even families that have done well in the past decade are acutely aware of the increased threats they face.

Just as economic change and competition quicken, corporate America is failing to make investments in research, development, and new technology. Short-term profits, long-term debt, and unprecedented managerial effort are being directed into unproductive mergers and acquisitions.

Innovations from American laboratories are being developed, commercialized, and marketed by firms overseas. We run the risk of becoming just the world's library, not her most advanced factory. At this time of crisis in corporate management and competence, leadership is sadly lacking. One "captain of industry," whose enterprise "out-sources" the manufacture of automobiles abroad, endorsed trade protectionism one week after depositing his $23 million bonus check.

With America's families on the ropes, and our corporations unable or unwilling to peer past the next quarter's bottom line, should not the national government be alert to the danger? This administration, as a matter of ideology, will not lead; it opts instead to repeat the rhetoric of past legislative "victories" that it alone still celebrates. It extols the virtues of the "the engine of free enterprise," while refusing to take any steps to maintain and modernize that engine.

The so-called recovery has been a pawnbroker's paradise financed by credit. In 1986, our economy spent $900 billion more than we did in the recession year of 1982. We produced, however, only $800 billion dollars more worth of goods and services. No new economic theory is needed to explain this trick—we borrowed $100 billion from abroad to make up the difference. Every foreign dollar we borrow is a dollar not spent on American exports—it is an extra dollar added to the trade deficit.

Indeed, our trade deficit mushroomed in four short years not because of a sudden decline in America's ability to compete, but because of a new player in the competition: the borrowing needs of a government living radically beyond its means. The other economic policies of this administration—and the Federal Reserve Board—compounded the problem. Curing inflation with tight money drove interest rates and the dollar up even further. Deficits, tight money, a laissez-faire approach to currency markets, and an utterly mistaken impression by senior administration officials that a strong dollar was good caused the dollar to soar and our trade strength to plummet. American companies were pushed out of markets abroad, and foreign companies got time to build markets here—and at subsidized prices, to boot.

It is not difficult to imagine the legacy this decade will leave. Its outline is visible even today. By 1992—if current policies continue—our nation will owe the rest of the world nearly $1 trillion. We are already the world's largest debtor nation, and the borrowing spree hasn't stopped. We're going to have to pay for these debts. Every year in the 1990s, interest on this foreign debt will be more than the money we sent OPEC on account of higher oil prices; it will be equal to the amount we spend each year on foreign cars; it will be greater than the output of the entire machine tool industry. And we will have to produce the goods and services to pay the interest with an older and less-sophisticated capital stock, because we will not have saved, but squandered, and will not have invested, but consumed.

These problems are not ours alone. Europe has faced inflation and then stagnation—20 million Europeans are still unemployed. Latin American growth has been halted by a debt crisis more appropriate to last century's world of bank runs and speculative collapses. Even the Japanese face economic troubles: Growth has plunged to less than half its 1960s levels, and for the first time in three decades, Japan's automobile and steel workers are being laid off.

We need now, as 40 years ago, leaders of vision and action—Roosevelts, Churchills, Marshalls, and Monnets. Leaders who understand that neither rigid ideologies nor scapegoating offers help or hope in America's search for a blueprint for revitalization. Leaders who recognize the truth of Lord Keynes's observation: "The difficult lies not in the new ideas, but in escaping from the old ones."

For now, the world looks to America to build a new economic order on the foundation of the old. History will judge the next generation of leaders by their ability to rally the imagination and energy of the nation to face challenges that have for too long gone unacknowledged and unanswered:

- The challenge of international economic leadership— Will our historic commitment to world growth and a fair trading system be replaced by protectionism and xenophobia?
- The challenge of making strategic investments in America's economy—Can we define a new, appropriate role for government in preparing us for the future?
- The challenge of expanding participation—Can we mobilize political leadership to expand opportunity at home and abroad?

These three challenges are inseparable. We cannot lead the international economy if we fail to invest in ourselves, expand economic participation, and guarantee democratic opportunity for our own people. Nor can we increase opportunity in our society without a strong world economy and investments in our people. Nor can an investment strategy succeed if it leaves behind a vast dependent underclass, untouchable and untouched.

CHALLENGE ONE: LEADING IN THE WORLD ECONOMY

Our first challenge is to reorient America's attitudes and economic policy in the new global economy. This requires more than policies for competitiveness. International trade is more than a swim meet among economies, with each industry a separate event and the trade balance the score.

International economic policy must become a central tool of America's foreign policy. Indeed, for the rest of this century and beyond, international economics may well be the most important lever for strengthening our alliances, advancing the cause of human dignity, and supporting centrist forces from Korea to Mozambique.

Indeed, world economic growth is the best defense against Soviet expansion. The Soviets have sought to spread their influence through the world by capitalizing upon poverty, hunger, and want. We can combat such adventurism with our most compelling weapons—democracy and opportunity. Our political future in the Third World does not rest on our ability to chase Cubans through Angola or to slip arms surreptitiously into Central America. It depends on our ability and willingness—with democratic allies—to help raise standards of living around the world.

Our stake in a free and open trading system is greater than it has been at any time in our national life—and the centrality of international economic policy to our foreign policy rivals only that of the days of the Marshall Plan.

Yet, irresponsible economic policies have not only hindered our use of these tools abroad, they have eroded support for enlightened internationalism at home. Record trade deficits and the appearance that other nations are getting rich at our expense are making Americans lose their patience. Many despair of our prospects on the world stage. Some wonder why the countries we helped rebuild after the Second World War now threaten us economically.

Some ask why we ever provided the help in the first place.

Well, that is the wrong question. The postwar recovery of Japan and Europe provided the foundation for three decades of unprecedented world economic growth. The question is not why we provided a Marshall Plan to stimulate growth in Japan and Europe. The question is how we and our allies can develop a new approach to achieve the same goals, this time with Latin America, Africa, South Asia, and even China.

Just as growth abroad strengthens us at home economically, slow international growth and the collapse of export markets can decimate American trade, and have. The Latin American debt crisis has cost hundreds of thousands of American jobs. Indeed, if American exports had held their own as a share of gross national product since 1981, our trade deficit would have been negligible.

We cannot turn back from the world economy and expect to prosper. And we can no longer dictate solutions to the rest of the world. We will need cooperation to revive world growth, to stabilize exchange rates, and to solve the international debt crisis. This point has been too long ignored: Governments must cooperate if economies are to compete productively.

We must begin and lead this cooperative process by reducing the federal deficit. The outlook for the next two years is decidedly grim. An out-of-touch president adopts a Soviet-style economic "bill of rights" as a public relations tool—evading concern or responsibility for a deficit caused by his own failed economic program. With no incentive to act against the deficit alone, the Congress responds with bluster but no action. It spends months trying to perfect Gramm-Rudman, a weapon that will allow them, like Bill Sykes, to use a "the knife, not I, killed the lady" defense.

It is incumbent upon all national leaders to state clearly and straightforwardly the truth—we must reduce this deficit, and it cannot be done without restraining defense spending and increasing non–income tax revenues. The president would, if he were accurately informed on the issue, discover this simple fact: If defense, taxes, Social Security, and, of course, interest payments are all off limits for deficit reduction, then the remaining spending—from education to Medicaid, from training to the FBI—would have to be cut nearly in half before the budget was balanced. From 1981 to the present, the administration has never proposed, must less built support for, such cuts. Yet, we still see the president happily waving his veto pen in the direction of tax increases or restraint in defense spending.

We must prove to the rest of the world that we can reintroduce a sense of national responsibility. But we must also insist that others join us in strengthening the world economy. Improving coordination and cooperation will go a long way toward this goal. Huge trade imbalances have been caused primarily by irresponsible macroeconomic and monetary policies. Japan, in particular, must stimulate its stagnant economy, help stabilize international exchange rates, and channel its surpluses to the capital-starved Third World—in particular, to important regional leaders like Mexico, Egypt, and the Philippines.

The international economy must resist a tidal wave of protectionism, and America should be leading the way by adhering to its 40-year commitment to a free and open trading system. Instead, we are offered a false choice between a purist's notion of free trade and protectionism. The hollowness of this choice is apparent.

The administration has clung to nineteenth-century laissez-faire, while watching American industry lose its competitiveness and American workers lose their jobs. This unwillingness even to consider a national industrial security policy—in the face of a disastrous $170 billion trade imbalance—reflects the administration's ideological rigidity, indifference to the suffering of dislocated workers, and lack of understanding of today's real world.

Meanwhile, too many politicians, including some in my own party, demagogue the trade issue—acting as if our strongest allies were our most bitter enemies. These new protectionists would confine America to a closed economic system barricaded behind our national boundaries. These new protectionists would build a Maginot Line of tariffs and quotas around overvalued products, aging capital equipment, and out-of-date production techniques. They would declare defeat in world trade.

Most of all, the new protectionists are pessimists: They are pessimistic about Americans and what we can do. They believe we're being outclassed and outplayed by countries like Taiwan, Korea, Malaysia, and Singapore—countries that are somehow smarter and better than we.

Americans, they hold, are now Gulliver, helpless before Lilliputians.

We must reject these policies—not on faith, but on evidence. The United States only seven years ago, in spite of the problems of that time, still enjoyed trade balance, growing exports, and an astounding $40 billion dollars in advanced technology trade.

We have not suddenly lost our ability, energy, and will to compete. Errors of policy have caused our competitiveness to fall. Most important, these errors can be corrected without relying on laissez-faire or a ruinous return to the Depression-prolonging, protectionist policies of the 1920s and 1930s.

Rather than stopping trade—in the vague hope that penalizing successful traders is equivalent to penalizing trade law violators—we must restore fairness to the system. That means strengthening sanctions, eliminating trade preferences, and cutting fair trade compensation for those who flout our trade laws. We must end trade concessions for countries that violate worker rights. We must cancel cutbacks in the Customs budget that make it more difficult to police dumping by our competitors. But we must not resort to percentage protectionism. Across-the-board cuts in trade, without regard to violations, must be exposed for what they are—outright protectionism.

We must create a strategy that strengthens us rather than weakens our trading partners. With our industries in crisis, rather than write a blank check of protection, our government should help organize their modernization and revival.

Experience has taught us in industry after industry that quotas and tariffs designed to provide "temporary relief" become permanent entitlements for outmoded management—unless they are accompanied by serious conditions. Time and again, protection has proved itself a temporary tonic for the corporate balance sheet, but of no lasting help to workers. We must face this reality squarely.

Industrial renewal must start with tough and realistic compacts among labor, management, and government. They should include goals for prices, output, productivity, and international market shares consistent with the industry's potential. I call such compacts Industrial Modernization Agreements.

These voluntary, negotiated agreements can form a blueprint of our national goals: a modern capital stock, greater worker participation on the shop floor, a program of universal worker training and retraining, and a system of research, development, and commercialization that will keep our industries at the forefront of technology for another century.

CHALLENGE TWO: INVESTING IN OUR FUTURE

The jargon of economic policy changes much more quickly than the underlying policies themselves. Today, when we talk about the trade crisis, we talk about competitiveness. But for much of the last decade, the debate over economic policy concerned how America could improve its productivity; indeed, our ability to compete depends on the ability of our workers and factories to produce goods and services productively. If we want more high-paying jobs, or to sell more of our exports in foreign markets, we must become more productive.

For a hundred years, we were able to boost productivity through inventing and implementing new technologies in our farms and factories. An expanding economy at home and a dominant position in the still nascent world economy ensured that these improvements would result in increased living standards—not lower wages or higher unemployment. Change proceeded at a pace dictated largely by American companies and workers.

But from now on, it won't be that easy. As the international economy, the family, the work force, and the workplace change, we must change our strategy. One change is the most important: We must invest in education, training, and other aspects of what some call "human capital" to ignite a new era of broad-based economic growth.

We know there will be shortages of two million workers to fill skilled-labor jobs in the factories of the 1980s and beyond. People will change jobs six or more times, and change careers two or three times in their lives. As today's workers retire, more women and more minority Americans must take their rightful places as computer technicians, machinists, and industrial repair people in the workplaces of the future.

It won't be a handful of lawyers, MBAs, and money managers who bring American industry into the twenty-first century. We're not going to recapture our competitive edge with the help of math majors, scientists, and computer geniuses alone. To increase productivity, employment, and wages, we must recognize that a modern industrial power requires a modern manufacturing base, energy independence, excellent schools, an efficient infrastructure, and superior laboratories. We must invest in our future.

At a time when this administration proposes spending billions of dollars on a bizarre technological umbrella it calls the Strategic Defense Intiative, I believe we should instead devote America's resources to a Strategic *Investment* Initiative (or SII). The Strategic Investment Initiative will not recreate the Great Society or the New Deal. Rather, it looks to government as a catalyst—to help forge an economy that can, once again, offer America's families the opportunity to prosper in a changing world.

The Strategic Investment Initiative begins with increased investments in education and training. For, as numerous studies have affirmed, our education system is in peril. Only a third of our high school students take a science course in any year. Twenty-five percent of current math and science teachers will retire in the next decade. Private-sector salaries are attracting vital teaching talent away from our schools. We need more teachers, better teachers, and teachers who have regained the respect and the support their mission requires. We need substantial new investments in the math, science, and computer skills of the coming generation of students.

Education can no longer end on some particular graduation day. The problems of international competition, automation, and technological change make education, by necessity, a lifelong endeavor.

Our society must make training as available to workers as public education is to their children. Individual training accounts, a reformed system of trade adjustment assistance, and expanding job training partnerships with the private sector will help ensure that our workers continue to upgrade their skills. Equally important, workers deserve a renewed social compact to cope with job dislocation. We must enact a strict community notification law for when plants decide to close. We should create a system of portable pensions, so that workers need not leave their retirement security behind when they have to change jobs.

The nation would make enormous strides in productivity with a smarter, better-educated, and more flexible work force. Policies making those goals a reality will enable millions of American families to look to the future with dignity and hope.

In addition to investments in human capital, the SII proposes increased investments in the physical assets that are at the very foundation of our economy. Without first-rate transportation, our industries will locate in the ports of the distant Pacific Rim before they will choose new sites on the Mississippi or near the Great Lakes. We need a long-term program to rebuild our infrastructure over the next 30 years. A revolving, low-interest loan fund to supplement existing infrastructure investment would help. Perhaps more important would be regulatory changes that would permit communities to receive loans and grants with fewer federal strings attached. Mature and sophisticated state governments should decide for themselves what highways, bridges, tunnels, or ports require repair or replacement.

Underinvestment in basic scientific research may cost us our most fundamental technological advantage. A vigorous national science program, with initiatives in space science, health research, and basic physics and biology, will attract America's brightest young talents. We cannot continue to squander our best minds and scarce resources on Star Wars or merger wars.

The SII must be part of a balanced package of deficit reduction and increased investment. Any responsible package to reduce the deficit substantially must include additional revenues, such as an oil import fee, luxury taxes, and extension of the income tax bracket for families earning more than $200,000. Military reform for our conventional forces, at first important for national security, is now a tool of fiscal policy, for the days of explosive expansion in the defense budget have clearly passed. Any substantial domestic savings must also be found—for example, reductions in payments to huge corporate farms and savings in Medicare reimbursements to physicians.

Reducing the deficit will lower interest rates, make credible our pleas for macroeconomic coordination, and help reduce our trade imbalance. Equally important, the deficit makes impossible investments that promise more than marginal changes in our economy. It is a barrier to prudent economic investments. Deficit reduction and strategic investments must proceed simultaneously.

CHALLENGE THREE: EXPANDING ECONOMIC PARTICIPATION

The third challenge is to combat our age-old adversaries— poverty, discrimination, economic isolation, helplessness, and despair. Economic empowerment—around the corner and the world—is basic to our system's survival. Our military security, economic vitality, and moral leadership depend on it.

We can no longer think of poverty as a problem neatly divided into domestic and international components. Our own economic future depends upon raising global living standards and increasing participation in the world economy. We have nothing to gain from a world where nations are too poor to buy our goods and too backward to serve our markets with their production. But we have everything to gain by leading a world where all nations can use their resources to create economic hope.

Simply and clearly, it is better to have prosperous neighbors than poor ones.

Here at home, opportunity and participation are not luxuries, but must be central to economic renewal itself. We need the productive efforts of all our citizens. Over the next 20 years, we face shortages of educated and skilled labor. We long ago passed the point where the frontiers of our economy were geographic—we now must realize that those frontiers are demographic.

We must refuse to accept a subculture of poverty, of isolated economic homelands within the United States—in urban slums, in Appalachia, in rural communities. Our task is not to maintain them at poverty levels, but to integrate them into our system, through improving literacy, through providing training and effective social services that make them a part of the economy of the future.

To promote opportunity, we must strengthen the family. Between 1981 and 1987, nearly three million more children fell into poverty. This is simply unacceptable in a great nation that claims for itself the moral high ground.

Defining a new social agenda for expanding economic participation is a key challenge. Strategic investments must be targeted to the neediest people—whether that means a major set of investments in inner-city education or new forms of sliding support for licensed child care. The solutions are not free—substantial new expenditures will be needed over a long period of time if we are to address these issues seriously.

For economic empowerment to work, workers must be regarded as partners in, not victims of, the economy. For if employees have more stock and say in their own companies, if they have a sense of owning their jobs, they will be far more productive and satisfied. Through employee stock ownership plans, quality of life programs, and gain sharing, America is coming to recognize that most often, the true interests of labor and management rise and fall together.

CONCLUSION

World economic leadership, investment in our people and our nation, opportunity, and participation—this is America's economic agenda toward the twenty-first century. But this agenda, so crucial to America's future, will remain unfulfilled without new and effective leadership.

Leadership in the corporate boardrooms and the executive suites. Not just complaints about government regulation, but leadership to persuade managers and MBAs that their actions affect the national interest, not just this quarter's bottom line or tomorrow's stock quotation.

Leadership in America's classrooms. Not just higher salaries for teachers or better equipment for students—even though both would help—but a new commitment to standards and a willingness to defer gratification on behalf of excellence.

And leadership from a progressive government—not devoted to dominance, but committed to being a catalyst. A government devoted to the national interest, clear blueprints, and an unwavering commitment to challenge the future.

A progressive government that directs public investment and private capital to help retool factories and upgrade the skills of American workers.

A progressive government that removes obstacles to capital formation and growth, without running ruinous deficits or sustaining programs that have outlived their usefulness. In this international economy, only a strong national government can negotiate clear, strictly enforced rules for balanced trade or currency alignments—and make them stick.

Realizing this American agenda for growth and opportunity will require informing our people about the choices we face and trusting their judgment and courage. The easy rhetoric and false choices some offer mask a simple truth: The future is promising, but it isn't free. In the words of President Kennedy:

> What is at stake in our economic decisions today is not some grand warfare of rival ideologies which will sweep the country with passion, but the practical management of a modern economy. What we need is not labels and clichés, but more basic discussion of the . . . questions involved in keeping a great economic machinery moving ahead.

CHAPTER 7

New Directions for the American Economy

The Reverend Jesse L. Jackson

FOR THE LAST FEW years, I have traveled across America, talking to young people in high schools and colleges, and working with people in union halls and on assembly lines. I have met with community leaders and elected officials, in places ranging from state capitols to church basements. I have met with the dispossessed and the dislocated, the locked out and the sold out. I have marched with farmers in Chillicothe, Missouri, with steelworkers in Homestead, Pennsylvania, and with television newswriters in Manhattan.

Everywhere, I have heard the same concern for the future of our nation—not just about the loss of jobs, but about the loss of hope; not just about the closing of factories and the auction of farms, but about the death of communities and the disintegration of families. And I have heard, too, renewed determination that we can turn our country around. We will not give in to economic violence or spiritual despair. There is a way up—and out—but we must be smart enough to forge it.

Ronald Reagan's economic and budget policies—tax cuts for the rich and spending cuts for the poor, military expansion and Social Security contraction—have worked to set us one against another. In the space of a single administration,

89

he has made America the world's biggest debtor, mortgaging our future to forces outside our political control. Every time we go to borrow, foreigners finance more than half. When they stop paying and cash in, we are going to lose.

He leaves us an America that is growing apart. The rich are getting an even bigger share than ever before: The most affluent fifth of the population get 46 percent of the income, while the poorest fifth get not quite four percent. There are 32 million Americans in poverty. The national poverty rate was higher in 1986 than in any year prior to this administration. One out of every five children under the age of six lives in poverty. That is the legacy this administration has left to us.

My vision of the nation includes the rich, the middle class and the poor; the white, the black, the red, the yellow, and the brown. It is a vision based on the American dream of a healthy, growing, productive, and full-employment economy; of equal opportunity and equal protection under the law for all Americans; and of special concern for the poor, the powerless, and the dependent.

Our priorities must be clear. As a nation, we must never compromise our need for a strong defense and must guard our national security interests. But we can cut the bloated, wasteful, nonessential, and ineffective aspects of President Reagan's attempt to achieve military superiority—through an unprecedented peacetime military spending spree—without cutting our nation's legitimate defense needs.

While we must always fight for an adequate and efficient defense, in order to meet the critical issues of our day, we must fight for a dramatic shift in the nation's spending priorities. Such a shift would include priority spending in the creation of a full-employment and balanced growth economy; the creation of an education system that would prepare all of our citizens for the world and the world of work in the future; the provision and maintenance of adequate, safe, and affordable housing for all of our citizens; and the struggle against the hunger, malnutrition, drug addiction, and illiteracy that plague even the richest nation on earth.

We must turn the perverse incentives of the Reagan years around into new incentives for American development—incentives that will produce a national economic policy that makes sense and shows that the administration understands that America's people are her best resource and her future. I have put forward a number of specific policy proposals for revitalizing America's economy:

- A National Investment Program to use a fraction of America's pension fund assets to reinvest in America's infrastructure, retrain America's workers, and reindustrialize America's production
- A Trade and Competitiveness Program that distributes the burden of adjustment to international change equitably, both at home and abroad, and that addresses the problems and potential of emerging, stable, and declining industries
- An Agriculture Program to end the ravaging of the family farm by providing emergency help, debt restructuring, parity, and management supply to America's farmers
- An Energy Program centered on the cooperation and resources of this hemisphere through a Pan American Energy and Environmental Security Alliance

THE NATIONAL INVESTMENT PROGRAM

Our challenge is to build an action plan that sees a vision of a new future for America. A future in which Americans manage our own savings to provide our own jobs, our own housing, our own transportation and our own education to prepare our youth for the future. A future in which American money rebuilds American infrastructure, providing the most precious gift of all, jobs. For a job is as much a part of a person's infrastructure as the house he lives in, the street he walks on, or the school he goes to.

The National Investment Program will be the first step toward making this vision a reality and making America more competitive. I have proposed two specific mechanisms in such a program:

- A system to pool small investments to back securities that will carry federal guarantees
- An American Investment Bank to leverage pension fund capital for investing in the infrastructure and research and development (R&D) throughout the country

Pension funds are a fast-growing source of investment capital. There are about $2 trillion in pension funds available for investment—about $600 billion in public funds and $1.4 trillion in private funds. I am proposing using only a small part of those funds—10 percent—for investment in America's infrastructure and job creation.

Many investment advisers and pension investors agree that what is lacking is a mechanism to bring together pension funds and investors in need of capital for housing development or job creation. At the moment, it is easier and more common for pension funds to follow the traditional route of purchasing stocks and bonds of private corporations than to direct their assets into improvements in public and private infrastructure, because many of the housing or job creation investments are too small or too new in concept to be easily marketable.

The guarantee program is intended to fill the gap between small projects and large pools of capital. It would do for low-income housing and urban infrastructure investments what Fannie Mae and Ginnie Mae did for the residential mortgage market—that is, take a huge number of small, economically viable projects and pool them into amounts large enough to back a marketable security the fund can buy and sell at will.

The program also meets the needs of pension funds, whose obligation is, of course, to make sure there are pensions for workers as they retire. The securities the pension funds will buy (which will finance this infrastructure investment) will be guaranteed by the federal government. As such, they will be as close to risk-free securities as are available on the market. The return to the pension fund on those securities will be determined by the market, taking risk into account, as it is, for example, with Ginnie Mae securities.

This mechanism not only satisfies pension funds' criteria for secure investments, it also makes capital markets more efficient. By pooling projects and using them to back securities that meet the investment criteria of pension funds, it broadens the market, bringing in new investors and allowing capital to flow to these investment opportunities.

I have asked America's mayors to come up with the investment proposals to go into this pool. Together with their governors, they would establish public benefit corporations, governed by leaders from business, labor, and the public sector, to oversee the operation of these infrastructure projects. These groups would ensure, for example, that low-income housing built by the investment of pension fund money would be run in a professional manner, covering its costs of operation, yielding a competitive rate of return, being properly maintained, and not discriminating against any potential purchasers or tenants.

The creation of an agency to issue and administer the government-backed securities would be the responsibility of the federal government.

Finally, each individual pension fund would decide how much of which securities it wished to purchase. It is my strong hope that even those funds that do not have employee representation on their boards of trustees will consult with employee representatives over this crucial decision. After all, it is the employees' money.

Americans have every right to insist that the federal government support efforts to reinvest in this country. When New York City tottered on the brink of bankruptcy, the federal government provided guarantees on the bonds sold to the city's pension funds. Similarly with Chrysler. There is no reason why the federal government should not provide guarantees to pension funds providing American savings to reinvest in America. It won't cost anything to do it; it will be very costly to America if we do not.

The second mechanism, the American Investment Bank, would be a permanent financing arrangement for urban and rural economic development. I envisage a domestic equivalent of the World Bank, which would leverage a small capitalization from the states by selling bonds to pension funds. As with the international model, each state would pledge an amount of capital, although only a fraction would have to be subscribed up front. That capital, with the pledges of the states behind it, would back bonds floated on the open market and purchased by both public and private pension funds.

The bank would invest its borrowed capital according to priorities established by a tripartite board representing business, labor, and government. A professional staff would screen a wide variety of proposals for investment projects and would also be available to work with states and localities to help them develop feasible projects. Such an institution would represent a unique cooperation between public and private knowhow.

This proposal would bring the states together in a new kind of federalism. It would encourage cooperation, rather than the cutthroat competition that currently exists among the states for job location, a major concern expressed by the nation's governors in July 1986, as they bemoaned the outdated competition between the "Rustbelt" and the Sunbelt. For example, a development project in the South can be required to use R&D, suppliers, and new technology from other parts of the country. In this way, each region of the country gets some piece of the action, even when major development projects are located elsewhere.

THE TRADE AND COMPETITIVENESS PROGRAM

Fundamental changes in the world economy are confronting us with unprecedented challenges. The way we respond will shape the future of prosperity and social justice not only in America, but around the globe.

At stake is the relative prosperity so many in America enjoyed during the first three decades following the Second World War and the progress made during that period in the direction of greater social justice.

I am convinced that successfully meeting the challenges of a changing world economy will require us to find "the moral equivalent of war." Throughout history, humans have accomplished prodigies of cooperation in killing one another. I believe that solving the immediate problems before us today requires a new vision of peoples and nations cooperating in the work of life, rather than in the work of death.

America suddenly finds itself part of an international economy, as it never was before. American multinationals are roaming the globe looking for cheap, and even militarily repressed, labor. Our jobs are not being taken from us by foreigners. More often than not, they are being exported by companies flying the American flag who care about the bottom line, not about the workers they leave behind or the workers they find abroad.

The multinationals are a new beast—a new factor shaping our economic life. These firms, with their ability to move money across borders, defy national regulations and create conflicting national economic interests. For them, borders are written in fading ink. They find it in their interest to roam the globe looking for the cushiest deal, with very short memories of what their present community has done for them.

We have a right to demand a higher standard of behavior from firms that we have aided in many ways. Many communities have provided American multinationals with infrastructure and tax breaks. The federal government has let them feed at the trough of federal R&D grants through the Defense Department. We have created special measures, including tariff codes, that permit them to lower their costs of producing in the United States. We even have special offshore corporations that large multinationals can use to shelter part of their overseas earnings so it will not be subject to U.S. taxes. But still they close down American plants, throwing workers out of jobs and impoverishing whole communities.

There are those who would blame foreign workers for stealing our jobs. But, for example, South Korean workers— many of them women—are not taking jobs away from American workers. It is multinational corporations that take the jobs away. South Korean cars, made by workers who are kept from effective union organization by military force, are a hot item in the American market. The corporate names of two of the biggest sellers are General Motors and Ford. The brand name is as American as apple pie. But the product is made by people denied the basic rights Americans treasure.

Is the problem foreign workers who help the multinationals make superprofits? Or is it the multinationals themselves? Are American and Korean workers struggling against each other? Or are American and Korean workers together struggling against the multinational corporations? These corporations are not satisfied with exploiting labor in the Third World. They want to bring the Third World to the United States. They want to drive American wages and living standards down to Korean levels.

But the products of repressed labor in South Korea can be sold, because there is a market in the United States. Indeed, the United States now buys fully 65 percent of all manufactured products exported from the Third World. But if we turn this country—and the Europe of Margaret Thatcher and Helmut Kohl—into another South Korea, where will anyone sell anything?

We now know, for example, that the debt of Latin American countries is a threat to the United States. To earn the dollars they need to pay it, they have to sell us more than they buy from us. And that means that they can't buy anything from us. By playing debt collector for large American banks, the U.S. government has supported wrenching austerity policies in Latin America and, in the process, has destroyed one of this country's most important export markets. Even the Reagan administration finally realized the problem and told the International Monetary Fund that it was against forcing the Third World to pay off its debt quickly.

The point is that we have to think globally. We have to look for a global reflation. A commitment to helping the Third World overcome its poverty would create jobs and contribute to prosperity in the United States. Under the Marshall Plan, after World War II, the United States, in the name of anticommunism, gave, or lent cheaply, the money that allowed countries devastated by the war, including our former enemies, to rebuild. And once they had done so, they bought the hardware of modernization right here.

We can link international decency and American self-interest. We already did it once. But this time, let us do so in the name of democracy and disarmament, not in the name of anticommunism.

A major cause of our trade deficit is the Reagan administration's record budget deficits, which drove up the value of the dollar and made our products expensive and uncompetitive in world markets. Although the value of the dollar has declined to where it was before Reagan sent it soaring, the damage has been done. Markets have been lost, and it will be much harder to get them back than it was to lose them. Climbing back up the hill of international competitiveness is going to be harder work than falling down it was.

We will need an explicit trade policy in addition to getting the exchange rate right. Trade policy has to begin from the interests of working people in the United States as well as in the rest of the world, and has to contribute to international prosperity, not international austerity. We need a trade policy that furthers social justice in the world, not one that destroys it. We need a trade policy that serves human rights, not one that promotes human degradation.

International trade is, and should be, managed trade. The issue is not whether or not to manage trade. We have no choice but to manage it. The issue is only in whose interests trade is managed and how well it is managed.

Free trade, the policy of the Reagan administration, is trade managed in the interests of the multinational corporations. Free trade is a code for letting the corporations do as they choose regardless of the consequences for workers in the United States or in the Third World. It is—judged by the values of prosperity and social justice—grossly mismanaged trade.

In the short run, we must support policies that cushion American workers, their families, and their communities from the blows of slave-wage competition. The flight of American corporations overseas and the flood of imports that followed have resulted in thousands of closed factories and hundreds of thousands of lost jobs and shattered lives. Individuals have thus been forced, unjustly, to bear the costs of adjustments to a changing world economic order.

By law, communities and workers must receive sufficient notice to prepare and adjust to plant closings. We have to provide communities with a full range of technical and financial help to ease such transitions. Displaced workers and their families have to be provided with the continuation of health insurance and unemployment benefits during the adjustment process. Training programs to provide workers with marketable skills as well as help in finding new jobs need to be a central feature of such short-run adjustment programs.

We must also support trade policies that make the transitions that are under way in the world economy today more gradual and more orderly. The changes taking place in the world economy have been devastating in part because of their suddenness. No set of adjustment policies will be able to cushion American workers from these destructive forces unless it is complemented by trade policies that control the pace of industrial transition.

Such policies involve tough international negotiations, within and outside the General Agreement on Tariffs and Trade. They are not meant to stop the transition now under way in the world economy. They are meant to exercise control over what have become international markets, international capital, and international technology.

We must also make labor conditions more subject to international scrutiny and international sanction. The provision of workers' rights and decent working conditions in countries with which we trade works to the benefit of all. If we declare the brutal repression of workers' rights in South Korea and elsewhere an unfair trade practice, that is a way of showing our solidarity with those workers and our opposition to the behavior of the corporations that exploit them—including American multinationals. It will also state clearly that the United States is committed—politically, economically, and morally—to raising the standard of living of people around the world.

In the long run, we must find new policies that address our trade and competitiveness problems at the fundamental level: the level of the industries themselves. We have three types of industries: emerging industries, which we admire because they exploit American technology in new areas and have done very well despite the constant threat of competition; industries that are doing well or are able to hold their own in international competition; and industries that are clearly failing or close to failing. Our trade and competitiveness policies need to be tailored to each of these groups in order to succeed.

For emerging industries, any of which are technology-based, we need to have a policy that takes innovation and product development into the civilian realm and away from the overwhelming dependence on military spending. We need to limit the ability of firms to exploit these new areas by simply licensing them to foreign companies. Companies should have the carrot of tax benefits and employee training assistance, but only when they are wiling to respond to the stick of limits on foreign investment and rapid price reductions aimed at creating a real market for new goods in the United States. In the computer field and other technology-dependent areas, I support the creation of a National Technology Office to provide information about new technologies to U.S. firms. I also support more incentives for the formation of joint ventures between U.S. firms and between U.S. and foreign firms.

For industries that are holding their own, I would call together industry leaders, and with the help of industry analysts, labor and management, I would develop a way to heed the public's will that prices be kept stable and that the import threat be stabilized. At the same time, I would use all the force of the government, including low-interest loans and technical assistance, to get American firms to agree to upgrade their equipment and retrain their workers.

For industries that are failing, often because of the sizable competition they face from abroad, we need to work out an industrial readjustment strategy with other nations and with our own firms, labor leaders, and affected communities. If some plants can no longer survive in the face of competition, then the communities that are affected should have access to technical experts and funds to change the local economic base and provide a fighting change for survival. If a community is really in distress, some workers may need assistance to be relocated to other cities so they can learn a new job. Where factories have some fight left in them, we should do the most to help them become competitive again, providing low-interest loans and helping to win support for efforts at retraining and upgrading machinery.

In sum, in the long term, we need an entirely new trade and competitiveness policy geared to the respective problems and potential of emerging, stable, and declining industries and their workers.

THE AGRICULTURE PROGRAM

Today, while he poses as a great defender of traditional American values, Ronald Reagan is presiding over the end of one of our most basic family traditions—farming. All over our fertile land, our nation's farmers are telling a grim tale. In the most productive farmland in the world, we see farm foreclosures and forced liquidations at record levels. More than 120,000 farmers went under from 1982 to 1984 alone. Nearly a third of borrowers from the Farmers' Home Administration cannot afford to repay their loans. Suicides, mental illness, and family breakups are some of the consequences that farm families face when they lose their farms. These families are losing more than a piece of land—they are losing a piece of themselves and of their heritage. Rural towns are becoming ghost towns. We cannot turn our backs on these tillers of American soil.

Unless policies are changed soon, family farming will be gone forever. And with the devastation of the family farm, there will be a ripple effect; the impact will be felt in our small towns, small businesses, jobs, and schools. We live in an interdependent society and an interdependent world.

Ranchers and farmers have fed America and the world. They deserve our understanding and compassion. We must work to provide solutions to the life-threatening problems inflicted by our current economic policies. American farmers need a moratorium and a restructuring of their debt, supply management, parity, and open markets. Farmers don't want a handout—they want a helping hand. If we can bail out Chrysler and Continental Bank, and Europe and Japan; allow a $17 billion cost overrun on the B-1 bomber; propose to spend $40 billion on two carrier fleets for the navy; and construct 21 MX missiles they now say will not work—then we are more than capable of addressing and meeting the needs of the family farmer.

Farmers need parity, not charity. Unemployed workers need to go back to work, and farmers need to farm. When people lose their land, and thus their livelihood, starvation is sure to follow. The demand for 90 percent of parity for storable commodities means simply that farmers must get a fair price for what they produce. They must be able to meet their production costs so they can continue to provide us with an abundant food supply. All those who work are entitled to a living wage in return for their labor. Farmers are no exception. It is to everyone's benefit to keep the family farmer farming. Guaranteeing a fair price is a necessary step in that process.

Finally, my plan includes a proposal to convene an international conference on food and agriculture in Chicago, at the Trade Center. The forum would focus on increasing stability in world food processing and production, through programs similar to those we have for the oil industry. The conference would also give priority to increasing the production and availability of agricultural products to meet the needs of the more than 700 million starving and undernourished people in the world.

Agriculture, not bombs and missiles, must be our most strategic defense, for it supplies the most basic necessities of human life. And it creates healthy allies, fed on American grain, who will always remember that America came to their aid in a time of crisis.

THE ENERGY PROGRAM

Under the Reagan administration, this nation has an incoherent and unenforced energy policy. Today, we trade away American jobs for dependence on an explosive part of the world. We turn our backs on opportunities to negotiate, and find ourselves embroiled in confrontation. I am proposing an energy policy that means security—job security for American workers, energy security for our people, national security for this country, and the security of peace in this hemisphere.

This policy means jobs for oil-rig workers in Oklahoma, for landmen in New Mexico, for seismic crews in Colorado, and for oilfield pipe manufacturers in Ohio. It means jobs for West Virginia coal miners and business for heating oil suppliers in Massachusetts.

Under this energy policy, all Americans will be secure in their ability to heat their homes. Farmers will be able to fuel their tractors and feed our families. Remember the rationing tickets printed by the government for distribution to farmers during the embargo in the 1970s? Our energy policy will assure that those tickets, stockpiled by the federal government, are never needed.

My proposed national energy policy rests on three points: a Pan American Energy Security Alliance; development of domestic energy resources in a manner that makes sense regionally as well as nationally; and, as a last resort, and with sensitivity to our neighbors in the region, an emergency temporary oil import fee.

This plan is important because it will serve more than just our own needs. In fact, therein lies its strength.

It will provide our neighbors with a market for their goods, an opportunity to pay off their debt, and the benefits of trade. Nonproducing nations of the Caribbean and Latin America would also benefit from a secure energy supply.

The alliance is a concept that directs us to safer sources of energy. I would not suggest that our sole source of energy be the producing nations of the Western Hemisphere. But a shift to increased energy trade with our neighbors would serve the needs of all concerned.

Negotiated agreements could also provide that in times of energy crisis, our energy supply, and that of the rest of the Western Hemisphere, would be secure at a certain price.

As threats of embargo and price swings are lessened, stability in the world energy market will encourage investment in domestic oil and gas development and create more jobs here at home. By putting our own people back to work, we reduce our deficit. By trading with our neighbors, we reduce their debt.

The reduction of Latin American debt is essential to avoiding economic and political chaos in those countries. A debt moratorium would allow revenues from trade, energy, and other sources to create new jobs and stabilize their economies. Economic growth is the only engine strong enough to power repayment of their debt.

Naturally, questions arise as to the quantity of crude oil reserves in the Western Hemisphere. The Pan American Energy Security Alliance is feasible. In effect, our neighbors were the ones who kept this country working during the oil embargo of the 1970s. To Canada, Mexico, and Venezuela, we owe a debt of gratitude. They have proven themselves as worthy trading partners.

Recent conservative estimates set Venezuela's reserves at 55 billion barrels, about equal to Mexico's. However, other estimates, which include production capacity in Venezuela's Orinoco Belt, run as high as 267 billion barrels, eclipsing Saudi Arabia's 167-billion-barrel reserves.

Even at the most conservative estimates, assuming no imports from outside the hemisphere, these reserves would serve the eight-billion-barrel annual consumption of the entire hemisphere for almost 20 years.

Of course the alliance would not exclude oil imports from other parts of the world. It would only redirect our attention to trade with our Western Hemisphere neighbors.

This is not a new concept. Mexico and Venezuela are signatories to the San José Accord, which commits crude oil to nonproducing Central American and Caribbean nations. We could be sitting down at the table with groups like the Organization of American States.

The development of the Western Hemisphere's resources in a coordinated and mutually beneficial way, coupled with the concerted development of U.S. energy sources and promotion of energy conservation, will provide a stable energy base for the entire hemisphere.

Complementing the Pan American Energy Security Alliance should be the development of our domestic energy resources according to a resource management plan. Such a plan would address not only oil and gas, but ethanol, methanol, coal, solar, and other energy alternatives. It also would increase the emphasis on energy conservation R&D. Federal spending for R&D in 1987 was allocated to the military (71 percent); health (nine percent); space (seven percent); energy (four percent); general science (three percent); agriculture (two percent); natural resources and environment (two percent); and other issues (three percent), including education and training, housing, and urban development (0.9 percent).

What are the priorities in the way our tax dollars are spent? Of every tax dollar, 55 cents goes for military spending, two cents for housing, two cents for education, and two cents for food and nutrition. Our best minds are being misused to develop bombs and missiles instead of the Pan American Energy Security Alliance.

Our national energy policy will be structured to recognize the strengths of our different regions, while assuring adequate energy supplies for the entire country. Each area of the United States boasts of particular resources, but no region is totally independent; all are united and share the bounty as well as the burdens.

We need an energy policy that is flexible enough to promote the development of oil and gas in the producing states, solar power in the Southwest, ethanol in the farm belt, coal in the Appalachian region, and hydropower in the Northwest. By emphasizing our regional assets, we design a national energy policy whose sum is greater than its parts.

During the oil embargo of the 1970s, Americans were taught the value of energy conservation. But it is a lesson we are forgetting all too quickly. Think back to the National Energy Act of 1978. We can learn as much from its high points as from its low ones.

The five separate pieces of legislation that made up that act brought energy conservation into its own while instituting a federal energy research program and bringing alternative energy sources to our attention. This country is at its best when there's cooperation between the private and public sectors.

Finally, it may be appropriate for this country to approve a temporary oil import fee, as an emergency measure, to get our domestic oil and gas industry back on its feet. Just as the American farmer in Iowa deserves a price floor for the products of his labor, the wildcatter in Oklahoma may need the stability of an import fee to attract investments. Food and energy are too basic to the wellbeing of this nation for us not to provide for the security of both. Home owners and consumers in the Northeast and farmers in the Midwest may need a federal energy tax rebate to ensure fairness and to avoid further economic disruption in their lives. Such a fee, however, must be negotiated and discussed with our hemispheric neighbors in a spirit of friendship, cooperation, and mutual dependency.

This is a rational, balanced approach to filling the federal energy policy void. It's a policy that envisions Americans living and prospering with our neighbors. It's the leadership that has too long been missing from America's energy policy.

CHAPTER 8

A Rendezvous with Reality: The New Global Economy

Congresswoman Patricia Schroeder

THIS COUNTRY IS ABOUT to embark upon the process of electing a new President to lead America to the threshold of the 21st century.

I want to speak today about the economic challenges that will confront the person taking the oath of office on January 20, 1989.

The strength of America and its capacity to provide for its people depends on the strength of its economy. Whether one cares about our capacity to defend our country from our adversaries, to educate our people, to provide for those least able to provide for themselves, or to sustain hope for the next generation, our economy must be strong and growing.

It's for that reason I believe that the next president should be a Democrat. A Republican President will not be able to reverse policies of the past seven years which have jeopardized the economic security of today's average American family, and put in doubt the future prosperity of our children.

The time for happy talk is over. We can no longer run away from our problems: our national credit card has exceeded its limit.

The central issue of the upcoming campaign is whether America is ready for a rendezvous with reality.

I think it is.

But before I outline how we can come to grips with the reality of the global economy, let me make two general comments about economic policy.

ECONOMICS AND MORALITY

First, the economy is meant to serve people, not the other way around.

The "laws" of economics are not a set of fixed mathematical relationships; they are shaped by human values and aspirations. Morality should matter to economics: equity is just as important as efficiency.

We need to face the fact that the economic policies of the past seven years have been fundamentally immoral; that there is something terribly irresponsible about borrowing from the future and from abroad in order to maintain a standard of consumption that we cannot earn through our own hard work.

The economic policies of the Reagan administration are not conservative policies; they are the policies of ideological radicals who are outside the mainstream of American tradition and values.

THE GLOBAL ECONOMY

Second, we must understand that there are no longer any sharp distinctions between the domestic and the international economy.

The steel mills of Lackawanna weren't transformed into a virtual ghost town because its 20,000 workers suddenly forgot how to produce. It happened because competitors across the border in Canada, and across the oceans, began using efficient continuous casting technology, and we didn't.

The economy of New York's Southern Tier is substantially affected by Corning's ability to sell fiber optics all over the world.

This summer a green and white Fuji blimp flew over

plants employing tens of thousands of Kodak workers, flashing its message to buy Fuji film and tapes. Kodak "retaliated" by sending its own black and yellow dirigible over Mt. Fuji, Japan.

Blimp wars may be harmless, but the sponsors are engaged in a deadly serious competition, and the economy of Rochester hangs in the balance.

IBM, with headquarters in Armonk and installations throughout the Hudson River Valley, is suddenly vulnerable to products made throughout the world.

Foreign competition also confronts many other New York industries, and their workers, their families and their communities.

And the story is the same all across the United States.

NO PLACE TO HIDE

While economists, editorial writers, and soothsayers anxiously search the horizon for the elusive "J curve," our trade deficits continue to mount, and the fact becomes increasingly clear that our industries have no place to hide.

Relocating corporate headquarters from New York to Greenwich won't help; and cheaper labor in right-to-work states will never compete with Third World wages.

The competitive pressures first started in the 1970's with basic manufacturing, then moved to high-tech in the early 1980's. The same pressures will soon be squeezing the services sector.

As the value of the dollar falls, our manufacturing industries should theoretically be helped. But a lower dollar also means greater value for assets denominated in yen, marks, and other strong currencies.

We have no reason to believe that the Japanese will be less resourceful or less successful in a role as bankers to the world than as producers of goods.

You need only walk down the street in New York City to see the foreign banks moving in—now almost 400 strong.

And we have no reason to believe that the whole "Selling of America" will diminish, with New York real estate and

New York stock exchange issues remaining very attractive bargains.

For a short time New Yorkers may benefit from this "sale of the century." But at some point in the future, the absentee owners will either assert control, or liquidate the holdings.

At the very least, rents from American buildings and interest on American securities will be providing "social security" to foreign countries for many decades to come. And reducing the standard of living for Americans.

That is the reality of the global economy today.

BENIGN NEGLECT FOLLOWED BY ACTIVE DELUSION

How did we get into this mess?

For most of this century, the United States, with its great natural resources and huge domestic market, had not been greatly concerned about international trade.

We were the world—or so it seemed.

By 1980, warning signals were all around, but we refused to recognize reality.

The only international competition the Reagan Administration recognized was a military competition with the Soviets. We would spend the Soviet Union into the ground, until they couldn't afford to compete any longer.

But we didn't bother to consider the consequences to our own economic fortunes.

The Reagan administration glossed over our increasing basic manufacturing problems by characterizing them as part of an inevitable (even welcome) transition to a high-tech or information-based service society.

Instead of recognizing that most of our problems were "made in America," and pulling together to meet the challenge, we chose delusion and division. The national economy split along smokestack versus high-tech lines, and national politics was divided along rustbelt versus sunbelt constituencies.

Instead of competing, we dissipated our advantages. We didn't do enough to keep our workforce the best educated and most productive; we heavily skewed our research and development priorities toward military applications; and we turned the most efficient capital market system in the world into a casino society where "paper entrepreneurs" and short horizons held sway.

And all along this path we have masked the inevitable consequences to our standard of living with happy talk that it is "morning again in America," and an unprecedented borrowing binge from abroad, which will only make the eventual reckoning much worse.

IS AMERICA BETTER OFF?

In 1980, Ronald Reagan asked voters whether they were individually better off than they were four years previously.

In 1988, we need to ask whether the country is better off.

Since 1980, stock values have risen by more than $2 trillion; but the median income of American families still remains below 1980 levels when adjusted for inflation. Is America better off?

Since 1980, prices of homes have escalated beyond the reach of countless young families. Many baby boomers may never reach the same standard of living as their parents. Is America better off?

Since 1980, defense expenditures have increased by 40 percent, while domestic programs have been cut by 21 percent. Our fastest growing budget item is interest on the national debt—up 53 percent. Is America better off?

Since 1980, federal aid to education has been slashed. College students—and their parents—are faced with the prospect of enormous loan repayments. Some choose not to continue in school. Is America better off?

Since 1980, we have gone from the world's greatest creditor nation to its greatest debtor. At this rate, we'll be a trillion dollars in the hole by the early 1990's. Is America better off?

VOODOO ECONOMICS REVISITED

As we celebrate the 200th anniversary of the Constitution, it is worth a bicentennial minute to ponder both the history of our national debt since George Washington, and the history of our international debt since Ronald Reagan.

You will note that our national debt stood at $1.2 billion in 1900. It stood at $258 billion after World War II, and $998 billion in 1980.

By the time it leaves office next year, the Reagan Administration will have almost tripled the debt amassed by all previous administrations.

In 1914 the United States became a creditor nation. Over the next 67 years, it built up its international investment position to a net $141 billion. By the end of this year, we are expected to owe the world approximately $400 billion—a reversal of almost $550 billion in just five years, and the pace is accelerating.

It's not enough to start reducing our trade deficits; we need to start running surpluses.

Against this reality we should remember the campaign promises of 1980.

On the domestic side we were told we could slash taxes, increase defense spending, and magically balance the budget.

On the international side, we were going to sit back, read Adam Smith, and get out of the way.

We should have known better. That famous New York investment banker, David Stockman, later confessed that the whole charade was simply "trickle down economics" in disguise.

You would think that given the reality of the record, the Reagan administration would be embarrassed to keep insisting upon the need for a balanced budget amendment to the Constitution.

What needs changing is not the Constitution, but the people running the government.

VERSAILLES OR THE WHITE HOUSE

This administration deeply resents constant references to "Reaganomics," so I have been trying to think of a new description of what is happening in Washington.

What comes to mind is Louis XIV.

Like eighteenth-century France, today we have a government out of touch with how common people try to manage their daily lives.

Concentration of wealth increases dramatically, while the middle class struggles, and one out of five American children lives in poverty.

Instead of ornate palaces, our monuments to extravagant waste are hidden away in cylinders deep below the ground, deeper below the oceans, and, if SDI becomes reality, aloft among the stars.

Our courtiers are the defense contractors who produce gold-plated weapons that don't work. We have an aristocracy of the rich and well-connected. Influence peddling abounds.

And, most of all, we have a total disregard for the consequences. Senator Moynihan recently described the 1980s as a time when "America borrowed a trillion dollars and threw a party." He could have been describing Versailles.

SETTING THINGS STRAIGHT

Let's put the happy talk aside—it's time for straight talk.

Let's break the cycle of management blaming labor; labor blaming management, and everybody blaming foreign competitors. All the finger pointing doesn't do much good, and it distracts us from getting our own house in order.

Success in international competition can be traced to a few essentials: a productive workforce, the efficient use of capital, skillful management, advanced technology, and an effective partnership between the public and private sectors.

We used to have the most highly skilled, highly educated workforce in the world. We don't anymore.

We used to put our capital to the most productive use in the world. We don't anymore.

We used to have the best commercial technology in the world. We don't anymore.

We used to have far-sighted management. Now, they are obsessed with quarterly profits and golden parachutes.

And we don't have an effective government policy to help

our industries and workers produce efficiently at home, and to make sure that American goods and services are treated fairly abroad.

TOUGH CHOICES NEEDED: VINCE LOMBARDI REPLACES LOUIS XIV

The solutions to our problems are known—there are no secrets. What we need is the political leadership to confront reality.

We need a clear call to accept some difficult changes now, in return for greater prosperity in the future.

I don't generally use sports analogies to make political points. But I think people in New York will understand what I mean when I say that we need to replace "Louis XIV economics" with "Vince Lombardi economics."

Vince Lombardi began his career as one of Fordham's "Seven Blocks of Granite," and went on to become the greatest football coach of his era. He did so by preaching and practicing the virtues of hard work and commitment.

The American economy needs to get back to such basics.

We need the best trained, best conditioned, and hardest working players.

We need the most dedicated and loyal coaches, and the most inspired leadership.

We need the most aggressive strategy and the driving commitment from top to bottom to win over the long haul.

Nothing fancy—just the basics.

But we've got to get moving.

CHANGING PRIORITIES

Overcoming our problems will require a drastic change in economic priorities for all levels of American society. Tomorrow's new realities will require major changes in how government, business and ordinary American citizens relate to their economy.

Citizens must accept the new realities of the international

marketplace: If we are not ten times as productive as those in Third World countries willing to work for one-tenth our wages, then we cannot maintain today's wage rate. This is not a call to cut workers' pay and benefits, but it is a call for American workers to accept the need for new ways of working to bring out the tremendous productive potential of our workforce.

Corporations also must confront new reality: It is simply no longer good enough to serve existing markets, work up new advertising strategies to sell the same old products, and squander executive talent on financial speculation, mergers and takeovers. Corporations must recognize that they are in a long-term struggle for survival, a struggle which will be won by 9-hour days, not 3-hour lunches.

Any government must finally face the reality that today's budgetary, financial and international economic policies are woefully out of step with new international realities. Our federal budget deficit, combined with our low savings rate, sucks in imports from the rest of the world.

Central to government's task is getting the budget deficit under control. The deficit both frustrates efforts at creative confrontation with new realities, and transfers the burden of today's excesses onto future generations.

Getting the budget under control does not mean the rigid formulas and mindless targets of Gramm-Rudman, which could throw our economy into a recession.

Getting the budget under control *does* mean setting a steady, responsible course of deficit reduction, while changing our spending priorities toward investing in the future.

Let me highlight a few of the many policy changes that are needed. First, we must insist that our allies share more of the burden for their defense.

Any realistic view of the choices before us makes it clear that we cannot have a world-class workforce, technological leadership in advanced products and a reasonable balance between consumption and savings while trying to carry much of the burden of defense for our allies on our shoulders.

The Reagan administration has ushered in a new form of isolationism. It likes to claim that "America is standing tall;'' but actually we are standing alone—our troops, our ships, our money.

The United States now spends approximately $175 billion in defending the security interests of our European and Asian allies. It seems absolutely preposterous that we should be underwriting the national security costs of our economic competitors at a time when we are borrowing billions of dollars a year from them, and losing our economic independence as a result.

Governor Cuomo has called for a new realism in our relationship with the Soviet Union. And he is exactly right. But we need to deal directly and honestly with our allies as well.

We need to sit down with our allies and tell them that the free ride is over.

Acting tough with our trade competitors during public negotiations, and privately accepting contributions from them for the Contras is not my idea of "burden sharing."

Second, we need to develop a family policy that addresses the realities of today's working families.

The fact is that most women have to work. Families feel increasing pressures in order to balance work and family responsibilities.

If we want to increase the productivity of current workers and invest in our future labor force, we must establish effective national policies that deal with parental leave, affordable day care centers, and latchkey children.

Third, the United States needs to increase substantially its commitment to education. Trade competition will ultimately be won or lost in our schools.

Our biggest asset is our people. The world is changing rapidly. The future belongs to the educated. Those who have only the minimum skills will be condemned to low wages and dead-end jobs, if they can get any job at all. What is true for individual Americans is true for the country as a whole. Without world class educational institutions, there will be no world class economy.

Fourth, we must reverse our current research and development priorities. In 1980, the federal government's basic research budget was apportioned 50-50 between military and civilian applications. In 1987, the apportionment is expected to be closer to 80-20 in favor of the military. That division is inconsistent with our long-term national interests and should be changed.

Fifth, we need a new Marshall Plan for the Third World. The only way that our exports can significantly expand is if Third World markets are growing rapidly. With current debt payment requirements, this is impossible. Although the United States cannot afford to unilaterally fund such a growth plan, we can provide the political leadership to encourage Japan, Germany, and other nations with trading surpluses to participate in a multilateral effort to provide the necessary financing.

A SENSE OF SHARED FORTUNE

America's most successful social and economic policy of the twentieth century was the New Deal. It's over partly because it succeeded so well.

If America is to successfully enter the twenty-first century, we need to recapture the spirit of the New Deal, to recapture the sense of shared fortune.

During the summer of 1787, 55 Americans had the inspired genius to strike a deal which has bound this society together for 200 years . . . Coloradans and New Yorkers; workers and shareholders; producers and consumers; students and retirees.

But that traditional cohesion is beginning to come apart under the strains of the new economic reality, strains unlike any since the Depression.

NEW IDEAS, OLD IDEALS

In 1932, New York sent its governor to Washington, and FDR and the Democratic Party helped to make the American dream a reality for two generations of American families.

(It probably wouldn't be fair to call upon New York to make that same sacrifice again so soon.)

The goals that FDR set forth for the Democratic Party and the country remain: A decent job for all who can work, a home for one's family, the opportunity to help the next generation, and some measure of security in retirement.

Some have suggested that we should step back, and let the Republican party reap the whirlwind. But we can't wait for 1929 to come again before repairing the damage.

In the real world beyond Hollywood, we can't "go back to the future." We can only move forward, and that's where the Democratic party needs to lead the country.

The next president must summon the best in us, the most noble, the least selfish. And most of all, the next American president must reaffirm that timeless essence of our party: that we are one society, that we are all in this together.

TOWARD THE NEXT CENTURY

Let me leave you with this last thought. In trying to lead America into the next century, we would do well to heed an ancient Indian saying from my part of the country:

> We do not inherit the earth from our ancestors;
> We borrow it from our children.

The simple message of this Navaho proverb should guide not only our environmental concerns, but our economic, social, and military policies, as well.

And, if we use this ethic as a moral compass, then our rendezvous with economic reality can also become a rendezvous with opportunity, and a better future.

CHAPTER 9

Let's Put America Back to Work

Senator Paul Simon

ETCHED IN A WALL on the House side of the U.S. Capitol there are words that describe what made this nation great:

> Labor is discovered to be the grand conqueror, enriching and building up nations more surely than the proudest battles.

Yet, in our good and great country today, too many seem to have forgotten the importance of work to each American.

We have become too willing to accept a level of unemployment that is costing us money through the federal budget deficit. It is a drain on productivity, a companion of illiteracy and crime.

We must make unemployment a national priority if we hope to address these ills.

Note: Portions of this text are adapted and reprinted with permission from Senator Simon's book *Let's Put America Back to Work*, Bonus Books, Chicago, 1986.

THE PROBLEM

Unemployment will not disappear by our wishing it away. We must march on it, because a massive waste of humanity is taking place each day, and it is slowly but certainly eroding our economic future.

Although there has been some month-to-month variation in joblessness, the overall rate has increased by more than one porcentage point each decade since 1950. Senator Daniel P. Moynihan has accurately noted, "Rates of unemployment that were thought intolerable in the early 1960s are thought unattainable in the 1980s."

Nothing restricts the future as much as our failure to use our human resources more fully. Why has Japan made such tremendous strides, moving from income that was 5 percent of the average American's income in 1950 to surpass us in 1987? Japan, a nation the size of California, and with half our total population, has few resources. Yet, Japan has announced a goal of having the world's highest per capita income by the year 2000, and few discount that possibility.

The agony of joblessness is still a stranger to most Americans because we do not know it personally. Even though we may not encounter joblessness in its full harshness, it touches us every day in a multitude of ways. We face the indirect spin-offs of unemployment: high crime rates, and tax money going for welfare, prisons, and unemployment compensation.

Unemployment leads to poverty, and the poverty statistics are not pleasant. In 1984, one in seven Americans lived in families that fell below the poverty line of $10,609 for a family of four. In 1968, the poorest fifth of U.S. families had 91 percent of the money needed for basic requirements; but 15 years later, they had only 60 percent. Most of the poor are white, but blacks are three times as likely as whites to live in poverty; Hispanics are more than twice as likely. Thirty-four percent of those living in female-headed families are poor.

In all, we have at least 10 million people unemployed or significantly underemployed (working two days or less a week when they want to work full-time). Ten million people is almost twice the population of Switzerland. If Switzerland suddenly would have no employment, the U.S. government would galvanize our resources to help the Swiss people. But when more than twice the employable population of Switzerland is unemployed within our own borders, we have yet to make it a matter of major national concern.

From 1979 to 1984, 11.5 million Americans lost their jobs because plants had shut down or moved, or production techniques had modernized, or demand had decreased. Of that 11.5 million, more than a million have simply dropped out of the labor force. They are no longer counted among the unemployed. Of those who were able to find new jobs, over half found themselves earning less money.

Politically, the gravity of what unemployment means to those who face joblessness has not penetrated deeply—nor is there a widely held belief that government action can change the picture much. Inaction is tolerated, and the misery is accepted or ignored.

The Reverend Dr. Martin Luther King, Jr., once said, "In our society, it is murder, psychologically, to deprive a man of a job or an income. You are in substance saying to that man that he has no right to exist." The nation's highest commitment—our most important national goal—must be to guarantee a job opportunity for everyone who wants to work.

UNEMPLOYMENT IS EXPENSIVE

When we fail to provide employment, the costs reach far beyond the jobless.

In Peoria, Illinois, Caterpillar employed 32,770 people in 1980, but only 18,000 in 1985. Real estate taxes paid in the three immediate counties dropped $1 million over the same period. The value of homes plummeted. How many people in grocery stores and clothing shops and car dealerships and hardware stores lost their jobs as a result of the Caterpillar layoffs? No one knows. Thanks to hard work and good leadership, I sense that Peoria and Caterpillar are starting to rebound. But in the meantime, thousands of people have been hurt.

While the depression in sectors of the agricultural economy is not the same as unemployment, its economic impact, reaching beyond those immediately hit, causes unemployment. The havoc of unemployment is more visible in a small community, but economic suffering is felt in any community where there is joblessness.

Not surprisingly, areas of high unemployment are also areas of high crime. The cost of crime in economic terms is huge. The cost of crime in agony to the victims is even greater. By tolerating unemployment and the resultant poverty, we also tolerate a discouragingly high crime rate. One of every 40 black men born in the United States will be murdered; one of every 131 white men will be murdered.

Rockford, Illinois, is in many ways a typical American city of medium size (population 139,712). Until recently, it had significantly above-average income. The economic recession of the early 1980s, together with a depression in the machine tool industry, sent incomes plummeting and unemployment skyrocketing. The author of a comprehensive study of a new phenomenon in Rockford, youth gangs, wrote: "Rockford unemployment has been the single most contributive factor in the rise of youth gangs, youth offenders, and youth at risk."

Unemployed youth have time on their hands and abundant energy, and when a job does not demand that time and energy, something else will. Sometimes it is crime. Since 1981, there has been both national population growth and growth in the total number of jobs, but the number of full-time jobs held by teenagers has dropped almost 30 percent, and this decline is a major cause of crime.

Children who grow up in families where no one works do not learn basic attitudes and work habits that are essential to performing effectively in our society. In a real sense, unemployment can be "inherited."

Business is obviously harmed by unemployment as well.

People who do not work do not buy new cars or air conditioners or suits. Tax incentives to stimulate business investment sometimes can be effective, but creating an economic climate in which people are working and buying always stimulates the economy.

The federal treasury suffers also. President Reagan uses the figure that one million people unemployed costs the federal government $28 billion. Others in his administration use the figure $35 billion. Let's be conservative and say that the federal expenditure for food stamps, welfare, unemployment compensation, Medicaid, and a host of other benefits—plus loss of revenue—amounts to $30 billion for each one million unemployed. If we had programs that reduced the number of those unemployed from 10 million to five million, the net savings to the federal government would be $150 billion.

Cutting unemployment in half would also result in at least a four percent increase in our gross national product, or approximately $700 for every man, woman, and child in the nation. What a tremendous economic loss we suffer through our indifferent acceptance of high unemployment!

Even that great financial impact is not as important as the psychological cost. Three thousand years ago, Solomon said, "There is nothing better than that a man should rejoice in his own work." Three centuries before Christ, Aristotle wrote, "The happy life is thought to be virtuous; a virtuous life requires exertion." And two hundred years before that, the famed lawmaker Solon warned, "An abundance of laborers should not be left idle." Plato wrote, "A state is not one, but two states, the one of poor, the other of rich men; and they are living on the same spot and always conspiring against one another." Machiavelli said much the same thing. To the extent that a government can avoid hopelessness among the poor, the two states can become one state.

Those who are unemployed feel left out of society. They do not have a feeling of contributing, of belonging. Yes, they can vote, but in a very real sense, they feel disenfranchised. There is a growing sense among them that their voice is not being heard.

THE SOLUTION

Our free system can eliminate unemployment if we try, and we must try. We have to make a higher priority of putting our people to work. The time is near when the United States can show that a free society can tackle unemployment and win.

An opportunity to work gives people self-esteem, something we all need. When self-esteem disappears, alternatives that are not good for society emerge. People without self-esteem cannot convey self-esteem to their children; people without hope cannot give hope to others. After more than three decades of public life and working with people who have every variety of problem, I have learned that the great division in our society is not between black and white, Anglo and Hispanic, Jew and gentile, or rich and poor. The great division is between those who have hope and those who have given up. There is nothing like a job to raise self-esteem, to make you feel that you are contributing something to society and to your family. For too many in our society, hopelessness and joblessness are the same.

THE OUTLINE OF THE PLAN

The Guaranteed Job Opportunity Program will work like this:

The governor of each state will appoint a committee of seven to hold hearings to establish boundaries of appropriate governing districts within the state, which may be the geographic districts of the Private Industrial Council of the Job Training Partnership Act (JTPA), or may be different.

In each district, an executive council of 13 people will be appointed: four by the governor (two Democrats and two Republicans); four by the mayor of the largest city within the geographic district (two Democrats and two Republicans); and five appointed jointly by the chief executives of the other government units within the district (no more than three from any one political party). At least four of the 13 must represent the business community, and at least four must represent labor unions.

The 13-person council will be authorized to employ an administrator and necessary support personnel, but in no event will the administrative and personnel costs exceed 10 percent of the money paid for putting unemployed people to work. The personnel employed in a professional capacity within the district will be subject to the restraint-from-politics restrictions now applicable to federal civil service employees. At least one person in administration will be a counselor. Careful auditing will be required.

Jobs will be provided on a project-by-project basis, following guidelines established by the secretary of labor. Within those guidelines, the local council can select projects. Any project may be vetoed if two labor union council members or two business members file an objection with the district council.

Supervisors will be employed on a project-by-project basis and will be paid the local prevailing wage.

To be eligible to work within a district, a person must have resided there at least 30 days and must have been out of work at least 35 days.

No one will be eligible for the Guaranteed Job Opportunity Program without showing evidence of having tried to secure employment in the private sector. No one can stay under the program without providing evidence of that continued pursuit.

No more than two people in any one household will be eligible for a job. No one whose household income exceeds $17,000 annually will be eligible.

Those eligible must be citizens of the United States or aliens legally authorized to work.

Those who are hired will work a maximum of 32 hours per week. They will be paid either the minimum wage (currently $3.35 per hour, $107.20 per week), 10 percent above what they receive under welfare, or 10 percent above what they would receive under unemployment compensation, whichever is higher. When they become ineligible for either welfare or unemployment compensation, they will continue eligibility for the 32 hour program at the minimum wage until they are once again employed full-time.

A person given a job under this program may work up to 16 hours per week in another job or jobs.

Only those who either are high school graduates or are nongraduates 18 years of age or older will be eligible. Those between 18 and 25 who are not high school graduates will be required to take tests to determine their verbal and mathematical skill levels. They will receive counseling and be required to attend evening or weekend classes until they receive their high school equivalency diploma.

All applicants, of whatever age, will be tested for basic reading and writing ability. Those who cannot read or write or have limited skills will be encouraged to improve themselves. Brief but basic training in applying for a job, how to prepare a résumé, and the practical steps to take to search for a job will be provided all applicants. "Job clubs" will be formed, where people will get together to discuss what they are doing and to encourage one another.

Transportation and equipment for a project cannot exceed 10 percent of its cost. Anything above that in equipment needs or construction material must be provided by the state or local government.

Those employed under the program will receive medical coverage (the "green card," if they meet standard eligibility requirements) unless they have coverage through private, part-time employment, other government programs, or other members of their family.

Whether people on welfare will be required to sign up for the Guaranteed Job Opportunity Program when it is fully implemented will be up to the individual states. States will find that the voluntary movement off welfare will be significant. Eventually, most states will probably require that all but mothers with children under two or three must sign up for the program. Oklahoma now requires "Workfare" for mothers within weeks of the birth of a child.

Food stamp regulations will remain unchanged. Some people working under this program will be eligible, some will become ineligible because of increased income. The same will be true of energy assistance.

Supervisors may give job references. These will be the first references some program participants ever will have had.

Those given jobs under the program will receive Social Security coverage to maintain eligibility for both retirement and disability programs, but will not be covered by unemployment compensation.

People eligible for retirement payments under Social Security, Railroad Retirement, or any other program will not be eligible to participate in the Guaranteed Job Opportunity Program, unless their retirement benefits total less than $400 a month. Those old enough to receive Social Security but not eligible for retirement payments can work long enough to become eligible.

The program will be administered by the Department of Labor. No new federal agency needs to be created.

THESE ARE NOT DEAD-END JOBS

These are not dead end jobs, in the sense that there is encouragement to move from them to private-sector jobs that pay more. Testing and educational incentives and counseling will be offered with these jobs so that a person's potential can be tapped.

But it should be added that millions of Americans work in what many people consider dead-end jobs. Digging ditches may be viewed as a dead-end job by some. But it is a useful and needed function in our society. And there are hundreds of thousands of Americans right now who would welcome an opportunity to earn money by digging ditches.

The easy categorization of some needed functions in our society as dead-end jobs is usually done by white-collar people whose contributions sometimes are less beneficial than those of the people who perform these "dead-end" jobs. Someone has to sweep the floors; someone has to clean the toilets; someone has to dig ditches. In several ways, this program is also different from the public-sector jobs welfare recipients often perform under programs known as workfare, which have the image of being punitive and mean-spirited, not offering a real lift to those who work:

- It will give people an incentive to work by paying them more than they would receive under welfare or unemployment compensation.
- It will make counseling available to help a person improve his or her economic lot.
- It will require careful educational testing so that those needing assistance to improve verbal or arithmetic skills can receive that, or those needing a high school equivalency or other training program can receive that. Those over 25 would receive more limited tests, but would be encouraged to improve themselves educationally.
- It sometimes will offer special services such as day care and transportation. Workfare ordinarily does not offer such assistance.

If by dead-end jobs the critics mean positions in which people stand around and do nothing, that is not a valid criticism of the Guaranteed Job Opportunity Program. That criticism had some validity for the Comprehensive Employment and Training Act (CETA), under which people were assigned to a unit of government, whether there was something meaningful to do or not. Sometimes CETA workers had nothing to do and were paid for doing nothing—precisely what we do under present welfare policies. Under the project-oriented Guaranteed Job Opportunity Program, people will not be assigned indefinitely to a unit of government, but will be assigned to a project. When the project is completed, there will be a new assignment.

The Guaranteed Job Opportunity Program gives people a chance to contribute to society in a meaningful way and to learn good work habits.

BUILDING AND REBUILDING OUR BASICS

Accompanying the Guaranteed Job Opportunity Program should be a plan to work on the infrastructure—the mass transit systems and highways and bridges and sewers and water systems—of our country. By meeting these real needs, we also put people back to work.

There are also less-obvious needs.

Within my lifetime (I am 59), I have seen rural America change from a land that was largely dark at night, with no electric refrigeration and other conveniences, to an attractive area where life is not appreciably different from life in the cities and suburbs. That did not happen accidentally. Someone had to have a dream.

Clean drinking water is now almost as universally available as electricity. Someone had to dream of having clean drinking water.

We should include telephones in our dreams of the future. For almost seven million American homes, a telephone is still an unaffordable luxury.

Telephones can now be set so that you can use them only for local calls, not long-distance calls. If we were to put a two percent surcharge on our long-distance calls and use the money to provide phones that do not have long-distance ability to the less-fortunate among us, we could reduce crime, help ensure safety for a health or fire emergency, enrich the lives of many of our citizens—and provide jobs to tens of thousands of people.

A six-cent increase in the gasoline tax would provide $7 billion in revenue. One-third could go for rural roads and bridges, one-third for state highway systems, and one-third for our mass transit systems. That would include all costs and put more than 200,000 people to work. More than half a century ago, Senator George Norris of Nebraska said, "I would rather have the government build highways and give men jobs than take the same amount of money and give it to charity to people who are without jobs."

In thousands of communities, water systems need to be repaired and extended, and sewer systems that were designed to take much smaller loads are decaying, in addition to being inadequate. A similar growth in expenditure—$7 billion—could produce a similar number of jobs, (200,000).

Congressman John Seiberling of Ohio pioneered an effort to establish an American Conservation Corps, a program similar to the Civilian Conservation Corps of the 1930s, designed to help the nation's parks and forests and to give young people a chance to contribute for a modest wage. For less than $200 million a year, 85,000 young people could be given that opportunity. Educational enrichment should be part of this. Teenagers are only seven percent of the work force, but their unemployment rate exceeds that of all other groups except the disabled. The unemployment rate for black teenagers is 40 percent and for Hispanic teenagers is 24 percent.

Initiate these four programs, and more than half a million Americans can go back to being productive and paying taxes instead of receiving taxes. When these people work, they purchase cars and clothing and television sets. Additional hundreds of thousands of people are put to work.

But these jobs are no substitute for the basic program, the Guaranteed Job Opportunity Program.

THOSE WHO BENEFIT FROM THE PROGRAM

The jobless will have new hope under the Guaranteed Job Opportunity Program. Even if they are the only beneficiaries, that alone will be worth the effort. The United States cannot hope to regain its momentum in world competition with a sizable portion of our population nonproductive, nonparticipatory, and increasingly dissatisfied. Greater participation and contribution by the lower one-fifth economically will not happen unless it is planned.

An *Atlantic Monthly* article on life in a West Side Chicago ghetto concluded that a jobs program is the only hope. The author observed:

> The great advantage of such a program is that it would enter the lives of ghetto kids when they were 18 or 19 and would affect them at a time when most still feel more hopeful than resigned, even if some have been overwhelmed by the traumas of growing up in the ghetto . . . . It is not a wacky scheme requiring a departure from the whole American political system; it is something that

America has already done once. It worked and, just as important, it is widely remembered as having worked.

Employees will benefit through the increased economic activities that will be generated. They will also experience appreciably lower unemployment compensation costs.

When the Guaranteed Job Opportunity Program is in place, money will be fed into areas that currently are severely depressed.

The program will encourage greater stress on educational attainment, which is good for those involved, good for the nation.

The Social Security system will be strengthened. The system had to be buttressed a few years ago for two reasons: unemployment and inflation. Offering work to millions of nonworking Americans will eliminate one of the two threats to Social Security.

Reduced crime helps all citizens and assists budgets of government units at every level. One writer has noted, "One advantage [of a jobs program] is that criminals can be treated as criminals, without residual guilt about the availability of jobs." Offer people—particularly the young—an opportunity to earn money rather than steal it, and many will seize that opportunity.

WE CAN LEARN FROM EXPERIENCE

It may be trite, but it is true: We don't need to reinvent the wheel. That applies to a jobs program.

In the 1930s, this nation had a huge unemployment problem, but, fortunately, it also had leadership with the wisdom to understand that the unemployment liability needed to be turned into a national asset. That leadership did it with a program called the Works Progress Administration (WPA). President Franklin D. Roosevelt created the program through executive order in May 1935, and by December of that year, 2,667,000 people were working in it. There is not a community in this nation over 50 years old that is not better for what the WPA did.

The good work of the WPA remains. That includes the building or modernizing of 125,110 schools, libraries, and park lodges; the construction or improvement of 651,000 miles of highways; and the installation of 16,100 miles of water line and 24,300 miles of sewer line. Hot lunch programs were started in schools where the poor were concentrated. More than 1.5 million adult Americans were taught how to read and write. Over a period of time, that alone paid for the program.

We still live in a land rich with the potential of unemployed people and loaded with things that need to be done. Both unions and businesses are better organized than they were in 1935, and some of the projects would have to be handled differently today. But we could teach many more than 1.5 million adult Americans to read and write; we could plant 200 million trees a year. There is no shortage of needs; there is no shortage of personnel. What we have a shortage of is creative and courageous political leadership.

In commenting on the WPA programs, Joel Drake, president of the Iron Workers Union, observed: "It's a sad commentary on the state of things that almost nothing done in the jobs and public works area in the half-century since [the WPA] has come close to making such a lasting contribution to our national economy . . . . We need a strategy to provide a good, economically productive job to every man and woman who needs and wants one."

Public employment experiments with recipients of Aid to Families with Dependent Children, with ex–drug addicts, and with ex-convicts all point to the public employment alternative as a successful way to lift people, as a wise investment.

Then why don't we do something about it?

The answer is political. When you help people who particularly need a helping hand, the results are not uniformly favorable. One of the reasons some people are down economically is that they are poor managers. When you're dealing with homemakers who have had a struggle with alcohol, with people who have not learned to work—with a host of others who could be mentioned—some of them are not going to turn out to be success stories. Newspapers will run articles about some person who abused a program; perhaps we will see a shot on television of some people loafing on the job. So the political leader, in order to avoid being identified with the abuse of a program, tolerates a much ·greater abuse: using taxpayers' money to pay people for being nonproductive, abusing the least-fortunate by not giving them a chance to be useful members of our society.

This is not to suggest that only the most desperate or the poor managers are unemployed and would be participants in the program. When a plant or mine suddenly closes or reduces its work force—often because of imports—many find themselves unable to get employment. They are citizens who have paid their taxes regularly with little or no complaint and who have accumulated enough in limited savings to be ineligible for welfare. They deserve something more than being pushed into poverty before they are helped.

Harry Hopkins, who helped direct the WPA during the 1930s, summed it up well: "Work relief costs more than direct relief, but the cost is justified. First, in the saving of morale. Second, in the preservation and creation of human skills and talents. Third, in the material enrichment which the unemployed add to our national wealth through their labors."

For several years under CETA, we provided jobs for hundreds of thousands of Americans who needed them. They were paid little, but the program was modestly successful in raising earnings, especially for women and others in the job market. Because it was not project-oriented, as the Guaranteed Job Opportunity Program is, it aroused opposition from the government unions, who feared substitution and experienced some of it, as well as criticism from the more traditional forces that oppose any move to help people in need. That combination proved fatal. There was some abuse—abuse that cannot be defended—and, unfortunately, some substitution. Instead of correcting the wrongs and keeping what was good, CETA was killed. Killing it was good politics but bad public policy.

CETA was succeeded by JTPA, a program that is more popular, in part because of the lessons learned from some of

CETA's mistakes, but in part because JTPA has been more selective in choosing people to serve. JTPA, for example, so far has served 18 percent fewer people without a high school diploma than did CETA, but 11 percent more high school graduates. Pick those to serve carefully, and the results will improve; there will be fewer public relations disasters.

The Guaranteed Job Opportunity Program is not designed to take the place of JTPA. JPTA should serve all it can, but those not served by JTPA and other programs—the millions who now fall through the cracks—should have better alternatives than welfare or impoverishment or crime. The Guaranteed Job Opportunity Program will give them a chance.

ENCOURAGING THE PRIVATE SECTOR

The Guaranteed Job Opportunity Program is not a substitute for doing everything possible to encourage the private sector to provide employment. I believe in the free enterprise system, but the private sector by itself is not able to provide all the jobs that need to be created.

Experiments unrelated to any present program should be carried out to encourage private job placement of those who have been out of work for a long period. For example, those unemployed more than 60 days might be given vouchers entitling employers hiring them to reimbursement of a set amount per hour for a period of months. The short-term unemployed are more likely to find employment on their own.

Other ideas should be tried. The nation has 50 laboratories called states. For the most part, business leaders want to demonstrate good citizenship, but they also have a responsibility to show profits. If we can devise more and better methods of providing assistance without diminishing profits, much more of the business world will join the effort.

But enlisting the support of the private sector is not a substitute for the new safety net the nation needs: the Guaranteed Job Opportunity Program.

A HELP ON INCOME DISTRIBUTION

We are quietly, undramatically, but unquestionably creating some long-range problems for ourselves through a shift in income distribution. In the last few years, I have heard a growing number of speeches that pit class against class, leaving me with an unsettling feeling that something basic to the nation is coming unglued.

Even a 1986 report from the Joint Economic Committee of Congress divides the people of our nation into four categories: the super-rich, the very rich, the rich, and everyone else.

It is not hard to find the source of our problems. During the past decade, the top 10 percent of our population has shown growth in income; the bottom 90 percent, loss. For the first time since the Great Depression, we have a shrinking percentage of Americans owning their homes, a smaller percentage belonging to the legendary middle class. In West Germany the difference in average income from the top 10 percent to the bottom 10 percent is only six times, and in Japan it is an even smaller difference. In 1969, the middle 50 percent of our population (the third through seventh deciles) had 39 percent of the income. By 1982, that share had dropped to 34 percent, and it is still shrinking.

Unfortunately, the massive overhaul of the tax code completed in the fall of 1986 will widen the gap between the more fortunate and the less fortunate. The more fortunate are much better lobbyists than the less fortunate!

Labor unions performed a major role in creating a healthy middle class, but as manufacturing slipped from 36 percent of private employment in 1965 to 24 percent in 1985, the power and numbers of labor unions also slipped. Manufacturing as a percentage of our gross national product has been fairly constant since the Korean War; but in part because of flawed trade policies, employment in manufacturing has been decreasing dramatically.

The United States today has a substantially smaller percentage of workers unionized than most democratic countries. The combination of the massive loss of jobs due to imports and the decline in power of the unions has resulted in growing numbers of poor and a shrinking middle class. The appointees of the Reagan administration to the National Labor Relations Board (NLRB) have made that body the most antiunion NLRB in history, and its rulings have reflected that strong bias. Traditionally, under both Democratic and Republican administrations, the NLRB has been fairly even-handed, without too much of a tilt toward either labor or management. That shift under the Reagan administration is an additional cause of union membership loss. Those who view the decline of labor unions as a healthy development may awaken some morning to find sizable numbers of American workers demanding much more radical alternatives. The inevitable result of a continually widening gap between rich and poor will be a radicalization and polarization that can mean only serious upheavals at some future point.

Even at the present minimum wage level, the numbers living below the poverty level would be reduced under the Guaranteed Job Opportunity Program, and the chance for many to move up the economic ladder would be increased.

Assuming that the minimum wage is increased perhaps 30 cents an hour during the next administration, whether Democratic or Republican, under the Guaranteed Job Opportunity Program, the huge disparity between the most fortunate and the least fortunate in our society would be modestly decreased even further. That increase in the minimum wage is overdue. Since the last increase in the minimum wage, in 1981, inflation has caused a decline of 26 percent in its effective rate. In noninflationary terms, relative to the rest of the economy, the minimum wage is now at its lowest level since 1955. While a 30 cent hourly increase in the minimum wage may not seem important to many readers, to those struggling to get by on a minimum wage, that extra 12 dollars a week (for 40 hours) can make a huge difference.

The wisdom in avoiding a society with too many poor and a few very wealthy is not some profound truth that suddenly descended on humanity. Four hundred years before Christ, Plato wrote, "There should exist among the citizens neither extreme poverty nor, again, excess of wealth, for both are productive of evils." And 14 years before the Declaration of

Independence, Jean Jacques Rousseau observed, "Allow neither rich men nor beggars. These two estates . . . are equally
fatal to the common good; from the one come the friends of
tyranny, and from the other tyrants. It is always between
them that public liberty is put at auction; the one buys, the
other sells." Both Plato and Rousseau wrote before any
country had developed the large middle-income group that
this nation first developed. So long as there is that sizable
middle-income group, a society can tolerate those with
great wealth; in fact, those with wealth serve as a stimulus
and model for hard work and creativity and risk taking. But
at some point, if the people of limited means become too
numerous and feel put upon, then a society has an explosive
situation. Writing from France, Thomas Jefferson told James
Madison of the concentration of wealth "in a very few
hands," with long-term consequences that would not be
good for France. He hoped that our nation could avoid that
danger. He might well have been writing to us today.

The main reason for supporting the Guaranteed Job Opportunity Program should not be to avoid political explo-
sions in the future. We should favor it because it makes
sense for the economy of the nation, and it is humanitarian.

The program is prudent insurance for the future of our
political system, and we should develop a sense of urgency
about providing that insurance. You would not drive your
car without automobile insurance. We should not drive our
government without protection for the unemployed, both
because of humanitarian reasons and because of what could
happen to the system.

Franklin D. Roosevelt once said, "The test of our progress
is not whether we add more to the abundance of those who
have much; it is whether we provide enough for those who
have too little."

PART TWO

The Goals and Principles of the Democratic Party

Free speech may best serve its highest purpose when it induces a condition of unrest, creates dissatisfaction with conditions as they are, or even stirs people to anger.
—Justice William O. Douglas

CHAPTER 10

Democratic Capitalism: A New Response to Economic Change

Governor Charles S. Robb

THROUGHOUT MOST OF THIS century, Detroit—probably more than any other American city—has exemplified our country's industrial might. More recently, of course, this city came to be portrayed in a less-flattering light—as the capital of America's ailing "Rustbelt."

But now, with advanced manufacturing companies sprouting up along "Automation Alley," Detroit is caught in the crosswinds of a dramatic economic change. In this essay, I'd like to speak to that change—and to its social and its political implications.

An economic and political order forged largely during the 1930s, and institutionalized by the New Deal, has largely run its course. What's needed, it seems to me, is a renegotiation of the social compact in the light of new economic realities.

As the industrial order yields to a new one, so, too, does the old political order that it shaped and sustained—a fabric

Note: The text of this essay is based on remarks by Governor Robb to the Economic Club of Detroit, March 2, 1987.

139

of social and economic relationships woven largely in the 1930s.

Facing a general economic collapse and, particularly, its social and political implications, Franklin Roosevelt was forced to take drastic steps to restore public faith in our economic system. In the place of untrammeled, predatory capitalism, he indeed offered the American people a New Deal: Government would now harness the raw energy of capitalism to serve broad social ends.

Government would regulate the market economy in the public interest, to cushion people against adversity and to spread the wealth more equitably. Social security, unemployment insurance, federal housing assistance, and, later, the G.I. Bill—all of these policies flowed from the new social contract that Roosevelt forged. The New Deal was a masterstroke that at once saved our free enterprise system and welded together a diverse but durable coalition that dominated American politics for half a century.

Roosevelt had redeemed the central promise of America— the promise of opportunity. And so, because Roosevelt was a Democrat, in the eyes of most Americans for nearly 50 years, Democrats stood for prosperity, while Republicans stood for austerity.

Starting in the late sixties, however, and culminating in 1984, all that changed. With some justification, Democrats began to be seen as being so preoccupied with wealth distribution that we didn't notice that the economic pie had stopped growing. People also began to take a less-benign view of government, seeing it less as the champion of national purpose and more as the captive of narrow interests.

The late historian Teddy White put it this way:

. . . My thinking is that by the time of the 1980 election, the pursuit of equality had created a system of interlocking dependencies, and the American people were persuaded that the cost of equality had come to crush the promise of opportunity.

Without that promise—without the glue of economic populism—the New Deal coalition simply came apart, and

Democrats surrendered the mantle of growth and opportunity to the Republicans. Yet now, after more than six years of borrow-and-spend policies, people aren't so sure that the Republicans have the answer either. There's a nagging sense that we're living on borrowed money and on borrowed time, that we're foreclosing future opportunities for our children, and that this administration simply doesn't comprehend the most urgent threat to our economic well-being.

That threat is not a cataclysm, like the Depression, but a kind of economic entropy, a slow and steady sapping of our economic vitality as we falter in world markets. I'll spare you the usual grim statistics on our ballooning budget and trade deficits, and on the geometric growth of our national and international debts, although I feel very strongly about them. But I do want to underscore the problem of lagging productivity growth, because it goes right to the heart of our ability to keep alive the promise of opportunity in the years ahead.

After World War II, our productivity grew at a rate that would double our standard of living every 24 years. But in this decade, growth has been so sluggish that our standard of living won't double again until the middle of the next century, in 2046, more than 60 years hence. And even many of our children may not be around to enjoy it.

It's obvious that this anemic trend is going to have to be reversed, because common sense tells us that America cannot have both high wages and low productivity for any extended period. The only way to compete without lowering wages, as well as our standard of living, is to become more productive.

Our ultimate goal, then, is not just to become more competitive, which we can certainly do simply by becoming poorer, but to have a competitive economy producing a standard of living that is second to none. That, I would submit, is the real challenge we face.

I believe America is in the economic fight of its life. And it is a fight we can—and we must—win if we are to maintain our position of world leadership. We certainly don't claim to have all the answers, but I'd like to offer at least some thoughts on how I believe this country ought to respond to economic change.

In my judgment, there are three things that we should not do. One is to retreat into economic isolation by erecting barriers to our markets. We need to compete, not to protect. Another is to allow further erosion of our manufacturing base. We've got to excel at producing high-value products, whether they're autos or semiconductors or industrial robots. Last, and perhaps most important, we can't be content with tinkering. So-called competitiveness legislation may well be useful, but new laws alone won't reverse the erosion of our competitive strength.

As far as I'm concerned, what's really needed is a profound change in our capitalist culture, a fundamental change in the way our entire society is organized to do business. Just as we did in the New Deal, the time has come for Americans to negotiate a new social contract, to insist on economic growth with economic equity, and to create a vibrant, democratic capitalism that puts our people and their productive potential first.

No longer can a high-wage economy like ours depend on standardized mass production. Let's face the facts. With the easy movement of technology and capital around the world, low-wage countries can mass produce steel, textiles, and televisions more cheaply than we can.

The rules of the economic game have changed. Where the old manufacturing model was capital-intensive, the new model is knowledge-intensive. Where the old manufacturing model was hierarchical and highly centralized, the new model is decentralized and spreads decision-making power widely. Where the old manufacturing model was rigidly geared to volume production of standardized goods, the new model emphasizes flexibility, innovation, and short production lines. And where the old manufacturing model divided management and labor into two distinct and often antagonistic classes, the new model makes close collaboration a virtual requirement if we are to have any real hope of success.

The view that sees workers as interchangeable parts, as disposable drones, is simply obsolete. I believe this point is critical. Notwithstanding occasional Republican fantasies to the contrary, we cannot rely solely on a small, elite corps of entrepreneurs to bail us out of our economic dilemma.

If we are going to be able to adapt successfully to a rapidly changing economic marketplace, we've got to make sure that the capacity to innovate, to think independently, and to learn and apply new skills is distributed widely throughout our work force. Our comparative advantage as a nation hinges on how well and how quickly we transform ideas into better products. And that, in turn, depends on the cumulative expertise of great numbers of people.

From the front office to the factory floor, all workers have got to add value to the goods and services we offer. In their collective ingenuity lies our best hope to keep ahead of the competition and to keep our wages and our living standards high. And every person who remains underemployed, unemployed, or stuck in poverty and dependence will subtract from our ability to generate value and wealth.

This new emphasis on resourceful and versatile workers, on teamwork and innovative capacity, implies major changes in the way our industries are organized for production. It means close cooperation among everyone involved at all steps of the process. It means less-stifling routine. It means less bureaucracy, fewer people who can say "no" to new ideas. And it means the end of an aristocracy of management and the beginning of a democratic capitalism characterized by a new egalitarian ethic in the American workplace.

As we renegotiate the industrial compact, both labor and management will have to discard some ingrained habits of the past. For labor, adaptability is the key. Rigid work rules and job classifications, resistance to new technologies that transform the workplace, wage demands divorced from long-term company performance, and a relentlessly adversarial stance toward employers—all of these today are anachronisms, and they ultimately work to the disadvantage of working men and women.

For management, a new standard of success is needed—a standard based on long-term market strength, not slavish devotion to the bottom line. After all, if U.S. companies can't compete, their managers aren't managing well enough.

Once the very model of brisk and exacting efficiency, the typical big American corporation today has grown flabby—more acquisitive than productive. Often it seems to lack the intensely competitive psychology that's necessary to take on lean and hungry foreign rivals.

Something is terribly wrong when U.S. workers can build products more efficiently under Japanese management than they can under American management. Yet, it's happening in our auto industry. As you know, the Japanese are making more and more cars here to get around the so-called voluntary quota on imported cars. By one estimate, the Japanese auto plants in this country enjoy a 15 percent cost advantage based on superior management alone.

Our managers ought to be risk takers, not risk avoiders. They ought to make patient, long-term investments, and not just chase quick returns and short-term gains. They ought to solicit workers' ideas, and not simply hand decisions down from on high. And they ought to be rewarded on the basis of production and the creation of new wealth, not of speculation and the shuffling of existing assets.

It all boils down to this: All Americans ultimately must share in the risks and the rewards of economic competition. That is the essence of democratic capitalism. Its purpose is to help America achieve three urgent social and economic goals: promoting higher employment and job security, giving workers a greater stake in their jobs, and making U.S. industry more productive and more competitive.

We need to start by creating a sound and stable environment for enterprise. That's government's primary responsibility. And nothing is more important than tackling the budget deficit and shifting the bias of fiscal policy from consumption to investment. Regulatory policy, particularly in the financial realm, also needs to be tailored to the new realities of global competition.

And government has a further obligation to assure the unrestricted flow of goods and services in a free and fair world trading system. We need to combat protectionism both at home and abroad.

Given the right economic climate, we can hasten our evolution to democratic capitalism by taking these three steps:

- First, link pay to performance.
- Second, practice democracy in the workplace.
- Third, make strategic investments in our human resources.

First, I think that if workers see a direct link between their pay and their performance, they'll work harder. Therefore, we ought to encourage business—and government—to move from fixed wages to a flexible system of bonus pay.

And I'm not just talking about bonuses for management, particularly not those that are awarded regardless of how the company performs. I'm talking about a bonus pay system for all managers and all workers, so that all share the rewards if their company fares well, and all share the pain if profits fall.

For example, I have trouble finding the logic in the decision by General Motors in early 1987 to set aside $169 million in bonuses for executives, even though profits fell by 25 percent in 1986 and were apparently too low to allow bonuses for hourly workers. But I see eminent good sense in Ford's rewarding hourly workers with bonuses, when company earnings outstripped GM's in 1986 for the first time since the Model T ruled the roads.

Experience both here and in Japan confirms what common sense suggests—that when workers and managers are rewarded on the basis of performance, effort, teamwork quality, and innovation all improve.

And pay-for-performance has another benefit. Some economists believe that a bonus system would move us closer to a full-employment economy. If firms have an alternative to laying off workers when times are bad, they will have an incentive to hire more workers when times are good. Bonuses that vary with a company's economic performance, provide that crucial flexibility.

Preventing layoffs also can help moderate downward

swings in the business cycle. If fewer workers are laid off, output will fall less sharply. So will demand, since purchasing power will remain higher than if layoffs are widespread.

Finally, some economists believe that a flexible pay method would dampen wage-driven inflationary pressures, since workers' pay would be tied to real economic performance. Even though pay for performance provides an incentive to work harder and better, however, it will be unavailing if workers remain virtually powerless to change their work environment or the way they perform their jobs.

So, it seems to me, the second thing we need to do is to practice democracy in the workplace—to give people the opportunity to improve their own productive efforts. This kind of "people power" has paid off dramatically at Ford, where workers participate in decisions affecting work schedules, equipment changes, production flow, and quality control. To encourage higher quality, workers are allowed to stop the assembly line when something is wrong.

Another promising development, in my judgment, is the Saturn agreement between GM and the auto workers, under which Saturn workers will be paid on a bonus system and will have a say in the plant's strategic decisions. The company has offered new job security provisions, and workers have agreed to a dramatic reduction in the number of job classifications. Also, worker-manager distinctions will be minimized. The Saturn plan reportedly provides that there will be no time clocks, no reserved parking, and one lunchroom for all employees.

Like any departure from the status quo, such far-reaching agreements are bound to meet resistance. It's been suggested that government can offer incentives that would help ease the transition to democratic capitalism.

For example, to entice both business and labor to embrace pay-for-performance plans, MIT economist Lester Thurow has proposed that bonuses be exempted from the payroll tax. I'm inclined to believe we'd have to front-load a percentage of the wage portion, so as not to lose any more of the revenue stream for Social Security—but the principle is sound.

The third pillar of democratic capitalism is strategic public investment.

We need to lift the general level of public education, so that every child receives the quality of instruction now available only to the brightest students. We need a national policy of rapid labor redeployment, one that includes job training and retraining, safe and affordable child care, and innovations that aid worker mobility and independence, such as individual training accounts and portable pensions.

We need new, targeted initiatives designed to help the poor free themselves from dependence and move into the productive mainstream of our society.

And we need not only more research, but also better ways to speed the transfer of new technologies from the laboratory to the factory and the office. An excellent example is the Michigan Modernization Service, which helps companies and workers take advantage of emerging technologies. In fact, it's an example of democratic capitalism at work, giving Americans the incentives, the opportunities, and the tools to succeed in a new economic era.

As far as I'm concerned, America faces a historic opportunity to become preeminent in the new economic order of information and knowledge, just as it dominated the previous industrial era. But few nations have successfully undergone such a transformation. History is replete with examples of powerful states that, refusing to bend to the winds of change, developed a deep bias against the uncertainties and disruptions of economic and social change. Clinging rigidly to the old ways, hoping to make time stand still, they were, inevitably, in time eclipsed by new and more dynamic societies.

I believe our nation stands at such a crossroads today. We can either master economic change or be undone by it. So far, our response has been ambiguous.

Let me add that I have had the opportunity to witness firsthand some of the extraordinary efforts industries in Michigan have made to adapt to a new economic era. The move toward advanced manufacturing; the strategic leadership of Governor Blanchard and the state commerce department; your research institutes, strategic fund, and modernization service—these are examples of public/private cooperation that convince me that the real economic innovation is taking place at the state level around the country.

And what I have seen here reinforces my own view that to block or retard economic change is ultimately to condemn our people to diminishing opportunities and our society to certain decline.

At the same time, we have an obligation to help our people to adjust swiftly and smoothly to the wrenching effects of inevitable change. We can't simply let them founder helplessly in capitalism's gale of creative destruction.

Instead, I'd much prefer to see us enlist all Americans in a new partnership for national prosperity. I'd like to see us forge a new social compact, to make our capitalist system more democratic and more productive. And I'd like to see us once again make the American economy a marvelous engine of growth and opportunity. I believe we can do it.

CHAPTER 11

The Crucial Dilemma and the Democratic Response

Stuart E. Eizenstat

A DEMOCRATIC PRESIDENT IN 1989 will have to confront cruel trade-offs in domestic policy: between what needs to be done for the disadvantaged, left in the backwaters of neglect by eight years of Reagan administration indifference, and what the country can afford to do with lingering deficits from the Reagan era; between the urgency of advancing economic and social justice and the imperatives of managing the American economy in an efficient, noninflationary manner; between the microeconomic needs of individual sectors of society and the macroeconomic realities of a brutally competitive world; between what our hearts tell us we should do and what our heads may require us to do.

There is an undoubted need to address problems that have been ignored or exacerbated by the policies of social Darwinism implemented by this administration:

- The social safety net for the needy is in tatters, as programs for low- and moderate-income Americans have been cut to the core. Construction of housing units for the poor is at a virtual standstill (outlays for housing assistance were $1.8 billion lower for 1982–1985 than

149

the 1981 baseline estimate), funds for job training for disadvantaged and displaced workers have been slashed, job placement efforts for welfare mothers are slated for elimination, and employment programs have been reduced by almost 60 percent of what they would have been before the 1981 budget cuts.

- Long-term investments in our young people have been deferred, with education programs at the elementary, secondary, and higher education levels slighted, day care forgotten, and efforts to arrest the alarming increase in infant mortality stymied by reductions in nutrition programs for pregnant women and infants (1982–1985 outlays for child nutrition programs were reduced 28 percent relative to the 1981 baseline projections).
- The combination of Reagan budget cuts, impacting primarily on the poor, and tax cuts, disproportionately benefiting the wealthy, from 1981 to 1985, resulted in a reverse Robin Hood effect. In 1980, the number of persons below poverty level was 8.6 million; in 1983, the number rose to 9.9 million. The average reduction in cash benefits was generally more than twice as large for those with incomes below $20,000 than for other income categories.
- Federal personnel have been cut in key agencies, like the Federal Aviation Administration and the Environmental Protection Agency.
- By the time the next president of the United States is sworn into office, in 1989, it will have been almost eight years since the minimum wage for the working poor was increased.

And, yet, Democrats face a grave dilemma. We have lost four of the past five presidential elections. A Democratic president has been in the Oval Office only four of the past 20 years. I believe firmly that one of the crucial reasons is that the American public lost confidence in the ability of our party to manage the economy and the American welfare state effectively. If, in the 1988 presidential campaign, we treat the Reagan era as an unhappy aberration; if we are perceived to want business as usual in domestic policy; if we suggest increasing funding for everything the Reagan administration cut, we will lose our third straight presidential election.

Whether unfair or not, our economic and domestic policies are associated in the minds of many with rampant inflation and a mismanaged welfare state. We can be certain the Republican Party will use this as a 1988 campaign theme, pointing to the record of the last two Democratic presidents.

The low rates of inflation enjoyed by Americans during the fifties and early sixties ended during the administration of Lyndon Johnson, as he delayed too long in seeking the revenuos to pay for the escalating Vietnam War on top of the added spending for the War on Poverty. His surtax was too late. An inflationary spiral commenced, as inflation rose from 1.3 percent in 1964 to 5.4 percent in 1969—high by the standards of that era. Inflation has yet to return to the levels prevalent under John F. Kennedy.

Soaring inflation likewise bedeviled the next—and last— Democratic president, Jimmy Carter. From a level of 5.8 percent in Gerald Ford's last year in office, 1976, inflation went to 6.5 percent in 1977, to 7.7 percent in 1978, to 11.3 percent in 1979, and finally, to 13.5 percent in 1980. The oil price shock of 1979–1980, resulting from the Iranian Revolution, was a major contributor to the double-digit rates of inflation that helped lead to the Carter administration's political demise. But inflation had already begun to rise significantly because of a combination of rising food prices, sluggish productivity growth that failed to keep in step with wage increases, and various policy decisions. These policy steps, of which I was very much a part, included an increase in the minimum wage from $2.30 in 1976 to $2.65 in 1978, and to $3.35 in 1981; two tax cuts, in 1977 and 1978; and a stimulative fiscal policy early in the Carter administration to reduce the unemployment rates inherited from the Nixon-Ford years, by means of major public works and public jobs programs through the Comprehensive Employment and Training Act (CETA).

Indeed, there are many parallels between 1976, the last time a Democrat was elected, and 1988:

- In each case, after eight years of Republican rule, there were tremendous pent-up and justifiable demands by the Democratic Party's constituency groups—mayors, minorities, labor, environmentalists, advocates for the poor—to rectify the regressive domestic policies of the Republican predecessor by boosting domestic spending. As in 1976, these constituency groups now constitute the core of party activists who must be mobilized if we are to win the primaries, and to whom commitments for increased spending are made.
- In both instances, inflation was moderate but the trends were rising, with downward pressures on the dollar.
- In each—indeed, even more so in 1988—necessary and desirable Democratic initiatives were constrained by the realities of rising budget deficits and inadequate real growth.

Now our candidates are being pressed to make commitments to support the first minimum wage increase in seven years; to restore Reagan cuts made in programs for the poor and for our nation's cities, counties, and states; and to increase farm income by higher subsidies or production controls.

Our party's nominee must not fail a key litmus test for presidential leadership—the capacity and willingness to manage the economy in such a way as to restrain inflationary pressures that ultimately will stall growth. Inflation is the great political equalizer—infuriating and adversely affecting the poor and the rich, the young and the old. Inflation makes it more difficult to educate children, raises barriers to home ownership for young couples, and upsets retirement plans for senior citizens.

The Democratic presidential candidate must also restore the shaken confidence of the American people in our party's capacity to efficiently manage the modern welfare state. The Great Society was by many measures an enormous success. Poverty levels were drastically reduced, health care fears of the elderly were mitigated, malnutrition was virtually wiped out, housing was improved, equal rights of minorities were guaranteed. But the War on Poverty could never match President Johnson's soaring rhetoric and promises.

The Democratic Party in the last two decades has been transformed from the party of opportunity to one of guarantees, from one that under President Kennedy challenged its citizens to contribute to the society to one that emphasizes government entitlements. We have concentrated on spending more, rather than setting clear priorities, stressing effective delivery of services, streamlining our federal programs, and providing needed flexibility to states and localities and to the private sector.

The American people do not want to dismantle the basic New Deal and the Great Society programs, nor did they elect Ronald Reagan to do so. Since the first half of his first term, even when Republicans controlled the Senate, he has been stymied in emasculating the American welfare state. But voters in the United States do want to be assured their tax dollars are spent on programs that work.

Just as we have an obligation in 1988 to demonstrate we can competently manage the economy without stimulating inflation, so, too, we must show the country we can make social welfare programs work effectively. We can win on a platform that promises not only more, but better.

I believe it is possible to fulfill these obligations in ways that are fully compatible with the historic Democratic commitment to a more compassionate and just society. Indeed, unless we can meet these challenges, we will not be given the opportunity by the voters to use government to help the disadvantaged enter the mainstream of American life, to revitalize American industry, and to make our society more competitive.

A Democratic president must first establish a sound, progrowth, anti-inflationary fiscal policy as his key priority. This will mean telling our constituency groups early and often that funds are more limited than we would like for new spending initiatives. We must be able to demonstrate we can pay for what we propose. This does not mean we should support artificial efforts like balanced budget amendments to the Constitution of the United States, line item vetoes, or inflexible Gramm-Rudman deficit targets. But it does mean establishing credibility in domestic and international monetary markets with a sound, sensible fiscal policy aimed at keeping the ratio of federal budget deficits to gross national product in the range of 2.5–3 percent. A Democratic president must avoid overstimulating the economy through excessive spending—or he will surely follow the unhappy political course of our current administration. Once the economy is on a sound, noninflationary growth path, we can do more of what desperately needs to be done in the domestic area to reverse the results of the Reagan era.

There will be occasions early in the president's term when he must confront the dilemma of taking a step that may be mildly inflationary but seems necessary to achieve a more just society. The need for the first increase in the minimum wage in almost a decade is an example. But even here, we can send a signal we are serious about controlling inflation. For example, the initial increase could be modest, and further increases could be tied to productivity increases in the economy, rather than to inflation, thereby sending a broad signal to the private sector that we expect wage demands for all workers to be in line with productivity improvements.

Moreover, we can suggest that the indexing both of taxes under the 1986 Tax Reform Act and of programs tied to inflation, like Social Security, commence only after a minimum floor is deducted. This would reduce inflationary pressures on the budget and emphasize the importance of fighting inflation.

Second, a Democratic president of the United States must signal that our emphasis will be less on providing new entitlements than on requiring a reciprocal performance from recipients of government benefits if we are to have both a more humane and a more competitive society. There are myriad ways in which this message can be underscored and implemented:

- Companies should be encouraged to link a percentage of their employees' salary (not just top management bonuses) to the profitability of the enterprise, as Professor Martin Weitzman, of the Massachusetts Institute of Technology, has suggested. This provides a less-inflationary way to reward workers, encourages productivity, and demonstrates the need for performance to be the *sine qua non* of reward. It encourages employers to retain workers in downtime and to enhance their incomes handsomely when times improve.

- Certain social welfare benefits should be linked to performance by the beneficiaries. For example, recipients of Aid to Families with Dependent Children (AFDC) should be expected to engage in job training and accept work as a condition of their welfare benefits, while the government has an obligation to provide day care for their children, transportation assistance, and meaningful job opportunities. Likewise, workers eligible for extended unemployment benefits or trade adjustment assistance should have benefits tied to participation in job retraining and placement, a practice followed in much of the rest of the industrialized world. In this way, government is helping achieve self-sufficiency, rather than simply providing income support.
- College federal aid recipients should contribute a period of public service in return for their assistance.
- Industries that seek import relief under Section 201 of the 1934 Trade Act should be required to propose and abide by industry readjustment plans as a condition for relief. My experience at the White House was that industries would pressure the president for protection from import competition, but might use the benefits of relief in wholly unintended ways—as U.S. Steel (now USX) did when it purchased Marathon Oil rather than modernizing its steel mills. These adjustment plans should demonstrate how management and labor propose to be more competitive—through capacity rationalization, management improvements, work rule modifications, and wage concessions during the term of the government relief.

Third, a Democratic president must stress programs that invest in human development and better prepare our citizens to be self-sufficient, contributing members of society. This means increased investments in education from the preschool to the elementary and secondary levels, from college to graduate school. But these additional federal investments should be made in a more responsive and accountable education system. The report of a Carnegie Foundation committee chaired by former Democratic Governor Jim Hunt of North Carolina furnishes a blueprint for reform. A human investment program will also stress job training programs, so badly cut by this administration, to provide our workers with the job skills for a rapidly changing economy.

Fourth, a Democratic president should demonstrate our party's willingness to make the welfare state both more just and more sensible by implementing major reforms in our federal system in which duplicative programs are synthesized and states are given more discretion in managing them. Income support programs, like Medicaid and AFDC, should have more uniformity and federal involvement, while we devolve to the states many of the infrastructure and economic development programs that can be better run at the state level. The report of a commission cochaired by former Virginia Governor Charles Robb and Senator Daniel Evans of Washington, on which I served, offers a model of a creative federal-state-local relationship far different from the Reagan administration's efforts to strip the federal government of its major social responsibilities and drop them on the states.

I have confidence that we have learned the lessons of our political exile and that the Democratic Party will present an optimistic vision of a party prepared to make the hard choices and to provide firm guidance to the nation's domestic affairs in the new interdependent world economy of the 1990s.

CHAPTER 12

The New, Painful World of Public Policy

Governor Richard D. Lamm

THE UNITED STATES AND the Democratic Party face a new, painful world of public policy. I suggest that four major revolutions have taken place over roughly the last 15 years in America that will immensely complicate the life and solutions of the Democratic Party.

First is the growth of the international marketplace. America is no longer a continental economy, but is competing in a new international economy that is imposing on us a new economic world. Between 1982 and 1987, we bought over half a trillion dollars more in goods from abroad than we sold abroad. We now face staggering trade deficits and have become the world's largest debtor nation.

Second is that politicians no longer have a growing pie to divide. We cannot count on a growth dividend to solve as many social problems as we have historically been able to. The average American family earned less money, adjusted for inflation, in 1987 than they earned in 1969. The United States, which used to have a productivity growth rate that would double American real earnings every 20 years, now has the lowest rate of productivity growth in the industrial world, and the current rate would double real wages every 80 years. Politicians increasingly divide a static pie.

Third is the explosion of the elderly population. The average age in America has gone from 25 to 31 and will soon be 37 (the average in Saint Petersburg, Florida). The population of the United States has tripled since 1900, but the number of those over 65 has increased eight times, and of those over 85, 21 times. America has had a grandparent explosion, and those grandparents vote in greater numbers than any other demographic cohort. They also have among the highest disposable income of any cohort in America.

Fourth has been the expansion of medical technology. We have dramatically increased the procedures and machines in the health care industry, so we can now keep hearts beating and lungs breathing long after any meaningful life has gone.

These four revolutions, I suggest, will test the Democratic party and test America in the years ahead. Democrats are great at dividing a growing economic pie, making sure it is produced under safe and sane working conditions, and dividing it as justly as politically possible. Furthermore, no one's political Richter scales are more sensitive to issues of social and economic justice. Whether the issue has been minimum wage, health benefits, worker safety, rural electrification, rights of workers, or consumer or environmental protection, whatever the social injustice, the Democratic Party has been there with a thoughtful solution. The glue that has held together this diverse, eclectic group of people is that we care.

However, the public policy challenges are always changing. Time turns history's kaleidoscope and is always presenting us with a new pattern of problems. Yesterday's challenges and solutions are seldom tomorrow's.

America faces the new challenge of restarting our economic engines. The new international marketplace requires us to become more competitive as a nation. We must learn how to stimulate the growth of the economic pie, and not merely divide it. We will be judged as a party by our ability to meet the total challenge of our society, and this challenge will consist only partly of our historic issues of social and economic justice. We must put a new emphasis on policies that create economic wealth and firm up our ability to compete in the international marketplace.

This will be much more difficult than any recent challenges to face the Democratic Party. It is not merely a matter of adding a new emphasis to please a new constituency group. It will mean more than a new plank in our party platform. The dilemma that we face is that finding solutions to these new realities will require us to amend, and even repeal, some of our other planks and agendas. It will require more than coming up with some new solutions, it will require painstakingly integrating these solutions with our historic constituencies.

Painful as it will be, we must realize that part of tomorrow's agenda will inevitably upset some of our historic friends. Simply said, our current constituency is often at odds with our historic idealism.

Examples are numerous. Take the issue of catastrophic health insurance, which has become the new staple of Democratic speeches. The elderly are one of the most powerful groups within the Democratic Party. The Democratic Party is rightly proud of the myriad programs we have developed for the elderly, and the fear of a catastrophic illness certainly is a real fear. But why do we have programs based on *age* rather than *need*? The real health needs of our society are among the children, who are America's new poor. Medicare, which is one of the proudest planks of the Democratic Party, pays billions of dollars for the health needs of the rich elderly, while we don't begin to cover the health needs of the poor. Medicare made sense (or at least more sense) in 1965, when 23 percent of the elderly lived in poverty. But our programs for the elderly have succeeded beyond belief. Now, instead of being mostly poor, the elderly have the lowest rates of poverty of any age cohort. Today, the average elderly family has twice the assets of families below 30. Today, 23 percent of our children live in poverty, many without even basic health care; yet, only 11 percent of the elderly live in poverty.

It no longer makes sense to build our public policy around age as opposed to need. It does not make sense to have survival to age 65 be the only qualifying event for public benefits. On any day in America, vast resources are denied the poor and spent instead on well-to-do elderly whose only justification for receiving the benefit is that they are over 65. We pay medical benefits to rich retired doctors in Saint Petersburg that are desperately needed for poor children in Saint Paul. That hardly represents the historic Democratic value system. We can better care for the needy, be they aged or young, if we better focus our limited resources.

Under the new catastrophic health care program, we are going to be spending vast amounts of public resources on high-technology medicine for the elderly, when 37 million American families don't have health insurance, and when one out of eight American families was denied some level of basic health care because they couldn't afford it. When 20 percent of our children haven't had polio shots, and when over 30 percent of the children in America have never seen a dentist, do we really want to be using our public resources to give heart transplants to 75-year-old ex-smokers?

This painful dilemma is not limited to health care. Painfully but inevitably, the Democratic Party must confront the fact that today, more than half of all federal social spending goes to those over the age of 65, and nearly all of these federal dollars are distributed without regard to need. We pay Social Security to retired millionaires and extend Medicare benefits to wealthy retired doctors, and sanctimoniously hold these programs inviolate to challenge. The party that had the idealism and sensitivity to develop these programs is forbidden by its constituency groups from reforming them.

Social Security, too, illustrates the point. Our fathers and mothers often got back 20–30 times what they paid into Social Security, but our children will be lucky to get their money back. There is clearly a question of intergenerational equity in these programs. The average person retiring today on Medicare has actuarial benefits some 7–12 times what he paid in, but the system is clearly heading for bankruptcy. It isn't a question of *if* it goes bankrupt, it's merely *when*. At the same time, there are 254,000 millionaires who are on, or qualify for, Medicare, and 700,000 people who get a Social

Security check every month who have other retirement income of $30,000 a year. Millions of working poor pay one dollar out of every seven they earn into a Social Security system that immediately transfers a significant portion of it to people who are wealthier and better off then the person paying the tax. We blindly defend these programs that we should be taking the lead to reform.

Immigration is another example of Democrats' ignoring the public interest and the public demand, and caving in to a small constituency group. All polls have shown for the last 10 years that the public has wanted something done about illegal immigration. Three times, significant and balanced immigration reform passed the Senate that would have controlled illegal immigration and also granted amnesty to millions of illegal aliens living in the United States. The polls have shown that over 80 percent of the public, including a vast majority of Hispanic citizens, have wanted action. But the Democratic House, giving in to a few vocal Hispanic leaders, failed to pass it year after year. And when legislation finally did pass, the Democratic House added myriad crippling amendments. Along the way, Hispanic activists got an anti-immigration plank inserted into the Democratic platform and cowed our 1984 presidential candidate into opposing immigration reform. As we so often do, we let a small group of activists define our agenda. Our heart is stronger than our backbone.

Farm policy is yet another example. No sector of the federal budget has risen faster in recent years than agricultural subsidies. They have risen 540 percent since 1982 and will exceed $30 billion this year, up from $4 billion in 1982. But this is not enough for the Democrats. Pushed by their extremes, they up the bidding with higher subsidies or new schemes to control production that will pass massive costs on to consumers. Kika de la Garza, chairman of the House Agriculture Committee and one of the Democratic Party's leading spokesmen on the issue, seeks a federal agricultural program that will not "sacrifice one single farmer." As one wag has observed, that's like saying we want cuts in the defense industry but without cutting a single defense worker. It is not possible, but if it were, it would not be good public policy. Farmers are victims of a changing economic world, and they deserve sympathy and transition help. But to place them in a sacrosanct place, above hundreds of thousands of steel, textile, shoe, and other workers who have also been victims of economic dislocation, is not possible nor just. We can place a safety net under individuals but not under whole industries. In a country that borrows 20 cents out of every federal dollar it spends, no one deserves a permanent place on the federal payroll.

Do we really want to give one group in America the right to determine the level of direct government support by merely voting in a referendum? What happens if one commodity votes to impose mandatory controls, and others in interrelated industries reject them? Do we really want to give the government the authority to determine production, price, and consumption levels in the name of increasing farm income? What will this do to exports?

Comparable worth is another lofty goal that has become a litmus test for Democratic politicians. Every Democratic constituency gets its ticket punched. Equal pay for equal work and affirmative action have not solved the problem of male bias in our society. There is truly a long way to go to incorporate women into the American mainstream, but that does not justify every "solution" that comes down the road. Do we really want to get the lawyers and the courts in the business of comparing salaries between job categories? We already have the most litigious society on the face of the earth, and two-thirds of the whole world's lawyers practice in the United States. The Democratic Party should be finding ways to reduce litigation, not multiply it. We should be looking at no-fault insurance and alternative dispute resolution, not new and imaginative ways to burden already overburdened courts. There is a "legalflation" at work in America that adds immense costs to American goods and helps make them uncompetitive in the international marketplace.

Thus, the Democratic Party lumbers through current history, adjusting itself not to the new realities but to the new interest groups. We have union leadership define for us what is good for the workers and the economy, and the National Education Association and the American Federation of Teachers define for us what is good for education. There is endless room under the Democratic tent; all a group has to do to get in is push and make noise. Whatever is boldly asserted and plausibly maintained finds its way into the Democratic platform, even if it is against the public interest and the public desires.

America needs a bold and imaginative Democratic Party. It needs to follow its instincts more and to follow its funding sources less. Fund-raising realities have put a "For Sale" sign on all American politics. That we are marginally better and purer than the Republican Party should offer us little solace. We still dance to tunes played by our constituency groups and bow to their wishes.

America faces a day of reckoning. We are consuming more than we produce, and importing more than we are exporting. We spend more than we save, and we are promising more than we can deliver.

We are running massive federal deficits and massive trade deficits. We have the lowest rate of productivity growth in the industrial world, and our kids are testing in the lower third on all international comparisons. Simply put, our problems are outrunning our solutions.

We are faced with many challenging problems needing our best thinking. No nation spends more per capita to educate its children, yet on all international exams, our children score in the lower third. A Swedish 17-year-old knows twice as much math as an American 17-year-old. New York City graduates only 25 percent of its students from high school, and nationwide, 50 percent of Hispanic students never graduate from high school. We have the largest number of functional illiterates of any industrialized nation. We spend far more per capita on health care, yet American males are 15th in life expectancy, and American females are eighth. Our welfare system produces the largest number of illegitimate children and the largest number of broken homes. Should we not get more for our money? Should not the Democratic Party take the lead in reforming and revitalizing our increasingly dysfunctional institutions?

Our Democratic "solutions," even if adopted, will not

solve our nation's problems. They are clearly better than those put forth by Republicans, but often only marginally better. We lack the objectivity and the courage to offer real solutions. Our old friends often keep us from facing new realities.

All human institutions tend to become captives of their constituencies. They all tend to become smug, risk aversive, complacent, and self-satisfied. The same programs and policies that made a party great will not keep a party great. Circumstances change, and so should the cutting edge of policy.

CHAPTER 13

The Democrats' Promise of Prosperity

Robert B. Reich

POLITICAL DISCOURSE IN MODERN America usually proceeds on one of two levels—either slogans ("It's Morning in America") or specific policies (individual retraining accounts). The vast area between, where slogans are connected to policies, and policies are linked to one another, is often the most important but the least discussed. Here is forged a public philosophy.

A public philosophy offers, among other things, a coherent answer to the central economic dilemma of democracy: how to achieve both social justice and economic growth. Americans insist upon having both. Prosperity for some at the cost of dire poverty for others is morally offensive. Equality at the price of stagnation has no greater political appeal. Social justice and prosperity together define the American dream. Any political candidate who aspires to the presidency, or even to more humble office, must credibly promise to deliver both.

In the quarter-century following World War II, liberal Democrats did just that. They offered a compelling public philosophy that successfully married the modern welfare state to principles of Keynesian demand-management of the economy. As public spending stimulated demand for all

165

sorts of goods and services, it became clear that active government intervention on behalf of poorer Americans was not just compatible with economic growth but essential to it. The spectacular performance of the American economy during that interval demonstrated that social justice fit hand in glove with continued prosperity.

As the American economy slowed after 1970, liberal Democrats continued to speak of social justice, but they were oblivious to the emerging problem of economic growth and the failure of government-as-locomotive to continue pulling the economy forwards. (Even when it showed some spark, the Keynesian locomotive disconcertingly tended to pull in products made abroad.) To be sure, liberal Democrats persisted in offering an abundance of slogans and detailed programs. But in the absence of a credible and coherent message about how to achieve both social justice and economic growth, the normative vision lying between the slogans and the politics seemed increasingly muddled.

By taking the economy for granted precisely at a time when many Americans began to worry about its fragility, liberal Democrats ceded the very ideal that rendered their vision of social justice palatable to the majority. Without economic growth, the liberal Democratic call for social justice became something akin to charity. At worst, it became a demand for preserving economic relationships as they were when times were better: erecting tariffs and quotas against foreign imports, regulating factory closings, limiting direct investment abroad, and investing public funds in dying industries.

Conservative Republicans, meanwhile, were busily seeding this fertile terrain. Through countless articles, books, academic studies, and conferences, they concocted a relatively coherent public philosophy that purported to combine economic growth and social justice in a new way. Their message was wonderfully simple. It could be expressed in 30 seconds, even drawn on a napkin. But it also possessed a coherence and consistency, and a semblance of intellectual rigor, which gave it a degree of respectability: Prosperity, they said, depends on creative individuals, motivated by the prospect of private gain. Any effort to redistribute wealth directly from rich to poor must necessarily reduce such incentives and therefore limit economic growth. Thus, if government would only refrain from interfering and give free reign to entrepreneurial energies, then ultimately all Americans, including the poor, will share in the benefits of the resulting prosperity. Prosperity, in the memorable words of Republican theoreticians, will "trickle down."

The beauty of this formulation extended beyond its simplicity and internal consistency. It also gave context and meaning to a variety of specific policies that conservative Republicans had been advocating all along. These included efforts to reduce income taxes, to eviscerate government regulation of business, and to give over to the private sector responsibilities that had been public. Now these separate initiatives could be understood as part of a grand design. They fit within a coherent whole. Slogans and policy prescriptions were linked together in a public philosophy that, at the very least, was more comprehensible than the Democratic alternative.

The absence of a coherent Democratic notion of how to combine social justice and economic growth and, by contrast, the clarity of the Republican vision have had a significant impact on American politics and on the manner in which Democrats and Republicans, respectively, have governed the nation. The Carter administration exemplified the Democrat's quandary: Without a clear idea of where the nation should be headed, there could be no priorities. Every effort at solving the problems of poorer Americans and every policy aimed at restoring economic growth demanded equal attention, while every failure or mistake along either trajectory suggested incompetence.

Ultimately and inevitably, with no overarching philosophy to guide its policies, and the public therefore expecting achievement along every front, the Carter administration found the two values of social justice and economic growth in bitter conflict. President Carter spoke eloquently about the problems of the poor, and took a number of initiatives designed to ameliorate them. But then, with inflation raging out of control, he felt he had no choice but to appoint Paul Volcker as chairman of the Federal Reserve Board and to watch passively as Volcker choked off the money supply, plunged the economy into recession, and thus imposed the heaviest casualties in the inflation fight upon America's poor and near-poor.

Ronald Reagan has demonstrated the reverse side of the same phenomenon: With a coherent public philosophy, it has been possible for him to accomplish (or at least take credit for) a few key economic objectives, like tax reform and deregulation, and to be forgiven the countless misadventures that have characterized his administration. All told, the American public has been remarkably willing to allow the Reagan administration to sacrifice social justice, as exemplified by the steadily widening gap between the nation's rich and poor, without much evidence that Reagan's economic policies have spurred growth. Jimmy Carter's brief administration ended with double-digit inflation and interest rates; Ronald Reagan's will end with double-digit homelessness in America's largest cities and 12-digit indebtedness to the rest of the world. The evidence of overall progress is debatable. But many have been able to overlook this gulf between Reagan's promise and reality because the promise has been consistent with an overarching rationale, intoned repeatedly: Reagan's policies will bring prosperity to everyone, eventually. We need only have enough faith and patience to stick with them.

What is the lesson of all this for liberal Democrats, now that the 1988 election looms? One part of the lesson—that any new Democratic public philosophy must acknowledge the central importance of economic growth—seems to have been learned, perhaps too well. Democrats are now embracing economic growth with a vengeance. These days, no Democratic candidate fails to speak of the importance of improving American productivity, and to offer several policies designed to accomplish just such a feat. All now talk of making America more competitive, and provide a host of measures calculated to do so. Every one celebrates entrepreneurship, and solemnly suggests ways to spur it. In the history of the Democratic Party, there has rarely been such unanimity of purpose.

But the larger lesson—the importance of providing a coherent, normative vision of how economic growth and social justice fit together—may not yet be fully understood by Democrats. It is not enough for them to argue simply that they favor both greater prosperity and greater equality—that they are now hardheaded as well as softhearted, business strategists who are also compassionate. They must also show how both values can be achieved. In particular, they must have an answer to the conservative Republican claim that government cannot hope to redistribute wealth and simultaneously maintain the private incentives necessary to generate it in the first place. If Keynesian demand-management of the economy can no longer justify massive spending on social programs, then what is the new Democratic vision for combining prosperity and social justice?

The danger for liberal Democrats is that the American public will hear no new public philosophy at all, just a rather watered-down version of what conservative Republicans have been advocating for several years. Liberal Democrats will be left with a tepid theme: They want more redistribution than Republicans want, but not so much as to seriously imperil economic growth. Democratic slogans and policy prescriptions alike will call for greater productivity, competitiveness, and entrepreneurship, but they will be indistinguishable from Republican slogans and policies calling for the same things. Democrats will also speak of the importance of compassion and social justice; but without any inherent connection to the first part of their message, these sentiments will tend only to undermine Democrats' credibility as hardheaded guardians of economic growth. The Republican message will be more credible, because its premise will be more coherent: Aim first for economic growth, and social justice will follow.

It is vitally important, therefore, that as liberal Democrats embrace economic growth this time around—as they should, as they must—their slogans and policy prescriptions stand for something fundamentally different from, and far closer to the reality of modern America than, that which conservative Republicans proffer. The fashionable homilies about productivity, competitiveness, entrepreneurship, and the like must be embedded within a public philosophy that gives these goals a context and meaning inherently connected to social justice—not as an afterthought or as a hoped-for eventual consequence, but as intrinsic to their achievement. Genuine prosperity is possible only when the means of achieving it, as well as the fruits of it, are widely shared.

The challenge of improving American productivity, for example, can mean vastly different things, depending upon the ultimate objectives to be served. If the aim is to improve the productivity of American business—helping our corporations produce more products and services per worker—that goal can be readily achieved by encouraging American business to slim down. Policies that help (or make it easier for) corporations to cut their work forces—by, for example, replacing skilled workers with automated machines, laying off long-term employees without incurring high severance and pension costs, and substituting full-time workers with part-timers—all contribute to this renowned objective. If fewer workers can produce the same amount as was being produced before, then—presto!—each remaining worker is more productive.

Conservative Republicans have tended to understand the challenge of improving productivity in precisely this way. Using the butcher metaphors of modern management, they speak glibly of "trimming the fat" from our work places and becoming "lean and mean." But they conveniently fail to note that this form of productivity improvement also can boost unemployment and reduce personal incomes overall. Farmers are becoming ever-more productive. So are our automobile workers. Yet, unless there is something more productive for ex-farmers and ex-automobile workers to do, they will not necessarily share in the new-found prosperity. Between 1981 and 1986, productivity gains in American manufacturing averaged about four percent a year, but about two million manufacturing jobs were lost in the process. A majority of the workers who lost these jobs found new ones that paid substantially less, and that generated far less real wealth, than the ones they left behind.

Liberal Democrats should support measures to improve American productivity, but the normative vision surrounding and defining such a goal should be quite different from the prevailing Republican view. The ultimate aim should be to enhance the productivity of every employable person in the nation—rather than the output of American corporations per employed worker—and thus increase prosperity across the board. This goal demands a fundamentally different set of policies, designed to continuously upgrade the skills of American workers and to aid them in shifting to ever-more productive jobs. The emphasis should be on education, training and retraining, child care, and public transportation that enables employable workers to get to productive jobs, and on the use of automation to give workers more discretion and responsibility rather than to substitute for skills. These policies should be viewed not solely as means toward social justice and equal opportunity, as Democrats have tended to view them, but as measures to help all of us by enhancing everyone's productivity.

"Competitiveness" is another term that now trips lightly over the tongues of Democratic and Republican politicians alike. But here again, there are two quite different meanings, depending upon the larger normative vision within which the term is employed. If the ultimate objective is to improve the nation's trade balance and the profitability of American corporations, America can become more competitive by getting foreigners to buy more from us, while we buy less from them. And the easiest way to achieve this goal is to cut or hold back Americans' real wages and to allow (or encourage) the value of the dollar to decline relative to foreign currencies. These measures will improve the trade balance, because they will make our goods relatively cheaper in global markets.

But this formula also has a discomfitting side effect. It will reduce the standard of living of most Americans. A competitive strategy dependent on reductions in real wages—through, for example, give-backs and other concessions of unionized workers; two-tier wage contracts, which give new workers lower pay; reductions in the minimum wage; and subcontracts to nonunionized workers—will be successful ultimately when the take-home pay of American workers drops to that of workers in Brazil or South Korea. Allowing or encouraging the value of the dollar to drop will have much the same effect, because everything we purchase from abroad will then become that much more expensive. By the time a Japanese car sells here for $30,000, we will surely be more competitive, but most Americans also will be much poorer.

Conservative Republicans have tended to understand the challenge of becoming more competitive in this way, and have cheered as wages have stagnated and the value of the dollar has dropped. They speak of the wondrous means by which free markets in goods and currency, left to their own devices, inevitably discover what each nation can do best. They blissfully ignore the dramatic successes of Japan, South Korea, and other Pacific-rim nations over the past decades in shifting their economies toward higher valued products, and they turn a blind eye to the overwhelming dominance of sovereign governments in managing global trade. Liberal Democrats must eschew this free-market blather, but must also avoid sounding as if the only alternative is to protect American jobs from foreign competition— which will make everything we purchase from abroad even more expensive.

The Democratic goal of competitiveness must be to improve the nation's trade balance while enhancing overall living standards. This objective can be achieved only by increasing the skills of every employable person in America, while shifting the nation's industrial base so as to make use of the higher skills. We will need to move out of mass production, large-batch production, and primary commodities, all of which less-developed nations with lower-skilled work forces are coming to dominate. We should move toward more customized, flexible, and technologically sophisticated production, which depend to a greater extent on knowledge services, like engineering and marketing. Such a transition is already occurring—as exemplified by everything from steel mini-mills to customized semiconductor chips—but the pace is too slow to maintain our standard of living free from debt to the rest of the world. In addition to continuous education and training, a more speedy transition depends on policies designed to quickly transform basic research and inventions (like superconductors) into new products and production techniques.

Finally, we hear politicians of all stripes rhapsodizing

these days about the wonders of entrepreneurship. But if
they are alluding to the sort of maverick inventors, financiers, and tough-guy chief executive officers (CEOs) whose
autobiographies now grace the shelves of bookstores, they
are trading perilously close to the conservative Republican
vision. There is no secret to stimulating entrepreneurs like
these. Just pay them princely sums, reduce their taxes, and
move regulations out of the way.

The Democratic vision of entrepreneurship must be fundamentally different, and more closely tied to the ways in
which groups of people are motivated to do their best. In an
advanced economy as complex as ours, innovation and
growth have come to depend less on lone geniuses and char-
ismatic CEOs than on creative teams with common commitments. The evidence is all around us—in small, highly
successful companies that have shared both the responsibilities and the benefits of success among all their employees;
in cities and regions that have turned around their economies through partnerships among firms, unions, universities, and grass-root citizen organizations; and in previously
moribund American factories that have been revived by the
Japanese, like the General Motors assembly plant in Fre-
mont, California.

To foster a more collective vision of entrepreneurship,
workers need to have more of a stake in corporate America.
Big differences in remuneration and responsibility between
those at the top and those at the bottom of companies reduce
team spirit and divide enterprise into "us" and "them."
The emphasis should be on policies designed to enhance
worker participation and spread the benefits of productivity
improvements: tax incentives for profit sharing and gain
sharing, employee stock ownership, and worker buy-outs.

Productivity, competitiveness, entrepreneurship. Every
American politician who aspires to higher political office—
which includes almost all of them, Democrats and Republicans, liberals and conservatives, neos and paleos—now
speaks with conviction about the need to spur these marvelous things; every candidate comes equipped with a list of
policies ostensibly calculated to do so. But the slogans and
policies can imply radically distinct visions of where America should be headed. The conservative Republican vision

emphasizes the importance of reducing overall labor costs and of stimulating a relatively few individuals to great feats of entrepreneurial daring. This is a public philosophy that promises immediate prosperity for a few, and asks us to trust that others will share in the prosperity eventually.

The liberal Democratic vision must be sharply distinct. When liberal Democrats speak of the importance of achieving economic growth, they should not subordinate social justice as a value to be traded off against growth or to be added on when growth is achieved. In the Democratic vision, a more egalitarian society should be understood as a means of achieving prosperity and as intrinsic to it. Rather than aim to reduce labor costs, Democrats should focus on the importance of increasing labor's value. Slogans and policies should be linked to this core purpose, so that their meaning is amplified and their intent is clear.

Such a public philosophy implies three related precepts: First, with adequate education, training, and logistical support, far greater numbers of Americans can be rendered more productive members of society. As a larger number of us become more productive, every one of us gains. Second, the evolution of our system of production is a public as well as a private responsibility. Corporations can compete either by reducing labor costs or by investing in new skills and higher valued production; the nation as a whole has a strong interest in encouraging the latter. The third and related precept is that a more egalitarian workplace can generate greater wealth for all. Large disparities in power and remuneration undermine collaboration and teamwork, and thus inhibit productivity. Efforts to reduce such disparities and to democratize the workplace can yield significant economic benefits.

Therefore, in reestablishing the connection between prosperity and social justice, Democrats can offer a new vision of where America should be heading. They can talk credibly of a nation whose new prosperity will be widely shared, precisely because the means of achieving it will be widely shared.

CHAPTER 14

Growth, Productivity, and the Federal Budget: Advice for a Presidential Candidate

Alice M. Rivlin
The Brookings Institution

IT IS TIME FOR a presidential candidate to try a novel approach to political rhetoric on the economy: straightforward common sense aimed at grown-ups. This daring maneuver might even generate applause, votes, and a workable economic program for the next administration.

First, the candidate should resolve, despite all temptations to the contrary, to avoid the more egregious sins of past political rhetoric on economics. Here are four rules:

1. *Avoid exaggeration.* The U.S. economy is not in desperate shape, in danger of imminent collapse, or about to be relegated to Third World status, but it is not without flaws either. We have great strengths to build on—natural resources; an educated, adaptable, and mobile labor force; a free market system that mostly works; a strong entrepreneurial tradition—but these do not justify our lapsing into euphoria. We have urgent problems to be solved—the budget deficit, the trade deficit, lagging productivity growth, and an increasingly isolated under-

class—but there is no need to act as if the sky were falling or the problems were unmanageable.

2. *Avoid villains.* The Japanese did not cause our trade deficit. Jimmy Carter did not cause the oil shocks that did so much to generate inflation. Ronald Reagan is not uniquely to blame for the budget deficit, but neither is the Congress. Blaming foreigners or the past is appropriate only to a candidate who does not have a clue how to set things right.

3. *Avoid magic potions and quick fixes.* The American public is not naive enough to think some hitherto untried gimmick is suddenly going to revolutionize the whole economy. The exaggerated claims that discredited supply-side economics ignored the commonsense observation that government policy has, at most, a marginal influence on how individuals and companies go about their business. Changes in tax rates, for example, can have a small influence on how much people work, save, or invest, but are not likely to dominate all the other factors that influence these decisions.

4. *Avoid economists who think they know all the answers.* There is a great deal about the economy that economists have to admit is simply mysterious. It is hard to explain the recent persistence of the trade deficit in the face of the falling dollar. No one knows exactly why productivity growth slowed so drastically in the seventies in all the developed countries or exactly what to do about it. No one knows what policies would raise private savings in the United States. All in all, a bit of humility is appropriate.

Being a presidential candidate is a teaching role. The candidate has a chance to get across a few basic ideas and to explain why they are important, how they relate to each other, and what policies might help move the nation in the right direction. I would urge the candidate to focus on three main economic lessons: (1) why productivity growth matters; (2) why it is generally good to live within one's means; and (3) why the United States should be a leader in world growth and development.

WHY PRODUCTIVITY GROWTH MATTERS

Productivity growth just means getting more output—more bushels of wheat or tons of steel or medical services—from the same inputs of raw materials, hours worked, and capital investment. Productivity growth matters, quite simply, because it determines how much our standard of living will rise in the future, and how much will be available for satisfying private desires for a better life, improving public services, and investing in future growth at home and overseas. Productivity grows when technology is advancing, savings are being invested in improved methods and processes, people are working more energetically or effectively.

Whose productivity matters? Everybody's. There was a time when most Americans were farmers and the general standard of living depended heavily on agricultural productivity. But farm efficiency rose so much that plenty of food could be produced by very few people. More recently, the same thing has been happening in manufacturing, where productivity increases have made it possible over the years to produce more cars, toys, and breakfast cereal with a declining portion of the work force.

Agricultural and manufacturing productivity still matter, especially in international trade, because we can compete with lower-wage countries in world markets only if our productivity is higher than theirs. Nevertheless, what will do most to increase our future standard of living is rising productivity in the areas of the economy outside agriculture and manufacturing, the areas that most Americans now work in. If we all want to live better, we have to figure out how to increase the productivity of teachers and nurses, bank tellers and waitresses, computer programmers and electricians, as well as farmers and automobile workers.

WHY WE SHOULD LIVE WITHIN OUR MEANS

The huge federal budget deficit has been a conspicuous feature of the 1980s. We have a government that has been living beyond its means: spending substantially more than it has been taking in, and borrowing the difference.

Big federal deficits mean that the national debt is rising rapidly and, with it, the burden of interest that has to be paid out of government revenues before they are available for defense and domestic programs. Even more serious, big deficits mean that the government is borrowing a large portion of the nation's savings; hence, less is available to finance productive investment.

The United States must have substantial investment if we are going to modernize factories, offices, and other facilities to ensure the productivity growth we need for the future. That investment can come from only three places: the private savings of individuals and companies, savings of the government, and savings of foreigners. Our government has not been saving, but borrowing. Investment would have collapsed if foreigners had not been willing to invest in, and lend to, the U.S. economy from their savings. The government deficits made the United States economy dependent on foreigners. Not only is the government living beyond its means, the nation collectively is living beyond its means and building up future obligations to the rest of the world.

It is vital to get the budget deficit down—desirable even to run a surplus—so we will have plenty of domestic savings to invest in increasing the productivity of our own economy. Then we will not be in the precariously dependent position of having to gear our own policies to ensuring a continued flow of funds from abroad, nor will we be passing on to our children such heavy obligations to pay interest, dividends, and profits to foreigners.

WHY THE UNITED STATES SHOULD BE A LEADER IN A GROWING WORLD ECONOMY

Politicians sometimes talk as though the world economy were engaged in a win-or-lose game in which it was crucial for the United States to beat the other players, especially the Japanese. But in this increasingly interdependent world, each depends on the economic health of others. European countries, Japan, and the United States will each be better off if all are growing. Moreover, the advanced countries need to ensure that Third World countries are developing and are able to export, to pay their debts, and to buy goods and services from us.

The United States cannot hope to recapture the position of world economic domination into which the accidents of history thrust us at the end of World War II. But we can and should be the leader of the group of advanced countries working for reduced trade barriers and orderly development of Third World economies.

SPECIFIC POLICIES

There is no sure prescription for attaining any of these goals. But, fortunately, a whole list of policies would contribute at least a small amount to several goals at once. The most obvious first step is to get the federal budget deficit down; indeed, it is a scandal that we have waited this long. Almost any combination of spending cuts and tax increases will do for this purpose. Of course, it would be best to cut "wasteful" spending—for example, eliminating costly military programs that may be making a negative contribution to national security (the Strategic Defense Initiative comes to mind) and phasing out uneconomic domestic activities (selling national forest timber below cost, for instance). It would also be best to raise revenue from taxes that discourage consumption rather than ones that discourage saving. It would be particularly good to discourage consumption of cigarettes and alcohol, for health reasons, and gasoline, for conservation reasons.

But we should not be too picky. We should just find some politically feasible combination of tax and spending measures that will get the deficit behind us. Moreover, discussion of the deficit is a good place to invoke the "no exaggeration" rule. Approximately $50 billion each of spending reduction and tax cut (for a total of two percent of the gross national product) would cut the deficit to manageable proportions and drastically reduce our dependence on the rest of the world for capital. Surely we can find that without excessive strain.

Besides reducing the budget deficit, what should we do to enhance productivity and growth? Everything we can think of: measures that encourage research development and innovation, improve the scope and quality of education, increase the flexibility and adaptability of people and institutions. In part, this means resisting and dismantling policies that protect and perpetuate inefficiency—many agricultural subsidies, make-work union rules, overencrusted building codes, and, above all, protection from international competition that retards, rather than encourages change in domestic industry.

Since some of these moves will hurt specific groups and industries, measures to ease transitions and reduce the pain of change are called for, but these should meet the twin tests of temporariness and effectiveness in moving people and resources toward productive activities, not away from them. Moreover, the United States should get something from the rest of the world in return for its willingness to face up to reducing the budget deficit and cutting subsidies. We should use the strong bargaining position that we have by virtue of our huge market for the world's goods, our position at the world's financial hub, as well as our role as major contributor to the common defense of Western Europe and much of Asia. If we use that power skillfully, we can get the barriers to growth and trade coming down in other countries as well as our own, and avoid the risk of an escalating trade war in which all would be losers.

None of this sounds like wine and roses, but there is just a chance that voters are tired of being talked down to and offered magic bullets, or sops to their own selfish short-run interests. A candidate who is brave enough to take a broader view; to explain why productivity, fiscal responsibility, and world growth are important; and what sacrifices need to be made to get them might just find the voters listening with new interest. It's worth trying.

CHAPTER 15

Toward a Pragmatic Federalism

Thomas J. Downey

FEDERALISM, THE UNIQUE AMERICAN experiment launched by a group of young, pragmatic thinkers and politicians at the end of the eighteenth century, celebrated its two hundred birthday last year. As our nation has grown and matured through 20 decades of internal and external threats, the central paradox of our system of government has endured. As Woodrow Wilson said in 1908, "the question of the relation of states to the federal government is the cardinal question of our constitutional system . . . [and] every successive stage of our political and economic development gives it a new aspect, makes it a new question."

From my perspective of 14 years in the U.S. House of Representatives, debates about federalism sometimes ring hollow in the Capitol's chambers. Whether the states or the federal government should have the flexibility to determine the speed limits on our highways ultimately gets answered by another question: What is my best for my constituents?

However, operating behind individual votes on such matters as the Clean Water Act, the Federal Highway Aid program, or the reauthorization of the Community Development Block Grant program is the same theoretical question that has been asked since the demise of the Articles of Confederation: What level of government is empowered and best equipped to promote the general welfare? Despite our parochial interests and the pressures of a given moment, we are back to Wilson's "cardinal question."

Scholar Morton Grodzins has used two metaphors to describe our "neither wholly national nor wholly federal" system of government. One sees our system as a layer cake with two distinct levels acting independently of one another. The other envisions the system as a marble cake, in which the line between the layers is blurred, and a slice reveals an "inseparable mixture of different-colored ingredients."

With some notable exceptions, the historical, political, and legal precedents of the pre–New Deal era brought the layer cake structure of federal and state relations to life. It was generally acknowledged, in both theory and practice, that individual states had the constitutional right and obligation to carry out those tasks that the Tenth Amendment reserved to them. As recently as 1976, the Supreme Court recognized, in the case of *National League of Cities v. Usery*, that a delineation can be made between "traditional governmental functions" at the state and federal levels.

However, it is clear that throughout our history, there has been movement toward a greater federal role at the expense of the role of the states.

In the 1970s, great hay was made during the political and constitutional debate over the payment of Revolutionary War debts. The issue was settled by a political deal in which the *quid pro quo* was the establishment of the nation's capital south of the Mason-Dixon line.

Questions about the federal government's authority to levy taxes, such as tariffs, whiskey excise taxes, taxes on states, and a national income tax, have ultimately been settled in favor of the federal government. The forums have been court decisions, congressional action, and the ballot box.

Other federal-state issues that have been resolved in favor of the federal government include the power to improve infrastructure, to preserve the union, to regulate interstate commerce, to dictate desegregation and equal rights for non-whites and women, to set minimum wage and maximum hour standards, and to establish educational systems for handicapped children with the promise that they constitute the "least restrictive environment."

In fact, in overturning its earlier states' rights decision of *National League*, the Supreme Court said in *Garcia v. San Antonio MTA* that there are no intrinsic and immutable divisions of power and responsibility in American federalism. In his opinion in that case, Justice Harry Blackmun wrote that Wilson's cardinal question is one that is best answered by the "political process."

Let others decide if the federal cake is marbled or layered; the taste in the mouths of most Americans is the icing of federal dominance.

Today's conception of federalism is based on large intergovernmental programs. Under this system, the federal government writes the rules and provides much of the cash for service programs that are implemented and partially funded by the states and local governments. These programs range from Head Start to the Clean Water Act to the Federal Highway Aid program.

The winners under this system have been the poor, who benefit from the social welfare programs created out of the desperation of the 1930s and social activism of the 1960s. The oppressed, to whom the American dream was an American nightmare of discrimination, segregation, and deprivation, have also benefited. Cities and local governments, too long ignored in state capitals, can now bend ears on Capitol Hill. Liberal ideology—which holds that bigness, aggressiveness, and centralization are government virtues—has triumphed.

The losers have been conservatives, who fear the welfare state, big government "intrusion," and neglected individual initiative. States, bridling under the weight of federal mandates and regulations, have witnessed the neutering of the amendment that keyed their acceptance of the original Constitution.

With the best of intentions, have we created a monster? Public support for safety-net programs to protect our children, poor, elderly, and disadvantaged remains high. Providing other services, including national defense, maintenance of our highways, protection of our environment, community development, and education also remains a high priority. Moreover, the government has a moral and legal obligation as defined by the Constitution, the Congress, and the courts to maintain the civil rights protections won over the past 30 or 50 years.

But public support also drove the 1981 tax bill, the largest single federal tax cut in our nation's history. The result is a $150 billion federal deficit and little political will to increase federal taxes.

Thus, the massive intergovernmental programs that characterize federalism as we know it today have been on the budget cutter's chopping block for several years. Since 1978, these programs have been cut by nearly $30 billion. Having once made up 16.5 percent of the federal pie, they make up barely 10 percent today. This inexorable erosion will, because of fiscal pressures, continue.

Yet, there are many people who think that if a Democratic president is elected, if the budget climate changes, if, if, if. . . . It is time to face some facts. We will live with these budget deficits and the fiscal constraints we currently face for as far as the eye can see. And while I do not have 20/20 vision anymore, I can still see pretty well.

Our federal system is broken. How do we fix it?

We must return to the age-old question. What level of government can do which tasks most effectively? Throughout various eras of federal laissez-faire, state and local governments have filled the void left by federal inaction. For instance, the Progressive Era was marked by enlightened policy conducted largely by states. The last seven years are no exception. The Reagan Revolution has led to a counterrevolt at the state level. As columnist David Broder, one of the more prescient observers of the Reagan years, has written, "the initiative on education, social, and most economic and environmental issues now rests in state capitals rather than in the U.S. Capitol and the White House."

So there is reason for hope. Federalism has been successful because it is flexible and adapts to changing political, economic, and social circumstances, as Broder comments. The trick is to involve the federal government where it is uniquely equipped to perform well, and to involve states and localities where they can best meet the need. Federalism today must be dictated not so much by history or ideology or constitutional imperatives, but by pragmatism.

Pragmatism should not be confused with expediency. Pragmatism, in my vision of federalism, can equal good public policy.

Let us try to answer Wilson's cardinal question. When should the federal government play the dominant role in a particular policy or program?

Primarily, the federal government should take priority when nationwide standards and uniformity are demonstrably necessary, as is the case with civil rights law. When diversity of policy finance and administration is important, or experimentation is desirable, states and localities should take the lead.

I put these important principles into legislation that I introduced last year with the state of Washington's senior senator, Daniel Evans. Our bill treats poverty as a "great and aggregate" issue that is in need of national solutions. It would expand the federal contribution to two basic income support programs, welfare and Medicaid, to 90 percent of the tab. These programs are currently financed on a patchwork basis in which individual states share varying degrees of the financial burden with the federal government. The bill would also greatly expand the eligibility for welfare among those who are demonstrably unable to work, and would provide health care to every poor child under the age of 16.

The legislation would establish a welfare-to-work program, leave wide state discretion in administration of these programs, and provide fiscal capacity grants to those localities and states that are most in need.

Furthermore, the bill calls for a termination of the federal role in most community development, infrastructure, and social service programs, since these can be best financed and managed at the local level. They are what Madison called "local and particular" concerns.

Our bill is, and will remain, revenue-neutral within the federal budget context. However, the social contract is not revenue neutral. As we shift the federal domestic budget more toward income maintenance, we will also shift this nation's priorities. That will be a welcome change. Revenue-neutrality is necessary at this time in order to get the type of hearing this proposal deserves. Revenue-neutrality is simply a means to reform the crazy quilt of intergovernmental programs that make up our current concept of federalism.

This particular elixir for our federal system may not on its face be embraced by the Congress as the cure we want to take for our fiscal woes. But its basic framework of trading safety-net programs for social and domestic service programs is representative of an approach that is gaining popularity. In fact, this legislation was the product of a report prepared by a bipartisan group of public officials, corporate executives, and academics. The authors included Democrats and Republicans, conservatives, moderates, and liberals. The recognition is out there that something can, must, and will be done.

Will this reform be done in a sensible, coherent form, or will it be a halfhearted reaction to fiscal constraints? I, for one, hope it is the former.

PART THREE

America's Agenda
for the 1990s

If we get sufficiently interlaced economically, we will most probably not bomb each other off the face of the planet. For example, I suggest that we are so economically intertwined with Japan that if we have any problems with Japan today, we are going to work them out. I think the same will be true globally. We should welcome increased trade with the Soviet Union, all the developed nations, and the Third World, as world trade moves us closer to world peace.

—John Naisbitt, *Megatrends*

CHAPTER 16

A Time of Decision

By U.S. Rep. William H. Gray III

WHEN AMERICANS GO TO the poles later this year, they will do far more than select among candidates for president, Congress, and state and local offices. They also will engage in a referendum on issues that are likely to dominate public policy through the end of this century and into the next.

The transcendent question then, is not only who will hold political office, but what is their vision of America's future and the problems that must be solved along the way?

Perhaps not since 1932 will the outcome of an election do more to influence the overall course of United States policy. This is one of the legacies of Ronald Reagan. For over seven years, his personality has dominated the shape of our politics. But his popularity has had little to do with his policies, which have been inconsistent and incoherent, and increasingly have been rejected by the American people and their elected representatives from both parties. As we exit the Reagan era, the President's failures are forcing us to focus more closely on our difficult domestic and foreign policy issues. And what we find is that he has limited our options for responding to them.

Barring any severe international conflict prior to Election Day, the major concern for voters will be the nation's economy. On this front, the news of the last few years generally has been good. Americans have enjoyed low inflation, reduced unemployment, lower real interest rates. But while the Reagan administration boasts about the success of its economic policies, other signs—persistent budget deficits, record trade deficits, low rates of capital investment, etc.— are not so positive. Opinion polls show that the public is uneasy about the future course of the economy—and rightfully so.

As Chairman of the House Budget Committee for the past three years, I have had a close view of our mounting economic problems, and their effects on our citizens. What I have seen is a series of developments that is undermining the American dream — our shared hope for continued prosperity, social equality, and economic opportunity.

The secret of America's success over the past 200 years has been the promise of justice. As James Madison noted in The Federalist Papers, "Justice is the end of government. It is the end of civil society. It ever has been, and ever will be pursued, until it be obtained, or until liberty has been lost in the pursuit." Even when justice—social or economic—has been absent, we have rested our hopes on its continued pursuit.

But our ability to attain social justice depends on our resources as well as our commitment. President John F. Kennedy observed that "a rising tide lifts all boats." When the nation's economy is fundamentally healthy—as was the case through much of the 1960s and part of the 1970s—we rarely question its ability to accommodate the needs of most members of our society. However, when growth is sluggish, as it has been much of the past seven years, even the modest aspirations of some can be met only at the expense of others.

That is why the focus of the coming election, and the core of our country's agenda, must be our economy and the need to insure its long-term health.

THE BUDGET DEFICIT AND ECONOMIC GROWTH

In recent years the American economy has been buffeted by unprecedented federal budget deficits. The facts speak for themselves: from $78.9 billion in fiscal year 1981, the federal deficit rose to a record $220.7 billion in 1986. From 2.6 percent of the nation's gross national product, the deficit more than doubled to 5.3 percent of GNP. Although congressional efforts brought the deficit down considerably in 1987, it remains uncomfortably high compared to earlier years.

What has driven the deficit to such heights? Simply put, spending on the government's activities has increased significantly, primarily due to the defense buildup, while government income has not kept pace. The resulting difference between outlays and revenues—the budget deficit—has been financed by borrowing. That borrowing added more than $1 trillion to the national debt between 1981 and 1987. As with any household or business, the government must pay interest on its borrowing; consequently, expenditures on net interest have skyrocketed. Indeed, they have been the fastest growing component of federal spending; the increase in interest payments alone is equivalent to 1.0 percent of GNP.

Aside from interest, spending increases have been driven up largely by outlays on defense. Between 1981 and 1987, these outlays as a share of GNP rose 1.3 percentage points. At the same time, domestic spending on all other government activities (except interest) fell by 1.2 percent of GNP.

The federal government's revenues base has been eroded significantly, primarily as a result of the multi-year tax cut enacted in 1981. Revenues as a percent of GNP fell from 20.1 percent in 1981 to 19.1 percent in 1987, despite tax increases in 1982 and 1984. They remain lower in relation to GNP than the Reagan administration projected for its economic program in 1981. Moreover, while total revenues have been falling as a percent of GNP, taxes earmarked for special programs like Social Security and Medicare have risen. Taxes available for general government activities such as defense, public investments, and interest thus have fallen more sharply, from 13.9 percent of GNP in 1981 to 11.7 percent in 1987.

This gross misalignment between government spending and revenues has had severe consequences for the economy. The most prominent problem developed in the trade sector, where industries exposed to international competition, primarily manufacturing and agriculture, suffered a sharp erosion in competitiveness. The result was massive job losses and rising bankruptcies.

The budget deficit is linked to the trade deficit through its impact on interest rates and capital flows. Massive federal credit demands during the 1980s put upward pressure on interest rates in this country relative to those abroad. Those more attractive rates of return stimulated demand for U.S. assets, sharply increasing the demand for dollars and their value. Between 1981 and its peak in 1985, the dollar appreciated more than 50 percent against the currencies of our major competitors. This priced many American goods out of markets at home and abroad. As imports grew and exports declined, the trade deficit reached a peak of $175.9 billion—over 4 percent of GNP—in 1986, and exerted a noticeable drag on U.S. economic growth.

More than 2 million jobs have been lost in this country as a result of the trade deficit. And even though the dollar's value has dropped sharply in the last two years, the trade deficit has receded only slowly because trade flows adjust very gradually to changes in currency values, and lost markets and customers are difficult to regain.

The budget deficit has had other consequences that will continue to affect our economic prospects in the years ahead. Chief among these is the sharp run-up in our debt to foreigners. In 1982 the U.S. was the world's largest creditor nation, an enviable position built up since the end of World War I. By the end of 1985, that position had reversed, and the U.S. had become the world's largest debtor, with a negative foreign debt quadrupled to around $400 billion. So far we have been enjoying the benefits of this borrowing: we have consumed and invested more than we could produce; inflows of capital have kept domestic interest rates lower than they otherwise would have been; foreign capital has kept us fed and financed the budget deficit.

However, being hooked on foreign capital over which we have little control has its costs. Already we are experiencing some of these, as our financial markets become much more volatile. As we saw last spring, if foreigners feel less enthusiastic about holding dollars, interest rates must rise to maintain the necessary private capital inflows to finance the deficit. That slows economic growth and runs the risk of pushing the economy into a recession. We wind up in a vicious circle, because as growth slows, the budget deficit climbs higher, increasing our need for foreign capital, not reducing it. This is a very precarious situation.

The huge debt also threatens the nation's continued prosperity. Growing interest payments to foreign creditors drain dollars out of the economy that otherwise would be available for investment and consumer purchases. In the long term, this transfer of income will reduce the living standards of most Americans.

The budget deficit also has had adverse consequences abroad. Our high interest rates have increased substantially the burden of debt service for less developed countries, leading the large debtors to cut imports sharply. This not only has lowered their living standards, but has adversely affected U.S. exports, worsening our trade deficit. Similarly, high U.S. interest rates led European nations and Japan to hold their rates at higher levels than they would have otherwise; this combined with generally restrictive fiscal policies to keep their growth modest, further dampening demand for U.S. exports.

These problems in the international economy cannot be solved without a change in the policy mix at home and abroad. For our part, deficit reduction is a necessary condition to restore the basis for global economic growth, and it is for this reason it has dominated the economic policy discussions for the past three years.

BUDGETING IN AN ERA OF HIGH DEFICITS

Without question, we need to make further cuts in the federal deficit. Even those of the supply-side school of economics who argued that we could "grow out of the problem" have been quiet in recent years. The reason is that economic growth itself has been dragged down by excess government borrowing. Since 1984 the economy has grown at a disappointing 2.5 percent annual rate—well below the post-war average of 3.4 percent. A weak economy generates weak revenues and higher outlays, enlarging the deficit. Consequently, even though we have slowed the growth of spending significantly, the faltering economy has prevented substantial progress on deficit reduction.

The question before us, then, is not *whether* to cut the deficit, but *how*. No easy choices present themselves. Against a background of budget austerity, all national needs cannot be served at once; priorities must be established. In recent years, however, the administration's priorities and those of the Congress have differed sharply. A strong defense is necessary for the nation's security, but many of us in Congress, from both sides of the aisle, believe that the administration's rapid buildup of the Pentagon's budget has been excessive and wasteful. Similarly, many members of Congress believe that domestic programs that promote opportunity, health, and social justice are equally vital to our country's future and have blocked the administration's attempts to cut them deeply.

Moreover, many members believe that to pay for government programs, we should be using the mechanism established for that purpose: our tax system. The alternate is continued borrowing, which shifts the economic burden of current spending to future generations. Nevertheless, despite public concern about the size of the deficit, and in the face of overwhelming evidence that the electorate does not support *specific* spending cuts of the size required to solve the problem, President Reagan has persisted in his anti-tax rhetoric. He pays lip service to the idea of a balanced budget by calling for constitutional and legislative changes that have little support in Congress or among the public. But in practice he refused to confront the real need for deficit reduction, instead pursuing his ideological program and thereby putting the Nation's economic future at risk.

Because of the President's recalcitrance, it has become increasingly difficult to find the middle ground between the administration and Congress, and within Congress. With the obvious fat in the budget already eliminated, and the debate over budget priorities at an impasse, Congress has turned to "external" mechanisms to cut the budget deficit.

By mandating fixed deficit targets with automatic budget cuts if they are not reached, the Balanced Budget and Emergency Deficit Control Act of 1985 (Gramm-Rudman Hollings) focused Congress's energies on deficit reduction. And in the past two years we have succeeded in bringing the deficit down sharply from its peak in fiscal 1986. However, although targets may be fixed, the economy is not. Under Ronald Reagan, actual economic growth almost always has fallen short of administration projections at the start of the budget year, making it impossible to reach the fixed targets without irresponsible fiscal restraint and program reductions.

If the past few years are any guide, we probably will continue to tinker with the budget process and the deficit reduction targets and mechanisms. But our political task remains essentially the same: to progressively reduce the "structural" deficit each year, not by so much that the economy is thrown into recession, but enough to slow the huge buildup of debt that is draining our economic strength.

THE ROAD FROM HERE

The budget deficits of recent years have ushered in a new preoccupation, one in which the accounting principles of deficit reduction take on a life of their own, separate and distinct from the needs of the nation's economy and its citizens. This is a short-sighted preoccupation. Cutting the deficit is not an end in itself; it is only the means to getting our economy into better balance to achieve increased prosperity and social justice. I believe, therefore, that while we must keep the fiscal brakes on, we must do so in such a way that initiatives on growth, job creation, and investments in our country's future are not hopelessly sidetracked.

Much has been written in recent years about the need to rebuild America's competitiveness. While many of our losses in the international arena can be attributed to large budget deficits, I believe a number of steps in addition to deficit reduction are urgently needed if we are to regain our position in the next decade and beyond.

We must modernize the means of production through greater investments in research and development and new plants and equipment. We must rebuild our infrastructure. And we must make the rules of the marketplace more fair and less cumbersome. All these are necessary if we want to move our economy forward.

However, it seems to me that what has been the most neglected in discussions of competitiveness is our investment in people. Without educated and skilled citizens, we cannot compete in high tech or even low tech.

Our level of literacy is an international disgrace. Graduates of many of our high schools have reading and computing skills far below those of their foreign counterparts. The problems begin long before graduation, with inadequate attention to early childhood development, underinvestment in the teachers and schools charged with imparting the basics to our children. The skyrocketing cost of higher education and graduate school, together with budget-related cutbacks in student aid, leaves vast pools of the nation's future work force underdeveloped.

For example, since 1980 black college enrollment has been declining steadily. This trend has coincided with changes in federal policy that reduced the amount of aid available to needy students. This is shortsighted policy that saddles young people with so much debt that they opt for quick returns in high-paying careers rather than those, like teaching, that may have more long-term social and economic benefits.

It is in the long-term interest of our society for its best minds to percolate to the top. A careful nurturing of the nation's "brain power" from Head Start to graduate schools is as important as investments in weapons—maybe more so. A comprehensive plan to get America moving again must include revitalizing our education system, in a broad sense. The cost of education in the long run is far less than paying for unemployment and welfare.

Our welfare system is another area where we are not utilizing our people in an effective way. The present system is full of perverse incentives that discourage people from working because, in doing so, they would lose access to food, housing, and health care programs that are more valuable to them than the income from many of the jobs available to them. This poverty trap nurtures an underclass in our society.

After ten years of inattention, welfare reform is gradually moving back onto the policy stage. Experts increasingly emphasize the advantage of providing benefits through an employment relationship, stressing the obligations of recipients as well as the government. A good example of new directions is provided by the Massachusetts AFDC ET program, where state officials have committed themselves to aggressive job placement efforts for welfare recipients and to the necessary basic education and training, child care, and medical benefits. Other states are in the process of developing their own experiments. They should be encouraged to try new approaches that would convert their welfare systems into job programs. The federal government should encourage these initiatives by providing suitable resources and incentives.

The essential point is this: as a nation we are faced with tight budget constraints. Events of the past six years have reduced our long-term economic security and shown us the folly of trying to borrow our way into sustained prosperity. Reducing this enormous deficit is necessary if we want a vigorous, healthy economy.

However, some types of deficit reduction are better than others. I suggest we evaluate government spending programs in terms of their importance to the future of our nation, and that we give our basic resources—our citizens, and their education, training, and employment—the highest priority.

CHAPTER 17

The Borrow-and-Spend Economy: Just Say No

Senator Ernest F. Hollings

RONALD REAGAN'S CAMPAIGN THEME in 1984 was "It's morning in America." The hard reality for candidates in 1988—Democrat and Republican alike—is "It's the morning after." In the wake of seven years of borrow-and-spend fiscal policy and promiscuous "free trade," the man who said we should "stand tall" has brought America to its knees. The task before the next president is to clear away the Reagan wreckage and get our nation back on a firm footing.

The battle to restore America's economic and financial integrity will be fought on two fronts: fiscal reform and international trade. On the fiscal front, we must enact a package of spending cuts and revenue increases that will produce a balanced budget by the early 1990s. On the trade front, we must keep the door open to free trade and, at the same time, serve notice that America will no longer be the doormat for nations that export illegally while shutting us out of their home markets.

STICK WITH THE GRAMM-RUDMAN-HOLLINGS DISCIPLINE

Concerning the federal budget, the bottom-line realities are these: Among reasonable people, there is a solid consensus

198

that defense spending must at least keep pace with inflation. Ditto for Social Security and basic programs to aid needy citizens. Accordingly, if we largely agree that we need a trillion-dollar government, then we are going to have to pay for it. And that means not just greater discipline on the spending side, but adjustments on the revenue side.

Regrettably, the consensus for budget discipline is far from unanimous. The hard-core supply-siders seem genuinely to believe that deficits don't matter. Representative Jack Kemp, former Delaware Governor Pierre DuPont, and others skip merrily down the yellow brick road singing hosannas to tax cuts and perpetual economic growth. In the White House, the Wizard of the Free Lunch—the Father of our National Debt, as he will be known to future generations, his legatees—indulges in homilies and shopworn nostrums about the virtues of a balanced-budget amendment. To paraphrase George Bush, these people give "voodoo" a bad name.

The current Republican administration has practiced a kind of Keynesianism in drag, goosing the economy with unprecedented deficit spending. The challenge before the Democratic administration that will follow it is to summon the political courage to reverse this reckless course. We can balance the budget, but not by slashing taxes and begging the Japanese to continue financing our spending binges. If the budget is to be balanced, it will be done the old-fashioned way, by reining in spending and, yes, increasing taxes.

The only workable framework for accomplishing this difficult task is the Balanced Budget Act and Emergency Deficit Control Act of 1985—that is, Gramm-Rudman-Hollings. In 1985, when we passed the original version of Gramm-Rudman-Hollings, Congress and the president confessed that—absent some dire external threat—we were not willing to take the tough measures required to shrink the deficit. In passing Gramm-Rudman-Hollings, we said, in effect: "Save us from ourselves. Stop us before we kill again."

And, lo and behold, Gramm-Rudman-Hollings initially worked. It produced a virtual freeze on federal spending during fiscal year 1987. Consider that from 1965 through

1985, federal spending increased an average of 11 percent per year. But between 1986 and 1987, thanks largely to Gramm-Rudman-Hollings, spending increased only two percent—roughly equaling the rate of inflation.

But this very real progress was placed in jeopardy when the Supreme Court struck down the original Gramm-Rudman-Hollings sequester trigger. True, the government pretended to meet the Gramm-Rudman-Hollings target of $154 billion for fiscal 1987, but the smoke and mirrors fooled no one. The teacher had declared recess. The punch bowl was freshly spiked.

As we drafted the fiscal 1988 budget, it became frighteningly obvious that deficits were back on an upward path. In February of 1987, the Congressional Budget Office (CBO) foresaw a steady decline in future deficits—even without further budget cuts or tax increases—from $176 billion in 1987 to $84 billion in 1992. But by July, revised CBO estimates showed a deficit of $161 billion for 1987, increases to $181 billion in 1988 and $198 billion in 1989, and then a slow decline.

Yet, even in the face of these startling new predictions, the president intensified his campaign against a tax increase, and Congress declined to expand the menu of budget cuts. As in the past, the president and Congress bemoaned the killer deficits, but lacked the will to do anything to reduce them. Accordingly, in the summer of 1987, we restored the sequester trigger and, once again, strapped ourselves to the mast of Gramm-Rudman-Hollings.

The beauty and necessity of the Gramm-Rudman-Hollings sequester threat is that it has created a very powerful incentive for politicians to do their duty. We have seen it before: Faced with the potential debacle of a sequester, Congress and the executive branch can work wonders.

At the same time, though the 1987 reformulation of Gramm-Rudman-Hollings retreated from the original deficit reduction goals, nonetheless has set ambitious new targets, and—in concert with the new sequester trigger—puts us back on track toward a balanced budget in the early 1990s.

TALKING TURKEY ON TAXES

There is not a responsible politician in Washington who doesn't realize that new revenues are the indispensable key to real deficit reduction. Yet, for seven years, we have allowed Ronald Reagan to browbeat us on the issue of taxes. White House minions say that Congress wouldn't dare propose new revenues as part of a deficit reduction package. They boast that the president has "potty-trained" the Democrats on this issue. Meanwhile, the national press ridicules our cowardice, our fear of using the dreaded "T" word in polite company. This has been a sorry spectacle, reflecting the opposite of leadership.

The fact is, responsible Republicans and Democrats are more akin to the Cowardly Lion, who lacked courage, than to the Scarecrow, who lacked a brain. We know in our heads what needs to be done. The only question is: Do we have the heart and honesty to do it?

I know the conventional wisdom: that taxes are a setup and a trap; that the president will demagogue the issue, and the Republicans will use it to bludgeon and besiege the Democrats in 1988.

Maybe. But on this issue, the best politics is no politics. It is the duty of congressional Democrats to pass responsible budgets in 1987 and 1988—with a credible balance of spending cuts and revenue increases—offering real budget reductions and keeping the deficits on a downward path. Then, if the president plays politics by vetoing those budgets, and if the Republican presidential candidates demagogue the issue, so be it. They will be exposed as the budget busters, the big spenders, the ones who sabotaged genuine attempts at deficit reduction.

Let me be specific about the types of taxes I would favor. I expressly oppose any increase in individual income taxes. But, with that one exception, I believe we must be open to all possibilities. In early 1987, on the floor of the Senate, I proposed an alternative budget plan that included the following new taxes:

- An oil import fee of $10 per barrel, producing $60.2 billion in fiscal years 1988 through 1991
- Extension of the telephone tax, providing $8.7 billion in fiscal 1988–1991
- A reduction of business expense deductions from the current 80 percent to 50 percent, producing $9.8 billion in fiscal years 1988 through 1991.
- An increase in the percentage of the contract completion cost method—saving $5.7 billion from fiscal 1988 through fiscal 1991

Of course, with the exception of the oil import fee, these various taxes are not major revenue raisers. Alone, they would hardly dent the deficits. The real engine of my deficit reduction plan was (and remains) a 10 percent value-added tax (VAT) to begin January 1, 1989.

I am thoroughly familiar with the inevitable hue and cry to the effect that a VAT is a regressive tax. My proposal specifically exempts food, health care, and housing from the VAT. These exemptions would largely mitigate the impact of the tax on low-income individuals, as well as those on a fixed income.

I can hear the protest, too, that the VAT would weaken our economy or that it would raise too much money, which would then be squandered on new government programs. My response is simple. Essentially all of our European allies and many Asian nations have VATs. So crippled are their economies that they are currently competing us into the ground. Moreover, I advocate that all VAT revenues be earmarked strictly for reduction of the deficit and, eventually, retirement of the national debt.

My point is that if we truly hope to achieve a balanced budget, we need a tax on the scale of a 10 percent VAT that will bring in sufficient revenues to get the job done. If the VAT has the side effect of reining in Americans' debt-financed consumer spending binge, then all the better.

Our last, best hope is to stick with the Gramm-Rudman-Hollings discipline. This requires truth in budgeting, plus an honest, intelligent mix of spending discipline and tax increases. Mr. Reagan notwithstanding, the objective of

Gramm-Rudman-Hollings is not to dismantle government. The bill simply says: "Decide what government you need, then pay the bills."

FREE TRADE OR FAIR TRADE?

The United States today is at war—an international trade war in which, shamefully, we have not yet begun to fight. As has been the fashion with wars in recent decades, this war remains undeclared. But the reality of the conflict cannot be denied. Nor, in the face of recent years' massive trade deficits, can we deny our surrender, our abject passivity in the face of a determined onslaught from abroad.

Tragically, this trade war is being fought principally on American soil. Its toll is evident in abandoned factories, failing farms, and vast defeated armies of the unemployed. No sector of the U.S. economy has been spared the devastation: not agriculture, not manufacturing, not high tech.

America is in the fourth quarter of its biggest game. And we're not talking touch football here. We're talking about an all-out international competition for jobs, for standard of living, and for national security. Yet, the current administration continues to indulge in the conceit that international commerce is governed by something called free trade—a wonderful, objective, rational system that rewards the efficient and punishes the slothful. The free trade theoreticians lecture us that foreign manufacturers are more efficient and therefore deserve to take over the U.S. market.

Typical was a lead editorial in the New Republic that intoned grandly: "If foreign workers can make a product more cheaply than we can, it is to our benefit to stop making it here, and to buy it from the competition or foreign producer." This is the reductio ad absurdum of the free trade argument. After all, as a practical matter, what product cannot be made more cheaply abroad? Does the New Republic advocate that we simply disband American industry, lock, stock, and barrel?

This is an insult to American industry and the American

worker. According to the Bureau of Labor Statistics, U.S. workers rank first in the world in productivity; Japanese workers rank only eighth. America is hungry to compete. All we lack is a government as eager to compete as our people are.

Is there no limit to the current administration's innocence and naiveté? From the ivory towers of Commerce and State, it preaches a childlike faith in the "invisible hand." Meanwhile, our trading "partners" pursue a policy of the iron fist. Their nations are citadels of tariffs and barriers to trade. They gang together in consortia and cartels and "common markets" to protect their own industries and to plunder America's.

So let us be done with this free trade myth. The reality is that 99 percent of world trade today is government-to-government trade—trade conducted according to ground rules laid down between governments. It is time, at long last, for the United States government to go to bat and play hardball with the rest of them.

The old concepts of terms of trade and comparative advantage grow increasingly irrelevant. We live in a world where products from toasters to computer chips can be produced in South Carolina or South Borneo. So competition is no longer between the cultural and natural resources of different countries; it is between governments.

The nations of Europe and the Pacific Rim learned long ago that government participation is the key factor in successful world trade. Since World War II, these nations have counted on their governments to protect domestic industries, to stimulate research and development, to orchestrate trade strategy. And, not surprisingly, today's trade powerhouses are better known as Japan, Incorporated; Korea & Company; Taiwan Unlimited; and so on. Meanwhile, the United States plays the hapless role of Uncle Sucker—dumping ground and market of first resort for all the world's goods and merchandise.

The choice is not between free trade and protectionism. Every nation practices protectionism. As a matter of national interest, each country draws a line beyond which it will not permit foreign penetration and plunder. This notion may sound like heresy to the Reagan administration, but it is just elementary common sense to the rest of the world.

Indeed, one of the earliest acts of the First U.S. Congress, on July 4, 1789, was enactment of tariff legislation in response to dumping of goods by Great Britain. This was the first substantive legislation of the First Congress. The measure—championed in Congress by James Madison—levied duties ranging as high as 50 percent on some 30 commodities, including steel and tobacco.

George Washington, James Madison, and Alexander Hamilton all agreed that it was a legitimate and necessary responsibility of the new government to invigorate and protect American commerce and America's growing manufacturing ability. When Washington took the oath as our first president, he dressed in a suit of Connecticut-manufactured broadcloth, and he expressed the hope that before long it would "be unfashionable" for gentlemen to appear in any other dress. President Washington made a point of serving only American-made beer and cheese in the presidential house.

My own trade reform agenda focuses principally on putting teeth in the laws already on the books, while also toughening their enforcement. In the process, I hope we can avoid enacting more stringent trade legislation in the future. Accordingly, the target of my reforms is chiefly our own government—specifically, the president, the U.S. Trade Representative, and the Departments of Commerce and State. I want them to do their duty and enforce the law.

The following are several measures that I advocate (indeed, they are embodied in the Trade Enforcement Act, which I have sponsored in the Senate):

- Place clear limits on presidential discretion in enforcing unfair trade practices under section 301 of the Trade Act of 1974. The objective here is to take the politics out of trade law enforcement, to ensure that enforcement against countries that export illegally is swift and certain, and not a matter for endless temporizing and bickering, as it is now.

- Likewise, I would place greater limits on presidential discretion under section 201 of the Trade Act of 1974, which makes available temporary relief to domestic industries that are being seriously injured by imports. Currently, relief measures recommended by the International Trade Commission (ITC) may be altered or ignored by the president. I would make ITC recommendations mandatory.
- Improve antidumping and countervailing duty laws designed to stiffen enforcement. Many of these changes are patterned on the practices of our major trading partners.
- Ensure that persons or firms convicted of two or more customs violations within seven years are barred from importing into the United States.
- Restructure the import relief process to remove discretion from the president and make enforcement automatic by the ITC.
- Create a cabinet-level National Trade Council in the executive branch, with a national trade adviser assigned responsibility for coordinating trade policy.
- Require congressional approval of tariff concessions made by the United States pursuant to trade agreements.
- To encourage investment in research and development, I would offer two tax credits. First, a credit against taxes would give qualified businesses six percent for basic research, six percent for qualified research, and six percent for qualified development expenses. Participants would thus be able to claim up to 18 percent total credit on current research and development expenditures. Second, I would permit small businesses to claim an additional six percent credit for start-up expenses.

These measures are not protectionist. They are aimed at no particular country. But, collectively, they communicate our determination to enforce fair trade laws and to insist on fair treatment from our trading partners.

Moreover, it is important to remember that the United States ultimately holds the high cards in the great international trading competition of the late 1980s. If we finally show some backbone and insist that our competitors negotiate and obey reasonable trade agreements, they will toe the line. After all, America is far and away the world's richest consumer market. Our rivals would not dare place in jeopardy their access to the U.S. market.

Who has more to lose from an all-out trade war: Japan, which exports $85 billion in merchandise to the United States; or the United States, which exports only $27 billion in merchandise to Japan?

Who has more to lose: Taiwan, whose exports to the United States total $21 billion; or the United States, whose exports to Taiwan total just $6 billion?

Who has more to lose: South Korea, whose exports to the United States total $14 billion; or the United States, whose exports to Korea total only $6 billion?

The fact is, we have enormous leverage in the International marketplace—and it's high time we exploited that leverage to restore some measure of equity and fairness.

It is time to draw a line. American workers are eager to compete. American industry is eager to compete. Accordingly, we in government must be equally resolved to compete. And let the world hear our message loud and clear: We intend not only to compete. We intend to win.

REALISM AND DISCIPLINE

The weakness of our trade laws is only one cause of the decline of America's international economic position. Another important cause is the runaway federal budget. So long as the deficit remains at current levels, American business will be denied the capital essential to investment in research, development, and modernization. Clearly, our huge trade and budget deficits are twin phenomena; they are inextricably related.

Accordingly, the Democratic administration inaugurated in 1989 must wage a two-front war to restore our nation's economic health and integrity. On the budget front, we must work within the framework of Gramm-Rudman-Hollings to bring the federal budget back into balance—through spending cuts and tax increases. On the trade front, we must disabuse ourselves of the myths of free trade and insist on rigorous enforcement of our trade laws. In instances where countries chronically violate our laws or refuse us access to their markets, we must not be afraid to use our market leverage in order to change their behavior.

On both the trade and the deficit fronts, we must be realistic about the gravity of the threat to our nation. On both fronts, we must have the discipline to follow through with difficult and often painful solutions. At issue, quite simply, is whether we have the toughness and resilience to remain a great power into the next century.

CHAPTER 18

A Marshall Plan for the Nineties

Senator Bill Bradley

DURING THE LAST FORTY years, the Marshall Plan has become a legend, a talisman that proponents of ambitious government programs invoke to imbue their schemes with an aura of high-minded altruism. But legends can disappoint. When people who promise more than they can deliver invoke the Marshall Plan, they debase the concepts on which it was founded. My interest lies in exploring whether one of the pillars of the Marshall Plan, innovative collaboration among developed countries, is applicable to an issue many describe as one of our most pressing problems, but I prefer to think of as a strategic opportunity: Third World debt.

I believe that Third World debt is as imporant as the opportunity at Versailles after World War I, which slipped through our hands, and the opportunity in Europe after World War II, which we seized with the Marshall Plan. The debt issue contains the same potential for success: to recognize opportunity, to mobilize resources, to overcome obstacles, and to place national interests at the service of the larger common good. At the same time, we must also recognize that, as with Versailles, the costs of neglecting this opportunity will be inordinately high.

This is why we must be clear about the stakes. We are not talking just about debt. Nor can we afford to treat the debt crisis as an arcane financial matter, a bunch of numbers on a bank's quarterly report, or a country's national income accounts. We are talking about economic growth and prosperity, about security, and about democracy.

As citizens of the most prosperous and progressive democracy on earth, we are also asking ourselves what we owe to fledgling democracies like those in the Philippines and Argentina, struggling against powerful forces from the right and the left who want their democratic experiment to fail. I believe we owe them a chance to grow. This is not charity. It is self-interest. If they succeed, our own economies will benefit, and our collective security will be enhanced.

Take jobs. The debt-driven economic collapse south of the U.S. border has produced a devastating loss of American jobs. And it is only a hint of what will come if we do not get international debt under control. Latin America has flooded our markets with exports in order to get dollars to pay interest to banks. At the same time, U.S. exports to Latin America have collapsed. In economies with no growth, money that goes for interest is money not spent on goods and services from abroad. We have over one million fewer jobs in America today as a result of the Latin debt crisis.

Lost jobs are not the only reason for concern. The populations of Europe, Japan, and, to a lesser extent, the United States, are aging. By the year 2010, more than 40 percent of the people in Germany and Japan will be at retirement age, compared with 29 percent and 15 percent today. In the United States, pensioners will comprise about 26 percent of the population compared with 24 percent today. Contrast this with the situation in developing countries. In Mexico, for example, the population has doubled in one generation, from 35 million to 70 million, and will double again in the next. About half of these people are under 15 years old.

These demographics confront the world with an asymmetry of adolescence and maturity in the balance of payments that has enormous implications for world prosperity. The aging societies of Europe and Japan, in order to avoid their own economic stagnation, need the developing countries with young populations and high growth potential to thrive. This means that Europe and, especially, Japan should be exporting capital that developing countries need to finance their growth.

Yet many of the developing countries have lost, or failed to create, the political and financial infrastructure for attracting the capital on which robust growth depends. So, by default, the world's surplus savings are flowing to a handful of middle-aged societies in North American and Australia with big deficits, high consumption, and sophisticated financial systems. This imbalance carries in it the seeds of disaster. And the debt burden in the developing countries, which actually discourages investment and encourages capital flight, only makes things worse.

But more than our economic future is in jeopardy. The collective security arrangements that have served us well for the past 40 years may also be at risk. The Soviet Union has recently sought to capitalize on Western disunity with intriguing overtures in Europe, a growing presence in Central America, and an unprecedented diplomatic campaign aimed at the new democracies in Latin America. As of mid-1987, for example, General Secretary Gorbachev was planning to visit Argentina, Brazil, Mexico, Cuba, and perhaps other Latin countries. Never before had a Soviet leader set foot in that region. And in the latter half of 1987, most Latin countries were holding elections, in which the self-interest of foreign banks was a potentially inflammatory issue. We should also remember that the first all-Latin debt conference was held in the Spring of 1985 in Cuba. So, there is an international security dimension to the debt crisis as well.

If the democratic forces in Latin America and the Philippines fail, the United States is likely to get bogged down in conflicts that could divert us from still greater threats in Europe, Asia, and the Middle East. At a time of heightened uncertainty about the Soviet Union's goals and tactics, this outcome could impose costly, perhaps intolerable, burdens on the Western Alliance. So the stakes for all of us in avoiding this kind of strategic diversion are very high.

As I see it, the future of the Third World, especially Latin America and the Philippines, and our own future are being forged in the crucible of the debt crisis. If together, through innovative yet patient collaboration, we can work our way out of this crisis, we will be tackling the problem that darkens all hope of political regeneration and economic growth in the developing world—debt-induced poverty. And we will be laying the foundation of our own prosperity.

If, on the other hand, we neglect this opportunity we will surely pay a heavy price. The global depression of the 1930's was a catastrophe for the Third World. In South and Central America only two countries, Colombia and Costa Rica, managed to retain their political stability. Nor was the twilight of democracy confined to the developing countries. In Europe, lack of leadership in surmounting the economic crisis put out democracy's lamp and thrust the West into chaos.

As in the 1920s and 1930s, we face a stark choice: either we figure out a way to let cash-starved developing countries grow, or we risk upsetting the international financial order and plunging the world into severe recession and political upheaval.

Efforts to date have fallen far short of the mark. We have concentrated on scrounging up new money, on piling new debt on top of old debt when we should have been figuring out ways to stem the flow of capital from the developing to the developed world. President Alfonsin of Argentina, whose nation owes over $50 billion to foreign banks, put it dramatically when he spoke to the annual conference of the International Labor Organization in June 1987. He compared present conditions for repayment to trying to cure a hemorrhage by drawing blood from the patient.

It is time to put these mistakes behind us and get on with the job. There are some encouraging signs. The recent decisions by American banks to write off part of their Latin loans in effect admitted that some developing countries simply cannot sustain their current debt burdens. Although the banks stopped short of offering relief, they at least recognized reality. Also encouraging is the new proposal whereby Mexico swaps long-term bonds guaranteed by the U.S. for relief on its outstanding debt. These are necessary first steps toward a workable, long-term solution; next the benefit that has already accrued to shareholders must flow through to the debtor countries in the form of lower interest rates.

In coming up with a long-term solution, we need to keep certain basic concepts in mind. First, we have to recognize that governments have a critical role in debt management: they can coordinate relief. Creditor countries should agree which developing nations need and could put to good use interest relief and, in some instances, debt relief. They should ask the leaders of debtor countries to propose reforms that embody a clear vision of their economic future and that lay a foundation of hope for better lives for their people. And then they should urge all creditors to offer appropriate relief on a case-by-case basis. Creditors, both private and official, should offer relief to debtor countries that carry out meaningful reforms. And the relief they offer should finance and foster the reforms debtor countries need for growth and democracy. In turn, debtor reform should stem capital flight and attract nonbank capital flows and investment, assuming that the benefits of growth will go beyond the elite to the poor and middle class.

It is time to couple relief with reform. Right now, we only couple bridge loans with debtor threats. Relief and reform are more likely to produce real North-South partnership than loans and crises.

The particular mechanism for delivering interest rate relief is less important than agreement on the concept. Interest relief, and in certain cases debt relief as well, is the only option that deals with the banks' real problem in Latin America and the Philippines: that most major developing country debtors borrowed too much and invested too little in their own businesses and workers between 1974 and 1982. Developing countries' productive capacity did not keep up with their debt. Adding more debt to finance more interest payments does not reduce the gap between debt and productive capacity. And increasingly we see it causes capital flight, which makes the cash problem worse. The only way to fix the imbalance between debt and productive capacity is to reduce the debt burden.

But no single bank can offer relief by itself. In fact, no single country can effectively offer relief. Even if every U.S.

bank cut interest rates deeply for some developing country, the country might not benefit at all. Other creditors in Europe and Japan might simply collect more on their loans than they would have collected without U.S. relief. That is where the Marshall Plan concept of innovative collaboration comes in. We need governments to coordinate international debt management. Without international coordination, there is little hope for effective relief. And without relief, debtors that have fallen behind can only fall farther behind in the race to catch up to their obligations. Without relief, there will be little growth and a spreading risk of default.

Let me turn briefly to the subject of debtor country reforms. The issue is not just economic indexes and national income accounts but democracy and human rights. Growth is essential to achieving those goals, but as we have seen in Chile and South Korea, growth and democracy do not necessarily go hand in hand. So we in developed countries will have to learn a new language if we are serious about reform. We will have to learn a language that speaks directly to the victims of oppression and underdevelopment. We will have to insist, patiently and steadfastly, on their right to a take in the system and to a more humane and abundant future. Our debt policies, our trade policies, and our economic assistance should aim to empower these people, not prop up antidemocratic elites of the right or left. That means working with those who are trying to mobilize the people in support of such an effort, not allying ourselves with their oppressors.

The way we provide debt relief can make a difference. So far, our response to the debt crisis has relied too heavily on the cozy relationship between money center banks and central bankers. This has tended to reinforce the power of the state, Yet, in most nondemocratic, or even newly democratic, countries the state is so overgrown and militarized that it has become an intrusive policeman instead of a wise helmsman.

The kind of "conditionality" that we have been insisting on as the price of new money for debtor nations has been equally undemocratic. Instead of offering political leaders powerful incentives to implement difficult reforms, we have trumpeted ideologically bankrupt policies—run the economy through a wringer; shrink the public sector; throw people out of work; puncture the rising expectations of the middle class; doom millions to a future of poverty and despair—all just so long as the banks get paid.

It is time to look to the best of our own democratic traditions for guidance in dealing with the debt crisis. The genius of Western democracy is that power, both economic and political, is dispersed. In America the complex government machinery of our founding fathers was designed to do one primary thing—preserve and promote individual liberty. The weakness of countries struggling to become democracies is that wealth is concentrated and power is centralized. Changing this means seeking ways to reduce military authority and state control. Rather than propping up dictators, we need to look for ways of strengthening community-based institutions, voluntary associations, and civic groups. We need to ensure the spread of economic and political power throughout society and to narrow the gap between rich and poor.

For example, the United States should have used its economic influence in the Philippines during the Marcos regime. Marcos and his cronies were propped up by a network of trade and financial preferences that included GSP, a valuable allotment under the United States sugar import quota, eligibility for guarantees from the Overseas Private Investment Corporation, and loans from the World Bank and the Asian Development Bank. This preferential treatment facilitated Marcos's monopolization of the economy and perpetuated his political control. We should have conditioned these preferences on Marcos's implementing economic and political reforms. That might have resulted in a more efficient and productive economy and a government that was more responsive to the people's needs.

Important as debt is, it is still only part of the picture. We cannot deal with it in a vacuum. The developed world must put its own economic house in order first. Lagging growth and rising protectionism are sure signs of real trouble that signal disaster for the Third World. Complicating progress toward a solution is the fact that the structure of the world economy has gone through a fundamental change. The United States is the largest debtor ever—owing $240 billion. Japan has become the world's largest creditor. Prior to World War I, Britain was the linchpin of the international economic system. And as Britain's ability to export capital diminished in the 1920s, the United States became the major creditor power. Unlike Britain though, America clung to its nineteenth-century protectionist trade policy—with tragic consequences. Unfortunately, Japan seems bent on repeating America's mistake by refusing to adopt the liberal trade policy needed to allow the international financial system to work properly. As a result, there is currently no backup for the United States, and the big question is whether we will all recognize this and act in time to avoid a severe disruption triggered by the fall of the dollar, protectionism on a scale not seen since the 1920s, and a deep worldwide recession.

Frankly, if the Venice summit was any indication of the developed countries' capacity for innovative collaboration, the prognosis is not encouraging. Yet the course of action we must take is quite clear:

- West Germany and Japan have to import more, otherwise the inevitable contraction of the U.S. trade and budget deficits will further slow world growth.
- Japan has to play a much bigger role in financing growth in the developing world and it must adopt trade policies that harmonize with its world creditor status. Given Japan's aging population such action is the essence of long-term self-interest.

All of this is easier said than done unless we can summon up the political will to act in our collective interests, rather than retreating into myopic self-absorption. But if the political will eludes us, if we fail to see how our national economies fit into an international framework and act on that knowledge, a crisis seems unavoidable. And then it may be too late.

With leadership and patience we can avoid crisis. This goes to the crux of the matter, because leadership is exactly what is lacking. The Baker Plan is essentially defunct. The World Bank and the International Monetary Fund are struggling, so far unsuccessfully, to find new roles for themselves. There is a new chairman at the Federal Reserve Board who will have his hands full interpreting monetary developments and sorting out conflicting economic messages. If he does not already know, he will soon discover that he is not only the arbiter of international demand in the United States but also the lender of last resort worldwide. The Venice summit revealed that summits, as an institution, are bankrupt in the absence of self-confident, vigorous world leaders who share a common vision. So, it is not surprising that solutions to the debt crisis have been on hold and the potential for a coordinated effort remains largely untapped.

Therein lies the limits of the Marshall Plan model. We need bold vision and unifying leadership to combat the "hunger, poverty, desperation, and chaos" of our own time.

CHAPTER 19

Lessons of the Third World Debt Crisis: Building a Sound Policy

Congressman Charles E. Schumer

ON A HOT WEEKEND in August of 1982, Mexico publicly announced that it was going to have difficulty meeting the service payment on its external debt. The debt crisis had begun. Initially, it was perceived as a self-contained, short-term problem. By now it has become clear that, instead, the debt crisis has deeply affected our banking system and the international financial market. As Democrats formulate policy alternatives, we should reexamine the history of the debt crisis, and its domestic impact, and build on the creative solutions offered in legislation in the One Hundredth Congress.

HISTORY OF THE DEBT CRISIS

The causes of the debt crisis are rooted deeply in the economic history of Third World countries, and in their attempt to rapidly industrialize and increase production for export. These countries, using the rising value of their natural resources, especially oil, as collateral, borrowed money to fuel

218

economic development programs. In the mid-1970s, this money came directly from industrialized countries and from commercial banks that, flush with petrodollars and eager to find new investment opportunities, perceived these resource-rich countries as good credit risks.

Unfortunately, several hundred billion dollars later, the borrowing binge ground to a halt. Falling commodity prices, high interest rates, and worldwide recession combined to deplete the foreign exchange earnings of Third World nations. In 1980, Latin America alone found itself $221 billion in debt, with insufficient funds to meet even debt service obligations. Mexico was the first country to enter the crisis. By the end of 1983, a total of 42 countries were behind in their debt payments.

The initial response was based on the assumption that there was a short-term liquidity problem. As a result, the solutions worked out in the first few years were devised on an ad hoc basis. In 1984, the Mexican government became the first to enter into a more systematic debt restructuring, the method currently in vogue. Essentially, restructuring involves negotiations (between the debtor country and both the International Monetary Fund [IMF] and the commercial banks) that result in an agreement committing the debtor country to a host of economic reforms designed by the IMF in return for more favorable repayment terms; payments are rescheduled, and additional capital is advanced to cover interest payments coming due.

These negotiations and arrangements begin a cycle which I have elsewhere termed "Faustian Finance."[1] In this arrangement, each party in the negotiation has made a bargain with the devil. The country agrees to increase its overall debt burden, in return for maintaining the appearance that it is meeting its debt repayment obligations. The banks agree to increase their exposure (and thereby their vulnerability to default), in return for short-term profit that shows up on their books each quarter.

If the problem in the Third World had truly been a short-term liquidity crisis, the Faustian bargain would have worked. The countries would have regained their economic balance and resumed normal debt service payments, and the banks would have continued to record profits on their books.

However, the problem was not a short-term liquidity crisis. The changes in the international economy undercut the basis on which these nations were able to borrow such huge sums of money. Interest rates continued to spiral, and the prices of raw commodities continued to fall. The terms of trade (the rate at which a country's exports can be exchanged for imports) also continued to deteriorate, further depleting foreign exchange earnings. These external conditions combined with internal mismanagement of the economy and high ratios of capital flight to create the structural conditions that forced countries to choose between repaying the debt (at significant political and social cost) and maintaining economic growth. They could no longer do both.

DOMESTIC IMPACT OF THE CRISIS: CURRENT POLICY

The United States response to the debt crisis has evolved through three stages, the first two dominated by the administration, and the last by the Congress.

The first stage was characterized by a U.S. government policy of "benign neglect" (under the stewardship of then Treasury Secretary Donald Regan). At this stage, the IMF dominated efforts to manage the crisis. The IMF designed economic programs for debtor countries that included the twin tools of domestic austerity (cuts in government services and removal of food subsidies) and increased emphasis on exports in order to increase foreign exchange earnings.

The impact in the debtor countries of the IMF programs was severe. Per capita income declined dramatically. In Bolivia and Peru, for example, in 1983, the real per capita gross domestic product had fallen to the 1967 level. Brazil's standard of living that same year had declined to its 1977 level, while Mexico's had dropped to its 1979 level. Overall, between 1982 and 1987, according to various estimates, the standard of living declined by 15 percent in Third World countries, while the amount of debt increased by 60 percent. In human terms, this meant increased unemployment, increased malnutrition, food shortages, lower wages, and loss of social services.

It was not long before the political repercussions of the IMF programs were felt. Food riots became commonplace, and the IMF became a hated entity across the Third World. Government after government reneged on the structural reform package. Finally, it was also clear that despite austerity and emphasis on exports, the countries still were not able to meet debt service obligations. Every year, another country was held up as the model debtor, only to fall into disgrace.

It was at this point that the second phase of the U.S. response was initiated. At the 1985 annual joint meeting of the IMF and the World Bank, in Seoul, Treasury Secretary James Baker introduced a program that came to be known as the Baker Plan. This initiative rejected the IMF-style austerity policies and, instead, emphasized the need for economic growth as the long-term solution to the debt crisis. Baker's plan hinged on increased voluntary lending from the commercial banks and from the international financial institutions, in return for substantial economic reforms in debtor countries to encourage growth-oriented policies.

Secretary Baker called for $29 billion of new money for debtor countries. It was not long, however, before it became clear that the new money would still be substantially used to service the old debt. Given that as of late 1985, when the speech was made, the total amount of debt had accumulated to nearly $900 billion, the $29 billion figure hardly seemed adequate to meet the challenge.

The test case for the Baker Plan was the 1986 rescheduling of Mexico's debt. It took nearly one year to negotiate the terms, and over 100 banks refused to participate. It was clear that the plan did not have unqualified support from the commercial banking sector.

In the third phase of the U.S. response, the advocates of debt relief have claimed center stage. Public awareness of the larger implications of the debt crisis came with a speech in Zurich by Senator Bill Bradley, in which he pointed out the link between the debt crisis and the burgeoning trade deficit in the United States. This link is by now well demonstrated. The debtor countries, particularly the Latin American countries, were, until the late 1970s, the second-largest market for U.S. exports. As these countries were forced to cut back on their imports and increase exports, not only did a significant shrinkage in market opportunities occur, but in some instances, the United States found itself in competition with Third World countries for a share of the export market. Two critical studies by the Joint Economic Committee of Congress demonstrated that declines of U.S. exports in Latin America were directly related to the debt problem.

Bradley's solution linked internally generated economic reforms in the debtor countries with debt relief in the form of interest payment reduction combined with forgiveness of a principal. In a 1986 editorial in the London *Financial Times*[2], I proposed a plan, developed in cooperation with a Mexican economist and a California banker, that entailed a cap on Mexican debt payments to 25 percent of their export earnings. We demonstrated that while such a plan would require banks to forgive 30 percent of Mexican loans, this action would not result in fiscal chaos. These proposals immediately drew criticism from the major money-center banks and the Treasury Department, which argued that banks alone could handle the problem and that the rescheduling process was working very well.

Nevertheless, among a growing number of economics experts and within the U.S. Congress, support for debt relief increased. In order to determine the viability of different debt relief plans, Senator Bradley and I requested a cost-benefit analysis from the Federal Reserve Board. The analysis demonstrated that while debt relief would entail deep costs to the commercial banks, it would not destroy the financial system. The analysis also showed that no one solution would work across the board, but that a combination of solutions could be utilized to provide significant relief while keeping costs to the banks at a minimum.

Despite the mounting evidence in favor of debt relief, we in the U.S. Congress hesitated to offer legislation because of two obstacles. First of all, with the entrenched opposition of the administration to any form of debt relief, it was clear that any legislation would meet a veto. Second, because the problem is multilateral in nature, it was not practical or fair to formulate legislation that would mandate a solution for

U.S. banks, but allow European and Asian banks, which hold two-thirds of the debt, to continue operating in the old manner. This situation not only would place U.S. banks in an unfair position with respect to other international banks, it also would not provide the debt relief to the debtor countries.

It was not until early 1987 that the U.S. Congress saw a vehicle for debt relief legislation, in the form of the trade bill. In the Ninety-ninth Congress, the bill passed overwhelmingly in the House of Representatives, but was not considered by the Republican-controlled Senate. By the time the One Hundredth Congress convened, the trade deficit had grown even larger. Clearly, the problem could no longer be perceived as one of the banking community alone. Because of the decline in U.S. exports linked to the debt crisis, close to one million U.S. jobs had been lost, and major manufacturers that relied heavily on exports experienced deep declines in sales (particularly hard hit were manufacturers of farm equipment and other heavy machinery).

The trade bill was the natural place to attach debt relief provisions. Two complementary provisions were formulated and passed both the Senate and the House of Representatives. One provision called for the initiation of negotiations to create an international facility authorized to buy Third World loans from commercial banks at a discount and to pass the discount along to Third World countries in the form of relief. This solution provided the needed multilateral dimension.

The other provision, termed the Schumer Options Plan, called for immediate action to allow banks to take advantage of a "menu of options" that provide debt relief. This plan was designed to offer banks a nonmandatory way to provide debt relief to Third World banks. It capitalized on the fact that some banks, to meet debt payments, wish to choose other methods than lending new money. Under the options plan, each bank may still choose to lend new money, but it may reject that approach and opt to forgive a portion of the debt, forgo or reduce interest payments, engage in a debt-equity swap, or combine any of these options.

Under the options plan, the debt restructuring negotiations would continue. After the negotiations, the bank regulatory agencies and the Treasury Department would be required to publish a table of mathematical equivalences stating the amount of interest reduction, debt forgiveness, debt-equity swap that is equal to lending new money. Each bank would then choose the option that best suits its needs. This plan offers a true case-by-case approach, because it would allow debtor nations and creditors to choose different options at each rescheduling, rather than requiring all banks to follow one course of action (lending new money). Because the plan would be nonmandatory, it would remain fair to United States banks. It also would not rely on multilateral negotiations, but could go into effect immediately on enactment of the bill.

By mid-1987, it was clear that banks were already beginning to look for and create options to avoid lending new money at the time of rescheduling. The 1987 agreement with Argentina, for example, included an "exit bond" option, which allowed banks to exchange up to $5 million in debt for a bond (at an extremely low interest rate). The Philippines package included a debt-for-equity exchange option. More significant, however, as of mid-1987, the banks had finally admitted that the loans they held were not worth their full face value, and that they were not going to necessarily recoup full payment. This admission came when, starting with Citibank, most major money-center banks created loan-loss reserves to cover up to 25–30 percent of their debt. The European and Asian banks, because of easier tax and regulatory rules, had taken this step years before, and so in a sense, the playing field was now level. Furthermore, almost immediately, the creation of loan-loss reserves caused the stocks of these banks to jump up, proving the contention of the debt relief advocates that debt relief would not be detrimental to the banking system.

FUTURE POLICY GOALS

The creation of loan-loss reserves in May and June of 1987 led some of us to belief at first that the debt crisis was near resolution. Yet, by the middle of the summer, we were beginning to doubt our early optimism. The banks, in spite of the admission about the devaluation of Third World loans, still refused to take the next step and use the reserves to provide relief to the debtor countries. The Reagan administration, through the Treasury Department, continued to advocate a "muddle-through" approach, although they adopted an alternate "menu of options" language to disguise the old policy.

A Democratic administration will still have to confront the debt crisis issue and take courageous steps to restore balance to the international financial system. These steps will include relief to overburdened Third World countries, regulatory changes similar to those adopted for banks holding large amounts of farm and energy loans, and international cooperation among debtors and creditors to encourage economic growth in the developing world.

If the trade bill becomes law, its debt relief provisions can be used as building blocks of a sound policy. A Democratic president should first encourage banks to take full advantage of the options plan and offer banks regulatory incentives if they take the interest relief or debt forgiveness options. As banks use the different options, it is probable that the size of the secondary market for Third World debt will increase, at which time negotiations to create a debt management facility should be initiated. The facility, especially if it is structured to offer interest rate relief to debtor countries, can control the growth of the secondary market and channel the benefits to debtor countries.

This step-by-step solution would further the interests of all parties. Poor Third World countries will grow. Banks will not collapse, but will gain stability as the chances that they will be repaid increase, and because the market will continue to applaud their efforts to reflect the true value of their loans. And a major threat to U.S. security—the growing political instability in developing countries—will be countered. These are the proper aims of U.S. policy.

1. C.E. Schumer, "Faustian Finances" *New Republic*, March 11, 1985.
2. C.E. Schumer, "Mexico's Debt Problem—A Plan Which Is in Everybody's Interest," *Financial Times*, October 22, 1986.

CHAPTER 20

Market Wars: Regaining Competitiveness in the Global Economy

Pat Choate and Juyne Linger

IF THE UNITED STATES trade sector were a separate national economy, its gross national product (GNP) would be the fourth-largest in the world, following those of the United States, the Soviet Union, and Japan. With a trade sector valued at more than $630 billion, the United States is the biggest international trader by far. In 1984, U.S. merchandise exports exceeded $217 billion, while merchandise imports totaled more than $341 billion. American farmers sell 30 percent of their grain production overseas. American industry exports more than 20 percent of its manufacturing output, and one of every six manufacturing jobs depends on foreign sales.

At the same time, a fifth of all goods sold in the United States come from abroad. American consumers buy 36 percent of Japan's exports and 33 percent of Latin America's. They also purchase 60 percent of the manufactures that Singapore, Hong Kong, South Korea, and Taiwan export to the industrialized countries. Any significant reduction in United States trade would create havoc in the American economy and pitch our trading partners into economic, political, and foreign policy upheavals.

These economic links between America and the rest of the world have proliferated during the past 25 years, as the nation has shifted from relative economic isolation to global interdependence. By the mid-1980s, trade accounted for 20 percent of the U.S. GNP, up from 10 percent in 1960.

But as the United States became more deeply involved in the global economy, the nature of trade changed radically, and America's competitiveness in world markets declined sharply. Understanding the changing realities of global trade is an essential first step in adapting to them and regaining competitiveness in the world marketplace.

POST-WORLD WAR II TRADE PATTERNS

Current U.S. trade policies are locked in the 1940s, when Britain and the United States dominated the global economy, tariffs were the principal barrier to trade, and U.S. supremacy was uncontested in virtually all industries. Today, 75 percent of world trade is conducted by economic systems very different from our own, a growing array of barriers distort global trade flows, and nearly three-fourths of U.S. goods and services face stiff foreign competition.

Over the past 40 years, financial flows and trade in services and high technology have become increasingly important. Exchange rates are no longer fixed. The world financial system has been internationalized. As trade competition has escalated, developed and developing nations alike have succeeded in choking off foreign imports to help domestic industries. The nations of the Pacific Rim have replaced those of Western Europe as America's most important trading partners. Many of the less-developed nations—including Brazil, Mexico, Argentina, Portugal, and the so-called Group of 77 developing nations—have become effective competitors as they have based their economic future on aggressive exports of goods and services, both high-tech and low-tech.

Much of the world's trade is managed—that is, controlled

tightly—by governments. In most nations, particularly developing nations, governments plan and subsidize export production while sharply curtailing imports; this is the case, for example, in Taiwan and Korea. Some advanced industrial economies, such as Japan's, also operate with government guidance and support.

An estimated 20–30 percent of all global trade is in the form of barter (countertrade). Lacking hard currency to buy Western goods, Eastern Europe and most developing countries exchange local products and raw materials for needed merchandise. A growing portion of U.S. firms now participate in this ancient form of exchange. The Coca-Cola Company, for example, barters its soft drink syrup with Bulgaria and other Eastern European nations for local wines, which it then sells in Europe and the United States. General Electric was able to sell $150 million worth of nuclear power plant turbines to Romania when the company agreed to market $150 million worth of Romanian machines, steel products, and other construction materials.

Japan's domestic trade policies and global commercial offensive are also reshaping the world economy. Japan has captured more than 80 percent of the global market for videocassette recorders (VCRs), 35 millimeter cameras, and watches; more than 70 percent of calculators and microwave ovens; more than 65 percent of telephones; and more than 50 percent of cars, motorcycles, and color TVs. And this is but a partial listing of Japanese successes.

But while Japan exports a large part of its production, it accepts proportionately fewer imported manufactured goods than other nations, preferring to bring in raw materials and unfinished products instead. In 1983, the ratio of manufactured imports to GNP was only three percent in Japan, whereas it was six percent in the United States and 10 percent in most Western European countries. Japan's export successes, coupled with its closed markets, are setting the stage for a round of intense protectionism, particularly with the United States.

The four newly industrialized countries of East Asia—South Korea, Singapore, Hong Kong, and Taiwan—are becoming the next Japans. The combined GNP of the four dragons, as they are known in Japan, is less than 10 percent that of Western Europe, but their exports to the United States are almost two-thirds those of Western Europe. United States trade with Taiwan alone produced America's third-largest bilateral deficit in 1984, following those with Japan and Canada.

Manufactures—clothing, footware, electronic components, toys, games, and telecommunications equipment—constitute 96 percent of the four countries' exports to the United States. The ready availability of cutting-edge technology is permitting these nations to move quickly into the production of advanced goods and services. For example, Korea is exporting VCRs, and Taiwan is producing advanced microcomputers. The East Asian nations are sure to become even stronger global competitors, and very soon.

Finally, the terms of market access are changing. In a growing number of industries—including automobiles, consumer electronics, pharmaceuticals, and financing—international competitiveness depends on access to all global markets. In the past, market access was determined primarily by a firm's ability to export. But in the future, that access will hinge increasingly on the willingness of foreign governments to permit local investment and production. This is a particularly important new dimension of trade, since foreign investment is not covered under existing trade agreements, and U.S. citizens and firms have almost $250 billion invested in other nations.

In the absence of an international agreement, foreign governments distort investment flows. For United States firms to do business in virtually all other nations, they must meet one or more complex requirements regarding employment of local citizens, levels of exports, use of local resources and components, technological specifications for products, the export of technology developed in local operations, maintenance of funds in local banks, and the production of a minimum amount of goods. Many governments—Brazil's and Mexico's, for example—also force foreign firms to cede majority ownership of affiliates to a native company and produce for both the local market and export. Thus, to locate in these nations is to create one's own international competitor.

IBM's experience in Mexico illustrates what happens in the absence of global trade rules on investments. Success in the computer industry depends on worldwide market access, and Mexico is a strong emerging market for personal computers. Because the government requires that computers sold in Mexico be made in Mexico, U.S. firms cannot ship American-made machines across the border. IBM refused to give majority ownership of Mexican affiliates to local companies and was denied permission to build a facility in Mexico. Both Apple and Hewlett-Packard, however, complied with the government's demands and got access to the market.

Faced with competitive pressures, IBM finally made major concessions to the Mexican government. In exchange for maintaining 100 percent ownership of its facilities, IBM agreed to underwrite a $90 million investment, create a semiconductor development center for Mexican industry, purchase high-technology components from Mexican companies, produce in Mexico the software that will be sold throughout Latin America, train Mexicans in computer science, and create a Mexican dealers' network. In effect, IBM relinquished effective control to the Mexican government, and the company is now creating one of its own major competitors in Latin America.

MARKET WARS

America's trade competitors are competent and sophisticated. Most have mounted aggressive efforts that represent nothing less than a new form of societal competition, in which a nation's full economic resources are marshaled in the global economic sweepstakes. Japan, Korea, Taiwan, Brazil, France, West Germany, and other industrial and developing nations have created national economic combines of government, business, and labor. They select a few key industries that will be favored, reduce the risks of investing in these enterprises, and facilitate large-scale economies of research, development, and production.

Virtually no national effort is spared. Promising foreign

technologies are identified and secured. Basic research is cosponsored and shared. A leading foreign company, such as U.S. Steel, Texas Instruments, General Motors, or IBM, is selected as a model and economic pace horse. National cartels are formed. Generous long-term capital subsidies are provided. Workers are trained and retrained. Prices, specifications, and standards are jointly determined. Aggressive export drives are launched when the industry achieves world-class competitiveness.

In their zeal to dominate markets, many of America's competitors are fueling a dangerous spiral of destructive beggar-thy-neighbor practices. As they introduce protectionist trade measures, pursue rapacious export programs, and violate trade agreements, others follow. Increasingly, these conflicts are escalating into global market wars that threaten the well-being of all nations, industries, workers, and consumers.

These market wars are being fought with few rules. Postwar trade agreements have not been updated sufficiently to accommodate the vast changes that have transformed world trade. As a result, less than 7 percent of the total value of trade and financial flows is now covered by international agreements. The principal international treaty on trade, the General Agreement on Tariffs and Trade (GATT), still deals almost exclusively with trade in manufactured goods. It provides only limited coverage for trade in agriculture and does not cover trade in services, trade with nonmarket economies and developing nations, barter, foreign investment, or financial flows.

Existing trade agreements, moreover, are often bent, broken, and ignored. Thus, the flood of formal complaints of trade violations filed by the United States and European countries in recent years has overwhelmed the antiquated and impotent GATT mechanism for settling disputes. As tariffs have been reduced, nations have erected a wide array of other barriers—for instance, local content requirements, employment and investment mandates, and slow inspections of imports—designed solely to obstruct the flow of foreign goods.

Although the inadequacies of the existing GATT framework are obvious, most of the 90 member nations have resisted U.S. efforts to extend coverage. But while other nations balk at modernization of the global trading system, U.S. losses of jobs and firms continue to mount, and protectionist sentiment climbs. By 1985, almost 70 percent of the American public was ready to close off U.S. markets to imports even if it meant increased prices and fewer choices for consumers.

Americans have slowly come to realize that most nations operate on the philosophy of nineteenth-century financier and stock manipulator Daniel Drew, who said, "All I want out of life is a little unfair advantage." Even as other nations offer products and services, they are creating an extra competitive edge through "little unfair advantages" that limit foreign imports and promote their own exports.

To be sure, the United States aids and protects many of its own industries. The Export-Import Bank subsidizes some exports, helps underwrite research and development through tax credits and federal expenditures, and stimulates capital investment through a variety of incentives, such as accelerated depreciation of plant and equipment. Also, most states assist local industry directly and indirectly, by financing worker training and public infrastructure, among other measures.

Substantial aid is also given industry through old-fashioned protectionism. The Buy America Act forces certain federal agencies to purchase domestic products that are up to six percent more expensive than their imported counterparts, and 50 percent more expensive if the item is considered essential to national security. Some defense-related items cannot be purchased from foreign sources. Thirty-six states also have selected Buy American policies, and five states require their agencies to use U.S.-made steel. Almost 25 percent of manufactured imports, such as textiles and steel, are restricted by quotas and multilateral trade agreements. Professor Gary Hufbauer, of Georgetown University, estimates that this protectionism costs American consumers $50 billion annually.

In spite of these barriers, the United States is by far the most open market in the world. Indeed, it is ironic that while other nations closely regulate most of their markets, the United States is labeled protectionist when it even considers using market access—its primary bargaining tool in trade negotiations—to open foreign markets.

In reality and perception, other countries are proving far superior to the United States in adapting to, capitalizing on, and setting the terms of global competition. The automobile industry provides a clear example of how other governments stack the economic deck. Australia, for instance, limits auto imports to 20 percent of its market and requires that 85 percent of auto components be made locally. In Brazil, 90 percent of auto components that are sold must be manufactured there. In Mexico, the mandated local content is approximately 75 percent of vehicles sold. Altogether, 35 countries use local content requirements to control auto imports.

European countries tend to use quotas and value-added taxes (VATs) to restrict auto imports. France restricts Japanese cars to three percent of its domestic market and imposes a 33 percent VAT on all other auto imports. Germany limits Japanese cars to 10 percent of its domestic market and imposes a 13 percent VAT on imports. Greece requires 30 percent local content and charges a 25 percent VAT. Italy imposes a VAT of 18–35 percent, depending on engine size, and confines Japanese imports to 2,200 vehicles per year, the exact number of Italian cars that Japan imports.

Although Japan has no local content mandates, export requirements, or import tariffs on cars, it effectively blocks auto imports through a virtually impenetrable maze of inspections, standards, and certification procedures. The United States has also imposed restrictions on foreign cars—a four-year voluntary quota on Japanese imports that expired in 1985.

These examples are neither unique nor extreme. Japan carefully limits telecommunications imports. The Japanese have prevented imports of superior U.S. products, such as cellular telephones, by refusing to give radio frequencies for their application. Even the U.S. embassy in Tokyo has been denied a cellular telephone frequency for use in its vehicles. In France, foreign electronic components are subject to a 17 percent tariff and can be sold only to state monopolies. The "little unfair advantage" is often even greater in other global economic activities—trade in services, for example—in which there are no rules.

U.S. service exports—including insurance, banking, engineering, and technological and consulting services—already exceed $43 billion annually and could expand even more. Yet, in the absence of a global agreement on trade in services, foreign governments erect flagrant barricades even as they strive to build up their own capacities. West Germany and many less-developed countries prohibit foreign firms from telecommunicating operational data across their borders—a restriction that is intended to force companies to locate their research, administrative, and manufacturing facilities within that country. Foreign insurance companies must wait years to receive a license in Japan. Norway has not approved a foreign insurance company in more than 40 years. Taiwan gave U.S. insurance companies permission to open branch offices there in 1981, but has restricted their operations to insuring American citizens and 100 percent U.S.-owned firms. U.S. air carriers are denied access to the airline reservation systems of France and Germany. Thirty-two nations require that firms exporting to them use their ocean marine insurance companies; only U.S. Agency for International Development shipments are exempt from these discriminatory insurance requirements.

By any measure, America is the world's leading producer of agricultural products. Because farm trade is inadequately covered in existing trade treaties, however, most nations refuse to accept U.S. agricultural goods except under the most severe political pressure. Neither Norway nor Sweden, for example, will allow American apples into the country until the domestic crop has been depleted. In Korea, it is illegal to possess an American cigarette. Other products of interest to U.S. farmers require approval by Korea's Ministry of Agriculture and Fisheries. But the U.S. Trade Representative reports that many of these products—including fresh oranges and grapes, canned fruit and fruit juice, meat products, walnuts, chocolate, and wine—are almost never approved for import.

An increasingly important dimension of international commerce yet to be accommodated in global agreements is trade with nonmarket countries, such as the People's Republic of China. These nations subsidize goods by holding down labor costs, excluding many of the costs of raw materials and capital from the product's final price, and setting extraordinarily favorable terms of barter. Without evaluations of such transactions in market currencies, these nations can dump or engage in predatory trade practices invisibly and almost with impunity.

In addition to protecting their domestic markets, foreign firms, often with the cooperation of their government, have long used aggressive export promotion techniques that are in clear violation of existing trade agreements. The U.S. International Trade Commission has found a British firm guilty of illegally underpricing (dumping) large power transformers for sale in the United States. Italian companies have been detected dumping pasta; Japanese firms, glass; Belgian and Portugeuse companies, portland cement; Canadians, potassium chloride; and the French, aminoacetic acid.

Moreover, dumping is only one of the thousands of predatory trade practices, and these cases represent only a fraction of the trade violations by foreign firms.

Foreign governments also provide strong financial support for their exports. The United Kingdom and Japan, for instance, subsidize 35 percent of their exports with long-term loans for purchasers, cheap interest rates, and even outright case grants. More than 29 percent of French exports are similarly subsidized, as are 12 percent of West German exports. By comparison, the U.S. Export-Import Bank provides long-term financing for only six percent of American exports. Recent trends, moreover, indicate that financial support for exports is contracting in the United States while expanding abroad.

Altogether, the Office of the U.S. Trade Representative has identified over 2,000 "little unfair advantages" now imposed against imports of U.S. goods and services and against U.S. investment.

The global market wars, already fierce, are certain to intensify; their stakes, already high, are sure to increase; and the new protectionism, already pervasive, will doubtless expand. The protectionism fueling these wars offers an attractive short-term political solution to difficult economic pressures. At the same time, however, protectionism risks untold dollars of future sales, hundreds of billions of dollars of investment, and millions of jobs in every economic sector in nearly every nation.

AMERICAN LOSSES

One American industry after another now finds itself with its back to the wall, largely because the United States has failed to adapt to changes in the global marketplace. Most of these losses are in sectors where the United States has long been dominant—manufacturing, services, and high-tech goods. Foreign firms have captured more than half the U.S. domestic sales of computer-controlled machine tools. Since 1960, foreign manufacturers have been able to reduce the U.S. world market share in auto production from 48 percent to 26 percent; in chemicals, from 66 to 35 percent; in pharmaceuticals, from 62 to 35 percent; and in metal products, from 67 to 43 percent.

America is losing the global battle in the high-growth service industries—insurance, financing, aviation, shipping, travel services, engineering, management, and legal services, for example—which generate over 70 percent of all economic activity in the United States. U.S. exports of proprietary rights (such as patents, processes, copyrights, trademarks, and franchises) and other business services (such as banking, architecture, advertising, accounting, and communications services) tripled between 1973 and 1983. At the same time, however, France and the East Asian countries were becoming more competitive in these areas, reducing America's share of the $157 billion world trade in these services from almost 15 percent to less than eight percent. In the past, U.S. surpluses in proprietary rights and other business services have offset deficits in travel and transportation, producing a substantial overall surplus in services trade. But as the value of the dollar rose, a small U.S. surplus in travel and transportation in 1981 became an $8.8 billion deficit by 1984. Because surpluses in proprietary rights and other business services were barely large enough to offset this deficit, the U.S. trade surplus in services plunged from $9.6 billion in 1981 to $2 billion in 1984.

High-technology exports—including communications equipment, electronic components, aircraft, and office computers—have been another traditional source of America's economic strength. Although high-tech products account for a growing share of U.S. manufacturing exports—43 percent in 1984—the high-priced dollar and formidable competition from the Pacific Rim nations reduced U.S. high-tech surpluses from $26 billion in 1980 to only $6 billion in 1984.

The foreign competitive pressures on American firms will increase in the years immediately ahead. By 1985, more than 70 percent of all American-made products were fighting intense foreign competition in the domestic market—up from less than 25 percent in the early 1960s. By the end of the 1980s, virtually all of America's most productive and advanced industries will face aggressive foreign competition. The competitive battles will center on biotechnology, computers and other electronic devices, carbon fibers, telecommunications, lasers, industrial robots, commercial aircraft, space satellites, nuclear power facilities, ocean oil development, seawater desalination, high-performance polymeric materials, fine ceramics, amorphous metals, superalloys, and magnetic materials.

These industries are crucial to U.S. competitiveness. They define America's ability to revitalize older businesses, such as auto manufacturing; to enhance productivity in basic industries, such as steel and even agriculture; and to maintain an edge in fast-growing service areas.

America's economic losses suggest an important economic lesson—namely, that success in the global marketplace hinges on both the capacity of business to produce superior goods and services and the power of government to ensure American access to foreign markets. Although much remains to be done, many American firms have launched ambitious, broad-based efforts to improve their competitiveness. Government policies, however, remain trapped in a time warp of the late 1940s, out of touch with the vastly different economic realities of the 1980s and unable to assure U.S. access to overseas markets.

A TRADE STRATEGY FOR THE EIGHTIES

To prosper in today's global marketplace, the United States requires an integrated, flexible trade strategy—one that is far less ideological, more practical, and much more results-oriented than what exists today. The two requisites of such an approach are practical objectives that are centered on granting foreign nations access to U.S. markets on the basis of America's access to theirs, and a flexible negotiating strategy that facilitates parallel trade talks with one, several, or all nations.

The temporary closing of U.S. markets will hurt some American consumers, firms, and workers, but if other nations are permitted to shut their markets while enjoying unlimited access to ours, even greater long-term harm is likely.

If the United States is not willing to secure its borders as a means of negotiating the opening of other borders, then there are no alternative means available to induce other nations to unbar their markets to American goods, services, and investment. Hard-nosed, results-oriented negotiations centered on reciprocal access to markets is the best, if not the only, negotiating chip the nation possesses.

Equally important, the United States must pursue a strategy of holding concurrent discussions with any nation that is willing to talk. While multilateral negotiations are useful, they certainly are not the only way to open overseas markets. The danger in relying solely on multilateral negotiations is that numerous opportunities are missed. Moreover, multilateral agreements typically take many years to negotiate, but most issues cannot wait that long for resolution.

The most pressing trade issues can be addressed in bilateral talks with America's main economic competitors—Japan, South Korea, Taiwan, Singapore, and Hong Kong. U.S. firms cannot operate successfully in the global marketplace if they are unable to penetrate these markets while firms in those nations enjoy unrestricted access to the American market. Until trade with these economies becomes much more open and the Pacific Rim cultures are willing to accept competitive U.S. goods and services, trade with these nations must be managed—that is, targets are required for imports and exports as well as for permissible market shares, whether acquired through imports or direct foreign investment. High-priority bilateral talks are also needed with other nations on such sensitive issues as debt rescheduling (Mexico) and the removal of barriers to U.S. made machinery and computer Imports (Brazil).

At the same time, other issues are of Interest to several nations—counterfeiting and intellectual property rights, for example. While these countries may be unwilling to enter into broader multilateral negotiations, they might be willing to discuss select issues of mutual concern. Such plurilateral talks can be structured so that agreements can be integrated into a broader round of multilateral treaties later on.

Finally, multilateral negotiations are needed as longer-term means to open global markets and confront issues such as the lagging development of many nations. Responsibility for initiating these talks resides with the world's premier trading countries—the United States, the European Community, and Japan.

The creation of a coherent, flexible trade strategy—one based on reciprocal market access and parallel trade talks—will go far in helping American firms to reverse their losses and regain competitiveness in the global marketplace.

CHAPTER 21

Stretching the Flag Too Thin

Congresswoman Patricia Schroeder

WHEN I SUFFERED THROUGH this institution in the early 1960s, the world was a different place. There were precious few female lawyers, and Dean Griswold meant to keep it that way. The United States confronted the Soviet Union over missiles in Cuba, and because we had a near nuclear monopoly, the Soviets backed down. Vietnam was part of something called Indochina, and the cognoscenti knew that the French had gotten their comeuppance there. Camelot was flourishing in Washington, with the best and brightest this institution could produce bringing rationality to government and civilization to Washington. And the United States had nearly 300,000 soldiers stationed in Europe.

Times have changed. Harvard Law School is now producing female, as well as male, leaders of the legal profession. The American nuclear monopoly is gone. We have learned—and perhaps have forgotten—what the French learned in Vietnam: Massive military force is no match for the desires of the local population. The best and brightest made us yearn for the not-so-good and the not-so-smart. The United States, however, still has over 300,000 soldiers stationed in Europe.

Note: The text of this essay is based on remarks by Representative Schroeder at a Harvard Law School Forum, March 16, 1987.

I want to discuss American troops stationed in Europe and in Japan. Let me provide you with a few basic facts:

- The United States has 325,000 soldiers permanently stationed in Western Europe and 50,000 in Japan.
- The North Atlantic Treaty Organization (NATO) eats up somewhere between one-third and one-half of all American defense expenditures.
- Germany and Japan plead poverty when asked to increase their contributions to their own defense, but are beating the stuffing out of us in international economic competition.
- The United States spends about seven percent of its gross domestic product on defense; Germany spends about three and a half percent and Japan spends one percent.
- The government is likely to spend $200 billion more than it collects in 1987, and the balance of trade is the worst in American history and continues to worsen.
- Over the last 20 years, the United States has been involved in military conflicts and threats of conflict in Central America, Southeast Asia, the Middle East, and the Persian Gulf—everywhere, in fact, except in Europe.
- The administration asked in its 1987 budget submission that the cap on the number of troops stationed in Europe be lifted so that more can be stationed there.

I do not advocate that the United States cut loose and run from its commitments. Rather, I think there are strong arguments that now is the time to begin reducing the number of troops we have stationed abroad. And this argument does not come from any recurrence of isolationism or a Fortress America mentality.

The history of the conversion of our postwar army of occupation into permanently stationed troops committed to the Atlantic Alliance is rich. The turning point came in 1951, after communist forces invaded Korea. The debate focused largely on whether Germany could be trusted with military power. Administration officials took pains to point out that the troop commitment was not perpetual. The decision to dispatch four divisions to Europe came on the heels of the communist invasion of Korea. And it came just as Europe was starting its recovery from World War II. Even while the Marshall Plan was helping to rebuild, no one could argue that the defense of the European landmass against a massive Soviet invasion could be handled by European countries.

While times have changed, the stationing of a huge American army in Europe has not. The economies of our European allies have recovered to a point where they are able to compete—and often to defeat us—in world trade. The Soviet threat has not diminished; yet, 35 years of experience has taught us a great deal about how, where, and under what circumstances Soviet expansionism and adventurism is likely to be expressed. Few military planners consider the risk of a World War II–style tank blitzkrieg over the soil of Europe high.

While the initial justification for the huge American military commitment has vanished, that is not, as they say in law school, dispositive. What about new justifications? Let's examine a few.

To begin, let's look at whether our stationing huge numbers of troops overseas makes budgetary sense. Since the current big defense buildup began in 1979, defense spending has gone from $105 billion, or 4.8 percent of gross national product (GNP) a year, to $300 billion, or 6.4 percent of GNP a year. The deficit has gone from $40 billion, or 1.6 percent of GNP, to $200 billion, or 5.5 percent of GNP. The American people have indicated to pollsters and at the polls that the current level of defense spending is either high enough or too high. While defense spending is not the sole cause of the massive deficit, it is surely a large contributing factor.

The problem is that the Pentagon buys on the installment plan. We ordered ships, planes, and tanks in the early eighties, but we have to pay for what we ordered during the late eighties. The costs of manning these ships and training pilots to fly these planes guarantee that defense spending will increase for the rest of the century. In other words, cutting or even holding steady defense spending will not be possible unless we reduce the number of military personnel. And troops stationed abroad cost more—far more—than troops stationed at home.

Unless we are willing to admit we made a mistake and mothball a $4 billion carrier or two, there is no plausible way to reduce the navy's personnel needs. Indeed, in the next few years, the navy's personnel needs will grow beyond anything we can realistically afford. As for the air force, strategic deterrence and control of the skies require maintaining approximately current levels. The army, on the other hand, has 780,000 active-duty troops and another 800,000 in the national guard and the reserves. Why do we have a standing army of 780,000 men and women?

A conventional war of attrition, such as World War II, would be fought with a massive army, but one mobilized when the need arose from reserves and through a draft. American soldiers made the difference in World Wars I and II; yet, there had been no American troops stationed in Europe before either war. In the nuclear age, however, a conventional war of attrition is a fairly remote possibility. And in an all-out nuclear war, there obviously is little use for a large army. Rather, it appears that the main reason we maintain a large standing army is to be able to station large numbers of troops in Western Europe. If there is no good military reason for doing so, would it not make sense to reduce the number of active-duty troops and, thereby, make substantial defense savings? While the budget deficit should not cause us to endanger our national security in any way, it makes us scrutinize and rethink the motive behind all expensive government policies.

So, let's examine our troop commitment from a military point of view. What I would like to see happen is for the United States to reduce its forces in Europe and Japan and to have our allies fill in those needs. Our allies have been somewhat lackadaisical in meeting promises to increase military spending. Indeed, no NATO country, besides the United States, has met the commitment to increase defense spending by three percent per year. And it is not clear that a reduction in American commitment to NATO would be met with increased spending by NATO allies. On the other hand, a reduction in the number of American troops stationed on the Iron Curtain would require our NATO allies to take more responsibility for their own security needs.

There is an oft stated, but not unquestioned, view that the Western Alliance could not, in a conventional manner, resist a Warsaw Pact invasion of Western Europe for more than a couple of days. This alleged truth leads to two conclusions: first, that the NATO allies will trust our commitment to protect Western Europe only if we have a third of a million troops stationed there; second, that the presence of this American trip-wire means that a Soviet attack will be met with an American nuclear counterattack, ensuring that the Soviets think long and hard before crossing through the Iron Curtain.

I think each term of this logical chain is faulty. If the Warsaw Pact were able to mobilize in secret and launch a full-scale, surprise blitzkrieg across the middle of Germany, it is possible that the "two days until Armageddon" scenario might play out. But this is not realistic. Our intelligence, both human and technical, is good enough to learn of any mobilization. And advance knowledge would give us the ability to blunt the Soviet attack. In the ensuing war of attrition, each side would have advantages. The Warsaw Pact has greater numbers of troops and tanks, while we have better-quality reinforcements, control of the seas, likely control of the air, and better smart munitions. If the Soviets failed to destroy the Western infrastructure in the first few days, the need for resorting to the first use of nuclear weapons would dissolve.

As to the conclusion that an American trip-wire is essential to reassure our allies, I think it is clear that the United States could not long survive with economic freedom and democracy if Western Europe fell to the Soviet Union. Whether we have 300,000 or 300 Americans in Europe, the American trip-wire exists. No one seriously believes anymore that a Fortress America could survive in a hostile world. Our commitment to the protection of Western Europe is so much in our self-interest, the claim that troops are needed rings hollow. Our commitment to Europe should never be measured by the number of soldiers we have stationed there.

In Europe we have thousands of nuclear warheads: in planes; on ships; on short-range, medium-range, and long-range missiles, guided and ballistic. They are called theater nuclear weapons for good reason: They are theatrical props, designed not for actual use, but to make a point. While we huff and puff about first use in peacetime, the presumption against their use is so strong that it would take a truly extraordinary set of circumstances for us to push the button. The argument that Europeans demand a trip-wire of American soldiers to ensure the credibility of an American threat of first use of nuclear weapons in the event of a Warsaw Pact invasion is bizarre. Europeans are well aware that nuclear war in Europe would destroy their homelands.

One more military factor should be noted. In the last decade, the United States has pre-positioned in Europe huge stocks of equipment and weapons. So, instead of its taking 3–6 months for reinforcements from the States to be ready to fight in Europe, as was true in World War II, it is now a matter of a week or 10 days. In other words, if we reduce the number of American troops stationed in Europe, we still have the ability to deploy and fight an effective conventional land war in very short order.

So, the historical reason for our troop commitment has evaporated, reducing that commitment is one direct way to deal with the deficit, and there is no compelling military reason for continuing the huge American presence in Europe. But how about our foreign relations?

From an international relations point of view, it makes a great deal of sense for us to announce our decision to slowly reduce troop levels. Up until now, we have been Uncle Sucker; indeed, we have been stretching the flag too thin. We protect Pacific sea lanes so that the Japanese can concentrate on selling Subarus to our ski team. We provide security to Germany so the Germans can build supercomputers faster than we can. It is not surprising that many of our allies do not want us to reduce the number of troops we have stationed in their countries. If they had to spend more of their own resources on defense of their own territories or lines of commerce, their ability to thrash us in international trade would be weakened. The strong popular opposition to a large American presence in Spain and Greece tells us that many Europeans consider the presence of American troops and nuclear weapons on their land more of a threat than a Soviet invasion would be.

I oppose protectionism in trade. I think that any trade barriers we erect will be matched by reciprocal barriers by our trading partners. Still, it is a bit silly that we are such free traders, we subsidize our competitors by paying the cost of their own defense.

The final aspect of this issue is arms control. Richard Perle came before the Armed Services Committee in March of 1987 to say that troop withdrawal would be particularly bad if an INF treaty were signed. At the same appearance, he also pointed out that we would handle a ban on intermediate-range nuclear missiles by placing the same number of warheads on short-range missiles. Since short-range missiles can go up to 600 miles, such a transition would ensure that insofar as the use of tactical nuclear weapons in response to a Soviet blitzkrieg would be necessary, the military equation would remain about the same.

For the past fifteen years, American and Soviet negotiators have been meeting to discuss mutual and balanced force reductions. These talks have never gotten off the ground. Perhaps, the United States should table a plan to reduce the number of American troops stationed in Europe as a way to entice the Soviets to join in real troop reductions at the Iron Curtain. Troop reductions could be a great opening to further breakthroughs on arms control.

In sum, I believe the arguments for withdrawing troops from Europe and reducing our military commitments in the Far East are persuasive. It is not in our interest to bankrupt our country to do for our allies what they can do for themselves. I strongly support our relationships with Japan and the Atlantic Alliance. But, like all relationships, they are strongest if they are based on equality and fairness. There is nothing fair and equal about these relationships now.

I have talked about the past, but I prefer to talk about the future. It's almost the twenty-first century; in fact, the turn of the century is closer in time than my graduation from Harvard Law School. We should ask what kind of world we want to live in after the turn of the century. The United States cannot afford to police the world. And our allies cannot afford to allow us to continue to patrol their borders. It is in our interest, in the interest of the Europeans and of the Japanese, and in the interest of world peace to develop a more cooperative, a more equal partnership among members of the Western Alliance. Ideally, the world I would like to see in the twenty-first century is one without nuclear weapons, without superpower conflict, without the gnawing, ever-present threat of destruction of humanity. This goal may elude us; a goal we can attain, however, is a fair and equal partnership with our allies and a reduction of tension with the Soviets.

In 1988, we are facing a key presidential election. Candidates have too often in the past gotten away with mouthing shopworn platitudes in answer to questions about East-West relations and war and peace. I hope that we can force a more serious debate on these issues in the coming months.

CHAPTER 22

Revitalizing America's Economy Through Economic Conversion

Congressman Ted Weiss

THERE ARE TWO FUNDAMENTAL imperatives that should draw our attention to economic conversion. First, we must reverse our nation's current economic decline. Second, we must bring a halt to the nuclear arms race, which threatens to extinguish life on this planet.

The current state of the American economy is cause for serious concern. While the unemployment picture has moderated somewhat from its worst levels, joblessness remains at epidemic proportions. The nation's infrastructure is in disrepair, and many of our key industries are collapsing in the face of stiff foreign competition. And the federal deficit remains at absolutely unprecedented levels, contributing to a massive trade imbalance and threatening a long-term decline in productivity.

How can we turn our economy around and fight this distressing decline in American industrial competence? Conventional wisdom, endorsed wholeheartedly by the current administration, suggests that military spending is a powerful spur to economic growth. If we reduce this spending, the argument goes, we may severely damage our economy and eliminate the prospects for growth.

Nothing could be further from the truth. A growing body of evidence explodes the myth of prosperity through continually increased arms production. Slowly but surely, people around the country are beginning to realize that military spending is not the solution to our economic ills, but a major cause of industrial decline.

It is apparent to all that we are shifting the burden of paying for our military hardware to future generations through deficits of massive proportions. These deficits are themselves a severe threat to our nation's economic future. But Seymour Melman, of Columbia University, and other economists have described unique elements of the military economy that have also contributed to a growing economic crisis.

The military economy is unique in that the money spent on the military has left our economy for good. Production focused on defense creates nothing of value for consumers or producers. No one will ever ride a Trident II missile to the office or live in a Minuteman silo.

Moreover, increased productivity is sacrificed when more and more resources are devoted to military, rather than civilian, purposes. In other words, not only are the dollars in the military budget unavailable for other uses, but the added benefits that commonly result from civilian production are lost.

There is also compelling evidence that military production creates significantly fewer jobs than comparable spending in the civilian sphere. For instance, total employment per $1 billion spent is estimated at 20,715 for guided missile and space vehicle production. This compares with 30,394 jobs created in the motor vehicles industry and 71,550 in education services, according to the Bureau of Labor Statistics.

The time has come to recognize that the military budget is an oppressive drag on our economy. The vast production resources exhausted by the arms race would, if applied to the civilian economy, encourage productive development on a national scale, reversing the current dangerous decline of key industries. Economic conversion provides us the means to achieve this crucial transformation.

However, economic conversion is not only an economic imperative. It is also essential if we hope to make meaningful progress toward arms control.

We are all aware of the overwhelming challenge facing this nation and the world. The nuclear arms race is in an extraordinarily dangerous phase that threatens the human race with extinction. In order for us to survive as a species, we must halt and reverse the worldwide arms race.

Despite this urgency, we have become accustomed in recent years to monstrous defense budget requests. Many of the weapons approved by Congress are unnecessary for the defense of our nation, and some actually increase the risk of war.

Everyone agrees that proposals for increased military spending should be assessed on their merits for the defense of our nation. Far too often, however, the deciding factor is not merit, but the ability of a particular weapons system to preserve or create jobs.

Year after year, as crucial votes on defense matters approach, members of Congress are urged to approve weapons—not because they are needed for the defense of our nation, but because they will create jobs in the members' home districts. The B-1 bomber, for example, is said to have survived because its components are manufactured in more congressional districts than any other weapon. And during debate of the MX missile, members of Congress circulated on the House floor urging their colleagues to support that missile on the basis of the number of jobs that would be created in their home districts.

In an era of chronic unemployment, concern about joblessness is legitimate and understandable. But when it serves to encourage the approval of unneeded weapons of mass destruction, it becomes a tragedy for all involved. It is a tragedy for the workers who produce these weapons, because their interests would be better served by appropriate civilian spending. And it is a tragedy for all people around the world, who face a likelier prospect of nuclear annihilation because of this added fueling of the arms race.

By creating viable alternatives to military spending, economic conversion would assure the millions of workers in military-dependent industries that their jobs will not be sacrificed in the effort to achieve meaningful arms control. As a result, proposals for increased military spending would more likely be assessed on their merits, rather than for reasons of job creation. This would significantly enhance the prospects for ending the nuclear arms race.

There are now important signs that economic conversion is gaining attention and support. As of the summer of 1987, two congressional hearings had been held on this subject, and more than 50 members were cosponsoring my bill, the Defense Economic Adjustment Act. I am hopeful that once the Congress has been fully educated on this issue, it will move to consider seriously the enactment of an economic conversion program.

The bill I have introduced, H.R. 813, recognizes that conversion to alternative production is a complex, multiyear process, which must be planned at different levels: at the national level with respect to capital resources; and at the enterprise and factory level for the detailed blueprinting of alternative products. The bill also calls for the involvement and expertise of planners at all of these levels. The cornerstone of H.R. 813 is the Alternative Use Committees it mandates in each military facility of 100 workers or more. These committees, composed half of labor and half of management, are charged with developing detailed blueprint-ready plans for civilian manufacture. Without careful planning for conversion, a decision to halt or reduce military production would create little else than increased unemployment and economic disruption.

Local conversion planning in the Alternative Use Committees would be coordinated at the national level by a Defense Economic Adjustment Council. The council would include cabinet members, the chairman of the president's Council of Economic Advisors, and representatives of labor unions and the nonmilitary business community. It would develop concrete plans for public projects that address human needs, and act as a clearinghouse on existing federal programs relevant to communities affected by military cutbacks. In addition, the council would develop a conversion guidelines handbook as a complete how-to guide for local conversion planners.

The council is purposely conceived of as a distinct federal entity and not a part of the Department of Defense, since we are seeking to transform portions of the military economy to civilian production, not to militarize the civilian economy. The Department of Defense has condoned the practice in military-serving industries of maximizing, rather than minimizing, production costs. Unless we can successfully retrain employees who have been participants in that process, the civilian enterprises they engage in will not survive in a competitive marketplace.

H.R. 813 also calls for one year's advance notification of plans to cut back or terminate a defense contract or a military base. The Defense Economic Adjustment Council would be responsible for informing the appropriate local officials and Alternative Use Committees of pending cutbacks.

Finally, the bill provides assistance for communities and workers while a conversion is under way. Communities seriously affected by defense cutbacks would be eligible for federal planning assistance. Similarly, individual workers would be eligible for adjustment benefits, including unemployment benefits, maintenance of pension and health benefits, and funds for retraining.

The provisions of H.R. 813 would be supported by an Economic Adjustment Fund. Defense contractors would be required to pay 1.25 percent of their gross revenues into the fund annually. In addition, the government would pay 10 percent of the projected savings from cancelled contracts into the fund. Because the only government contribution would come from cancelled contracts, this funding mechanism will not contribute at all to the budget deficit.

Here's how the plan would work: If Congress terminated a military contract, the local Alternative Use Committee would be notified in advance. This committee would then put in motion its existing plan to convert the affected plant to civilian production. The federal government would provide guidance and support for the workers and their community, but the new enterprise would receive no subsidy and would have to compete on its own in the marketplace.

A number of military contractors have attempted to produce civilian products without engaging in the kind of planning that is mandated by H.R. 813. Without exception, such attempts have failed, precisely because the firms involved did not engage in conversion planning. Yet, it is exactly these failures that conversion opponents point to in asserting that conversion will not work. These opponents—including the Reagan administration's Department of Defense—fail to distinguish between real economic conversion that is backed up by the mechanisms contained in H.R. 813 and some defense contractors' willy-nilly attempts to experiment with civilian products.

The case of Boeing-Vertol, a division of the Boeing Company located in Philadelphia, is particulary instructive. Primarily a producer of military helicopters, Boeing-Vertol won orders for electric trolleys and subway cars in the early 1970s. However, because the firm did not engage in any organized form of conversion planning, the product was a spectacular failure. In his book *Profits Without Production*, Melman reports on the status of trolley cars ordered for use in Boston:

> By June 27, 1979, the [Massachusetts Bay Transportation Authority] gave the following accounting of the 175 vehicles that had been ordered from Boeing-Vertol in 1973. On the previous day, 30 of these vehicles were in service. Of the rest: 40 were never delivered, 35 were returned to Boeing, 19 were extensively damaged, five were under modification, 24 were awaiting maintenance, five were awaiting parts, three were awaiting inspection, and 14 were in maintenance.

It is clear from Melman's description that the project failed because Boeing-Vertol maintained production techniques associated with military aerospace technology instead of adjusting its techniques for civilian design.

The Defense Department, using twisted logic, contends that Boeing-Vertol's experience demonstrates that economic conversion is not feasible. But if H.R. 813 had been enacted into law, Boeing would have planned for an alternative product and retrained its workers for civilian enterprise. Success, though not guaranteed, would have been far more likely.

Rather than leave conversion planning to the whim of the companies involved, H.R. 813 mandates that the prerequisites for a successful conversion be fulfilled by every military contractor. The comprehensive plan for economic conversion contained in H.R. 813 would provide a significant impetus for meaningful arms control. It would free us from the tyranny of jobs blackmail in the approval of military contracts, and allow us to pursue a lasting peace wholeheartedly without sacrificing our commitment to full employment. It would also contribute to our nation's long-term economic survival by providing the resources for the revitalization of basic industries and the repair of our infrastructure.

Economic conversion would also be a strong unifying force in our society, for it bridges the gap between two of the most important progressive movements in our nation—the labor movement and the peace movement. These groups have traditionally been cast as adversaries because of the loss of jobs resulting from the cancellation of military contracts. But economic conversion provides for their cooperation—a cooperation that is essential if we are to return sanity to our foreign and military policies.

Moreover, conversion could unite the peace and labor communities behind a single candidate or party. Thus, it could operate as a formidable electoral weapon. The Democratic Party should recognize that the way to stand for jobs *and* peace is to include economic conversion as a key element of its program for the future. And it must recognize that doing this will yield electoral benefits. The way to convert the White House to Democratic hands is to adopt a plan to convert our bloated military economy to civilian production.

Economic conversion provides the hope that humanity will manage to survive into a peaceful and prosperous future. I have high hopes that the conditions for a successful conversion program can be created if we join together to raise this issue to the top of our national agenda.

CHAPTER 23

Toward Real National Security: The Reagan Legacy and Defense Requirements for the 1990s

Gordon Adams

THE LEGACY OF THE REAGAN-WEINBERGER BUILDUP

Six years, seven defense budgets, and $1.8 trillion after the election of Ronald Reagan, a chorus of criticism surrounds American national security policy. Performance failures, acquisition waste, contractor fraud, and contradictory policies have all been targets. The underlying problem, however, has been the absence of a clear, concise, and carefully framed rationale for policy. The Reagan-Weinberger approach to national defense has been fiscal, but the rationale has been so broad as to permit unlimited expenditures.

As Secretary Weinberger stated in 1983, "it would be a grave mistake for our strategy to focus only on what seemed the most dangerous threats, or the most plausible ones." Rather, the United States should be prepared to fight "across the entire spectrum of conflict" from terrorism to nuclear war in virtually any theater.[1] As the Pentagon's *Defense*

Guidance described it, American security was best ensured by having the ability to fight and prevail in a protracted nuclear war, to bring war directly home to Soviet ports, to open a second front against the Soviets in Asia, to engage in major combat in the Middle East, to maintain control over the high seas, and to intervene rapidly and in force in combat situations in the Third World.[2]

Moved by the apparent popular mandate for this program, Congress provided 95 percent of the Pentagon's requested budgets between fiscal year (FY) 1981 and FY 1985. By 1985, the Pentagon budget had doubled from $144 billion to $295 billion; average annual growth was 9.3 percent after inflation. In FY 1987, despite deficit reduction efforts under Gramm-Rudman-Hollings, defense spending was higher, in constant (uninflated) dollars, than it had been in any peacetime year since 1946.[3]

Thanks to its limitless policy and virtually unlimited funding, the Reagan-Weinberger Pentagon has left a dangerous legacy for the next administration:

- A buildup meant to convince the Soviets they could not surpass U.S. military strength and should negotiate arms control has neither halted Soviet military spending nor produced a strategic arms control agreement. According to Pentagon and Central Intelligence data, the U.S. buildup has done little to change the quantitative military balance between U.S. and Soviet military forces.[4] While the Soviets have made substantial negotiating concessions on European nuclear weapons, verification, and deep cuts in strategic forces, only a symbolically important but militarily meaningless agreement on intermediate-range nuclear forces in Europe has resulted. Though the Strategic Defense Initiative (SDI) may have helped bring the Russians to the table, Reagan has refused to negotiate on this program, making it a limited incentive for real progress. The Pentagon now hopes to push SDI to the point of abrogating the most significant existing arms control agreement with the Soviets—the Anti-Ballistic Missile (ABM) Treaty.[5]

- Although salaries, morale, and personnel quality in the armed forces have improved, training, readiness, and the ability to sustain combat are paying the price as the defense budget has focused on adding new hardware. The army has not grown, and the navy is now roughly 30,000 behind in its manpower needs for what approaches a 600-ship fleet. The rate at which new combat hardware is being added is well below the rate at which funds are being spent on that equipment.[6] Spending for ammunition and spare parts is low, while other measures of readiness and sustainability have not improved to the degree they should have, given the investment.[7]

- Quality and performance problems plague much of the new military equipment: wing cracks on the F-18 fighter; technical problems with the Aegis ship radar system; performance failures on the (now cancelled) DIVAD air defense gun, the Bradley fighting vehicle, the B-1 bomber and MX missile.

- Actual military performance in Lebanon, Grenada, and Libya has revealed weaknesses in planning and execution that are evidence, in part, that interservice rivalry and bureaucratic parochialism are hampering military effectiveness.[8]

- Despite deficit reduction efforts, actual defense spending has continued to grow. The Weinberger budgets focused on hardware, funds for which are spent slowly, leading to a growing spending backlog. As a result, outlays continue to rise, and the Defense Department is losing flexibility to adjust its program and make changes in its budget plans.[9]

- Throwing money at hardware programs has led directly to Pentagon and industry waste, abuse, and mismanagement, which will have to be brought under control.

- Current Pentagon research programs are bringing a whole new generation of weapons into production in the next three years: the Trident II, Midgetman and advanced cruise missiles, Stealth bomber, C-17 cargo plane, SSN-21 submarine, LHX helicopter, and new air force and navy fighters. This will mean a whole new "bow wave" of defense procurement in the 1990s,

with unpredictable costs and a need for significant
new operations and support funds.

- Rapid growth in defense spending has aggravated an
  unusually large federal deficit, forcing harsh trade-offs
  between defense and funds for vital domestic needs.
  Myriad measures of domestic security—including
  poverty rates, infant mortality levels, and homelessness—indicate that some standards of economic and
  social well-being have deteriorated since 1980.

- Finally, the continuation of military conflict in a wide
  number of areas suggests that the world is hardly a
  safer place under the Reagan Doctrine. U.S. defense
  policy has exacerbated the conflicts in Central America
  and Angola, while it has been powerless to encourage
  peaceful resolution of conflicts in Ethiopia, Iran and
  Iraq, Lebanon, Afghanistan, or South Africa.

THE NEED FOR A COHERENT, REALISTIC ALTERNATIVE

The 1988 presidential elections offer an opportunity to define a policy that can provide greater security for the United
States through greater stability in U.S.-Soviet relations, a
reduced risk of military combat in Europe, and a more responsible U.S. role in the Third World. Through such a
stability-oriented policy, we can reduce our reliance on strategic weapons for anything other than deterrence of nuclear
attack, restructure European forces to provide assured security at less cost, and decrease naval forces and redesign
lighter land forces responsible for contingencies in other
parts of the globe. The U.S. military would be leaner, while
adequate to ensure national strength, more closely tailored
to security requirements and to available funding, and more
efficient.

What is needed is a commonsense security policy between the extremes of a "tough talk" school, which tends to
portray the Soviets as 10 feet tall and calls for greater U.S.
military spending to catch up, and a "utopian" school,
which goes too far in seeking to cut back the military in a

dangerous and difficult world. Such a new national security policy needs to meet one overarching standard: It must, within the limits of available resources, defend the United States and protect its interests, while seeking to ensure global stability. This policy needs to confront and deal with four critical dilemmas:

(1) How can the United States deal with the reality of Soviet military power while making arms control an integral part of national security policy, reducing the risk of nuclear or conventional war between the superpowers? What forces and what agreements will ensure stability and mutual security in the U.S.-Soviet relationship?

(2) How can the United States help Europeans on both sides of the Iron Curtain find new ways to ensure security and stability in Europe with fewer nuclear or conventional military forces?

(3) What can the United States do to limit the ferocity of armed conflict in the Third World and prevent such conflict from escalating to a superpower confrontation?

(4) How large should the defense budget be to sustain the forces needed to achieve these goals, and how can the acquisition and operational activities of the Pentagon be managed to acquire and use such forces more effectively?

RELATIONS WITH THE SOVIET UNION: THE SEARCH FOR STABILITY

The Soviets are six feet tall, not 10, but they are militarily powerful, politically ambitious (generally, cautiously so), and internally troubled. By and large, U.S. armed forces, in combination with our allies, are a more than adequate deterrent to the Soviet military. Our central defense problem in this arena involves strategic nuclear forces. The existing U.S. arsenal is as diverse and survivable as can be expected in a world where all nuclear forces are vulnerable. U.S. (and Soviet) strategic policies, however, are pushing toward the next generation of nuclear technology, with less visibility, greater accuracy, longer range, and higher speed. Defensive technologies promise phantom security, but deliver the reality of an accelerated race between offense and defense.

United States policies should seek to ensure the survivability of both the U.S. and the Soviet deterrents, moving away from the temptation to use nuclear weapons first. Such policies should also eliminate incentives for either side to develop or deploy the next, destabilizing generation of offensive strategic weapons. The opportunity for successful diplomacy is now as ripe as it has been since 1945. It is important to make arms control and nuclear weapons policies integral parts of strategic thinking, since arms control gives us access to and influence over Soviet choices.

A new administration should develop a serious arms limitation and reduction strategy, including confidence-building measures in strategic command and control, a formal consultative process on treaty violations, mutual exchanges of information on verification, agreements on a nuclear test ban, and a permanent antisatellite warfare ban (strongly in the interests of both superpowers, who depend on satellites for verification of each other's military developments).

With respect to overall strategic forces, U.S. policy should focus on deep reductions in the strategic arsenals of both superpowers, which could lead to the following major changes in the U.S. arsenal over the next decade:

- The gradual elimination of all strategic nuclear systems that are inherently destabilizing because of their range, speed, accuracy, or stealth: the MX missile, any heavy, multiple-warhead version of the Midgetman missile, and nuclear sea-launched cruise missiles
- Limitations on the deployment of the Trident II missile, with counterforce capability[10]
- Serious reexamination of the current plans for the Midgetman missile, which (with only one warhead) has less counterforce capability than the MX, but remains highly vulnerable, despite plans to make it mobile
- Review of the role of the strategic bomber force, based on the B-52 and the B-1B, carrying air-launched cruise missiles, and possible elimination of the potentially

destabilizing stealth bomber and advanced cruise missile programs

- Continued research on the Strategic Defense Initiative only at a far lower level, in the framework of an arms control agreement

EUROPE: ENSURING INCREASED STABILITY

U.S. policy continues to define Soviet intentions in Europe as aggressive and Warsaw Pact conventional forces as significantly superior to those of NATO. Nuclear arms control, it is argued, will make major U.S. and European expenditures necessary in order to ensure that NATO continues to deter the Warsaw Pact.[11] It is tempting, from this perspective, to call for beefing up conventional forces and to "bash" the allies for their presumed failure to make up the conventional military deficit.[12]

In reality, for more than two decades, the North Atlantic Treaty Organization (NATO) has maintained active-duty military forces numbering well over five million, including 325,00 American troops, along with large military reserves. NATO antiarmor forces, fighter aircraft, and surface naval forces surpassing those of the Warsaw Pact, and the alliance substantially outspends the pact on defense. Moreover, the allies make a signficant contribution to NATO's forces.[13]

U.S. policy toward Europe should seek to continue and deepen the military stability of the European theater. Negotiations to reduce U.S. and European active-duty military forces, in common with the Warsaw Pact, would both add to such stability and save budgetary resources.[14] Other defense policy changes should follow:

- U.S. nuclear policy should move to a "no first use" position in Europe. Through arms control negotiations with the Soviets, intermediate-range nuclear weapons (ground-launched cruise missiles and the Pershing II) should be removed. In addition, the United States will begin to denuclearize its ground, air, and naval forces assigned to NATO.[15] Such nuclear capabilities provide little security, since their use would devastate the battlefield and move a conventional combat situation toward a strategic nuclear exchange between the superpowers.

- Conventional arms control should be integral to U.S. policy, both as a way to constrain Warsaw Pact options and to limit the resources the United States and its allies must spend on conventional defense.[16] Confidence-building measures between the two alliances are already proceeding, and there are significant signs that the Soviet Union is prepared to move on conventional force reductions talks. Some U.S. forces should remain in Europe in order to fulfill NATO's other mission— ensuring that the West Germans do not expand their own conventional forces because they feel the United States is no longer committed to their defense.[17]
- Doctrine and weaponry for existing NATO conventional forces need to be rethought, with an emphasis on defensive positioning, reinforcing NATO capabilities to withstand tank charges, and elimination of destabilizing "deep strike" weapons. In order to reinforce the defensive capabilities of the alliance, NATO spending could increase for ammunition supplies, antiarmor rounds, U.S. military equipment prepositioned in Europe, hardened airfields, and sealift capabilities.
- The navy need not expand to 15 carriers, since its mission of attacking Soviet naval ports would disappear.[18]

THE THIRD WORLD: CENTER OF STRESS AND CHANGE

U.S. defense policy assumes that the right mix of economic assistance and military intervention, equipment, and training is the best recipe for defending American interests in Asia, Africa, and Latin America, since virtually any change (other than an authoritarian dictatorship) not only has been detrimental to U.S. interests, but has benefited—or even has resulted—from Soviet intervention.

This approach leads to constant U.S. intervention and ignores the fact that change is a basic reality in the Third

World, as less-developed countries search for structures of government that make sense internally; face natural calamities that shred fragile economic fabrics; depend on developed countries for investment capital, economic aid, and markets; negotiate frontiers inherited from the colonial era; or sort out ethnic groups and tribes from nations.

The central U.S. interest is to continue to have working relationships with all countries regardless of the party in power. Global U.S. military deployments and covert intervention increase the risk of direct U.S. involvement and of the escalation of conflict to a superpower confrontation. The United States should do what it can to assist peaceful change, while ensuring, as far as possible, that no local conflict becomes the "Sarajevo" from which global conflict grows. Rhetoric to the contrary, U.S. (and Soviet) leverage over the outcome of such conflicts is minimal.[19] This is not to say that the Soviets and Cubans do not meddle in the Third World, but the impact of such meddling is secondary to the domestic forces at work in those countries.

A new administration has a unique opportunity to bring coherence and change to U.S. policies toward the Third World:

- A redefined policy does not require a 600-ship navy, though such will be its size by 1989. Additional carriers are unnecessary. Rather, resources might be put toward strengthening submarine and antisubmarine warfare capabilities, and large carriers could be replaced by smaller ones, carrying vertical, short takeoff and landing aircraft, as military reformers propose.
- Large U.S. conventional forces already exist for those U.S. military activities in the Third World that may be appropriate; more are not needed. Existing forces could be better coordinated and trained, as the experiences of Lebanon and Grenada suggest. The Marine Corps is a highly skilled and adequate body for most contingencies U.S. forces could face; new army light divisions are wasteful and unnecessary.

MANAGING THE PENTAGON TO MEET THESE GOALS

Better Pentagon management is crucial in order to create a more effective deterrent and fighting force, scaled to meet commonsense military missions in the framework of achieving a more stable world:

- Four decades of Pentagon box shuffling has not substantially improved planning or management. Most important today are changes that more closely connect the definition of military goals and missions, budgetary planning, and program management. Joint commanders, who have an overview of the military requirements for a given theater, should be given a more central planning position, and there may be merit, in the long run, in exploring the possibility of restructuring the four services along mission lines, thereby eliminating redundancies and rivalries.
- Some basic changes would make an important contribution to Pentagon efficiency. Honest "should cost" reporting by contractors, plus serious independent cost analysis in the office of the secretary of defense, would help the cost control and waste problem. The investigative work of the Defense Department's inspector general's office should be continued and expanded. Contracting incentives should be restructured to reward contractors for lower cost production. Greater competition in contracting is still needed. Over the long run, serious consideration might be given to removing the military services from the process of negotiating, signing, and supervising contracts for research and development and procurement of weapons and supplies, and having the military focus on military, rather than bureaucratic, combat.

This national security alternative would provide greater stability in the three central theaters of U.S. concern, as well as a different defense force, emphasizing reduced reliance on strategic weapons for anything other than deterrence of nuclear attack, restructured European forces that provide stability and assured security at less cost, and a reduction of naval forces and restructuring of lighter land forces for contingencies in the Third World. The globe would be more stable, and the U.S. military would be leaner, but more efficient and more closely tailored to security requirements.

There would be budgetary advantages to such a policy as well. The major error of the Reagan-Weinberger defense policy was to assume that more resources meant better security. An overflow of resources has, instead, encouraged unrestrained budgeting, poor planning and priority setting, and loose management in the Defense Department and the defense industry. A more restrained defense budget, designed to reconfigure the force structure to meet appropriate goals, would do more than help reduce the federal deficit: It would encourage rethinking the relationship between national security policy goals, missions, and forces; improve priority setting; and foster more effective management of scarce resources.

---

1. Department of Defense, *Annual Report to the Congress, Fiscal Year 1984*, U.S. Government Printing Office, Washington, D.C., pp. 15–18, 31–40.
2. Quoted in detail in R. Halloran, *To Arm a Nation: Rebuilding America's Endangered Defenses*, Macmillan, New York, 1986, Chs. 7 and 9. This guidance bore little relationship to Pentagon procurement planning. According to an analysis of this strategy by the Joint Chiefs of Staff, in order to carry it out, U.S. armed forces would have to grow from 16 to 23 army divisions, from 13 to 24 aircraft carriers, from 24 to 44 air wings, and from 304 to 1,308 airlift aircraft, while the defense budget would have to contain $750 billion more than the five-year forecast through FY 1988.
3. In wartime, only peak spending for the Korean War (in 1953) and the Vietnam War (in 1968) have surpassed the 1987 level in constant dollars.
4. See: Department of Defense, *Soviet Military Power*, annual volumes, Washington, D.C., 1981, 1983–1987; and J. Collins, *U.S.-Soviet Military Balance, 1980–1985*, Congressional Research Service, Washington, D.C., 1985.
5. See the interpretation of the ABM Treaty offered by Senator Sam Nunn in *Congressional Record*, March 11, 1987, pp. S2967–2986; March 12, 1987, pp. S3090–3096; and March 13, 1987, pp. S3171–3173.

6. See: L. Aspin, *Defense Budgets Up—Whither Security?: What Have We Gotten for a Trillion Dollars?* House Armed Services Committee, Washington, D.C., 1985; and Congressional Budget Office (CPO), "Defense Spending: What Has Been Accomplished?" staff working paper, Washington, D.C., April 1985.

7. See: Aspin, op. cit.; CBO, op. cit; and staff report of the House Defense Appropriations Subcommittee, in House Committee on Appropriations, Subcommittee on Defense, *Department of Defense Appropriations for 1985*, Part 1, U.S. Government Printing Office, Washington, D.C., pp.663–1039.

8. See: R. Gabriel, *Military Incompetence: Why the American Military Doesn't Win*, Hill & Wang, New York, 1985; and R. A. Stubbing, *The Defense Game: An Insider Explores the Astonishing Realities of America's Defense Establishment*, Harper & Row, New York, 1986.

9. The Office of Management and Budget estimates, for example, that while 27 percent of FY 1980 defense outlays were "uncontrollable" because they grew out of made in prior years, contract obligations, that share would rise to 40 percent by FY 1988.

10. The rationale for the Trident II is ambiguous. As a sea-based system, it is less vulnerable than ICBMs, hence stabilizing. As a more accurate upgrade of the Trident I missile, it is a counterforce weapon, hence destabilizing. Deployment of the Trident I, which is equally invulnerable, but less accurate, might be preferable.

11. Some Democrats endorse this version of the European security problem. See: Democratic Leadership Council, *Defending America: Building a New Foundation for National Strength*, Washington, D.C., 1986; Democratic Policy Commission, *New Choices in a Changing America*, Democratic National Committee, Washington, D.C., 1986, and J. Glenn, B. Carter, and R. Komer, *Rethinking Defense and Conventional Forces*, Alternatives for the 80's Paper No. 8, Center for National Policy, Washington, D.C., 1983.

12. Some analysts go so far as to argue that the United States ought to pull all or a significant part of its forces out of Europe, in response to this alleged unequal sharing of the defense burden. See: Halloran, op cit., pp. 253–256.

13. See: J. M. Epstein, *The 1987 Defense Budget*, The Brookings Institution, Washington, D.C., 1986; *The 1988 Defense Budget*, The Brookings Institution, Washington, D.C., 1987, pp.36–45; and T. Gervasi, *The Myth of Soviet Military Supremacy*, Harper & Row, New York, 1986, Ch. 4.

14. See: J. Dean, *Watershed in Europe: Dismantling the East-West Military Confrontation*, Lexington Books, Lexington, Mass., 1986.

15. See: M. Halperin, *Nuclear Fallacy: Dispelling the Myth of Nuclear Strategy*, Ballinger, Cambridge, Mass., 1987.

16. Such arms control would minimize the need for the vast multitude of new weapons systems the services wish to purchase in the

1990s, making it possible to set priorities within the framework of more limited defense resources.

17. Halperin, op. cit., argues that current U.S. force levels committed to Europe should be guaranteed, to help ensure that the West German military does not feel the need to expand. In a wider framework of conventional force reductions on both sides of the Iron Curtain, this may not be necessary.

18. See: Epstein, *The 1988 Defense Budget*, op. cit., pp. 45–49.

19. Although it has improved, Soviet global power projection cannot be compared to the 13 U.S. carrier battle groups, military airlift command, airborne infantry units, and Marine Corps.

CHAPTER 24

Making America Work: A New Social Contract

Governor Bill Clinton

THE JOB OF GOVERNING any state is defined in large measure by the economic realities of our time. Some states and regions are doing well; some are not. Within each state, some people are doing well; some are not.

Clearly, many of our present problems grew out of the painful truth that we were largely unprepared for the onslaught of global economic competition over the last decade and a half. Too many of us for too long took it for granted that America's position as the world's dominant economic power was permanent. Now we know better. Since 1973, real wages have declined 17 percent. Forces of international competition have disrupted the equilibrium of our society and called into question President Kennedy's adage that "a rising tide lifts all boats." Between 1981 and 1986, while several million jobs were added to the economy, 40 percent of Americans suffered a decline in real income, 20 percent held steady, and 40 percent enjoyed an increase.

America has split in other ways as well. Prosperity has a distinctive geographic feature. It can be found largely in the states along the Atlantic and Pacific coasts, and in certain urban areas in the heartland. Most of America's continuing economic distress is found in our "deflation belt," in the states from Canada to the Gulf of Mexico with economies based on agriculture, energy, mining, timber, and import-vulnerable manufacturing.

There have been deep and troubling ruptures in the fabric of American society. In 1985, for the first time ever, the percentage of our elderly citizens living below the poverty line dropped below the percentage of the nonelderly in poverty, a remarkable achievement, of which our country can be proud. Unfortunately, this development was paralleled by a dramatic rise in the number of single-parent households, often headed by divorced women whose incomes dropped markedly after divorce; huge numbers of young women and children in poverty; millions of adults unemployable in today's economy because of their low level of literacy or lack of skills; and high rates of welfare dependency, teen pregnancy, school dropouts, and drug and alcohol abuse. The consequences of these developments can be seen most vividly in the swelling number of the homeless throughout America.

The news is, of course, not all bad. Since 1981, our country has gained about 12 million new jobs, a far greater number than our competition in Europe. There is evidence in virtually every state that more and more manufacturers have been willing to make the hard decisions necessary to increase productivity to internationally competitive levels. And the results of the last few years of effort in education are paying off. Our schools are getting better, and our children are learning more.

It is important for governors to note that many of our problems and some of our sectional prosperity are rooted in international economics and national politics and, therefore, are beyond their direct reach, if not their influence. For example, much of our current trade deficit is a function of the depression in Latin American economies. If the growth rates of the 1970s had prevailed in Latin America in 1986, our trade imbalance would have been 19 percent less. The high value the dollar held until late 1985 worked to subsidize imports and tax our own exports. Furthermore, the dramatic increases in defense spending over the last several years have helped some state economies much more than others.

Government cannot replace or control that moving force within individuals that causes them to abuse drugs, get pregnant while they're teenagers, drop out of school, or remain illiterate or on welfare. Government cannot be a savior, but government cannot be a spectator either. We need a government that can be a catalyst and a partner—one that offers the people the right to participate in the American dream in return for their willingness to assume the responsibilities of citizenship.

MAKING A DIFFERENCE

When I became chairman of the National Governors' Association in the summer of 1986, the governors had been working hard for four years on education reform—one of the most fundamental issues of our time. Our association had just issued a report, *A Time for Results*, on what governors should be doing for the next five years to keep the reform bandwagon rolling and our schools improving. Yet, I assumed the chairmanship with the haunting sense that as critical as these efforts were, we could and should do more.

As important as our education reforms are, they will not reach millions of Americans who face barriers that prevent them from taking full advantage of better schools or even from becoming productive citizens.

As important as it is to prepare our people to succeed in a highly competitive world, education alone will not guarantee them opportunities. They also need sound economic policies to provide good jobs.

Because we plainly have both people problems and economic policy problems that must be addressed before our efforts in education can bear full fruit, I asked the governors to face our responsibilities in these areas—not with more studies, but with action plans and programs.

I appointed the Task Force on Jobs, Growth & Competitiveness to develop solid strategies for state and regional economic development activities, to highlight successful programs, and to explore the extent to which programs in place in prosperous areas would or would not be likely to help more depressed regions.

I also established a welfare prevention project, composed of five task forces dealing with the most widespread and crippling barriers to productive lives in America today: welfare dependency, school dropouts, teen pregnancy, adult illiteracy, and alcohol and drug abuse. The plans developed by these task forces emphasize prevention and are designed to enhance the ability of our people to live up to their God-given capacities and, in so doing, to provide the critical contributions we need from them. The plans are described in the report *Bringing Down the Barriers*.

Together, these two reports comprise the project Making America Work: Productive People, Productive Policies.

The policy recommendations in these reports included many actions already successfully taken in some states. Not all of them are appropriate, or even possible, for other states. But every state will find something of value in the reports, areas in which more can be done to speed the processes of economic transformation and human development, which are critical to our future.

As governors have seen in stark, personal terms, barriers to individuals' productivity entail costs not only to those who live in their shadows, but to the rest of us as well. We must work to break down these barriers, because our capacity to promote economic opportunity is limited by the incapacities of our fellow citizens.

There is no one solution to all the issues dealt with in the Making America Work project, but there are some clear conclusions that any governor, or any American, will reach from reading it.

(1) No matter what burdens or benefits the international economy or national policies may bring to states, practical problem solvers can take steps to reduce the human loss from welfare dependency and other barriers to full development, and to accelerate local economic growth.

(2) It is, therefore, unacceptable for any governor today to sit on the sidelines and avoid tackling these issues head-on.

(3) While we have learned the hard way that we in government cannot solve these problems alone, we have also learned we can't leave them alone. Partnerships with the private sector have enabled states to make progress in other areas. They are essential here, but governors must take the initiative.

(4) We do need some help from Washington—most immediately, a good welfare reform bill and a sustained commitment to reduce the deficit.

(5) While citizens have a right to insist that the states move aggressively in these areas, they also have responsibilities to help the efforts succeed. The heart of the welfare reform proposal developed by the governors during 1986 and 1987 is the contract that conditions the right to benefits on the assumption of personal responsibility to pursue a path to independence, through education, training, and work. The governors' welfare reform proposal is making its way through Congress, and we are continuing to work with congressional leaders to ensure that the measure emerges with our essential proposals in place.

Similarly, local leaders have a right to expect the state to offer every available and affordable economic development initiative, but unless they assume responsibility for making something happen in their hometowns, the state's efforts will be to no avail.

I believe this model could be used to address other national problems. For example, we might increase, rather than decrease, student loans to college students, but require that in return for the right to the loans, students assume the responsibility of spending a few hours each month performing such public service as teaching illiterate adults to read.

(6) Indeed, this model should be at the heart of our efforts to develop a new national agenda, because welfare prevention and competitiveness, like education reform, are issues of interest to all Americans. We cannot maintain our standard of living—or, perhaps, even our security—if we have more incapacitated or underutilized people than our competitors have. That's why investment bankers and defense contractors should care about distressed farmers and at-risk children. We're all in this together.

MAKING A COMMITMENT: A NEW SOCIAL CONTRACT

I believe Americans are coming together on these issues because we want to preserve the American dream. And we know it cannot be done if we continue to behave as a swarm of isolated individuals oblivious to the pain and untapped potential of our fellow citizens.

I believe most of our people are ready to do their part to build a new politics based on a very old idea: a social contract between government and the people in which no right can be asserted without a citizen's being willing to assume a corresponding responsibility. That idea is at the heart of the governors' welfare reform proposal, which requires a person, in return for the right to receive benefits, to assume the responsibility to move toward independence. It is at the heart of our best education reforms, which require of teachers more accountability in return for higher pay and require of students more effort in return for more opportunity.

The states are going to do their part, but we also need an agenda of national unity that will be committed to these new partnerships and will embody neither the uncritical generosity of our past nor the penurious neglect of the present. The principles that guided the governors in developing the Making America Work project should be a part of that agenda.

When I was a small boy, I was taught, as so many of my generation were, that I had to get a good education and work hard so that I could do better than my parents and grandparents had done. Citizens of that time took the overall economic health and strength of America for granted and worked to make sure their children could benefit from it more than they had.

Today, I want my daughter to get a good education—not only for her own benefit, but for me and my generation as well. And I know we need her classmates, some of whom are from very poor families, to do well too, because the future of our great American experiment depends on it.

That is perhaps the fundamental lesson of our time: America won't work if Americans can't work, or learn, or believe in the promise of tomorrow.

CHAPTER 25

National Economic Competitiveness: Ohio's Response

Governor Richard F. Celeste

A *WASHINGTON POST* ARTICLE titled "You Want to Compete with Japan? Ask Ohio" correctly observed that the competitiveness programs in place today were "not the product of Washington wizardry." The states, the article said, are leading an "upheaval in the way America is learning to compete economically in the world."

Across the country, states are carrying out competitiveness strategies using their own resources. With little support and no recognition from the federal government, states are vigorously pursuing far-reaching economic policies in their historic role as laboratories for policy experimentation.

Ohio has developed a strategy involving government, industry, and universities. States like Ohio now recognize that for the United States to hold its own in foreign markets, we must learn from the competition. Just as Japan and Western Europe have demonstrated the benefits of linking universities and industrial bases, states have learned to make the most of their native resources and direct them toward the world market.

Ohio's Thomas Edison Program promotes technological

275

innovation through the cooperation of every major university in the state and over 450 companies. This homegrown effort has three components: seed capital grants, technology incubators, and research consortia. All funds granted by the state must be matched by a firm. This provision stretches the state's investment and serves as an indirect market test for a proposed technology. If the private sector does not want to match the investment, the area is probably best not pursued.

The seed capital program, known as the Edison Seed Development Fund, has backed 73 individual applied research projects. It allows the Edison program to work with any firm in the state and has included the smallest of start-ups, as well as corporate giants such as National Cash Register and General Electric. Technologies have ranged from nonsmear newspaper ink to colorectal cancer probes. Grants are from $50,000 to $250,000, and are made to universities that execute research for and with the corporate partner. If the state-aided research is successful, the business commits to producing the new technology in Ohio.

In December 1985, for example, the University of Dayton received $250,000 to help Rodger Gamblin's Saranda Corporation develop and commercialize an ink that will not rub off on furniture, clothes, or people. The dye-based ink will be virtually nonsmudgeable, while also being cheaper to use.

Newspaper publishers complain that ink smearing is the number-one technical problem they face. The Neighborhood Cleaners Association in New York says that newspaper rub-off generates two percent of dry cleaners' business. To solve this problem, newspapers can replace printing presses with a new type of press, which is expensive and requires complete staff retraining. Or they can use a nonsmear ink, like Saranda's.

The ink has already been tested at the Columbus *Dispatch*, the Akron *Beacon-Journal*, the Louisville *Times*, the Fort Wayne *News-Sentinel*, the *Washington Post*, the Fargo *Forum*, and the Houston *Chronicle*. Reaction to the ink has been positive. James McVeigh, press plate manager at the Fort Wayne *News-Sentinel*, called it "absolutely smudgeless" and the only "zero-rub" product he has found.

Encouraged by the results of these trial runs, Saranda has purchased a 20,000 square foot plant in Newark, Ohio, to produce the ink. The company will be able to produce 30,000 gallons of ink a day. The business has already created eight jobs, and Gamblin projects that by 1990, another 37 Ohioans will be employed by his company. The state investment will be repaid through a royalty arrangement with Saranda.

The second component of the Edison program is technology incubators. These six enterprises provide a safe harbor to new companies during the difficult initial legs of their voyage.

The incubators attempt to leverage a large domestic supply of venture capital, and they rely heavily on the combined support of academic institutions and corporations, including special arrangements with seed and venture capital funds. Over $119 million in public pension funds have been invested since Ohio became the first state to authorize their use as venture capital.

Historically, the failure rate of start-up companies has been as high as 85 percent. In one and a half years of operation, this rate has been reduced for incubator tenant companies to 10 percent. A total of 67 tenant companies now employ over 200 Ohioans, and seven of these companies have graduated to their own facilities.

When Chartwell Technologies, a pharmaceutical research and development (R&D) company, was founded in 1985, the chances were slim that it would survive. Chartwell not only survived, it grew in an Edison Incubator—the Business Technology Center (BTC) in Columbus.

When Chartwell moved into its 750 square foot space at the Business Technology Center, it had a staff of three with large research goals. Chartwell's mission was to research new methods of drug delivery systems, as well as to continue fundamental chemical research. Through the business support services, the network of consultants, and the research ties with Ohio State University provided by the BTC, Chartwell was able to realize its goals.

Chartwell has hired seven more employees and will soon establish a 4,000 square foot development lab in Columbus.

In addition, the firm has three patents pending and was expecting to request two more by the end of 1987.

Finally, eight Edison technology centers have been established, and a ninth is on its way. These university-industry consortia are located throughout the state and are expanding Ohio's traditional strengths in polymer engineering, advanced manufacturing, welding, animal biotechnology, and information systems.

Among the least understood aspects of manufacturing is welding and joining. Yet, it is a critical factor in product quality, and the failure of welds is the most common fault of manufactured goods. In contrast to the governments of Britain, the Soviet Union, East Germany, and Japan, the U.S. government has done little to develop advanced welding technologies or transfer those technologies to American industry. As a first step toward providing this support, the Edison Welding Institute (EWI), located in Columbus, has joined forces with 161 corporate members to launch this nation's first welding technology and development effort. EWI was founded by Battelle Memorial Institute, the British Welding Institute, and Ohio State University to develop new welding technologies and to teach engineers and materials scientists about them.

EWI is the largest welding center of its kind in North America; in a little over two years, it has completed more than 300 research projects. A key industry journal, *Welding Design and Fabrication*, wrote of EWI in November 1985, "If this country is ever to have one top-notch welding development organization, this is it."

Facing national competition to become the exclusive supplier of an advanced technology for the navy is a big order for a small firm like Welded Beam Company of Perry, Ohio. But with the assistance of the Edison Welding Institute, the company was chosen as the sole supplier of a specifically designed welded beam for navy vessels.

EWI's assistance was essential. Although the company had developed a new, more economical welding system, the Navy Sea Systems command requested the shipbuilder to document performance of the new process. EWI was able to conduct sophisticated tests that were beyond the scope of Welded Beam. Once the results of these tests were presented to the navy, Welded Beam qualified as the only company in the country to supply the high-frequency-welded T-beams. This has already resulted in the addition of new jobs for Ohioans and could lead to \$30–\$50 million in Naval contracts for the Welded Beam Company.

Another center, the Edison Polymer Innovation Corporation (EPIC), was founded by Case Western Reserve University, the University of Akron, and corporate giants such as Goodrich, Goodyear, and Firestone. Although only 25 miles apart, these two outstanding programs had never worked together prior to the Edison Program. EPIC's 400 researchers serve a burgeoning polymer industry; over 12,000 polymer-related companies are located within 100 miles of the center. An EPIC-developed synthetic wound dressing has recently received a great deal of attention from the medical community.

Although many states in addition to Ohio have had success in the support of applied research, the federal government has yet to wake up to this. Consider three developments.

• In 1985, the National Science Foundation (NSF) created the Engineering Research Center program. Its goals and objectives sound very much like those of the Edison technology centers. Despite the similarity and potential for cooperation, the NSF set up centers that directly compete with existing centers. When asked why the NSF didn't seek to cooperate with the existing state centers, the NSF replied that "competition is good."

• In October of 1986, the U.S. Congress passed the Federal Technology Transfer Act, which created Federal Laboratory Consortia for technology transfer throughout the country. Although we strongly support the goals of this initiative, it has left federal officials struggling to create their own technology transfer mechanisms with little or no input from the states.

• Finally, increasing defense R&D spending continues to benefit only a small portion of the nation. Ohio receives far less in federal R&D support than it sends to Washington.

The potential impact of federal dollars cannot be overstated. Economists understand that the boomtown prosperity of Route 128 and Silicon Valley is wholly dependent on an extraordinary concentration of military R&D that provides little benefit to the rest of the national economy.

If states are going to shape their own technological future, it must be with their own resources, and I believe that Ohio's Edison program provides a model for the rest of the nation in this area.

The fiscal 1988 federal budget congratulates itself for its economic competitiveness initiatives: a new civil space technology plan, the expansion of the Strategic Defense Initiative, and the creation of new U.S. Department of Energy programs. Each of these is sure to make a difference—to California and Massachusetts, but not to Ohio or the vast majority of other states.

The new federal budget proposes a 76 percent increase in money for scientific research between 1982 and 1988, but nothing to translate research findings into usable products and technology. How much of this research has needlessly been left on the lab bench? And how much of it has needlessly duplicated existing research efforts in other parts of the country? The United States cannot afford the incredibly wasteful practice of having the federal and state governments compete with each other.

In conclusion, there are many measures state government can take to address the competitiveness issue. States that squander their competitive resources on each other or the federal government won't have any left for our economic rivals abroad. To be truly effective, we must find creative ways to promote coordination between state competitiveness programs and the federal government.

More importantly, state policy-makers nationwide are going to have to make economic competitiveness a concrete fiscal priority, and not just a rhetorical whipping post. It's going to take vision and guts to throw off the quick-payoff blinders and make the tough decisions to better prepare for the future. But it will be a lot more painful in the long run if we don't. In Ohio, we have chosen to take positive action *before* the situation becomes a crisis. So far, we are encouraged by the results. In the absence of a comprehensive federal strategy, we feel that state governments can and should lead the struggle for U.S. competitiveness abroad.

CHAPTER 26

When Education Fails, Democracy Fails

Mayor Dianne Feinstein

A FEW YEARS AGO, when a Japanese financier was asked what he perceived to be America's problem in competing on world markets, he spoke first about "the tyranny of the quarterly report," then commented:

> You must understand that Japan's successes depend on the quality of its work and workers. Beyond being industrious, Japanese workers are well educated, informed about the world, self-sacrificing, fiercely loyal, and can play a role in determining policies for their companies. Too many American workers are uneducated, beer-swilling, television-watching louts who care only about their paychecks.

A harsh and glittering generality, yet from the Japanese point of view, one to be carefully considered.

A Time magazine reporter, Edwin Reingold, returned home to the United States after eight years in Tokyo, and contrasted Japanese civility and competence with American "bureaucracy, ineptitude, and lackadaisy," asking: "Where was the old American pride in competence, work well done, and pride in service?"

New York City's futuristic Commission on the Year 2000 issued its report in the summer of 1987. While optimistic about the economic prospects, it expressed grave doubts that the city's residents would qualify for jobs that will be produced. The commission's number-one recommendation: major improvements in the city's school system to give students the skills needed to compete for jobs. The report noted that today, one in three public high school students in New York leave school without a diploma.

The California World Trade Commission's policy specialist, Cary Walker, says "everyone seems to agree that our nation's quest for excellence must begin in the classroom," and warns that unless young people are better prepared—unless they develop "international literacy"—California's economic future is imperiled.

In terms of global competition, we as a people can be only as good as our education. Education is the lifeblood of our society and our democracy, the glue that holds us together, and the meat and muscle of our business and industry.

Unfortunately, while everyone agrees, little happens to change the situation. We race toward the twenty-first century with nineteenth-century schools. Education enjoys no high priority in Washington and only rarely commands attention in state capitals.

America's education system is not just a disgrace, it is a potential national disaster. The crisis in education is already creating problems for business, industry, the professions, and government, and indeed in the very fabric of our society.

The hungry, the homeless, the criminals, and the misfits of today's troubled America are largely those too poorly educated to get and keep jobs and lead useful lives. The teenagers who scrawl graffiti on city walls would have trouble writing their names.

When education fails, democracy itself fails.

How can we achieve international competitiveness when much of our population can't read, write, or calculate, when our people know almost nothing about the world around them—let alone its science, its business, and its competitive markets?

Education is defense. A national defense built only of guns and bombs and missiles is one-dimensional, short-sighted, and archaic. Without a strong education system, we are at the mercy of a more sophisticated world. Talking about national defense without first talking about educational excellence overlooks the most critical ingredient of defense.

This world is in a battle of brains, not bullets—but it is a battle, no less.

Does it make sense for us to splurge on defense and stint on education? Does it make sense to let American education slip when the other superpower—the Soviet Union—routinely requires every student to study physics and algebra for five years, chemistry and biology for four years, and calculus for two years? And when most U.S. students today don't take even a year of physics or chemistry, and only six percent take calculus?

How well are we preparing our children for their lives?

Ironically, many young Americans don't even know how ill equipped they are to compete in the global economies of today, tomorrow, and ten years from now. They think they can compete, but cannot—hence, their frustration and alienation are increased. Often, compared with the young of other countries, they have not learned the basics about the world in which they are destined to compete. They don't know its languages, its cultures, or its social values—let alone its technologies, its systems, and its trade practices.

Clearly, our schools fail in still another dimension: They fail to develop a work ethic. Thus, they compound their failure. And, unfortunately, many young people do not learn the strong values in their family life that will make them good workers and good citizens.

Consider the situation we find ourselves in:

- The President's Commission on Excellence in Education found that 23 million Americans are functionally illiterate by the simplest tests of reading, writing, and comprehension. Another 30 million were found to be only marginally capable of doing productive work.

- As recently as 1984, a full 20 percent of U.S. high school students could not locate China on a world map.
- Just 15 percent of American high school students ever study a foreign language, and only five percent of their prospective teachers take any course related to international affairs of other cultures.
- Twenty-five percent of American students never even finish high school. (And the number-one reason they drop out is boredom, according to a *Wall Street Journal* poll).
- The navy, testing its high school graduates, found 24 percent of them reading below the ninth-grade level.
- An estimated 500,000 Americans hold fraudulent college degrees, and a credential-checking service says one in every five resumes include some kind of bogus academic credential.

No one can say all of our country's schools are bad; we have some fine schools and universities. But they are the rare exceptions, and the great mass of American young people don't attend them. Clearly, too many of our schools have taken the path of least resistance. They are overwhelmed. Teachers are poorly paid, classes are too large, and homework and discipline are lax.

Moreover, the mediocrity of the education system has produced a society that neither values education nor understands its competitive importance in today's world.

America's workplaces today are computerized, systematized, and highly structured—with 55 percent of our jobs involving information processing. In a world of services and communications, a good education is essential just to understand how to use the tools of a trade. Without solid backgrounds in language, geography, and mathematics, students coming out of our schools are just not able to do the work.

Yet, despite this crying need for heightened skills, our high schools graduate students poorly equipped to compete. Only 15 of the 50 states require four years of our own language, high school English. Only ten require three years of math. Only four require three years of science, and not one—not one state—requires two years of foreign language.

It is a human tragedy that the bright young minds of America's children are being eclipsed by their schools—never to reach their full potentials, never to help fulfill their country's destiny.

In this fiercely competitive world, challenged in every way on every side, we risk our technological future by allowing our children to spend an average of 15,000 hours in front of the television—which is 2,000 more hours than they spend in school.

Compare what's happening in our schools with what our world competition is doing:

- Japanese students must study English for six years prior to their high school graduation.
- With only half as many people, Japan produces nine percent more engineers than the United States. And most people who get Ph.D.s in engineering in the United States today are foreigners.
- Japanese eighth-graders spend 243 days a year in school; our students are in school only 180 days—60 days fewer than Japanese students. Thus, when they graduate from high school, Japanese children have the equivalent of three or four more years of school than American children.
- While American students get three months for summer vacation, their Japanese counterparts get only 40 days.
- And while one out of four Americans drop out, only one out of ten Japanese students fails to graduate from high school.

The Japanese are not alone. Education experts also rate West Germany, the Soviet Union, and France above the United States in four out of five categories.

A CBS survey asked schoolchildren several simple questions: Who was Joseph Stalin? Which president got us into the Vietnam war? Who is Peter Ustinov? Students thought Peter Ustinov started the Russian Revolution, that Franklin Delano Roosevelt started the Vietnam War—and 10 percent thought Joseph Stalin was a Frenchman.

In another survey, California college undergraduates were

asked to identify Tom Bradley—who has been the mayor of Los Angeles most of their lives and twice a candidate for governor. Half could not identify him.

These kinds of stories are all too familiar. What should distress us most is that for all the years we've known such things, little has been done about them.

Our economic competitiveness—already badly battered—is going to fail completely unless we move quickly to remedy the rampant deficiencies in American education and to strengthen the American work ethic.

We are already paying dearly for educational failures. Xerox Chairman David Kearns has estimated that U.S. industry is currently spending $25 billion a year just to train and retrain poorly trained workers.

We pay dearly in other ways. The *Wall Street Journal* reported in February 1987 on Louisiana's troubled school system—a system that ranked near the bottom in almost every educational statistic. It was a portrait of failure—educationally, economically, and socially.

Here was the picture it portrayed:

- Employers refuse to come to Louisiana because its poorly educated work force scares them off. When the New Orleans Hilton opened in 1977, the hotel had to interview 12,000 people to fill 500 jobs—and then took eight times as long as usual to train them.
- Louisiana has the highest percentage of residents living below the poverty line.
- The state has proportionately the highest prison population in America.
- And it also has the nation's highest unemployment rate.

Quite obviously, these factors are closely related—related directly to poor education.

A former Louisiana chamber of commerce member described the state's schools as "factories for the underclass." The sheriff of Orleans Parish said he has five times as many prisoners as he did 12 years ago and that "unless we get them an education, they'll be right back in here."

Clearly, Louisiana is paying for its bad education because it won't pay for good education. And is it not fair to ask how many other states may be headed in that direction?

Is not America already suffering because its industries have failed to compete in a competitive world? Our country's trade deficit soars and our resources are drained away by debt, but Americans go on buying imported cars, watching imported television sets, and wearing imported clothes. Why? Because American products do not satisfy them.

American companies have been slow to retool, redesign, and modernize—and so our automobile and steel industries have been mortally wounded by competitors. In short, in many areas, America has not recognized that the competition is not us—border to border—but the world.

Too often, our companies have not taken the time to learn about other countries and cultures. There are an estimated 10,000 Japanese business representatives in the United States—and most speak English. Fewer than 900 American businesses are represented in Japan—and only a handful of their personnel speak Japanese.

An example of our lack of culture know-how turned up a few years ago, when General Motors discovered why its Chevy Nova was not selling in Mexico—because in Spanish, *no va* means "it doesn't go."

Ten years ago, a Toyota executive told a group of American business reporters his company did not really compete with American auto builders, it "looked for holes in the market and filled them." In other words, Toyota was giving other countries products their own manufacturers were not producing.

My question is how can all these things be reversed—when schools continue to turn out functionally illiterate graduates, when a quarter of the students drop out, and when millions of Americans lie about their educations to get a job? What does all this mean?

In my opinion, it means we all have a lot of work to do. We somehow have to convince our national and state leaders that America's standing as the world's number-one economy is at risk unless drastic action is taken to upgrade education and to strengthen working habits. What we get from

Washington are more cuts in the education budget. Unless that changes, we are in real danger of seeing our national standards go from bad to worse. And we are in danger of becoming a second-class economic power unless education gets a higher priority—the highest priority.

This country has been penny-wise and pound-foolish on education. If we are saving money for a rainy day, we should know it's pouring right now. In a world of increasing skills, the United States cannot settle for mediocrity in its schools. It is not enough that a few Americans—at great cost—can receive superior educations.

We are in a race for the future, a race we dare not lose.

You and I and all of us owe good educations to today's children and to children of the future. We owe it to all our futures.

CHAPTER 27

A Housing Agenda for America: A Federal-City Partnership

*Mayor Raymond L. Flynn**

DECENT, AFFORDABLE HOUSING IS the American dream. The task for the next president, and the next Congress, is to begin to fulfill the promise first made by Congress in 1949 of a "decent home" for all Americans.

In this article, I want to recommend three items that can form the basis of a new direction in federal housing policy. The first deals with homelessness; the second, with preserving the stock of subsidized housing; and the third, with expanding the supply of affordable housing.

During the past few years, the rising tide of homelessness has put the nation's housing crisis back on the front pages. The sight of Americans sleeping in alleyways and streets has stirred the country's conscience. It has led to a wide range of grass-roots efforts—by religious and other volunteer groups, as well as local governments—to provide the homeless with shelter and food. In Boston, for example, we have more than

---

*Raymond L. Flynn, mayor of Boston, is chairman of the U.S. Conference of Mayors' Task Force on Hunger and Homelessness, a member of the National League of Cities' Election '88 Task Force, and a member of the Democratic Party Platform Committee.

doubled the number of emergency shelter beds since 1984. Surveys conducted by the U.S. Conference of Mayors Task Force on Hunger and Homelessness, which I have the honor to chair, reveal that cities and volunteer groups are stretching their limited resources to provide basic services for the homeless, but the need far surpasses available resources.[1]

If the record numbers of people on America's streets had been driven there by a natural catastrophe, many areas would be declared disaster areas. But even though homelessness is a national problem, the Reagan administration has given only lip service to the issue, and has taken no responsibility for its role in swelling the ranks of the homeless through its cutbacks and policies.

Homelessness is a symptom of a much deeper problem—the nationwide shortage of affordable housing. This problem, in turn, is a direct result of the federal government's withdrawal from housing assistance.

Those of us on the front lines of the housing crisis see the impact of these cuts every day. We look at vacant buildings we want to rehabilitate. We look at empty lots where we'd like to see new construction. We look at skyrocketing rents, which force families to choose between such basic necessities as heat, food, and medical care. We see energy bills that could be cut by weatherization programs. We look at long waiting lists for public and subsidized housing. And we look at homeless people in our streets, alleyways, subways, and shelters, and see Americans who deserve decent, affordable, permanent housing.

In the late 1980s, however, housing is a growing concern among many sectors of our population. It is no longer simply a problem for the poor, but also for working-class and middle-class Americans. Because the housing crisis is widespread, we can now fashion a federal housing policy with broad appeal—one that can help restore the American dream and the promise of opportunity for all. Affordable housing must be a centerpiece of a new urban agenda.

Indeed, from the late 1940s through the late 1970s, the housing conditions for the American people steadily improved, thanks primarily to federal housing policies. During that period, the federal government was committed to improving the quantity, quality, and affordability of housing for all income groups and age-groups. Home ownership rates increased steadily, reaching 65 percent in the 1970s. Low-income Americans were served with a variety of programs to boost subsidized rental housing. The quality of housing improved as well. During this period, the number of Americans living in substandard units declined significantly. Of course, there was always room for improvement. But in that three-decade period, America set high standards for itself, and applied its talent and resources to reaching the goal of decent, affordable housing for all.

In this decade, however, Washington has transformed the American dream into a nightmare.

Since 1981, the federal government has all but dismantled the nation's housing programs. The number of new federally assisted units has plummeted from above 300,000 annually. Housing programs funded by the Department of Housing and Urban Development (HUD) have been cut from over $33 billion to under $8 billion—a 75 percent cut.

THE IMPACT OF FEDERAL WITHDRAWAL

The consequences of the federal government's withdrawal from housing have been disastrous. We have seen a steady erosion in the quality of life in our communities. Americans have begun to lose confidence in the ability of our economy to "deliver the goods." The housing crisis has become the number-one topic of conversation across the country. From posh suburbs to inner-city neighborhoods, from city halls to state houses, from corporate boardrooms to neighborhood bars, from young families to the elderly, the shortage of affordable housing is on everyone's mind.

Home ownership—the symbol of the American dream—is increasingly beyond the reach of the American people. In 1949, the average 30-year-old home buyer needed to spend 14 percent of his paycheck to afford the typical home. By 1985, the figure had risen to 44 percent. Since 1980, home ownership rates have fallen each year. For young families, in particular, this dream has become an illusion. The home ownership rate among 30–34-year-olds, for example, declined from 59.3 percent in 1981 to 54.7 in 1985. A recent report by the Joint Center for Housing Studies of the Massachusetts Institute of Technology (MIT) and Harvard University warned that "young households feel thwarted by the high cost of home ownership and alarmed about their prospects of ever being able to buy."[2] According to *American Demographics*, the proportion of young adults living at home with their parents is higher now than it has been at any time since the 1950s.[3]

The rise in home ownership costs has pushed many households back into the rental market. Because of this growing demand, rents have skyrocketed, rising much faster than income. Renters are thus paying a growing portion of their income for rent. (The average rent burden grew from 20 to 29 percent of income between 1970 and 1983.) This is particularly true for the poor, whose ranks are swelling nationwide, and who have the least discretion in allocating their limited incomes. According to the MIT-Harvard study, one-quarter of the poor pay over three-quarters of their income for rent. (The new tax law will make matters worse, by eliminating incentives to build new rental housing and by pushing current landlords to raise rents.)

The most serious consequence of this housing crisis is the rise in homelessness. A 25-city survey, results of which were released in December 1986 by the U.S. Conference of Mayors, found an increasing demand for emergency shelter across the country. Perhaps the most tragic finding was the growing proportion of families and children among the nation's homeless population.[4] A follow-up survey of 29 cities, released in May 1987, found that the number of families seeking emergency shelter had increased by 31 percent in two years. Every survey city reported that the number of families temporarily living with friends or relatives has increased.[5]

This epidemic of homelessness in our affluent society is a national scandal.

The housing crisis is also a problem for American business and the overall economy. High housing costs make it difficult for employers to attract employees. The chief economist for the Port Authority of New York and New Jersey recently told the *New York Times*: "Companies are not going to expand here when their employees can't afford homes."[6] The business community needs to become a more vocal advocate for affordable housing.

THE SEARCH FOR SOLUTIONS

During the 1980s, as the Reagan administration dismantled federal housing programs, state and local governments have assumed a greater responsibility for dealing with the escalating demand for affordable housing. Out of necessity, they have developed many innovative programs, combining public and private initiatives, including partnerships with foundations and community-based organizations.[7] Of course, there is no way that cities and states can fill the huge gap created by the federal government's withdrawal from housing. Only the federal government has the resources to meet this basic need. But many of the creative efforts of local governments can provide models for federal programs in the future. What is needed now is a partnership between the federal government and our cities, with the federal government providing the resources and the localities providing the initiative and talent.

In housing, the problem is not to get the federal government off our backs. It is to get federal dollars back in our communities. We need to create a broad, bipartisan coalition to support an expanded federal role in housing.

The Massachusetts experience suggests that it is possible to create a political climate that strongly supports housing. There is a broad constituency for affordable housing, which is led by Governor Michael Dukakis, and includes the state legislature, mayors, private developers, community development corporations (CDCs), unions, religious organizations, tenant groups, and neighborhood associations. The state's business community understands that to attract employees and to sustain economic growth, we need affordable housing. Business leaders have helped to create the Boston Housing Partnership and the Massachusetts Housing Partner ship, umbrella organizations of private-sector, government, and community leaders that have played key roles in expanding housing opportunities for low- and moderate-income people.

NEW DIRECTIONS: A THREE-PART APPROACH

What should federal housing policy look like in the post-Reagan period and through the end of this century?

Three components are necessary:

- First, emergency shelter and services for our most vulnerable citizens—the homeless and near-homeless
- Second, preservation of our existing subsidized housing inventory
- Third, a major supply program to build affordable housing, based primarily on nonprofit developers

Emergency Shelter and Services

As a nation, our first priority must be to help our most vulnerable citizens. In the 1980s, as noted earlier, we have witnessed an increase in the ranks of the poor, particularly among women and children. Almost one-quarter of children under the age of six live in poverty. In general, about one out of seven Americans live below the poverty threshold. Structural changes in the nation's economy have increased the number of low-wage jobs and working poor, people whose salary is below the poverty line.

Federal cutbacks have cut huge holes in the so-called safety net, leaving more and more Americans vulnerable and needy. For example, job training programs were slashed from $11.5 billion in FY 1981 to $2.4 billion in FY 1986. Further, with the growing vulnerability of Americans to layoffs and temporary (but often calamitous) poverty, the percentage of unemployed persons receiving unemployment insurance benefits hit a record low in 1986; it is now only about half what it was in 1980, when the unemployment rate was about the same level as it is today.[8]

The homeless are those who have suffered most from the widening holes in the safety net. The cumulative effect of federal cutbacks and reductions is the tragedy of growing homelessness and hunger in this wealthy nation.

America's homeless population comprises poor persons who, for a variety of reasons, cannot afford a permanent roof over their heads. A growing number of the homeless are families, particularly children, who must live the rest of their lives with the emotional scars and physical problems created today by America's failure to provide decent food and housing.

In addition, a substantial segment of America's homeless are mentally ill persons. They are victims of the policy of deinstitutionalization, begun in the 1960s, which emptied our nation's mental hospitals without providing adequate resources for community-based facilities. Nationwide, the number of persons institutionalized in mental hospitals declined from 505,000 in 1963 to 138,000 in 1980. The nation's homeless shelters are often filled with these mentally ill persons. For example, at the Pine Street Inn, Boston's largest shelter, between 50 and 60 percent of the guests on any given night suffer from mental illness. Many shelters have become, de facto, America's new mental institutions.

The most frustrating aspect of homelessness is that Americans have the will to address this most basic human need. Cities around the country are working with individuals and organizations who are giving their hearts and souls to others in need. I have been privileged to work with advocates such as Mitch Snyder, of the Community for Creative Non-Violence, and Robert Hayes, of the National Coalition for the Homeless, as well as many staff and volunteers in Boston's shelters and soup kitchens, who reflect the many caring people who give us hope for the American spirit.

We must give these people the resources they need to help the homeless. Private charity and local government cannot, on their own, provide these resources.

Our immediate response must be to restore the safety net for these vulnerable Americans. The One Hundredth Congress took important steps to provide this emergency assistance.

In the spring of 1987, the Congress passed a $425 million bill, sponsored on a bipartisan basis to provide funds for the homeless. House Speaker Jim Wright carried through on his pledge to "fast-track" the legislation. The bill, which will expand emergency shelter, food, and health care for the homeless, is a vital first step. It will help cities like Boston— that are stretching their limited resources, working with nonprofit groups and foundations—to add shelter beds, soup kitchens, rent subsidies, and mental health and health programs for those who live in the streets and in the shelters. Its swift passage was a fitting tribute to its cosponsor, the late Representative Stewart McKinney, (R.-Conn.), who died in April 1987.

In addition, Senators Albert Gore (D.-Tenn.) and Daniel P. Moynihan (D.-N.Y.) have filed the Homeless Persons' Survival Act. Working closely with the National Coalition for the Homeless, Senators Gore and Moynihan, with Representatives Mickey Leland (D.-Tex.) and Leon Panetta (D.-Cal.), drafted a bill targeted at $4 billion that would provide housing, food, and social service benefits needed to serve the many faces of homelessness.

In the FY 1987 budget, Congress approved $5 million to help cities create transitional housing for women and children. Transitional housing is designed to help women get back on their feet and become independent following a family tragedy—a divorce, an abusive domestic situation, widowhood, job loss, or eviction. It is a self-help approach that provides the support needed in order to live independently. It is an opportunity to leave a shelter and prepare for independent living. In Boston, we have worked closely with women's groups and social service providers to create transitional housing programs.

It is critical to expand resources to assist the homeless. The ultimate goal, however, is to eliminate the problem of homelessness altogether. The major step toward achieving that goal is to protect and expand permanent, affordable housing.

Protecting Existing Housing

The most valuable housing resource in the nation is the existing inventory of public and subsidized housing. During the past 40 years, the federal government has helped construct more than three million units of low-income rental housing. This includes approximately 1.3 million units of public housing and about two million units of private assisted housing.

The American public has a substantial investment in this housing inventory. There is absolutely no way to replace these units if they are lost as low-income housing; it is much more cost-effective to preserve this inventory than to build another 3.3 million low-income housing units. In addition, the social cost of losing these units—the displacement of families, the public funding to serve the families made homeless, the jump in welfare, and related public dollars—would be overwhelming. The federal government should protect the public's investment.

We cannot allow HUD to become simply an auctioneer at a garage sale.

Toward this end, the Reagan administration and Congress should abandon all plans to sell off public housing. A HUD-sponsored demonstration project is currently under way. Only a handful of public housing agencies even volunteered for the program. They recognized it as simply an effort to rid the federal government of its commitment to support public housing—in effect, to balance the federal budget on the backs of the poor. Allowing tenant groups the opportunity to participate in management is a useful concept. But selling low-income public housing to tenants—without safeguards against windfall profits or any attempt to replace these scarce units—is a flagrant misuse of public dollars.[9]

What makes more sense is to encourage tenant self-help and long-term affordability. To do this, HUD could help public housing tenants to transform their developments into resident-owned and managed limited-equity cooperatives. To make this feasible, HUD would have to provide tenants with the down payment, provide ongoing operating subsidies, and provide technical assistance to help tenant groups develop management skills. For the rest of the public housing stock, Congress must provide resources to guarantee these residents safe, decent housing and—through a variety of antipoverty programs—opportunities to lift themselves out of poverty.

A more pressing issue is the fate of the 1.9 million private, government-assisted housing units across the nation. This inventory is a ticking time bomb waiting to explode. Recent General Accounting Office (GAO) reports revealed that these developments face two related crises: First, project-based subsidies are scheduled to expire; second, 20-year use restrictions (which allow owners to opt out of their pledge to guarantee low- and moderate-income housing by prepaying the mortgage) are scheduled to expire.[10] When these restrictions expire, these low-income units could be turned into market-rate housing or (in weak markets) go bankrupt. Either way, tenants would be displaced and pushed into a tight housing market. Between now and the year 2000, most of the 1.9 million assisted units will be at risk as their subsidies or use restrictions expire. Between 200,000 and 900,000 units may be lost by 1995 alone.

Now is the time to plan for this inevitable situation. Policies must be devised to preserve these developments as affordable housing. Owners must be encouraged not to prepay mortgages, while funds must be allocated to continue the subsidies. The most cost-effective use of federal funds, however, would be to assist nonprofit groups and resident-owned cooperatives to purchase and manage this inventory, rather than simply pour more federal subsidy dollars into filling the gap between what tenants can afford and the rents needed for absentee private landlords to make a profit.

In Boston, we have had successful experiences transforming at-risk HUD-subsidized projects into cooperative and nonprofit housing. HUD, in fact, has occasionally seen the wisdom of this cost-effective approach by allowing residents to use their rent subsidies as equity for cooperatives, and by allowing nonprofit groups, through the Boston Housing Partnership (BHP), to buy distressed projects, rather than selling them off to the highest bidders. This approach saves taxpayers dollars, gives residents a greater stake in their homes, and guarantees the long-term preservation of affordable housing by removing it from the speculative market.

Congress must create incentives for current owners to either retain these units as low-income housing or sell them to nonprofit groups and tenant cooperatives. Congress should appoint a task force—with representatives of tenants, private owners, nonprofit groups, and local, state, and federal government—to develop a workable approach to protect this inventory. In the meantime, Congress should place a moratorium on prepayments—or at least require owners to give substantial prior notice of their intent to prepay—in order to provide time to find solutions that will preserve this low-income housing.

We must not allow this ticking time bomb to explode. If it does, the victims will be millions of low-income Americans, their neighbors, and the cities they live in.

THE NEW PARTNERSHIP: A COMMUNITY-BASED SUPPLY PROGRAM

We are a nation of builders and dreamers. To maintain our country's greatness, to expand opportunities for all, we must continue this legacy. We must build more housing to sustain the American dream.

We continue to suffer from a shortage of affordable housing. We see this not only in the expanding waiting lists across the country for public housing, and not only in the many housing vouchers that go unused because of a tight private rental market, but also in the growing demand for moderate-income homeownership. For example, the Bricklayers' and Laborers' Union recently constructed 17 brick townhouses in South Boston and sold them, at cost, for $70,000—less than half the market value. More than 200 persons applied for these units, which were sold by lottery. Soon after the union started construction on another 48 units, in Charlestown, more than 1,700 families applied.

The story is the same elsewhere—for example, the long wait in Brooklyn to buy a home through the Nehemiah Program (named after the biblical figure who rebuilt Jerusalem).

To meet this demand, we must expand the supply of housing, both rental and owned for low-income and moderate-income persons. An ambitious supply program will not only help satisfy this demand, it will also create many new jobs, help rebuild our communities, and restore confidence in our country's promise of opportunity.

The question is not *whether* to embark on a new supply program, but *how* to do so.

Fortunately, much can be learned from the recent efforts of local governments and community groups that—during these lean years of federal cutbacks—have found creative ways to build affordable housing. Across the country, the 1980s has been a period of renewed local initiative. In particular, many cities and states have nurtured community-based, nonprofit housing developers, who helped rebuild neighborhoods that the federal government and for-profit developers had ignored or abandoned.

These grass-roots efforts—by churches, neighborhood groups, unions, and others—planted many seeds. Local and national foundations, along with local government, provided financial support to help these seeds grow. The Local Initiative Support Corporation (LISC), launched by the Ford Foundation, and the Enterprise Foundation, headed by developer James Rouse, have worked closely with these nonprofit groups to develop new construction, rehabilitation, and financing techniques. In Brooklyn, a coalition of churches launched the Nehemiah Program, which is rebuilding a blighted neighborhood with low-cost housing for working-class homeowners. The churches provided interest-free construction loans, the city donated 30 blocks of vacant land and granted each buyer a $10,000 interest-free second mortgage, and the state provided below-market mortgages from a tax-exempt bond.

Across the country, these community-based, nonprofit efforts have now borne fruit. Thousands of units of affordable housing—sold at or below construction costs—are now in place that would not have been there without these initiatives. These groups have become sophisticated developers—

a vast improvement over some well-intentioned but naive nonprofit groups that emerged in the 1960s. This generation of nonprofit builders combine social concern with hardnosed business skills.

Some cities have formed umbrella organizations of community-based, nonprofit developers to improve efficiency and expand the scale of development. The Boston Housing Partnership (BHP), the acknowledged leader of this approach, is a consortium of private, community, and government leaders, whose board includes the heads of major banks, the directors of nonprofit CDCs, and top government officials. The city government provided $4.1 million in Community Development Block Grant funds,[11] and the private foundations contributed $430,000 for initial seed capital and acquisition; the state provided financing and rent subsidies. Through BHP, 10 nonprofit groups have renovated 700 units of low-income rental housing—a $38 million project. The BHP is so successful that a consortium of local and national foundations, including LISC and the United Way (which is supporting housing for the first time) has committed $4 million for a six-year support program. The BHP's next project is the rehabilitation of 950 apartments in HUD-owned buildings that were saved from HUD's auction block by community pressure.

New York City, Chicago, Cleveland, and other cities are developing similar partnerships.

These efforts are working well. But local governments, churches, and foundations simply lack the resources to turn these small success stories into a major new nationwide supply program for affordable housing. Only the federal government has those kinds of resources. It is now time for Washington to learn the lessons from these local efforts. What is needed is a partnership between the federal government and these community-based housing efforts.

The mechanism for realizing this goal is a National Community Housing Partnership program. Through this program, the federal government would provide matching funds to locally based, nonprofit housing initiatives. Federal dollars would be matched by local government, business, private foundations, the United Way, churches, or other entities. Matching grants are a good way to encourage local efforts by helping those communities that help themselves. This program is the best way to leverage federal funds.

First, the program would provide federal matching grants for seed money. This would enable local, nonprofit housing partnerships to start, or expand, their development efforts. The grants would provide these groups with up-front funds for staff to do planning and architectural work, put financing together, and acquire abandoned buildings for rehabilitation or vacant lots for new construction.

Second, the federal funds would provide capital grants to community-based partnerships for the construction of housing. Direct capital grants are much more cost-effective than the current approach. They reduce the long-term debt that escalates the cost of housing far beyond construction costs.

Ironically, the Department of Defense, which uses this approach to house military families, has a lot to teach us about housing development. Over the years, the military has constructed 400,000 units of family housing. It is financed and operated for the most part by direct capital grants appropriated by Congress—eliminating both the debt burden and the speculative resale that drive up the cost of conventional private housing.

Who can turn down an idea that draws on both local CDCs and the Pentagon for its inspiration?

Housing, especially for low- and moderate-income people, is expensive to build. But Congress need not carry the stigma of simply throwing money at problems. A National Community Housing Partnership program is a viable, cost-effective alternative to some of the wasteful federal programs of the past and the do-nothing approach of the present. By learning from the successes of grass-roots initiatives, the federal government can chart a bold new course in housing policy.

MAKING HOUSING A PRIORITY

This three-pronged approach to solving our deepening housing crisis—providing emergency shelter and services for the homeless, preserving the existing inventory of assisted housing, and creating a supply program linking federal dollars to community-based partnerships—provides an opportunity to place housing at the top of our nation's agenda once again. There is, across the country, a growing awareness that while there is much to learn from the mistakes of past federal housing programs, the answer is not simply to completely withdraw from housing. We need a new direction, one that will address the housing needs of our citizens, but do so in a way that is cost-effective, flexible, and sensitive to local approaches. Equally important, it should target resources to those who need it most—low- and moderate-income Americans.

Government must play a leadership role in expanding housing opportunities for all Americans. In housing, there is no such thing as a completely private free market. The private housing industry is aided by a wide (but often invisible) array of government supports—from tax deductions for builders and buyers, to insurance for lenders, to secondary market mechanisms. This support system is an essential component of our private housing market, and is responsible for the considerable housing progress our nation made during the three-decade period following World War II.

The federal government must extend, not reverse, this progress, by providing funds to build and preserve housing for low- and moderate-income Americans. It must do so in partnership with local and state governments that have demonstrated their capacity to create innovative approaches to housing, but lack the resources to meet the needs.

We still have a way to go to fulfill that promise, first made in 1949, of a decent home for all Americans. We should not stop our efforts until we have succeeded.

---

1. U.S. Conference of Mayors, *Responding to Homelessness in America's Cities*, Washington, D.C., 1986; and ——, *The Continued Growth of Hunger, Homelessness and Poverty in America's Cities*, Washington, D.C., 1986.

2. H. J. Brown and J. Yinger, "Homeownership and Housing Affordability in the United States: 1963–1985," Joint Center for Housing Studies of the Massachusetts Institute of Technology and Harvard University, Cambridge, Mass., 1986.

3. M. Riche, "Mysterious Young Adults," *American Demographics*, February 1987.

4. U.S. Conference of Mayors, *The Continued Growth of Hunger, Homelessness and Poverty in America's Cities*, Washington, D.C., 1986.

5. ———, *A Status Report on Homeless Families in America's Cities*, 1987.

6. T. J. Lueck, "Region's Growth Tied to Housing and Training," *New York Times*, March 5, 1987.

7. A compendium of state/local housing initiatives can be found in the following: J. Pickman, B. F. Roberts, M. Letterman, and R. N. Mittle, *Producing Lower Income Housing: Local Initiatives*, Bureau of National Affairs, Washington, D.C., 1986; M. K. Nenno, *New Money & New Methods: A Catalog of State and Local Initiatives in Housing and Community Development*, National Association of Housing and Redevelopment Officials, Washington, D.C., 1986; J. Sidor, *State Housing Initiatives: A Compendium*, Council of State Community Affairs Agencies, Washington, D.C., 1986; and National Governors Association, *Decent and Affordable Housing for All: A Challenge to the States*, Washington, D.C., 1986.

8. Center on Budget and Policy Priorities, *Smaller Slices of the Pie: The Growing Economic Vulnerability of Poor and Moderate Income Americans*, Washington, D.C., 1985.

9. H. Silver, J. McDonald, and R. J. Ortiz, "Selling Public Housing: The Methods and Motivations," *Journal of Housing*, November/December 1985; P. Dreier, "Public Housing for Sale," *New Republic*, August 4, 1986; M. J. Schussheim, "Selling Public Housing to Tenants: How Feasible," Congressional Research Service, Washington, D.C., December 1984; and E. J. Howenstine, "Selling Public Housing to Individuals and Cooperatives: Lessons from Foreign Experience," *Urban Law and Policy*, 7, 1983.

10. U.S. General Accounting Office, "Rental Housing: Potential Reduction in the Privately Owned and Federally Assisted Inventory," Washington, D.C., June 1986; and "Rental Housing: Potential Reduction in the Section 8 Existing and Voucher Inventory," U.S. General Accounting Office, Washington, D.C., October 1986.

11. This is a good example of the importance of federal Community Development Block Grant (CDBG) funds. The CDBG program provides flexible funds to help cities address their diverse housing, economic development, and human service needs. CDBG funds have been a major victim of Reagan's budget cuts. Instead, the program should be expanded in funding and scope.

CHAPTER 28

Compassion and Common Sense: The Urban Agenda in 1988

Mayor Edward I. Koch

I WILL NOT RUN for president of the United States in 1988. I enjoy too much meeting the challenges and fulfilling the responsibilities of the second-toughest job in America—being mayor of the city of New York.

But I do have a stake—a huge stake—in the outcome of the 1988 election. So does every other mayor in every other city, regardless of size, region, or party affiliation.

Mayors, you see, are the frontline managers, the day-to-day problem solvers, the officials held accountable for the effects, good or bad, of national policies set by the president and Congress. In an age of trickle-down federalism, mayors are the ones who get doused when federal policies go wrong.

And since 1981, federal policies have gone wrong. Washington has gutted federal program after federal program, broken federal commitment after federal commitment. Most cities have survived. Only a fortunate few, like New York, have thrived.

Will the next election reverse the bad fortunes that have swamped our cities since Ronald Reagan took office? Only if

305

someone speaks for America's cities. Will someone? If Democratic candidates don't, the White House will stay Republican in 1988.

Who needs cities? America does. Farms employ less than three percent of our nation's work force, while metropolitan areas employ 71 percent and produce 81 percent of the nation's personal income. Our farms may be where the wheat is, but our cities are where the economic action is. If they're strong and vibrant, so is America.

But they won't be strong and vibrant without Washington's help. Our next president must realize that for almost eight years, the stirring rhetoric of federal-state-city partnership hasn't been matched with the resources needed to make it work. The next president must put the resources where only rhetoric has been, especially in four areas—drugs, acquired immune deficiency syndrome (AIDS), homelessness, and housing.

DRUGS

Drugs have placed America at risk. Statistic after statistic serves as warning. So do the many terrible tales of abandoned and addicted babies, of senseless acts of drug-related violence, of lives wasted and lost because of drugs.

In 1986 alone, we arrested nearly 60,000 suspected drug pushers in New York City. In 1987, the city will spend more than a quarter of a billion dollars of local taxes in the war against drugs. We're doing our share to enforce the law.

The cities, however, can't do it alone. Heroin and cocaine aren't grown within U.S. borders. They are smuggled into the country. Only the federal government can interdict and stop the poison before it hits our streets. The Omnibus Drug Bill passed by Congress in 1986 provided a blueprint for the war against drugs. President Reagan proclaimed its potential when he signed it into law and said he was committed to fighting the scourge of drugs. But within three months, he gutted the bill by eliminating most of its funding from the budget. Our next president must put federal resources where, to date, only presidential rhetoric has been.

AIDS

AIDS has been diagnosed in more than 10,000 residents of New York City. That's a lot of people—about 29 percent of the nation's AIDS caseload. But while the number of New Yorkers with AIDS will continue to rise until a cure and a vaccine are developed, New York's share of the nation's caseload will continue to drop. By 1991, New York will have only 15 percent of the nation's caseload.

AIDS, in other words, has become a national problem. In 1987—20,000 deaths and six years after the Centers of Disease Control first identified the disease—the president finally created a national commission to examine the federal government's response to the AIDS epidemic. Better late than never, I suppose.

The commission faces a tremendous challenge, which must be met quickly. By 1991, the Rand Corporation projects, we may be spending up to $133 billion nationally on AIDS. The commission, then, must determine whether adequate federal funds are going to research to find a cure and a vaccine. But it must also ensure that the employment and housing rights of those who suffer from AIDS are not jeopardized; that reimbursement systems accurately reflect the costs of treating the disease; that the current two-year wait AIDS victims must endure before obtaining Medicare coverage is ended; and that taxpayers of cities such as New York and San Francisco, with already well-developed institutional responses to AIDS, do not bear the full burden of the nation's AIDS bill.

There's a tendency for the debate over AIDS to dwell on diversionary issues, such as mandatory testing. As with drugs, however, the real issue for our next president is putting federal resources where, to date, only presidential rhetoric has been.

HOMELESSNESS AND HOUSING

On an average night, the city of New York shelters over 10,000 homeless individuals and 5,000 homeless families—

or 25,000 people, many of whom are children. Often, these are people who've run out of alternatives—individuals who've been discharged from mental institutions into the community without adequate treatment programs; families evicted for nonpayment of rent.

Right behind them are hundreds of thousands of others at risk of becoming homeless—people living doubled up; people living in overcrowded, tense, and unsafe conditions; people living beyond their means and struggling to pay the rent from a fixed income. Their ranks will swell, and the middle class will be further diminished, if we don't act now to help those who have been shut out of the housing market in every city in America.

Since the Great Depression, both Republican and Democratic presidents have worked with state and local government to build low- and moderate-income housing. Not Ronald Reagan. In 1981, New York City received almost $2 billion in federal assistance for the creation of low- and moderate-income housing. In 1987, we'll receive just one-tenth of that amount. And it can be used only to maintain existing low- and moderate-income housing, not to construct new units.

In advocating the Federal government's retreat from the housing market the president argued that the private sector would pick up where Washington left off. It hasn't happened. Private developers earn a larger profit from upper-income housing than from low- and moderate-income units. No wonder the need for low- and moderate-income housing today is greater than it was in 1981.

Following Washington's retreat, the city of New York stepped forward with its own tax levy funds to meet some of our housing needs. Over the next 10 years, we'll spend $4.2 billion to construct, rehabilitate, or preserve some 252,000 units of housing—85 percent to go to New Yorkers with incomes below the city's median. Another 4,000 units of city-owned in rem housing will be rehabilitated each year for homeless and near-homeless families. Already, more than 13,000 units have been completed.

If we must continue going it alone, we'll never meet our housing needs, especially in a city with a vacancy rate of less than two percent. Washington has to get back into the low- and moderate-income market, where the private sector refuses to invest. As with drugs and AIDS, federal resources must be put where, to date, only presidential rhetoric has been.

Drugs, AIDS, homelessness, and housing—issues this president has been reluctant to address; issues our next president must address. But in an age of record federal deficits, is there any money to spare?

Well, money alone isn't the answer to these problems. Innovation is just as essential. Consider, for example, an approach the city of New York, in cooperation with church leaders and community groups, has developed to address the need for affordable moderate-income housing. It's called the Nehemiah Project.

In a neighborhood of Brooklyn that until recently was riddled with vacant lots, burned-out buildings, and abandoned cars, new three-bedroom homes are being offered for sale at just $53,000. A new home for $53,000? Think that's crazy? It's not.

Just ask the 800 families who've moved into Nehemiah homes. The city provides the home owner with the lot for just one dollar and a one-shot $10,000 grant for plumbing, sewage, and other infrastructure repairs. That, in combination with the home owner's $5,000 down payment to secure a $38,000 low-interest mortgage from the state of New York, makes the home affordable to families normally shut out of the new home market. Many Nehemiah families used to reside in New York City Housing Authority units. Their purchase of a Nehemiah home creates an opportunity for another family to move into the authority unit they've vacated.

And it saves money. Instead of assuming the traditional and costly 20- or 30-year financial responsibility for a family, we use our limited financial resources on a one-shot basis to help them get a stake in their community. Once they do, they'll pay taxes, thereby increasing city revenues, out of which more such opportunities can be created. It's an approach that gives the city more bang for its housing bucks.

In an era of limited federal resources, it's an approach Washington ought to consider.

Innovation alone won't provide us with all of the funds we need to solve the problems we face. Money is still critical. And until we tackle the national debt—already above $2 trillion—some will say there's no money to spare. If that view prevails, our problems may become insurmountable.

To date, many candidates have said what needs to be done by the next president. None have identified the resources with which to do it, except one—Governor Bruce Babbitt of Arizona. He proposes that we adopt a national sales tax dedicated to retiring the debt. I agree. In fact, I recently made a similar proposal in New Hampshire, one of the lowest-tax states in the country.

A four percent national sales tax on nonessential items would raise about $70 billion a year. I'd favor a 13-year limit on the tax. When it expires, it will have raised nearly $1 trillion. That $1 trillion would go a very, very long way toward erasing the debt and making it manageable again.

Will taxpayers rise in revolt? I don't think so. When New York City faced bankruptcy during the 1970s, we enacted a series of temporary taxes to help restore fiscal solvency. Once it was restored, the taxes were repealed. New Yorkers didn't oppose the taxes so long as they were being used for the purposes for which they'd been imposed. Americans won't mind a 13-year sales tax if it brings the debt under control.

The same approach ought to apply at the federal level. Identify potential revenue streams, dedicate those revenues to particular problems, and once those problems and the debt are manageable again, lower federal taxes.

Furthermore, untapped revenue streams do exist. Now that gasoline prices have again fallen below a dollar a gallon, for example, the federal government could impose a tax at 20 cents a gallon. After all, if we don't do it, OPEC probably will. Such a tax would bring in billions of additional dollars that could be used in the battles against drugs, AIDS, or homelessness. Coincidentally, it might also help reinstill a fuel conservation ethic, an ethic that has lapsed in recent years.

Consider another untapped stream. Fewer than 15 years ago, our tax collection system was a marvel. We achieved over 92 percent voluntary compliance. Today, there is less than 80 percent voluntary compliance. That means more than $100 billion in taxes are not collected each year. That's $100 billion in revenues unavailable in our battle against the problems we face.

In New York, the underground economy represents as much as $40 billion in business activity and $1 billion in lost tax revenue. Half of that $1 billion is attributable to illegal activity such as organized crime. These evaders belong in jail, not in tax court. But the other half-billion dollars is due to underreporting. We're going after the underreporters.

If we collected the $500 million we're owed, the city of New York could hire 2,750 new teachers, 1,900 new police officers, 1,400 new nurses, and 550 new sanitation workers, and could build 3,000 housing units. If that's what $500 million could buy in New York, just imagine what $100 billion could buy in the nation as a whole.

When Democrats launched the Great Society and the War on Poverty, we did so for good and decent reasons. We sought to fully guarantee equality of opportunity to all Americans, regardless of race, creed, color, or gender. We enfranchised many who'd never enjoyed the benefits of political power before. These are accomplishments of which we can all be proud, and that have vastly enriched and strengthened our society.

But in this process, parts of the Democratic Party began pushing the country down a path it did not want to travel. With each passing year, the clamor grew for unrealistic social goals. Democrats began the 1960s by promising their fellow Americans a better society. After our initial successes, all we delivered were burdensome taxes, burdensome regulations, and burdensome government.

Since 1981, the Republican Party has had a chance to build a better society. And for some Americans—wealthy Americans—our society is a better one now. But for many more Americans, the Reagan Revolution has been more hype than hope.

Democrats can offer real hope in 1988, but only if they adopt a simple principle—that their party's candidate will run on a platform of compassion and common sense. The Democratic Party has always been known as the party of compassion. The New Deal, the New Frontier, the Great Society—all are examples of a nation's stepping forward to help those most in need of help. Let's not forget that legacy in 1988.

But too often, the Democratic Party is seen as a party that believes government can solve every problem, big or small. That's not common sense. Government has its limits. The federal government can and should provide more funds to combat drugs, to find a cure and provide adequate treatment for AIDS, and to reduce homelessness while expanding our housing stock. But money alone won't solve these problems.

Our standard-bearer in 1988 must reawaken a spirit that's been sorely lacking in the last decade. It's a spirit that combines the resources of government with the talents, ideas, and energies of countless millions of Americans who, given half a chance, will work tirelessly to improve the schools, strengthen their neighborhoods, and reinstill values of cooperation, innovation, and dedication that are discouraged when government is seen as the be-all and end-all of a nation's problems.

Ours is a compassionate electorate in search of a compassionate government. But compassion without common sense is craziness. Craziness isn't what voters are looking for in 1988.

CHAPTER 29

Time for a National Urban Investment Policy

Mayor Joseph P. Riley, Jr.

IN THE DEPTHS OF the Great Depression, poor people from the rural corners and crossroads of this country flocked to the cities for jobs, food, shelter—and hope. This migration marked a watershed in American history: the irreversible movement toward becoming an urban nation, and the creation of a federal-city partnership to support the urban nation. This partnership was not the child of altruistic egalitarianism; it was a response to the realities and the demographics of an urbanized nation.

Over the past half-century, the federal government has played a central role in urban growth and development. It has helped find solutions to serious social, economic, and environmental problems, tearing down the barriers to neighborhood renewal, creating jobs and training opportunities, improving housing and the networks of street, transit, sewer, and water systems that hold our cities together. The federal investment in cities has been significant; it has enabled cities to leverage large amounts of private capital, undertake needed economic development projects, and provide quality public services that would not have been possible with limited local revenues alone. It has also helped cities respond to myriad costly federal government mandates.

313

From its beginnings in the Hoover and Roosevelt administrations, the federal-city partnership has been developed and fine-tuned by Democratic and Republican administrations alike. But in recent years, the federal investment in the cities has been jeopardized as the current administration and the Congress have cut, and in some cases eliminated altogether, the programs that for years have aided the people of America's cities, and that for years have helped cities move toward important national goals. Between 1980 and 1987, according to the Congressional Research Service, federal aid to local government dropped 38 percent. The Senate Budget Committee reports that between 1980 and 1986, federal nondefense spending declined from 16 percent to 15 percent of the gross national product.

Wise and thoughtful national leaders know they cannot look to the future without a sound trade policy, foreign policy, defense policy, and industrial policy. Why, then, is our national leadership moving from year to year without a semblance of a reasonable, fair, or creative urban policy? Three out of four of our citizens reside in urban areas, yet we have no urban policy—no policy to guide the development of the hundreds of major cities that, as a group, are the engine that drives the nation's economy—no policy to ensure that this engine runs smoothly, that it has what it needs to run without breakdown—no policy to ensure that there are people prepared to do the jobs that must be done, and that there are jobs for people when they need them—no policy to ensure decent, affordable housing, or reasonable mobility within and among our communities, or personal safety, or maintenance of health.

The time has come for this nation to adopt the urban policy that is so badly needed, and the 1988 presidential election provides an excellent forum for discussion of the policy. In the last election, cities were never mentioned by any candidate. In the upcoming election, they must be an issue in the campaign of every candidate.

In June of 1987, the U.S. Conference of Mayors convened its annual meeting in Nashville. Two hundred mayors and hundreds of other local government officials met for five days to examine our urban priorities, to discuss our most serious problems and the most promising solutions. Many of the major presidential candidates addressed this meeting, sharing their views on the future of the cities. The mayors were generally encouraged by what they heard from these candidates at this early stage in their campaigns, and look forward to working with them in the months ahead to help develop effective approaches to urban policy.

To aid in this process, at the close of the meeting the mayors ratified a National Urban Investment Policy statement which presents the official position of the Conference of Mayors on the issues that we all believe must be addressed by the candidates and the parties in the next election.

This is what we are saying.

THE CITIES AND COMPETITIVENESS

For the first time in recent history, we are concerned with the ability of the United States to compete successfully in the marketplaces of the world. There are unmistakable signs that our once secure—indeed, once dominant—position in the global economy has weakened. Attacking the current $170 billion trade deficit and restoring the United States to a fully competitive position will require an enormous national effort, one that enlists all sectors of the economy and all levels of government.

A sound national competitiveness policy must include a sound national urban policy: A competitive nation must have competitive cities.

Developing legislation to improve access to world markets and ensure fair trading practices is an important part of what must be accomplished, but it is only a part. Our central concern must be our ability to respond to world markets, and our own markets, with what is needed, when it is needed, with high quality and competitive prices.

America's cities make this response possible. We house the businesses, the industries, and the people that produce for the nation. We can provide the environment in which their production is efficient and profitable, but we cannot do it as individual cities, without a national commitment to support our efforts.

We are already pursuing a wide range of innovative approaches to development of new business and technology, often involving public-private partnerships. But for too many of our cities today, local resources are spread too thin to meet more than minimal capital spending and public service needs, much less numerous federal mandates, and will not support a nation's new competitive initiatives. A national urban investment policy, a policy to bolster the cities' many roles in improving national competitiveness, must be in place.

CHANGES IN AMERICA'S CITIES

The mayors of this nation are responsible for city governance and are the chief advocates for city residents at the county, state, and national levels of government. There was a time, a half-century ago, when mayors focused most of their time and effort on fixing the streets, collecting the trash, and assuring the public safety. Today, mayors and city governments must also be concerned with economic development, employment, housing for those who can pay and those who cannot, public health, clean air and water, recreation—the full range of services required to meet the needs of all the people. Over the years, city governments have had to take on more basic public services, including transportation and utilities, as private owners and providers of these services have withdrawn.

Meeting today's capital improvement and public service needs demands that partnerships be formed among all levels of government and the private sector. In cities throughout the country, this is happening: City government, private companies and foundations, the education community, religious groups, and others share in the responsibility for community well-being.

In 1980, the federal budget deficit was under $60 billion; by 1986, it had climbed to over $220 billion. The federal investment in housing, job training, neighborhood revitalization, public transportation, and the other essential elements of a strong urban America did not cause the enormous national deficit and debt, as some in Washington have claimed. In fact, as the deficit increased, federal spending for key urban programs decreased—dramatically. There is no question that this federal withdrawal from the urban partnership, if not checked, will prove to be one of the most damaging effects that the deficit has on this nation.

The partnership that has developed between cities and the federal government is concerned with meeting national challenges—with finding solutions to problems that are the result not just of local conditions, problems that are common to all cities, problems whose solutions exceed the ability of local governments, and problems that detract from the ability of cities to provide an environment in which our economy can grow and America's competitiveness can be assured.

In some areas, how and when problems are solved by the cities has been mandated by the federal government. For many years, local governments have been active partners in the development and implementation of national policy in areas such as nutrition, housing, education, public safety, civil rights, transportation, and clean water and air. Mayors do not oppose the presence of national policies established to ensure opportunities for, and the well-being of, citizens; but mayors do oppose the federal imposition of those policies with no federal effort to share in their costs. Mandated federal costs have contributed greatly to the financial burdens that must be borne by city residents. If there are goals that are truly in the national interest, worthy of federal legislation, then at least partial funding for them should come from the broad federal tax base.

THE ELEMENTS OF A NATIONAL URBAN INVESTMENT POLICY

The current national deficit and debt pose an enormous internal problem for the nation, but it is clear that a growing economy with reduced unemployment and reduced income dependency offers the best solution. A national urban investment policy that strengthens, not abandons, the federal partnership with our cities must be the heart of that solution.

The urban policy needed today must ensure that all cities and all citizens contribute, fully and fairly, to all the goals of the nation, be they goals of competitiveness, cooperation, or compassion. In the most basic of terms, this means each of our cities must do the following:

- Provide a climate, both fiscal and physical, that supports and encourages business and industry.
- Build and maintain a work force prepared to fill all the jobs of today and tomorrow.
- Make it possible to transport workers, raw materials, and finished products swiftly, safely, and economically.
- Provide housing and basic public services for all citizens in decent, safe neighborhoods.
- Protect the health of all citizens.
- Afford all citizens opportunities to improve the quality of their lives and realize their full potential.

These are broad responsibilities, and helping cities meet them calls for a national urban investment policy that is equally broad in its scope. In our view, such a policy must contain the elements described below.

TAX POLICY

National tax policy should provide revenues sufficient to reduce deficits and meet both defense and domestic needs, including the encouragement of investment and the creation of jobs. The federal government must recognize and accept the right of local governments to issue debt that is free from federal taxation. State and local taxes should remain deductible from federal income taxes, and the deductibility of sales taxes should be restored.

FEDERAL BUDGET

Federal spending and revenues must be brought in line through a realistic, multiyear effort that avoids severe economic and program dislocation. Significant progress toward achieving a balanced budget requires that the nation reduce military spending to a level consistent with national security and stem the growth in non-means-tested entitlements. Savings produced should be placed in a fund specifically earmarked for deficit reduction and, if necessary, augmented by an increase in federal revenues.

FISCAL ASSISTANCE

Unfunded federal mandates represent a severe and increasing burden on the fiscal capacity of local government to provide essential services. General Revenue Sharing, enacted in 1972 and allowed to expire in 1986, provided at least partial compensation for such mandates. A new program of compensatory federal payments to local governments, permitting maximum flexibility for use in meeting priority local needs, must be enacted to ease the burden of these mandates, and any new mandates on local governments that impose costs must be federally funded.

INTERNATIONAL TRADE

Trade law must be reformed to permit more effective action against unfair foreign trade practices in U.S. domestic and overseas markets, but this reform should not include domestic content requirements or other unwarranted restrictions that cause reciprocal trade barriers to be increased. The administration should negotiate trade agreements to open markets for U.S. exports, and cities should stimulate exports by helping small businesses overcome trade barriers.

PRODUCTIVITY

Mayors have worked with the federal government, states, academic institutions, and the private sector to disseminate new commercially applicable technology to their local firms, and will expand these efforts in the future. Federal support for technology dissemination should be increased in order to strengthen the international competitiveness of U.S. firms. Mayors have also taken the lead in encouraging local employers and the unions that represent their employees, in both the public and the private sectors, to improve productivity and quality, and federal support for these efforts should be increased.

WELFARE REFORM

The nation's welfare system needs to be reformed so that it encourages recipients to work—by providing education, training, and necessary support services, such as medical and child care—and establishes for those who cannot work a national minimum benefit, adjusted for regional differentials. In no case should it be more beneficial to remain on welfare than to work. As recipients move off welfare, child care and health care benefits and other supportive services must be continued so that there is an incentive to work. After a period of time, these benefits should be phased out gradually.

EDUCATION

Federal aid to education that meets the needs of all segments of the population, particularly minorities, the disadvantaged, and those who are illiterate, should be maintained. To prepare future generations to contribute to the competitiveness of the United States in the global economy, the federal government should provide funds directly to local school districts for improvement of instruction in basic skills, mathematics, science, computers, communications, and foreign languages.

Higher education must remain accessible to low- and moderate-income students through the maintenance of adequate, federally assisted grant and loan programs. Occupational education must be made available to any student who does not pursue a higher education.

EMPLOYMENT

Adequate levels of support should be provided to employment and training programs, including those aimed at young people and those that provide vocational and technical education. The nation's commitment to full employment should be renewed, and targeted federal grants and loans that create jobs should be provided. If sufficient jobs are not available in the private sector, the federal government, in cooperation with local governments and the private sector, should offer constructive employment to people in need, rather than resort to providing public assistance for them.

CHILDREN AND YOUTH

For far too many of America's children, the future is bleak. This nation must increase its support for programs that invest in the future of our children, and that strengthen the family, through cost-effective, preventive services—those that provide good nutrition, health care, education, employment and training, day care, and other social services.

THE ELDERLY

The nation's policies for the rapidly growing elderly population must promote independent living and the opportunity to continue to make contributions to the community. The income, health care, housing, nutrition, and social service needs of our elderly population should be addressed through the maintenance of Social Security and Medicare benefits and the provision of various forms of housing assistance. The Older Americans Act must be adequately funded, and city officials must be given a more effective role in the aging network's planning and coordination of community-based support services.

CATASTROPHIC HEALTH INSURANCE

America cannot allow the continuation of the current health insurance situation, in which many elderly and disabled Americans are forced into poverty by catastrophic illness. Adequate medical personnel and services must be made available to the medical personnel and services must be made available to the approximately 37 million Americans—three-fourths of whom are employed workers or their dependents—who have no private health insurance coverage and do not qualify for Medicare or Medicaid.

ACQUIRED IMMUNE DEFICIENCY SYNDROME (AIDS)

Current projections by the federal Centers for Disease Control indicate that 80 percent of the 46,000–91,000 new cases of AIDS diagnosed in 1991 will be reported from localities other than New York and San Francisco. Estimates are that half of these new cases are individuals already infected with the AIDS virus.

In the absence of a vaccine against AIDS, health education remains the only tool we have to persons at risk of the disease. The National Academy of Sciences recommends a spending level of $1 billion by 1991 to educate those at risk and the general public, and $1 billion for AIDS research. While the costs of such a concerted research effort and media/education campaign are high, they appear small when compared with the health care costs to be incurred if such efforts are not made. Though the cost of care per patient varies greatly from city to city, taking the average cost

($65,000) times the most conservative projection for new AIDS cases reported in 1991 alone produces a national health care cost of $2.99 billion.

HEALTH CARE FOR THE URBAN POOR

Many urban hospitals operate at a loss, even after local government subsidies are taken into account, partly because of the disproportionately large number of indigent patients they must care for. The federal government must support these hospitals as health care providers of last resort by giving incentives to providers who serve medically indigent and vulnerable people. In addition, enforceable penalties against "dumping"—the involuntary transfer of indigent patients from private to public hospitals—must be strengthened.

REDUCING HEALTH CARE COSTS

Though the general inflation rate as reflected by the consumer price index has been reduced, health care costs continue to soar. Home health care coverage should be strengthened and expanded under Medicaid and Medicare, thus avoiding the greater costs of hospital care. In addition, preventive medicine and health education should receive greater emphasis and funding at the national level, thus reducing the need for more expensive care in future years.

DRUG AND ALCOHOL ABUSE

With the passage of the Anti-Drug Abuse Act of 1986, the national government became the cities' ally in the war on drugs. That act provides a comprehensive approach to the drug problem: It strengthens federal laws and efforts, and provides much-needed support for local education, treatment, and enforcement efforts. Winning the war on drugs will require a sustained effort over many years. The federal government must provide an adequate level of assistance for state and local narcotics control efforts. In addition, the Department of Defense should be assigned the mission of actively searching for, and interdicting, smugglers attempting to bring narcotics into the United States by seizing drugs and arresting drug traffickers at U.S. borders. Funding for federal enforcement agencies such as the Coast Guard and the Customs Service should be increased so that they are better equipped to combat the flow of drugs into the United States.

CRIME

Crime and the fear of crime continue to be significant problems in cities. They compromise the safety and well-being of urban residents and hinder local economic development. While assuring the public safety is primarily the responsibility of local governments, the federal government must recognize that crime is a national problem with a national impact, and must assist local officials in responding to it. Federal law enforcement assistance programs that help local officials meet particular needs, such as the justice assistance and juvenile justice programs, must be continued. Federal laws that enhance local police efforts, such as those in the area of handgun control, must be strengthened.

CIVIL RIGHTS

The federal government must play a strong role in the enforcement of civil rights laws and the promotion of equal opportunity for all citizens. The U.S. Department of Justice should enforce existing civil rights laws vigorously. Affirmative action programs with specific goals and timetables are appropriate tools to provide and ensure equal opportunity for underrepresented groups and protected classes. Federal contracting should be expanded as a vehicle for the achievement of equal employment opportunities. The Equal Rights Amendment to the U.S. Constitution should be adopted.

The rights of citizens regardless of their sexual orientation should be protected under the law. Housing opportunities in the neighborhood of choice should be available to all Americans regardless of race, sex, age, religion, handicap, or family size; the nation's fair housing laws and the government's enforcement of them must be strengthened.

HUMAN RIGHTS

The strength of a nation and the principles of its people are often reflected in its policies toward other nations. Our national government must take a strong stand against those countries in which citizens are denied basic human rights, including Northern Ireland and Nicaragua. Because it is inappropriate for public funds to help sustain the racist apartheid system of South Africa, we urge the federal government to join American cities and withdraw any public funds now invested in institutions doing business with that nation. Mayors also believe that the leaders of the Union of Soviet Socialist Republics must respect the civil rights of Soviet Jews and all other citizens in its sphere of influence.

HUNGER AND HOMELESSNESS

All levels of government and the private sector have a shared responsibility to respond to the national problems of hunger and homelessness—painful problems that have become increasingly visible in cities of all sizes in every region. The national response to these problems must address both their short-term needs and their fundamental causes and should include (1) funding for emergency food and shelter; (2) adequate benefit levels of income assistance programs; (3) more permanent low-income housing and more transitional housing and housing with supportive services for mentally ill people; (4) discretion to use public assistance funds for the rehabilitation and construction of permanent housing; (5) more support for mental health, substance abuse, and social service programs; and (6) an adequate level of support for employment and training and education programs that assist people in preparing for jobs.

HOUSING

An all-income housing policy should be adopted to assure every American access to decent, safe housing.

Within the next decade, the lack of rental housing for low-income persons will reach crisis proportions. This is largely a result of rapidly increasing costs relative to personal income, the cumulative effect of years of cuts in federal housing assistance, and tax changes that have eliminated powerful incentives for construction and ownership of low-income housing. Coupled with little new construction is the problem of deterioration of public housing and other subsidized housing stock. Cities are responding to this situation with a variety of initiatives, such as housing trust funds and public-private partnerships, but an effective solution to the problem will be reached only after a national recommitment to low-income housing is made.

The federal government must provide sufficient funds for the maintenance and rehabilitation of existing low-rent public housing, and must provide increased support for operating subsidies and modernization. Mayors recommend a housing assistance block grant that will meet the nation's housing needs by ensuring a steady supply of newly constructed and substantially rehabilitated units. Local governments should be given authority over the allocation and distribution of the housing assistance funds, and innovation in their use should be encouraged.

COMMUNITY DEVELOPMENT

The Community Development Block Grant (CDBG), enacted in 1974, has proven itself a dependable and effective vehicle for the delivery of housing, economic development, and human services to low- and moderate-income people. Funding for CDBG must be increased to keep pace with the demand for services, not reduced, as it has been during the 1980s. (Between fiscal years 1981 and 1987, CDBG was cut by 34 percent in real terms.) With the number of cities receiving CDBG funds having increased by 37 percent, and with the program having to take on more local funding responsibilities as other federal programs have been cut, the Community Development Block Grant has become one of the most important, and needed, programs of the federal-city partnership.

ECONOMIC DEVELOPMENT

In the 1960s, America's urban problems were brought into sharp focus: Inner-city neighborhoods exploded on the front pages of newspapers and on the nightly TV news shows. Since that time, all levels of government have searched for the keys to the revitalization of depressed communities; as a result, many effective programs have been created.

The Urban Development Action Grant, Economic Development Administration, Small Business Administration, and Industrial Development Bonds have been critical to urban revitalization; mayors' support for expansion in each of these areas is stronger than ever, in light of the recent changes in federal tax law that have taken away incentives for private investment in economic development projects.

INFRASTRUCTURE

America's engines for economic growth, her cities, can run efficiently so long as they are livable. The infrastructure— the public works of America—makes the livability possible by providing citizens with mobility, clean air and water, power, and waste management. A national infrastructure financing program must be enacted to provide localities with the loan authority for repair and revitalization of their infrastructure systems.

Urban Mobility

Urban mobility, embracing public transit, roads and bridges, aviation and rail transportation, is a critical component of urban economic growth. The infrastructure for urban mobility, created through a partnership of federal, state, and local governments, must be maintained and developed. Further, a comprehensive multimodal mobility program that permits city officials to use available funds in support of community and economic development goals must be created. It is essential that, to the extent possible, federal funds targeted for urban mobility be allocated directly to local governments and be available for expenditure in a flexible manner, to meet the unique needs of each community.

Aviation

Funding for airport and airspace infrastructure should be maintained at levels consistent with the amount generated by the fund. The administration of the nation's airspace, a key to the nation's competitiveness, must continue to receive support from outside the trust fund. For cities to be truly competitive, the national airway and airport system, which is suffering from capacity and safety problems, must be mended. Full funding of airport and aviation programs is key to this process.

Rail

In order to preserve competitive pricing in rail transportation, maintain service, and ensure national safety standards, the federal government must continue its support of a national passenger and freight rail system. In many communities around the country, there is no feasible alternative to AMTRAK, particularly as interstate bus service has declined. AMTRAK support has been cut substantially in recent years, with resulting declines in service. This trend should be halted.

Roads and Bridges

For America to be competitive, moving goods within our nation must be more economical than bringing foreign goods into our nation. The funding for roads and bridges, therefore, must be maintained at levels supported by the Highway Trust Fund, including interest. Further, local government must be a full partner in the post interstate era of the national highway system. As policy is developed for this post-interstate era, new attention must be given to the condition and viability of local road systems, which have been largely excluded from the benefits of the Highway Trust Fund.

Public Transportation

America's cities house large groups of "transportation-disadvantaged" persons, individuals who do not have ready access to an automobile and are therefore more dependent on public transportation than is the population as a whole. These groups consist largely of the young, the disabled, the poor, and the elderly. Mayors' opposition to cuts in public transit operating assistance (40 percent, adjusted for inflation, over the past five years) and their support for funding at the levels that have been authorized by Congress are based in large measure on concern for these groups.

ENERGY AND ENVIRONMENT

Regional Approach

The role of the federal government should be to establish national goals in the protection of the nation's environment. However, the various regulatory agencies should not mandate national models as the means to attain national standards. Instead, the federal government should employ and empower its regional offices, in consultation with local elected officials, to develop regional models for the attainment of the national standards.

Clean Air and Water

Cities have traditionally accepted the responsibility of providing water and sewer services to their residents and leading the fight to preserve the region's air quality. But because air and water pollution know no political boundaries, the federal government must acknowledge that it has a shared responsibility—other than the imposition of unfunded mandates—for the protection of the nation's environment. Cities can no longer accept federal mandates that are not accompanied by the federal funds needed to satisfy them.

Waste Management

The disposal of solid waste has developed into a serious and costly problem for cities. With conventional methods of waste disposal no longer feasible in many cities, resource recovery plants are badly needed. Waste-to-energy facilities, alone or as components of integrated resource recovery systems, are superior to conventional disposal methods and are a necessity in many cities. The federal government must help, not hinder, cities' efforts to employ this technology.

Hazardous Waste and City Health

As advocates for both city residents and city economies, mayors must be consulted in any discussion of the transport, storage, or disposal of hazardous waste in their communities. Congressional inclusion in recent legislation of "community right to know" requirements covering the presence of hazardous material is laudable and should be continued. Further, the right of cities to prosecute those who pollute the air, water, and land must be maintained.

ARTS, CULTURE, AND RECREATION

The National Endowments

Arts, culture, and recreation are integral parts of both the quality of life and the economic development of a city and a nation. While cities make the largest government expenditure for these activities, the national government recognized the need for its participation when it established the National Endowment for the Arts, the National Endowment for the Humanities, and the Institute of Museum Services (IMS). But the National Endowments and the IMS have always been shortchanged in the federal budget. Cities creatively leverage small amounts of federal funds for the arts and humanities to achieve outstanding quality and excellence; this bare minimum has a significant impact upon the nation's cities. Thus, funding for these agencies, particularly support for local arts programs, should be increased, at least to keep pace with inflation until the federal deficit is under control. Subsequently, federal support for the arts and humanities should be strengthened further to supplement the exceptional efforts of cities in the areas of arts and culture.

Historic Preservation

Historic preservation has been a joint commitment of the cities and the national government since 1966, when a national program was established to provide incentives to the private sector to preserve or restore the physical vestiges of our national past. Funding from general revenues and from the tax code, however, has been under constant attack. Federal funding for historic preservation and federal tax incentives for rehabilitation—which, combined, form one of the best-targeted urban aid programs cities have ever had—must, at least for the present, be restored to previous levels of support; subsequently, they should be strengthened.

Urban Parks

The relationship between cities and the federal government in the parks and recreation area is important, exemplified over the years by such key programs as the Urban Parks and Recreation Recovery Program and the Land and Water Conservation Program. Since the bulk of the American population live in cities, the focus at the federal level should be on strengthening the ability of cities to meet the recreation needs of their large populations. A trust fund that provides support for local, state, and federal land protection strategies and for state and local recreation resource development and rehabilitation should be established to ensure a dependable source of funding and to make possible multiyear, comprehensive planning.

THE FUTURE

The cities of the future are what we make them, starting today. The National Urban Investment Policy we are seeking is a blueprint for the future that this nation can follow, starting today.

We must all recognize that this nation's economy is but a collection of the economies of her cities, and that a wise nation shares its resources with the great cities that create them. The urban scholar Jane Jacobs cautions: "People who relinquish the civilized art of maintaining creative cities are not to be entrusted with the risks of developing further. Societies and civilizations in which the cities stagnate don't develop and flourish further—they deteriorate."

History has shown that the nation's investment in her cities has been a good investment, yielding high returns to government at all levels. More importantly, this investment has produced high returns for the people of America, because the investment has been in the people of America.

CHAPTER 30

Openings to the New Texas

Mayor Henry Cisneros

THE CHALLENGE

THE SUBJECT OF THIS essay is at once challenging and optimistic, but it also must be grounded in some facts and some realities. Some of these are not so pleasant, so I apologize in advance for having to remind you of them. But the results, I feel, are worth the challenge. Allow me to begin by setting an important scene.

The place is Los Angeles. A quick analysis of the economy reveals that of the major weapons systems funded by the U.S. Government, the immense increase in defense spending over the last several years, virtually all or some part or all of those weapons systems are being developed in Southern California.

There is an amazing confluence of factors contributing to the economic success of L.A. One is a tremendous political influence for funding capabilities. Second is the influence of training and education and the ability to get talent. And third is the economic support system within the region at large, what economists call "agglomeration" economics, where there is a support system put in place that is known as the diversified economy. One might say that the story of Los Angeles is unique in California, that it is simply a coincidence, a random happening in a state that is otherwise nor-

333

mal. But Los Angeles is not unique. A trip several hundred miles north would take us to San Francisco; its port and naval center at Oakland make it a world class naval facility. Its nationally prominent financial center is so strong that the predominant fear of San Franciscans today is the Manhattanization of their 43 square miles, as new office buildings vie with hotels and retail facilities for space in that dense area. San Francisco's venture capital base that has spawned the greatest growth of biotechnology companies anywhere in the world is actually larger than the available venture capital of New York. Its international outreach is legendary. As of this writing, Mayor Feinstein is in the People's Republic of China, Hong Kong, and Taiwan developing business for San Francisco.

Travelling slightly to the south of San Francisco we find San Jose and Sunnyvale, Palo Alto, Cupertino, and Santa Clara. Arguably, here lies the greatest concentration of technological power in the world, which is virtually an honor roll of every company, including American, British, and Japanese firms involved in microelectronics development. The culture of high technology that sweeps across America today stems from that concentration of resources in the Santa Clara Valley. It extends from Northern to Southern California, from Sacramento—one of the fastest growing and most attractive communities in the country to the far south of San Diego—a sophisticated, livable city developing its strengths in education and biotechnology. This concentration of economic power is so strong that if California were a nation, it would be the sixth most powerful one on the globe.

I have started a discussion of Texas dangerously by daring to compare the experience of another state. The comparison has been made before, simplistically. On the one hand, Texas has relied on the bounty of the earth, the black oil that runs under our ground and on the topographical conditions that made it possible for us to raise cotton and sorghum, grains and cattle for the last 40 years. By contrast, California has focused on the bounty of its human capital to build the greatest set of higher education institutions and junior colleges, funding its public education.

In contrast to the big picture that I have just painted in California, if a similar tour around Texas were to start in the Golden Triangle—Beaumont, Port Arthur, Orange—we would find unemployment rates pushing 20 percent. If our drive were to take us then to Houston on our way down the Gulf Coast, we would find the effects of vacant office space, business foreclosures at a higher rate than ever. As we made our way past Corpus Christi, we would find the same result of closed refineries and the slowdown in petrochemicals. If our ride then took us to the borderlands, if we began in Brownsville and moved along Edinburgh, Harlingen, and McAllen, and out to Laredo, and to Del Rio and Eagle Pass, beyond to El Paso, what we would find there is not a 20 percent unemployment rate, but in many areas, unemployment approaches 30 percent. This includes a different reality, the border relationship, but the same fundamental problem, an overreliance on one major industry. Where the economy of the Gulf Coast and Golden Triangle has been petrochemicals, the borderlands has been trade with Mexico. Our ride could then take us to West Texas where in Midland-Odessa we would see the effects of the oil and gas turndown, to the high plains, to Lubbock, Amarillo, and again, we would see the problem in a slightly different variant, the stagnation of agriculture prices.

In contrast to that somewhat gloomy picture around the perimeter of the state is the central corridor of Texas. It, too, is hurt. But its pain—in Dallas, Fort Worth, Waco, Temple, Belton, Austin, and San Antonio—tends to be more cyclical, whereas the pain of the periphery of the state tends to be a more structural problem. The shape of the future economy of Texas is visible along the spine of the state that is IH-35. It is in the mix of education, government, technology, defense, electronics, tourism, wholesaling, transportation, and goods distribution, that we will see the shape of the future economy of Texas.

Perhaps I have overstated the case, but we must be ready to work through such comparisons—not to be maudlin nor for self-flagellation—but as a step toward understanding the larger world and the rest of the country. Fundamentally, we must be more open-minded. Indeed, I suspect that simple phrase, "to open," will shape our dominant attitude of the next few years.

In Texas, it is time . . .

—to open our economy and our approach to economic development;
—to open our attitude about the public sector and its relationship to economic problems;
—to open our financial practices and banking system;
—to open our international postures;
—to open access to education to all Texans;
—to open our ethic relations, to put some of the scars and wounds of the past behind us for good.

In this commentary, I would like to share further thoughts on this process of "opening up." I will concentrate on three dimensions of the future of Texas: (1) opening up economically, (2) opening up our politics, and (3) opening up the equity and social issues that confront our state.

OPENING UP ECONOMICALLY

Diversification is a word used much today to describe the challenge before our state. There can certainly be no question that we must diversify. I worry, however, that in talking about diversification, we miss an important point about the challenge before Texas. Diversification alone or in general will not be enough. What we will really have to do is to match a diversifying and changing Texas economy to regional realities. There must be different strategies for different regions of this state since our geography divides us into different topographical and climatic zones. We have everything from the High Plains, which are as different as night and day from the Piney Woods; the Big Bend and its rugged beauty to the black dirt farm districts of Caldwell County, and the palms of the Gulf Coast. Geographically, we are several different zones. So, too, is our economy really several different economies. It is the economy of the petro-chemical regions, of the Mexico relationship, of the agricultural base, and of the corridor down the center of the state.

How might we begin to think in terms of this regional diversification as we plan for the emerging economy for the new Texas? There has already been a visible major thrust to our economic future. It has been to focus on the emerging industries of aerospace, computers, microelectronics, and biotechnology. Although these efforts will largely benefit only Houston, Dallas, Fort Worth, Austin, San Antonio, and College Station, these industries are clearly important. At one level, we must focus on these new and emerging businesses as part of our economic strategy. A major reality of this focus is that we will have to advance a science and technology policy. We will have to recognize the underpinning role that education and research play in the development of this type of economy.

Unfortunately, there are many indicators today that Texas lags behind in developing a cohesive science and technology thrust. Research and development activity in Texas is at a level of about one half of the national per capita average. The combined research of all Texas universities is at a level just 79 percent of that done at Johns Hopkins University alone. The University of Texas system is involved in research and development activity at just 31 percent of that found within the University of California system. Although Texas ranks third among states in population, it is tenth in total expended R&D funds. Relatively speaking, Texas receives a smaller percentage of Federal R&D dollars than it did ten years ago. If R&D in Texas were conducted at just the national average, then a new and strategic $4 billion influx of capital would be added to the state's economy. Texas ranks 45th among the states in composite SAT scores today. Any economic strategy that will focus on these new and emerging industries—aerospace, computers, microelectronics, and biotechnology—will be highly dependent on improvements in R&D and education.

An economy based mainly on emerging industries dependent on science and technology will not be enough to reach all the regions of Texas. There will have to be a second layer or level of economic initiative. That second layer will build on regional strengths. In the border region, it will mean focusing on the maquiladora program. In the Gulf Coast, it will mean focusing on, for example in Houston, the space initiative. In Corpus Christi, it will build on the port facilities. In east Texas and west Texas, it will focus on timber and agriculture. This will require a job-creation role by the land-grant institutions, especially their extension and experiment services.

On this second level our economic strategy must be to build on regional strengths that may exist across the state. It is a targeted, segmented, economic development strategy that builds on the existing capabilities. It may also include expanding airports for new air routes, focusing on the development of university resources, such as those at Pan American or U.T. El Paso, or East Texas State, or West Texas State. It may include developing "main streets" and tourism. Indeed, a most attractive industry today is the development of tourism in smaller and middle-level cities. Those communities that have not considered themselves as attractive to tourism may need help from the state in funding community facilities. This is a type of economic development that we have often overlooked as an opportunity.

There is also a third level of our economic strategy that must reach down to every community in the state. I am convinced that no state or city in the country, including Texas, has yet properly mastered the relationship between economic policies and the stimulation of indigenous small businesses. Most of the analyses by experts such as David Burch of MIT tell us that on the average 80 percent of the new jobs created annually in a given community will stem from small business. While people like me and other public officials are waiting for that great Toyota plant in the sky to arrive, or the gigantic Saturn plant to suddenly materialize with 5,000 jobs, we overlook that most of the new jobs are created by small businesses within our communities. In 1983, when considering all of the moves by Fortune 500 companies in the United States—when all was said and done—the net number of jobs created was zero. But in that same year six million jobs were created in small businesses.

I am convinced that the State of Texas has an obligation to work on small business incubators, such as the Business & Technology Center that exists now in San Antonio. It has created 70 small businesses and about 200 jobs that did not exist a year ago. We just created the Institute on Entrepreneurial Development, not to focus on high technology or biotechnology, but to encourage individual entrepreneurs who want to grow. No matter whether they want to make tacos, do laundry, do pest control, or custodial services, the key is if they want to double or triple in size. Are they willing to work 18 hours a day for seven days a week if that is what it takes? Do they have the personality profile that will allow them to get the business to grow, to add branches, to expand a fast food operation? For many areas of Texas, particularly middle-sized and smaller communities, a strategy of small business development will be the most effective in these times. We have largely overlooked this opportunity.

More than these three levels of developmental strategy is needed. Overreaching all levels must be an initiative that promotes a state-wide plan for development. Although we Americans have often shied away from thinking in terms of industrial policy, there are states that have policies with a sense of strategy about them. Perhaps the state with the clearest sense of industrial policy is North Carolina. Several governors have nurtured not only the famous Research Triangle Park, but across that state, from Charlotte to Raleigh/ Durham, a sense of patience and planning, and an integration of resources. Massachusetts is another example, especially in terms of its investment in education. Enough has already been said about California. These are the frequently cited models of industrial development policies, the ones mentioned when one counters with examples of the American response to Japanese economic initiatives.

Other states will be models of economic development over the next five years because their current initiatives will put them in that position. Arizona is one of those states because of major initiatives in financing of higher education, including the excellent junior college programs that have been created in the Phoenix area. Arizona also has innovative policies in venture capital initiatives, development of air routes, and small business. Michigan, a Rust Belt state, is newly prosperous because of its targeting of investment resources, including pension fund monies, in the creation of start-up businesses. In Utah, Salt Lake City is a center of biotechnology, the base of Western Airlines, the site of the Jarvik heart development, and ahead in the development of technology jobs because they sought those gains. Minnesota, with a long tradition of public-private partnership, is often cited as the classic example of a state that cooperates with its private initiatives. Finally, Florida may outstrip us all in terms of its investment, not only in education, but also in conscious growth strategies that were the legacy of Governor Graham's tenure.

Texas has work to do. If we are to create a compact—a science and technology compact with a strategic focus on economic development—we have our work cut out for us. Our work will require cooperation with our federal delegation which we have not experienced in recent years. It will mean setting targets such as academic salary increases five percent above the average salaries in the ten most populous states in the country. This will cost money, but it must be done. Universities must work to try to protect, or regain, the indirect cost receipts from sponsored research. We must create a research-biased formula for university funding in addition to the existing formulas. Research must be increased in institutions across the state in such areas as supercomputers, molecular biology, materials research, manufacturing technology, microelectronics, agricultural genetics, and polymer sciences.

Still another set of policies must deal with capital formation. Texas has a conservative banking community relative to small business financing. We have a young, but growing, venture capital industry, yet a private investor community not accustomed to technology-related investments. Changes in law and institutional mechanisms will be required. Among those that merit pursuit are amendments to the state securities regulations to allow full disclosure, pension and trust funds to permit investment in venture capital pools, franchise tax deferrals for start-up companies with negative cash flow, and countless other actions that need to be considered by the legislature to open the financial community in Texas.

Up to this point, I have concentrated heavily on the need to open economic initiatives and opportunities in Texas. This has already been the focus of much of the public discussion on solutions to the current problems of our state and is being given new impetus by task forces now at work. Larry Temple's Select Committee on Higher Education will have much to say about what it will take to build our higher education system. The legislature has a full-time job on its hands to defend public school funding and add to it, as must be the case even with a $3.5 billion deficit, and the need for new revenues. The Science and Technology Council is producing a set of some sixteen recommendations that will reflect on several of the points that I have discussed here. There is due to be much more, discussion of economic planning in Texas.

OPENING UP POLITICALLY

We now have in Texas the emergence of a two-party state. There is no doubt that the potential exists beyond the Governor's Office for the creation of a fully competitive two-party system. It means that there will be contested positions and that neither party will be allowed to become complacent. Neither will be allowed to slip to the extremes; both will have to contest for the middle. But it also means that we have to be particularly attentive so that we can take advantage of bipartisanship in the interests of building Texas.

The role of bipartisanship for Texas must be pursued with a vengeance. It must be the dominant style of our political leaders as we work through the emergence of a two-party state.

A second initiative related to political culture must be to rethink the definition of the Texas conservative. The dominant coloration by which one gets elected in Texas is to say that he/she is conservative. It seems to me there are several kinds of conservatives. There are conservatives who will stand for no change and no expenditures, and that is the kind of conservative we have typically associated with Texas. There are also conservatives, who while they are conservative on a set of issues—social questions and others—understand the role of investment. They understand human capital and the role of corporate initiatives (be they public or private). These are the conservatives—investment-oriented conservatives—who are needed in today's Texas. This is not the conservative with a siege or bunker mentality, the cutback planner who refuses to acknowledge change, but the kind of conservative who understands the need for investment and development.

Texans are pragmatic. They do not want ideological solutions. They want results, and their number one priority for results is that four-letter word, "JOBS." If we start with the premise that our objective is to create jobs and growth, then work backward from there, many other problems become solvable.

OPENING UP SOCIALLY

The third area of opening up Texas has to do with our attitudes on matters of equity, social justice, and relations among the ethnic groups of our state. Last year, I had opportunity to attend a conference at the California Institute of Technology. I was asked to be a respondent to a study that was produced by Cal Tech on a difficult issue: the future ethnic mix of California and how to prepare for governance of a state that is changing so rapidly in this regard. In the 1940s, California was a state that was 80 percent Anglo. By the year 2010, California will be a state that has no definable ethnic majority. Estimates show that it will roughly be 25 percent black, 25 percent Asian, 25 percent Anglo, and 25 percent Hispanic.

The task of governance of such a population mix and the required new coalitions is immense. Cal Tech, a technological institution noted for its work in engineering and space, was taking the lead in trying to define at least the shape of the new demographics of California. Perhaps in this way, social scientists, public officials and leaders could begin to wrestle with the implications of this change. Much fear and concern resulted, for example, in the passage of the English-only referendum by a 2-to-1 margin.

I would assert that Texas has a better chance of getting a handle on this problem than California. Texas had two Hispanics on the ballot in 1986. One was offered by each party for statewide office. One of those, Raul Gonzales, was elected to the Texas Supreme Court. Of the 3000 Hispanic elected public officials in America, from New York to Florida to California, better than half, more than 1,500, are in Texas. There is something about our concentration of population, to look at it demographically, and perhaps even in the history of Texas, that allows Texas to have a better chance. But, I worry a great deal about how fast this process will occur and what price we will pay if we are forced to carry entire regions of Texas. There is no question in my mind but that if we focus only on that first kind of economic policy I described—i.e., science and technology—then the Valley of Texas is not likely to participate. If the Valley does not participate, then a large part of Texas will be left out of the economic mainstream. This has profound political consequences for Texas as a whole, not just the Valley, not to mention the human consequences of suffering and trauma that will be attendant to such oversight.

I recently met with reporters from the *Dallas Morning News* who were preparing a major series on the future of Texas. They asked me a question that I found interesting; it was whether Dallas could "go it alone." Is it possible for Dallas, because of its essential prosperity, to separate itself from the rest of Texas and be, in effect, an island economically, culturally, and politically. I suggested to them how that might be possible in the short run, but that I thought it would have immense negative consequences for Dallas in the long run. Consider, for example, that Dallas is the headquarters of the bank holding companies and, as such, is a *de facto* economic capital that cannot separate itself economically from the rest of the state. Realize, too, that even within Dallas the demographics are changing. The majority of schoolchildren in the third grade and below are black or

Hispanic. Neither Dallas nor any part of Texas will be able to separate itself from the demographic changes that are reaching every region.

Education is a critical part of the social agenda. This includes outreach by our senior universities to Hispanic and black students, the use of the community colleges as an integrated element of our education system, and equity in school financing at all levels. As a Regent at Texas A&M, with a student body with only between six and seven percent minority in a state where minorities are approaching 35 percent of the total population, I told my colleagues that for the good of the institution and the good of our state, an outreach strategy must be a part of the new Texas.

FACING UP TO CHANGE

In the final analysis, the dominant feature of our times in Texas is change. It is a change that is massive in its scale and so pervasive that it touches every dimension of our lives. It is a change that is rapid in its pace and, ironically, a change that has about it dimensions of permanence. It will be with us for a long time.

We are now living directly in the midst of a transformation to a new Texas. We are transforming from . . .

—an economy that had little foreign competition to one that lives in a world of heavy foreign competition;
—a Texas that once had only marginal domestic competition in the United States to a new Texas that now must compete among the other 49 states;
—a Texas where job growth was mostly in large companies to a Texas where job growth is in small and medium-sized enterprises;
—a Texas where job creation seemed to have been the responsibility of the Federal government to an era in which the states are on their own; if job creation is not a strategy in that state, then the state will do without;
—an era in which a minimally skilled work force was acceptable to an era in which a technically proficient work force is an imperative;

—an era that revolves around a gradual development of infrastructure to an era in which we have to have competitive infrastructure—telecommunications, electricity, roadways, and airports;

—an era of little investment in education to the challenge of now thinking of education as the preeminent element of infrastructure for our times; and

—living in a Texas where there was little concern about environmental issues to a Texas in which the quality of life deserves emphasis.

The competition shows little respect for our great Texas traditions and legends.

But let me conclude by describing a moving incident that recently occurred in my own city. I went to the West Side of San Antonio and listened to a group of Hispanic children recite a series of songs associated with the sesquicentennial celebrations at that school. They closed with a song that I think is beautiful. It is the state song of Texas, "Texas Our Texas." It was once learned in all the schools of this state. In tune and in words, it is just as inspiring as the National Anthem. The closing phrases of that song as those children recited it wide-eyed, innocent, and taught to say it while perhaps not even understanding the words are:

God bless you Texas and keep you brave and strong,
that you may grow in power
and worth
throughout the ages long.

As they recited the verses, I thought that the key phrase here was "throughout the ages long." Our Creator did not put Texas here to last for only 150 years. We know that it existed for thousands of years before that. If we had any doubt, James Michener made sure that we understand it is destined to be here for hundreds, or, hopefully, thousands, more.

The real question in this Sesquicentennial year is not the traditional "What have people done who came this way before?" as heroic as they may have been. It is instead the questions we must ask ourselves while penetrating our individual consciousness for answers. These questions are:

> What will we, as individuals, do?
> What is our legacy?
> What is this generation's contribution to the evolving history of Texas?

There is a temptation to think because William Barret Travis and Davy Crockett lived in an earlier era that they must have been giant human beings of immense stature and capability, of heroic proportions, and that the times in which they lived were uniquely decisive. But to face the facts, almost any single Texan chosen at random today will be larger physically, better prepared mentally, will live a longer life, and have better health than any of those who were present at the events of 1836.

What could be more decisive for today's Texan than living in this moment when Texas has to choose between mediocrity and excellence, between going into a siege mentality or realizing an investment opportunity? We must be prepared at this moment to seize the opportunity to make those decisions. I believe we are most fortunate to be living in these challenging times.

CHAPTER 31

Why We Must Save the Family Farm

Senator Tom Harkin

AMERICA'S FARM ECONOMY AND rural communities are in crisis. Debt and despair, foreclosures, and even suicides have swept across the heartland in recent years, turning entire regions into economic wastelands.

But it is not just a farm crisis. It is a crisis of values, resulting from a failure by our nation's political and economic leaders to recognize the importance of rural America to the stability and strength of our democratic society.

The real crux of the farm policy debate is this: How many farmers will society permit to own and work the land?

Do we want 2–3 million farm families owning the land they live and work on and preserving it for future generations? Or do we want our farms run like giant corporations, owned by absentee landlords and operated by day laborers?

The Reagan administration prefers to inaccurately portray the farm policy debate as the free market versus government control. For one thing, there is no free market in agriculture. Every nation in the world controls its production and prices through various subsidies and tariffs. Here at home, the mythical free market offers farmers only the freedom to go broke.

As far as government control is concerned, it seems the

347

president wants to have it both ways. President Reagan once bragged that he had spent more on farm programs than any other president in history. That's like Henry Ford's bragging about the huge production costs involved in the Edsel.

Despite all this administration's bold rhetoric about "getting the government out of agriculture," the fact is that an affordable and reliable supply of food is just as essential to our national security as are our military forces. For this reason, government has been involved in agriculture since the first spade of soil was turned over in this country—and it always will be.

What we need to decide is whose interests government will defend—whether those of the vast majority of farmers or those of the handful of large producers and agribusiness conglomerates. How we answer this, it seems to me, strikes at the core of who we are as a people and what we are as a nation—whether we will be a nation that continues to place value on human dignity and individual worth, or whether individual Americans are to be swept aside by the consolidation of economic wealth in fewer and fewer hands.

The human tragedy of families splitting up and breaking under the financial strain, post-Depression record rates of bank closings and small-business bankruptcies, massive layoffs in factories producing agricultural machinery, the economic devastation of entire communities, the erosion of our soil and pollution of our groundwater by excessive use of pesticides and fertilizers—all this, the administration would have us believe, is the inevitable cost of progress.

It is not inevitable. Nor is it progress.

It is the result of misconceived and mismanaged agricultural policies that create a destructive cycle in which farmers are forced to produce more and more for lower and lower prices.

In the 1970s, there was a brief period when—because of drought in the Soviet Union and other short-term factors—the world market could handle all the farm commodities the United States could produce. Prices stayed high, land values went up, and the farmer was prosperous. During this time, economists, government officials, bankers, and credit officials all advised farmers to expand and borrow.

But the prosperity of the 1970s could not continue forever. Then 1980 brought an explosion of food production around the world, particularly in the Third World. Suddenly, the world didn't need all our grain. To make things worse, the rising federal deficit effectively priced our commodities out of the market—even while it contributed to dramatically higher real interest rates at home. Inflated land prices—the basis for most farmers' equity—fell through the floor, and domestic commodity prices dropped well below the average cost of production.

At first, the victims were those farmers and outside land speculators who had vastly overextended their operations. As the farm crisis drags on year after year, more and more good, solid operators, through no fault of their own, are also being dragged down by this administration's blind faith in free market ideology.

The time has come to cast aside myths, face the facts, and develop a farm policy that is adequate to deal with the challenges and opportunities of modern world agriculture.

We ought to examine the potential (or actual) record of a farm policy in light of its effect on three key indicators: U.S. exports and international trade, the structure of our agricultural system, and the American consumer.

TRADE

A stated key objective of the 1985 Food Security Act was to improve the competitiveness of U.S. agricultural exports through the use of lower loan rates for feed grains and oilseeds, marketing loans for rice and cotton, and an aggressive export enhancement program. At the same time, it intended to protect farm incomes through a costly program of fixed target prices and deficiency payments.

This drive for exports raises two fundamental questions: What level of market share can the United States realistically expect to achieve? And in what sense does a nation gain by increasing export volume at the expense of lowering commodity prices (with or without increased federal subsidies)?

Since 1981, U.S. agricultural exports have fallen more

than one-third in volume and 40 percent in value. Despite projected increases in export volumes for our major commodities in 1987, revenues remain stagnant. To put the current situation in perspective: In 1981, feed grain export revenues were $10.5 billion, while 1987's total was $6.5 billion. Similarly, 1987 wheat export revenues of $3.1 billion compare with $8 billion in sales in 1981.

Indeed, the 55 percent share of world grain exports captured by the United States in the peak year of 1980–1981 was the result of a combination of very favorable conditions for U.S. agricultural trade that are not likely to be repeated.

Prospects for expanding the U.S. share of world agricultural trade in the near term are limited. While foreign trade will continue to contribute importantly to demand for American agricultural production, the halcyon growth of the late 1970s is not likely to be repeated.

This expectation is consistent with projections by both the National Center for Food and Agricultural Policy (NCFAP) and the Food and Agricultural Policy Research Institute (FAPRI) at the University of Missouri and Iowa State University, suggesting that the United States could possibly recover about 25 percent of lost agricultural export volume over the next three years. Even a gain of this magnitude, however, would still give us less than a 50 percent market share. Further, the rise in volume is projected to be accompanied by only a six percent gain in export value.

Looking at the long-term picture, NCFAP projects that the total volume of U.S. agricultural exports, which rose more than 10 percent annually during the 1970s, will return to a more normal long-term growth rate of 2.3 percent through the end of this century. NCFAP projects that U.S. grain exports will increase from 110 million metric tons in 1980 to 168 million tons by the year 2000. This projected 53 percent increase compares with a 300 percent growth in the 1970s.

Trade at any price does not necessarily make a nation better off. Studies by Andrew Schmitz, of the University of California, and other economists have shown that if the terms of trade are distorted by input subsidies and trade barriers, there may be no economic gains from trade (and, in fact, there will likely be losses) even though trade volume is large.

Why, then, do the United States and other exporting countries continue to subsidize exports? The bottom line is that multinational grain firms, the major players in international trade, profit from large trade volumes and price instability.

As the last few years have shown, the present program, with its export enhancement and marketing loan features, will not provide any real relief for our farm economy (without massive government payments).

President Reagan's proposal to eliminate all farm subsidies and move to a world free market agriculture through negotiations in the next round of the General Agreement on Tariffs and Trade will go nowhere. The idea that the European Community (EC) or Japan would agree to move to a system of unbridled, laissez-faire agriculture is utterly naive. It is also the wrong approach at the wrong time.

What world agriculture doesn't need is more of the boom and bust cycles of the seventies and eighties. What is needed is a process that will bring some order to our world agricultural trading system.

Certainly, we can all agree on the need to eliminate wasteful subsidies, but it must be done in conjunction with efforts to bring supply in line with demand, raise (not lower) world prices, and enhance farm income.

Many Democrats favor another option—negotiate with our trading partners to maintain higher world prices, equitable supply restrictions, caps on government farm support payments, and a fair sharing of carryover stocks. This is the approach embodied in the Family Farm Act, which Representative Richard Gephardt (D.-Mo.) and I have introduced.

The potential payoffs of this approach are high: Under the Harkin-Gephardt bill, for example, such agreements could result in an annual net gain in export revenues for seven major commodities of $12.3 billion over revenues resulting from the current "export-oriented" policy, for a total of $248 billion through 1995, as compared with $137 billion under the present program. In addition, under Harkin-Gephardt, the resulting higher world prices would raise domestic farm income to $59 billion by 1991, compared with $19 billion under the 1985 farm bill.

To those who say other nations will never go along with these kinds of agreements, I would point out that in 1983, the EC unilaterally offered to restrict its share of the world wheat market to 14 percent. None of the major trading nations agreed, so the EC continued to increase its market share, which today is 17.5 percent.

A frequent criticism of this approach is that it creates a cartel and that if OPEC didn't work, there is no reason to think this cartel will.

Let's see how badly OPEC failed. In 1973, the first year OPEC unilaterally established its own price, non-American producers of oil received an average of $3.39 a barrel. In 1986, even after a major worldwide energy slump, the average world price of crude oil was $15.35 per barrel. By contrast, the average corn price in 1973 was $2.55 per bushel; in 1986, it was $1.96 per bushel. Corn producers could use some of that OPEC-style "failure," though, unlike OPEC, we're not after an extortion price, only a fair price.

By refusing to exercise our tremendous potential power in influencing world markets, the United States and the other major grain trading nations have hurt only themselves and helped create a buyer's grain market.

Under Harkin-Gephardt, if nine months after negotiations with our trading partners begin, no multilateral agreement has been consummated, the secretary of agriculture would be mandated to use export payment in kind (PIK) or cash subsidies to maintain exports. I am opposed to unilaterally abandoning our export markets, but first we should at least attempt to reach cooperative, mutually beneficial trade relationships. This carrot-and-stick kind of approach can help us achieve the maximum negotiating leverage.

THE FAMILY FARM

The price of ignoring world trade realities in pursuit of a mythical free market is paid for by our farmers here at home.

If current policies are continued, the total number of farms in the United States will fall to 1.2 million by the year 2000, nearly 50 percent fewer than the 2.2 million farms in the nation in 1982, according to a 1986 study by the congressional Office of Technology Assessment (OTA).

Most of this loss will come among small and moderate-sized farms, which will plunge in numbers from 2.1 million in 1982 to 1.1 million at the end of this century, while the number of large farms (defined as those operations selling in excess of $200,000 in farm products) will increase from 122,000 to 175,000. Fifty percent of these megafarms "will account for 75 percent of all agricultural production by the year 2000," the OTA concluded.

"Who owns the land?" is becoming the key question as farmland held by the Farm Credit Administration, the Farmers Home Administration, banks and other lenders, and insurance companies moves back into the market and is snatched up in larger and larger chunks by outside, nonfarm investors, including some Japanese and Europeans. We may soon witness the virtual disintegration of the family farm system of agriculture. The effects will be felt far beyond the fenceposts.

In its 1986 report, the OTA concluded: "As agricultural scale increases from very small to moderate farms, the quality of life improves. Then, as scale continues to increase beyond a size that can be worked and managed by a family, the quality of community life begins to deteriorate."

A landmark study by the U.S. Department of Agriculture (USDA) in the 1940s compared two rural communities in California—Arvin and Denuba. Both communities had roughly equivalent dollar values of agricultural production. However, Denuba's economy was based on a large number of small family farmers, while Arvin's was based on a few giant producers.

Compared with Arvin, Denuba supported:

- About 20 percent more people, and at a higher average income
- A higher percentage of self-employed workers (in Arvin, fewer than one-fifth were self-employed, and nearly two-thirds were agricultural wage laborers)
- Twice as many small businesses and 61 percent more retail business
- More and better schools and public services
- Greater involvement in democratic decision-making groups

Thirty years later, Walter Goldschmidt, the USDA researcher, stated: "The vision of the future under increased corporate control of the land is the vision of Arvins rather than Denubas—indeed of super-Arvins."

So, it is not mere sentimentality to suggest that the family farm is worth preserving. The late Supreme Court Justice Louis Brandeis once said: "We can have democracy in this country or we can have great wealth concentrated in the hands of a few, but we can't have both." Political democracy cannot long survive without some measure of economic democracy, as the history of Central America has amply demonstrated.

If we want to know how to save the family farm, the answer is not elusive: Get supply in line with demand, reduce the surpluses, and allow market prices to rise to a level where farmers can make a decent profit.

Even the Reagan administration is belatedly coming to the conclusion that supply management is needed. Yet, it clings blindly to a belief in a nonexistent free world market, while spending billions on massive set-asides, huge diversion payments, and bonus payments—all terribly inefficient and ineffective attempts to reduce surpluses.

If supply management is needed, and clearly it is, why not implement it correctly and efficiently by eliminating budget-busting farm subsidies and providing farmers with a cooperative mechanism that allows them to produce only as much as the market will bear?

Under Harkin-Gephardt, farmers would have the right to vote in a nationwide referendum to decide what kind of farm program they want. Then, if a majority approved the referendum, farmers would be allowed to join together cooperatively in a market-certificate program to bring their supply in line with demand. The secretary of agriculture would set a national marketing quota for each commodity, based upon projected demand. Commodity loan rates, which guide market prices, would be set at 70 percent of parity (the standard measure of fair farm income) for 1987 and increased one percent per year thereafter up to 80 percent of parity.

Each farmer would limit his production on the basis of bushels, not acres—a feature that would reduce the incentive to pile on chemicals and fertilizers to achieve maximum production. The bigger farmers would reduce their production more, the smaller farmers would reduce less. In no case would the unpaid set-aside on any one farm exceed 35 percent.

Matching supply with demand would raise market prices above government support levels. Thus, all direct government payments to farmers, including target prices (deficiency payments) and diversion payments, would be eliminated. Surpluses would be eliminated over a period of five years, and farm income would rise to a level where farmers could afford to pay their debts and get back on their feet.

To deal with farmers' immediate problems, our bill would establish mediation services to get farmers and creditors together to work out an alternative to foreclosure and encourage restructuring of farmers' debts. These provisions were included in the 1987 Farm Credit Bill passed by Congress and then signed by the president.

The Family Farm Act represents a sharp departure from current policies, but it is by no means a radical new idea. In his 1960 presidential debate with Richard Nixon, President Kennedy stated: "In my judgment, the only policy that will work will be for effective supply and demand to be in balance, and that can only be done through governmental action."

Kennedy went on to suggest "that in those basic commodities which are supported, . . . the federal government, after endorsement by the farmers in that commodity, attempt to bring supply and demand into balance [and] attempt effective production controls."

Recent studies by FAPRI and by the Agricultural and Food Policy Center at Texas A&M University show that the Family Farm Act would dramatically increase net farm income while reducing costs to the federal government. According to FAPRI projections, the Harkin-Gephardt bill would cost the government $72.3 billion less than the current program over the nine-year period 1987–1995. Furthermore, according to FAPRI, our bill would raise average annual net farm income by 77 percent over that expected under the current program—to $48.2 billion per year, as compared with $27.3 billion.

The Family Farm Act would put more market-earned money in farmers' pockets, allowing them to purchase more goods and services, and creating a positive ripple effect that could revitalize our small towns and farm-dependent businesses.

This supply management program must be undertaken in conjunction with efforts to reach international trade agreements, so as not to put our producers at a comparative disadvantage. And we must also start now to address the demand side of the equation by developing new markets for our farm products.

The Senate has passed my bill, the Alternative Agricultural Product Research Act of 1987, which would authorize $1.5 billion over the next 20 years for long-term research to help discover nonfood uses for farm crops. What we're looking for, figuratively speaking, are 101 new ways to utilize or alter farm crops.

Perhaps the greatest promise lies in creating plant-based petroleum substitutes. By the year 2000, most economists believe, the price of oil will shoot up to $30 or even $50 a barrel. If we start to link our research and development efforts now, when that happens, plastics, oils, and sources of energy manufactured from plants could be positioned as the economic alternative to products made from expensive oil imports.

Another way to increase demand is to reexamine America's relationship with the Third World. Instead of pursuing a beggar-thy-neighbor policy, driving world prices down and bankrupting Third World economies, we ought to be seeking to increase worldwide demand by raising standards of living in developing nations.

Technical assistance and development aid to Third World nations should be expanded, not curtailed. And we ought to provide real debt relief (not just austerity plans) to Latin America, whose purchase of U.S. agricultural exports has fallen by more than one-third since 1981.

A report by the Curry Foundation on the relationship between U.S. agricultural exports and Third World development put it best: "It is not the hunger of the poor countries, or even their growing population size, that makes them better customers for U.S. farm producers. It is the purchasing power that comes from their growing wealth."

CONSUMERS

What about consumers? President Kennedy correctly saw the delicate balance that must be struck when he said, "It must be our purpose to see that farm products return a fair income because they are fairly priced. No farm program should exploit the consumer. But neither can it subsidize the consumer at the cost of subnormal incomes to the farmer."

An examination of the food-processing industry shows who is benefiting most from the current administration's farm program.

Profits of 29 food-processing firms surveyed by *Business Week* increased 13 percent from January to October 1986, a period during which farm prices fell nine percent.

Even compared with other industries, the food processors have come out far ahead. The 50 top food-processing firms listed in a 1986 annual survey by *Forbes* had increased their sales six percent and their profits 13 percent that year, while the all-industry averages showed sales increases of four percent and increased profits of three percent.

How did the consumer fare from all this increased "prosperity?" In 1981, the average retail price of a box of Wheaties was $1.04. The amount of wheat in that box totaled about 2.5 cents. By 1987, the price of Wheaties had risen to $1.41, but the wheat value had fallen to 1.5 cents—a 36 percent price increase to consumers, even as wheat prices had fallen more than 40 percent.

There's nothing wrong with food processors' making profits, but there needs to be equity so that the producers of food and fiber can make decent profit also.

The bottom line is that low prices and chronic overproduction are a sure-fire formula for only one thing—the concentration of land ownership and agricultural wealth here and abroad. Consumers and farmers alike will benefit most from an agricultural system that provides a stable and fairly priced supply of food.

The time has come for a new direction in our agricultural policy.

At home and abroad, we need to be more concerned with value than with quantity, more concerned with long-term growth than with short-term profits, more concerned with balancing the interests of all those who depend on our agricultural system than with just the vested interests of a few.

Government can be part of the solution, not the problem. One of the most successful government programs in history was the Homestead Act of 1862, which settled the West by giving land to families willing to turn their plots into productive farms. Why didn't the government just say instead to Cornelius Vanderbilt or Jay Gould or some of the other wealthy railroad barons at the time, "Here's the Dakota Territory. How much will you pay for it?"

Why didn't it do that? Because its leaders understood that it was better for society when citizens had an ownership stake in the economy.

Free market advocates argue such a course would not be efficient. But we need to consider social, and not just economic, efficiency. When we are told efficiency means only bigger and bigger agriculture, we ought to ask "Efficient for whom?" Who benefits from this efficiency? Not consumers, and certainly not the farmers and other residents of rural America.

The family farmers of America do not want handouts. They only want the opportunity to live and work in dignity on the land they love, raise families in peace and security; to support their churches, schools, and small communities, and to pass on to their children the culture—the "agri-culture"—of being stewards of God's creation. We owe it to ourselves as a nation to provide them with that opportunity.

CHAPTER 32

Grass-Roots Economic Development: From the Ground Up

Jim Hightower

IT'S POPULAR THESE DAYS to assume that family-farm agriculture in the United States is doomed. A few prognosticators go so far as to say that food and fiber production will fall to Japanese managers producing world staple crops on low-wage, high-tech plantations in Brazil and other "host countries."

A more common view—offered by such visionaries and pontificators as *National Geographic* and Earl Butz—is that the productive assets of American agriculture will shift quickly and inevitably from the hands of the independent family entrepreneurs into the control of U.S-based conglomerates. Theirs is a "Star Wars" concept, in which relatively few integrated management combines envelop and direct capital-intensive, computer-driven agricultural production centers that are industrialized, centralized, and monopolized. The role of the "farmers" in this system is to serve as contract producers operating under midlevel corporate managers.

We are already seeing the makings of deliberate govern-

Jim Hightower is Texas Commissioner of Agriculture.

ment policy to bring about the realization of such a vision. Make no mistake about it. The Reagan administration has an agricultural economic development policy. But it is a policy devoted to centralized, corporate agribusiness and conglomerate food processing and distribution. It is a policy carried out by polishing the shiny leaves on top of the food production tree while starving the roots.

A concentration of capital, market power, and land is occurring in the food and fiber industry at record rates. It is sucking rural America dry. The policies of the Reagan administration are sending a message to rural America that it can wither on the vine, it can dry up and blow away, it can cease to exist as a way of life—so that it can be transformed into one big corporate farm.

On the corporate farm, there is no sense of stewardship of the land. It is run for short-term profit. It is subjected to chemical saturation and biotechnological experiments, often developed by chemical companies owned by the same conglomerates that own the land. It is dedicated to maximizing current yields at the expense of the future. The message delivered by the Reagan administration is that rural America is not a place for families to grow, for communities to thrive, for hard work and independence, for the stable, productive, safe, and healthy practice of agriculture. The message is that rural America is a place for toxic waste dumps and the corporate farm.

Three companies now control two-thirds of the beef slaughter industry in this country. They are Iowa Beef Processor, which is owned by Occidental Petroleum; Excel Corporation, which is owned by Cargill, this country's largest agribusiness and one of five corporate giants controlling 80 percent of the world's grain trade: and ConAgra, which recently acquired Montfort of Colorado, a beef-packing firm, E.A. Miller, Inc., and half of Swift Independent. Since 1982, ConAgra alone has added to its poultry, grain, and farm chemical empire by buying over 50 companies with sales totaling $4 billion—including Banquet (a maker of frozen dinners), Armour (producer of processed meats), and dozens of makers of refrigerated foods and dairy products. Cargill, whose pretax earnings in 1986 showed a 66 percent increase over the year before, holds beef-processing operations in Brazil; pork-processing businesses in Illinois and Honduras; cornmilling, cotton, coffee, poultry, and seed operations; insurance companies; a Dutch cocoa processor; a Venezuelan pasta plant; and a Texas oil pipeline company to augments the feed mills, storage facilities and railroad and oceanic shipping of its grain operation.

These food companies have been assisted in their expansion in every way possible by the policies of the Reagan administration. While most farm prices fell between six and nine percent in 1986, profits for food-processing companies increased, on average, by 13 percent. While consumer food expenditures rose about five percent in each of the past six years, the farmer's share of the money spent on food dropped to 24 percent in 1987, from 25 percent in 1986 and 32 percent in 1976. Falling farm prices, dictated by Reagan's farm policy, have contributed to making food corporations attractive targets for takeovers. As an investment banker told the New York Times, "The antitrust environment under the Reagan administration is extraordinarily liberal and presents a window of opportunity for a major acquirer to expand its position in the domestic packaged-food industry." This is the thrust of the economic development program of the Reagan administration.

It has led to a concentration not just of food industry capital, but, increasingly, of farmland itself. There is a merger process taking place not on Wall Street, but on farm-to-market roads in Texas and Kansas and Iowa. Since 1981, the number of farms overseen by the 1,000 farm management companies in this country has increased by 40 percent, to 110,000. The number of acres managed by these companies has increased by an area the size of Colorado. A real estate developer from Mesa, Arizona, told the New York Times that he has bought dozens of farms in Iowa, amounting to 15,000 acres, and rents them to Iowans, sometimes former owners, making up to 12 percent return on his investment in cheap, foreclosed farmland. All this is part and parcel of the Reagan administration's economic development package, in which the food and fiber industry is controlled by multinational conglomerates. In these situations, farmers become tenants and serfs on land owned by investors and run by farm management corporations, and the human and natural resources of rural communities are sucked dry.

It doesn't have to be this way. It is neither sound nor permissible economic policy to destroy the efficient, competitive structure of family agriculture and turn America's food future over to either foreign or conglomerate interests. Rather than pursuing current federal agricultural policies, we should be adjusting our policies, technologies, systems, and bureaucracies to fit the productive needs of America's most efficient and competitive economic unit: the independent family farm and ranch.

This is not to argue that we should merely keep on with the same old ways of agriculture, but it is to argue that we should base a new, more sophisticated, market-sensitive agriculture on the people who have consistently proven their value to our economy. By planting a few new seeds of agricultural development and by nurturing them properly, we can revitalize our family-farm agriculture. It requires no massive wrenching of the economy, no heavy hand of government, and no artificial tampering with the marketplace. It requires the commonsense realization that our most fertile prospect for true economic diversity and growth is the hard work and enterprise of the people of this country.

It requires a commitment to change the way we use public resources to stimulate economic outcomes. These are now being used for the middlemen, the shippers and big processors who are making phenomenal profits while rural America struggles to hang on. Public resources can, instead, be used for the benefit of the family-farm producer. This means a government commitment to a system that values the blooming of a thousand flowers across the land rather than the unchecked growth of a single, voracious kudzu.

The role of government should be to serve as a problem-solving catalyst for enterprising family farmers and small businesses, assisting them in such areas as market development and penetration, capital formation, and technical expertise. This kind of modest government assistance to generate and nurture hundreds of grass-roots agricultural enterprises, when practiced on a nationwide scale, can help turn our agricultural economy around. Family farmers will no longer be locked into a system that takes their underval- ued commodities to generate corporate profit. By investing in grass-roots economic development, government can help reverse the cash flow that is currently rushing out of rural communities at record rates.

This means investment not in some high-cost, high-tech, pie-in-the-sky scheme, but in down-to-earth, here-and-now, profitable enterprises that rural Americans themselves can plant and grow throughout the country. Added together, these small and medium-sized agricultural ventures will help create billions of dollars in new income and millions of new jobs to help this country, and rural America in particu- lar, grow out of today's economic stagnation. If "productiv- ity" is the buzzword for economic growth in this decade, it makes the most sense to invest in the single most productive unit of agriculture, the family farm, and in the rural commu- nities built around family farms.

In Texas, we know that this grass-roots economic develop- ment approach will work, because it already is working in dozens of ventures that the Texas Department of Agriculture has been assisting during the past few years. Sixty-two such projects in Texas represent a capital investment of over $213 million and, when complete, will create over 5,000 jobs. Projected first-year sales are over $582 million. The income from these projects will not be divided up on Wall Street or in Europe or Saudi Arabia or Japan. It will remain in rural Texas, as will the jobs created.

The goal of these projects is to let the producers enjoy the fruits of their labor, giving them access to the profits in the food and fiber industry. This is accomplished by providing commodity producers with the means to diversify to meet market demand, to market their products directly, and to reap the value-added dollar realized through processing.

For example, we worked to help put together a coop of black farmers in southeastern Texas, not far from Houston. They were raising a Black Diamond watermelon—as sweet a melon as you ever put a lip on—but they were having 60 percent of their crop rot in the field because it had no mar- ket. What they did sell went for a penny a pound out of pickup trucks by the side of the road. At the same time, in Houston, one county away, Kroger's supermarkets had 106 stores bringing in melons from Florida. The Texas Department of Agriculture went in and convinced Kroger to deal directly with the coop that we helped organize. In 1984, the first year of the coop's existence, its members sold every melon they produced to Kroger—500,000 pounds of watermelon at seven and one-quarter cents per pound. They enjoyed a 165 percent increase in their incomes from watermelon as a result and by 1987, had tripled their watermelon acreage for sales to Kroger. We've got dozens of these kinds of coops around the state, selling directly into the profitable mainstream of the marketing system.

We've also been able to apply this direct marketing on an international level to help the family farmer. We engineered a sale of 12,000 dairy cows to Egypt, which is trying to build up its dairy industry. It resulted in a $24 million deal. And that $24 million did not go to Carnation or Pet Food. It went to a little dairy in Stephenville, Texas.

The Texas Department of Agriculture has helped family farmers diversify after they'd begun to go broke because the price they were receiving for the staple commodity they'd been producing was much less than their production costs. We've done market and production analyses for these farmers. By so doing, we've helped them develop an appreciation of the farming of such products as blueberries, pinto beans, redfish, and buffalo. A good number of these farmers have been able to take advantage of our research by diversifying from their single surplus-commodity production to the production of crops for which there is a demand.

We've also been working with family farmers and small-business entrepreneurs in rural areas to develop the processing for what the farmers produce. Most of the profit in the food industry is in processing. Family farmers and rural communities have been losing the money that could be made in small, decentralized processing business. These are job-creating businesses. They can support whole communities.

We have worked with wheat farmers in the Texas Panhandle to set up their own flour mill. They were going broke selling wheat that was going to a flour mill in Kansas. There wasn't a mill within 250 miles of those farmers. Now there is—they built and run it. When it opened, in August 1987, it milled the first flour produced in the Panhandle in a generation. The mill has the capacity to produce 300,000 pounds of flour a day and will put $10 million in first-year sales into Dawn, Texas, right outside of Amarillo, creating 14 jobs. That doesn't solve the unemployment problem in the Texas Panhandle, but it solves it in Dawn. The Texas Department of Agriculture has worked with a cattle rancher in setting up her own slaughterhouse to produce and market her natural beef. We have helped cucumber producers in the Lower Rio Grande Valley, who were shipping raw cucumbers to Ohio for processing, set up their own cucumber and pickle processing plant, which will eventually provide some 1,000 jobs in an area experiencing unemployment rates three times the national average. These are good examples of the way our economic development concept works—specifically, locally, where people live, creating new jobs and an incoming cash flow.

In addition, the Texas Department of Agriculture has worked with members of the state legislature to develop legislation that will make more capital available for grass-roots agricultural economic development. The legislation includes a loan-guarantee program administered by a Texas agricultural finance authority through the sale of bonds to encourage bank lending for businesses marketing new crops, processing food or fiber, or exporting Texas agricultural products. It also provides for a program of small, low-interest, long-term loans to rural and agricultural enterprises initiated by low-income and minority Texans.

The key to grass-roots economic growth is simply to make financing available. People are out there, ready to pick up the tools and make them work. The expertise is available. The markets are sitting there ready and waiting. With only a minute outlay of government money, development financing made available through local banks will build economic growth for the state's small farmers and small-business people and for the state's economy as a whole.

And that's the importance of grass-roots economic

growth. It creates jobs. It makes for a sound economy. It creates the opportunity for lower income groups to organize themselves for greater economic security. It matches jobs to the skills and resources of people in a particular community. The control of the jobs created is not in the hands of distant directors, who may decide to move the entire operation to another state or to Taiwan; it remains in the hands of local citizens.

What we are doing with food and fiber in Texas can be accomplished on a national level. Government can help small farmers and businesses overcome the current inequities of the economies of scale. It can develop market analysis and trade leads for small enterprises or cooperatives of small producers. Our international trade policy could be taken out of the hands of the international traders and developed to create more opportunity of access for all Americans. The federal government can set up programs to provide grants to localities to stimulate business creation; to provide training in business creation, in small industrial production, in coop creation and in management; and to provide direct loans and long-term loan guarantees. Greenlining, through investment in particularly troubled regions and economies, can provide affirmative action for small farms and businesses. Federally funded research can be redirected to serve the interests of those at the grass roots.

It's not the Rockefellers who are going to solve our nation's economic problems; it's the "little fellers." If we invest in the initiative and grunt-level work of the people of this country, they will generate wealth not only for themselves, but for their communities and for the nation as a whole. We didn't get where we are by asking Toyota to come solve our problems. This country's wealth is homegrown. If we invest in the dirt farmers and the small-business people of this country, we can grow out of the economic doldrums again. This is the opposite of the trickle-down theory of economic growth; it is, instead, a policy of "percolate up." It won't depend on the smoke and mirrors of ballooning debt and junk bonds. It will be built, brick by brick, from the ground up.

There is a moving company in Austin that has a slogan we like to use at the Texas Department of Agriculture: "If we can get it loose, we can move it." If government will help to get the economy loose at a grass-roots level, the people will move it for themselves.

CHAPTER 33

A Democratic Framework for Poverty Policy

*Paul Jargowsky
and Mary Jo Bane*

EVERY SO OFTEN, THE United States rediscovers its poor. We go through a cycle of shock, followed by concern, followed by legislation and programs. The next stage seems to be disappointment that we can't eliminate poverty and frustration; and, finally, there is a stage of resentment and retrenchment. In the last few years, the cycle has started again—with shock at the specter of homeless families roaming the streets, high levels of poverty among children, and the seeming development of an alienated ghetto underclass. We are moving now to concern and compassion, and soon we will move to legislative action.

Democrats, as they should, will take the lead in the policy response to our continuing poverty problem. Is there some way to prevent the negative end of the cycle—insufficient progress, frustration, and retrenchment? For if it arrives,

Note: Many of the arguments in this article draw heavily on the report of the New York State Task Force on Poverty and Welfare, *A New Social Contract: Rethinking the Nature of Public Assistance*, of which Jargowsky and Bane were the principal authors. This article, however, represents only their own views and not those of the task force.

those who led the charge will suffer along with those for whom the campaign was waged. To avoid the mistakes of the past, both substantive and political, we believe that Democratic policy proposals must be grounded in two basic principles:

- Poverty is not confined to minorities in the cities, but is a diverse phenomenon with multiple causes affecting different groups and family types. Policies must respond to this diversity to be effective.
- Poverty and welfare cannot be looked at in isolation, but are inextricably linked to larger issues concerning the economy, education, and the conditions of entry-level work.

The virtue of these ideas is that they bring the issues of poverty and self-sufficiency back to the larger community. By emphasizing our common cause with the poor and their children, these principles help to change the idea of our policies from charity to strategies that serve the interests of the whole community.

THE DIVERSITY OF POVERTY

The stereotype of the typical poor person is that he or she is a member of a minority group, lives in an urban ghetto, has never had a job and does not want to work, and lives permanently on welfare. While people like this undoubtedly exist, they make up a tiny fraction of those in poverty. Stereotypes lead to the impression among many Americans that aid for the poor is taking from "us" and giving to "them." Moreover, the poor in this stereotype are so different that many Americans feel no empathy. Democrats need to break down this barrier, and point out that many people in all walks of life—friends, neighbors, even family members—may be poor at some time in their lives.

Myth: Most Poor People Are Members of Minority Groups

In fact, the typical poor person is not a minority member; 57 percent of the nation's poor are non-Hispanic whites, 27 percent are non-Hispanic blacks, and 12 percent are Hispanic.

Myth: The Typical Poor Person Lives in an Inner City Ghetto and Is a Member of the Underclass

The recent upsurge in media attention to the plight of the homeless and poor is certainly welcome. Unfortunately, the coverage has focused for the most part on the inner-city poor, perhaps because they are the easiest to locate. It is misleading, however, to think of the typical poor person in this way.

- About 30 percent of the poor live in rural areas. In comparison, 43 percent live in central cities.
- In 1980, about 1.8 million poor people lived in the 100 largest central cities, in areas where the poverty rate was 40 percent or higher. These are the true ghettos, and they contain only 6.7 percent of the nation's poor.

The conditions in inner-city poor neighborhoods are truly disturbing. Still, it is important to remember that the typical poor person is not a resident of a high-poverty area.

Few residents of poor inner-city neighborhoods are like the alienated young men portrayed in newspaper and television accounts of the urban underclass. More than four in 10, for example, live in two-parent families, and nearly four in 10 live in families in which someone works.

Myth: Most Poor People Are Able to Work but Do Not

In fact, most poor people who can work do work.

- Nearly four out of ten poor people are children.
- More than one in ten of the poor are elderly.

- As a result, fewer than half of the poor are working-age adults.
- About five percent of the poor are too ill or disabled to work.
- Of the working-age adults who can work, 56 percent work at least part-time, and another nine percent are unemployed and looking for work. Only about one-third are neither working nor looking for work, and most of those are mothers with young children.

Most of those who can work are working. But the working poor—even many who work, full-year, full-time—have inadequate incomes and, often, inadequate health insurance. Low wages, intermittent unemployment, and large families mean that they are not able to escape poverty.

Myth: Most Poor People Collect Public Assistance

Again, the facts tell another story: Fewer than half the people who were poor in 1984 lived in households where someone received cash income from public assistance. Although virtually all the poor are eligible for food stamps, the majority of working poor do not participate in the program because of the perceived stigma, administrative obstacles, or other reasons.

THE IMPLICATIONS OF DIVERSITY

The astonishing diversity of the poor is matched by the diversity of reasons for their poverty. No single-stroke solution—like the negative income tax, cashing out benefits, or mandatory workfare—can simultaneously respond to the needs of the working poor, poor female-headed households, unemployed youth, the disabled, the elderly poor, the rural poor, the urban poor, and all the others who from time to time find themselves without adequate income.

To make strides against poverty, we are going to have to recognize and accept this diversity. We can't count on reforms of welfare, as necessary as they are, to do the whole job. Most of the poor are not affected by reforms of welfare, because they are not on public assistance or they receive minimal benefits. Thus, the most important implication of the diversity of poverty is that welfare reform alone is not enough. All of our poverty policies must be related to the state of the economy, the quality of education, and the opportunities for self-sufficiency available through work at entry-level jobs.

RESPONDING TO DIFFERENT TYPES OF POVERTY

The changes in the poverty rate over time almost perfectly mirror changes in the overall performance of the economy. Median income of fulltime, full-year male workers, a good measure of the economy's performance, is very closely correlated with the poverty rate: As median income goes up, the poverty rate goes down, and vice versa. The reason is simple: Most of the poor are working poor. Nearly two-thirds of the nonelderly, nondisabled poor live in households in which someone works.

Basically, the level of economic performance and the trends in real wages determine the extent to which there are opportunities for self-sufficiency. Real economic growth is a clear prerequisite to reducing poverty, and is one of the most important antipoverty strategies. Beyond this general strategy, we must address the specific causes of poverty in several different groups.

The Working Poor

Because so many of the poor are working poor, strategies to help them escape poverty and achieve self-sufficiency are very important. Such strategies have the secondary benefit that they make welfare reform easier by making the transition from welfare to work more rewarding for people on public assistance. A number of measures could make a substantial difference in the lives of the working poor:

- *Health insurance.* Persons on public assistance have Medicaid, and persons in good jobs have employer-provided coverage, but the working poor are often left uninsured. Two and one-half million poor families have no health care coverage, with the result that they receive poor prenatal care and poor nutrition, and have untreated health problems that only get worse. Those who are working and struggling to achieve self-sufficiency should have access to medical care. Meeting the health care needs of the working poor will be an expensive and complex undertaking, but is extremely important for both the working poor and those who want to make the transition from welfare to work.
- *Earned income tax credit (EITC).* Tax policy can help to supplement the earned income of the working poor to bring them out of poverty. Under the new tax law, the EITC only partially offsets the Social Security tax payment for a family of four at the poverty line in 1988. An EITC that fully offset Social Security taxes and was varied by family size would bolster and reward the efforts of parents to support their children by working.
- *Minimum wage.* The minimum wage has been severely eroded by inflation since 1981 when it was last increased; consequently, families with only one wage earner working at the minimum wage are almost certain to be poor. The minimum wage today is only 38 percent of the average wage, its lowest value by that measure since 1949. If we want to make it possible for families to earn their way to self-sufficiency, we must increase the minimum wage to make up for the erosion that has occurred and consider indexing it to the level of wages.

  ilies with two workers, assistance with finding affordable child care options can help to make self-sufficiency through work possible. The schools can help by providing more preschool education, fullday kindergarten, and, possibly, extended school days or years. Direct subsidies or tax deductions for child care may also ease the burden on working parents and reduce the number of children placed in unsafe or low-quality arrangements or, worse, left unsupervised.

Single-Parent Families

Not all the poor can be helped by economic growth alone. Poverty among female heads of household does fluctuate with the economy, but even in the best of economic times, the rate is very high. Female heads of household find it very difficult to achieve self-sufficiency through work for two reasons: (1) The wages for many jobs commonly available to women are very low; and (2) managing parental responsibilities alone makes it difficult for female heads of household to work full-time. Thus, it is very unlikely that a female-headed family will be able to escape poverty through work.

Yet, the fact is that every child has two parents, who should both be contributing financial support. A number of recent studies point out the atrociously low rate of child support orders and payments in the United States. The result—poor children and families forced to rely on public assistance—is unfair to mothers, children, and taxpayers. The situation justifies a major effort by states and federal government to increase the number of child support awards, their level, and the degree of enforcement. A greater reliance on child support stresses individual responsibility and could help to reduce poverty among children. Adequate child support combined with part-time work would often be enough to help single parents get off welfare and out of poverty.

Public Assistance Recipients

The chance that a person on public assistance will be able to become self-sufficient through work is determined mostly outside the welfare system itself. The state of the economy, particularly the level of unemployment and the level of wages, determines how many families will be able to achieve self-sufficiency. Public education determines how many poor people will be prepared to take advantage of opportunities for self-sufficiency. Tax policy and the availability of health insurance and child care have an impact on whether workers can lift their families out of poverty and into decent lives. Thus, changes in these larger arenas are prerequisites to successful welfare reform.

Like the poor generally, those on public assistance are diverse and have different reasons for needing public assistance. Nationally, 65 percent of the persons on Aid to Families with Dependent Children (AFDC) in 1985 were children. Of the adults, 11 percent were ill or incapacitated. Those who are employable are usually at the end of the queue when it comes to getting jobs, so that it may take time for the benefits of a booming economy to reach them. Many recipients are on public assistance for only a short time, after experiencing personal difficulties, such as a divorce, loss of employment, or a mental or emotional crisis. Others remain on public assistance for a long period of time and seem very far from achieving self-sufficiency.

Thus, our welfare reforms must also be focused. Education and training should go to those who can use them to obtain unsubsidized employment. Work opportunities should be reserved for those who have greater skill deficiencies and are not likely to become self-sufficient through a service delivery approach. Long-term income maintenance will still be needed for those who are physically or mentally unable to work.

Disaggregating the Poor

Our nation's experience with social programs has achieved a number of important successes, but many serious problems remain. We must get beyond the stereotypes of poor people to fashion effective policies. Poverty, taken as a whole, seems too huge a problem to ever be solved. But by breaking the problem down into discrete groups with discrete problems, we begin to see how we might address people's particular problems to help them achieve self-sufficiency. Seen in this way, progress against poverty seems not only possible, but well within our grasp.

By disaggregating the poor, we also see that poverty affects more of us, in all walks of life. The poor are people we know: a young set of parents working at two jobs but still struggling, an injured auto worker temporarily out of work, a teenager who got pregnant, a divorced woman down the street. Further, because there is a lot of turnover in the poor population, the annual poverty rate itself tells only part of the story. As many as one-third of the residents of the United States will be poor at some point in their lives.

THE ECONOMIC BENEFITS OF FIGHTING POVERTY

The primary reason the United States should fight poverty is moral: The only decent course for a nation as advanced and wealthy as the United States is to ensure that all citizens have the opportunity to share in prosperity. There are also reasons to fight poverty that would fall into a category of enlightened self-interest. We believe that an antipoverty strategy based on training and education must also be a vital part of our economic strategy.

The lack of basic education and skills among many of the poor is one of the principal causes of poverty. Fewer than half of the poor adults are high school graduates, compared with three-fourths of nonpoor adults. For the American economy to grow and be productive, it must increasingly concentrate on those industries that require highly competent workers. The inability of many of the poor to compete in this new labor market leads to unemployment, low productivity, and low wages.

Many analysts believe the economy increasingly needs literacy and flexibility rather than brawn and job-specific skills. More jobs are in high-technology industries, and service industry jobs tend to require basic literacy and communication skills. Even blue-collar jobs are becoming increasingly complex as technology is introduced into the workplace.

This emerging economy requires investments in the labor force that will result in better jobs and a higher standard of living for all Americans. If enough skilled workers are not available in the United States, many jobs may be lost to international competition. The productivity of the poor may be more important in the next few decades than it ever was before. By the year 2000, the number of young adults potentially entering the labor force will decline by more than 20 percent. Thus, we will need all young adults to be able to enter the economy and be productive workers.

Investments in the work force, particularly in poor and minority workers who have historically received less preparation for the labor market, will become increasingly important in the decade ahead as an economic policy. Individual firms in the private sector have no incentive to undertake such investments unilaterally. Thus, it is the responsibility of the public sector to make those investments in human capital that will be the basis for the prosperity of our nation in the years ahead.

RESTORING CONFIDENCE IN GOVERNMENT

Before Democrats can change the way Americans think about poverty and government policies to alleviate it, they must first convince the American people that the fight is worth fighting. Democrats must work to overcome the notion, held almost universally, that poverty programs have all failed, or even made matters worse. Poverty has not disappeared, it is true, but there are a number of notable accomplishments of which the nation should be proud. Recognizing those accomplishments is an important part of mustering the public will to go further. Among them are the following:

- The poverty rate for the elderly has decreased dramatically, and for the last several years has been below the national average. Social Security and Supplementary Security Income, which are indexed to inflation, and other programs, such as Medicare, are directly responsible for the improvements.
- A substantial black middle class has developed. The wage gap between white and black men has narrowed, and the wage gap between white and black women has almost disappeared. Minorities are now more visible in professional and managerial occupations and in

politics. A variety of programs and policies, from civil rights legislation to Head Start to Pell Grants, have all contributed to this trend.

- Quality and availability of health care for the poor have increased substantially. For example, the infant mortality rate for nonwhites, who comprise a disproportionate share of the poor, has declined dramatically. Programs such as Medicaid and the Special Supplemental Food Program for Women, Infants and Children have helped to increase access to health care.

All Americans can be proud of these historic achievements, and can be inspired by them to attack the problems that remain. These accomplishments show us that we have the capacity to create a better society, in which more of our people share in our nation's prosperity.

Yet, most people seem unaware of these accomplishments. One reason is that some politicians have exploited the fears and frustrations of voters with inflated rhetoric about welfare cheats and the dramatic changes that could be brought about through workfare. Some cheating and administrative errors do occur, as they do in any large organization. But errors in AFDC and food stamp cases, as verified by the federal government, have declined 65 percent since the mid-seventies. The rate of overpayment was six percent in 1984—much lower than the error rate for the Internal Revenue Service—and it has been declining steadily.

Yet, some political leaders continue to misrepresent the facts by presenting the exceptions to the rules as if they reflected the general case. They ignore the fact that the vast majority of recipients are eligible for and need the aid that is provided, aid that Americans say they support for people who actually need it. By distorting the facts, these politicians do a disservice to the American public and impede the development of sensible policies to address the problems that cause poverty to exist.

The myths and misperceptions about the poor, like the notion that all poverty programs have failed, did not just happen. These ideas came to be accepted because many politicians and academics argued them forcefully and were allowed to dominate the public dialogue. Until some of these myths and misperceptions are effectively debunked, the American people will remain ambivalent—or even hostile—toward the notion of helping the poor.

CHAPTER 34

Hunger and Poverty at Home and Abroad

Congressman Mickey Leland

I HAVE SEEN THE matchstick arms and legs of children who are malnourished and hungry in the United States, a land of plenty, and in the poorest countries of the world. Hunger at a full table or at an empty table is deplorable.

Children suffer from inadequate diets all over the world, and they are the most vulnerable to permanent damage from malnutrition. According to the United Nations Children's Fund (UNICEF) more than 40,000 children in the Third World die every day because they have not had sufficient nutrients and health care to resist disease. In our own country, the effects of poor diet are more subtle but still easily observed. Preschoolers taking part in the Head Start Program, which includes meals, are far more lively and active than poor children of the same age who are on program waiting lists.

Technically, hunger is a subjective, subclinical state. People are hungry when they miss meals and feel anxiety about food because they are uncertain of their food supply. Hunger is the gnawing desperation of a mother who denies her appetite so that her children will have a little more food. The widespread malnutrition that results from hunger is measured by physicians and recorded in clinical terminology.

People are not hungry because there is a global shortage of food. On the contrary, there is a glut of food in the storage bins of the world; most nations are able to produce enough to feed their own people. In the early 1970s, there was fear that population growth would outdistance the food supply. While the "green revolution" prevented that tragedy, mankind has not yet found a way to distribute food equitably. Worldwide, about 730 million people suffer caloric deficits, according to the Food and Agriculture Organization of the United Nations.

The major cause of hunger is poverty—people simply do not have enough resources to buy food. While catastrophes such as droughts and military strife occur and interrupt the food supply, causing terrible human deprivation, the numbers they affect are not nearly as great as the millions who don't eat enough day after day. The 1984 famine in Africa affected as many as 150 million people in 28 countries, but every day in India, more than 200 million are hungry. In our wealthy industrialized nation, over 30 million people live below the poverty level, vulnerable to hunger. Almost 13 million of the poor people in America live at less than half of the poverty level, or on an annual income of less than $6,000 for a family of four. These are the folks we find at the soup kitchens and food pantries that have sprung up in great numbers in the past decade.

Too many families cannot meet their needs for food, clothing, shelter, and health care. It is the inability to purchase food and meet other basic human needs that causes hunger. In India, after Mutafa has paid rent to the owner of the rickshaw he pulls for a livelihood, he has few rupees left to feed his family. In the United States, 80-year-old Mrs. Yates is hungry, because her retirement income, a few dollars above the Medicaid eligibility level, must be spent for expensive medicines and rent, leaving her short of food money.

Acknowledging the link between hunger and poverty, the World Bank recommends that hunger in each nation be determined by the availability of socially provided basic services, such as health care; the gaps between received and disposable income (what is available for food consumption); the relative prices and composition of the bundles of needed commodities; and the distribution of income.

These analytic measures establish the extent of hunger in a single country, but they do not tell us its causes or how to prevent or alleviate it. The causes of hunger are not confined to a single country, because we now live in a global economy, an interdependent community. However, national government policies and programs are effective tools for alleviating hunger. Studies by the House Select Committee on Hunger show that although a broad range of programs ameliorate hunger, those discussed below are most fundamental and urgent.

WOMEN, INFANTS, AND CHILDREN FIRST

In the United States

In recent years, economic and government policies in this country have given new meaning to the phrase "women and children first." They are first in the ranks of poverty and hunger. One in every five children under five in this nation live in poverty. These children must be given priority in any antihunger effort. Pregnant women, infants, and children are most likely to suffer long-term damage from hunger. Inadequate diet during pregnancy causes mothers to suffer anemia, loss of calcium, serious weight loss, and deprives the fetus of vital nutrients as well. Infants and children who are not properly nourished in the early months of life, when rapid growth and development take place, may be irreversibly damaged. This neglect creates future social costs.

If the infant mortality rate (IMR), deaths per 1,000 live births, is used as an indicator, the United States appears to be falling behind other industrialized nations in the care of pregnant women and infants. Although the IMR continues to fall very slightly, we now rank 18th among these nations, whereas once we ranked fifth. We are not progressing because certain vulnerable groups do not have adequate medical care and nutrition programs. The IMR among these groups reflects this failure. The IMR among blacks is twice that among whites; the rate for all races in rural poor counties is rising, and in many urban centers, it is much higher than the national average. Rising poverty affects these groups unduly and prevents an overall national decline in the IMR.

Low birth weight is the most likely predictor of infant death during the first year of life. Recent research by the Department of Health and Human Services confirms that adequate nutrition during pregnancy can prevent low birth weight. Similarly, a recent Department of Agriculture evaluation of the Special Supplemental Feeding Program for Women, Infants and Children (WIC) revealed that the integrated food, education, and medical care components significantly decrease the incidence of low birth weight. Yet, only one-third of the income-eligible reap the benefits of participation.

Similar evaluations have found Head Start participation effective in laying the groundwork for a healthy, productive life through early education supported by adequate nutrition. It is in these preschool years that sound bodies and good nutritional habits can be established.

It is entirely practical to expand the WIC caseload by an additional 500,000 for each of the next five years and, thereafter, to open the program to every person eligible by income. In the same way, the Head Start Program could add 80,000 children each year for the next five years, setting aside a special portion for Indian and migrant children, who are more likely to suffer hunger.

The critical nutritional needs of children do not disappear after preschool. In poor neighborhoods, school lunch and breakfast programs are the mainstays of the diets of most children. To know when the family larder is empty, just watch a child eat school breakfast on a Monday morning toward the end of the month (when food stamps and cash run low). The School Breakfast Program reaches only 3.2 million children from low-income families, while 11.7 million poor children receive free or reduced-price school lunch.

There is no reason that the United States could not provide free school lunches to every child. Japan does so, and the program there is considered not an income-based subsidy but an investment in the coming generation. Our competitiveness with Japan should extend beyond consumer goods to human investment, the basic source of productivity.

In Developing Countries

Protecting maternal and child health is critical in poor nations. Undernourished children are far more likely to succumb to infection, and, conversely, infection prevents them from absorbing nutrients. The Child Survival initiative of UNICEF seeks to reduce the terrible child mortality rates resulting from infection and malnutrition.

The UNICEF program has emphasized a set of four primary health care tools, called GOBI: growth charts, oral rehydration (simple salts used to restore children dehydrated by diarrhea), breast-feeding, and immunization. The UNICEF campaign has mobilized every level of society in a number of countries to achieve high rates of outreach and immunization. The international immunization campaign has been so successful that it was able to bring about a truce between warring government and rebel forces for a national immunization day in El Salvador.

Vitamin A has been recognized as a significant tool in lowering child mortality rates. Long known as a cause of childhood blindness, vitamin A deficiency is now known to inhibit the body's ability to recover from infectious diseases, especially measles and respiratory illness. Studies by Dr. Alfred Sommer, of Johns Hopkins University, indicate that vitamin A supplementation decreases childhood mortality by as much as 70 percent in certain circumstances.

Another powerful force in saving children's lives in less developed countries is maternal education. For each year of maternal education, there is a drop in children's deaths by six per 1,000. As children grow, they are better fed if their mothers have learned the importance of a balanced diet.

Female education is also a factor in increased food production, slower population growth, and generally improved nutritional status.

The House Select Committee on Hunger has taken the lead in obtaining greater funding for the worldwide immunization initiative, vitamin A supplementation, and basic education as part of the U.S. foreign aid budget. The majority of foreign aid, however, goes to military rather than humanitarian assistance. In 1980, development and food aid comprised 56 percent of the U.S. foreign aid budget, and military aid only 22.4 percent. (The balance of 21.6 percent was direct economic support of governments.) By 1986, military aid had increased to 38.8 percent, and development and food aid had declined to 37.3 percent. This trend reflects national leadership with little concern for human development.

DEVELOPING SELF-SUFFICIENCY

There are three groups of adult poor and hungry: the working poor, who are trying to provide for their families, but whose limited incomes keep them in poverty; the potentially self-sufficient, who with training and job opportunity could move from assistance to independence; and those who are unable to care for themselves because of circumstances beyond their control.

A national policy of full employment in jobs with adequate wages is clearly in the best interests of our society. We do not, however, provide the proper training and education for high-skill and high-pay jobs. As a consequence, more and more people are forced to survive in low-skill, minimum-wage jobs.

The phrase "working homeless" may sound like a contradiction in terms, but it defines a new social group. Approximately 20 percent of the people in homeless shelters are working or are children whose parents go out of the shelter to work. These parents work, but they are not breadwinners. They do not make enough money to afford food and shelter. The minimum wage has been frozen at $3.35 an hour since

1981. It provides a salary of less than $7,000 a year, $4,600 below the poverty level of $11,592 for a family of four.

There are 1.2 million heads of household now working full-time whose earnings fall below the poverty level. Many more people who are working part-time are living below the poverty level. These families with insufficient wages need additional food stamps to meet their nutrient needs. The Food Stamp Program is the one national income supplement available to the working poor. The allotment, which is based on income and family size, was designed to supplement the family food budget, not to be its sole source. As the benefits to poor people have been reduced during the 1980s, households have had fewer and fewer discretionary dollars to add to the food stamp allotment. Consequently, many supplement the family diet at food pantries and soup kitchens, especially as food stamps run out toward the end of the month.

A vast number of Americans lack marketable skills necessary to assure access to employment with wages that will allow them to be self-sufficient. Without the benefits of job training and placement services, many recipients of Aid to Families with Dependent Children (AFDC) benefits, workers suffering dislocation as a result of declining industry, economically disadvantaged youth, and persons who are homeless have no alternative to dependence on public assistance programs.

During this decade, Congress has enacted legislation authorizing states to implement programs to provide most of these targeted populations with training, education, and job search skills. These include the Omnibus Budget Reconciliation Act of 1981, which granted states unprecedented flexibility designing and implementing work-related programs for AFDC recipients; the Food Security Act of 1981, which requires that each state implement an employment and training program for food stamp recipients; and the Job Training Partnership Act, which establishes a network of job training services for economically disadvantaged and dislocated workers. Although the framework to enable self-sufficiency is in place, many individuals remain unserved.

Programs combining vocational training, remedial education, and job search and placement services are most successful in helping people into private-sector employment. Administrators of successful state programs, such as those in Maine and Massachusetts, contend that child care and transportation support services also are crucial. These are costly elements that have never been adequately funded at the federal level. Only when there is a national commitment and the political will can people have the opportunities to fulfill their potential and earn sufficient income to prevent hunger.

TRANSPORTATION AND RURAL POVERTY

Throughout the United States and the entire world, much hunger is unseen, because it is rural. Two problems generally afflict the rural poor—lack of income and inadequate transportation. As noted earlier, the infant mortality rate in the United States is increasing in poor rural counties. In Appalachia, on Indian reservations, on the tenant farms of the Mississippi Delta, and in the northern counties of Maine and Vermont, people must drive or walk miles to purchase food or obtain services. The food they buy will cost more, because it is transported great distances from wholesale distribution centers.

In poor nations, the problem is more acute, because roads are mostly nonexistent. In Haiti, for instance, only 40 percent of the people live within an hour's walking distance of health services. The isolation of the rural poor not only denies them basic services, it prevents them from coming together to organize and find solutions to their problems.

FOOD AND DEVELOPMENT VS. ARMS

Just as there is enough food in the world to feed every person, there are resources enough to enable every individual to live a decent life. Expenditures on armaments are staggering. The governments of the world invest $800 billion a year against the possibility of attack by external enemies, disregarding the threat of internal deterioration. The annual budget of the U.S. Air Force is larger than the total education budget for 1.2 billion children in Africa, Latin America, and Asia, excluding Japan.

In the United States, the fastest growing budget categories since 1981 have been interest on the debt and defense spending. With adjustment for inflation, defense outlays have increased 40 percent since fiscal year 1981. During the same period, the Food Stamp Program was cut by 13 percent ($7 billion) and school feeding programs were cut by 28 percent ($3 billion).

In developing nations, the infection of the international arms race has spread. Between 1970 and 1980, the total value of arms imported by developing countries—from the United States, the Soviet Union, France, Great Britain, and China—grew by 400 percent.

In 1980, Africa imported $4.5 billion worth of arms. In contrast, UNICEF has announced a project to immunize all the world's children by 1990 at a cost of $1.5 billion. The lives of three and a half million children will be saved, and countless others will be spared the crippling effects of malnutrition-related disease. If UNICEF can accomplish this with one-third of Africa's arms expenditures for one year, consider what might be done with the balance of $3 billion to meet educational, environmental, and food production needs. Investment in military hardware adds to the total of fear and violence in the world, while subtracting from the capacity to fight hunger and poverty.

Sufficient food, resources, and talent exist to defeat the scourge of hunger and poverty. We must confront the challenge. Like Martin Luther King, Jr., who succeeded in changing our lives and our country, we must "have the audacity to believe that peoples everywhere can have three meals a day for their bodies, education and culture for their minds and dignity, equality and freedom for their spirits."

CHAPTER 35

Rethinking the Approach to Criminal Justice

The Honorable Elizabeth Holtzman
(assisted by James Ledbetter)

MOST PEOPLE THINK THAT the criminal justice system in the United States is in serious disarray. Our courts and prisons are dramatically overloaded, and crime is on the rise. It sometimes seems that there is no relationship between law enforcement and crime; to some, the system appears out of control.

Moreover, public fear of crime remains high. Surveys have found that 45 percent of Americans worry about walking at night near their home. Almost as many fear that they will be the victim of a crime. These fears are not unjustified: a recent FBI study concluded that more than eight out of 10 Americans will be the victim of an attempted violent crime at some time in their lives.

Plainly traditional approaches to fighting crime have not worked well enough. Even worse many professionals in the criminal justice system have largely succumbed to despair about fighting crime; others offer simpleminded "solutions." But it is vital that we not throw up our hands and declare that nothing can be done about crime. We must reject a "business as usual" approach in favor of new ideas and methods that can work. As district attorney in one of the

389

largest urban areas in the country, I know that we can make the criminal justice system work better, if we are willing to be both bold and practical.

One new strategy that offers considerable hope for effective change is using modern technology—bringing the criminal justice system into the twentieth century. Too often, police and prosecutors are given antiquated tools with which to fight crime. Technological improvements can go a long way to help police, prosecutors, and courts do a better job.

New fingerprint technology, for example, promises to make a significant dent in apprehending some of the worst repeat offenders. Most people expect that when a fingerprint is found at a crime scene, the criminal is "done for"—that the police promptly compare the print with those of criminals on file and then, once a match is found, arrest the suspect—just as it's done in the movies.

Unfortunately, that is not the case in most of the country. In New York City, for example, there are some 1.5 million fingerprints of criminals with prior records in police files. To match a print taken from a crime scene against those on file requires a manual search, flipping through files one by one. To match any one set of fingerprints could take decades. Obviously, such comparisons are so laborious and time-consuming that fingerprints are almost never used to identify criminals, except after they have already been arrested.

This is intolerable. Computerized fingerprint matching technology exists that can solve such cases in minutes, but only a handful of jurisdictions are using them. The failure to use new technology means that many criminals, including the hardcore, repeat offenders who commit most of the crimes, are not being apprehended.

In San Francisco, where a computerized fingerprint system was installed in 1984, there has been a 26 percent decrease in burglaries and a 5 percent annual decrease in the overall crime rate. New York authorities estimate that a statewide computerized system could generate 10,000 additional arrests (mostly of serious, repeat offenders) in its first year of operation.

In addition to reducing crime, these computerized systems have fiscal benefits. California's sytem, for instance, is projected to save $2 million annually. Clearly, putting these systems into place throughout the country should be a top priority.

The federal government can exercise crucial leadership in this area, leadership that has been sorely lacking under the present administration. The federal government ought to be a pioneer in the development and use of new technologies. It should sponsor research to identify and test new anticrime technologies, and should encourage and help states to adopt systems that work. At present, however, it does nothing, leaving local prosecutors and local governments to discover and develop their own systems, a process that is too slow and haphazard to make a significant enough dent in crime across the nation.

Other technological changes also can make the criminal justice system run more smoothly, cheaply, and humanely. Victims of rape and child sex abuse, for example, are often traumatized by the prospect of appearing in a courtroom. Many victims, especially children, simply cannot face the ordeal of telling the story of their abuse in front of strangers (as in the grand jury), or in front of their alleged attacker.

New York State recently made it legal for prosecutors to videotape children in a comfortable surrounding and use the tape as testimony before a grand jury. The state also allows children to testify live using closed-circuit TV if the children would be emotionally traumatized by testifying in person. My office has found that, by easing the trauma of testifying, not only do we help victimized children, but we can prosecute abusers who otherwise may have gotten off.

Video technology can often have remarkable effects when used in the criminal justice system—in the arrest process, for example. Last summer, my office installed a two-way video link between a police precinct and the central booking room downtown where prosecutors draw up charges against defendants.

Normally, witnesses and police officers whose testimony is required in a criminal case must be brought to the downtown complaint room. This complicated procedure takes police officers off their patrols for lengthy periods of time, reducing their effectiveness in fighting crimes—and is costly as well. Victims and witnesses are faced with the enormous inconvenience of having to travel back and forth to the district attorney's complaint room, spending their own time and money. Not surprisingly, the inconvenience, especially after the ordeal of a crime incident, discourages many witnesses from coming forward early in the process to aid prosecution.

Under our new system, police officers, victims, and witnesses can give their statements to the prosecutors directly from their neighborhood precinct via the two-way video linkup that connects the precinct with prosecutors miles away. Police are back on the streets in half the time it took under the old system. The video linkup also makes it easier for witnesses to tell their story; many more come forward thereby improving prosecutors' ability to get the facts and charge defendants accordingly.

While this system is currently being tested in a limited capacity, its implications for the criminal justice system are far-reaching. If such systems were in place throughout the country, police could devote more time and resources to arrests and investigations, rather than to processing defendants. The technology may also offer ways of improving the arraignment process. Taken collectively, these changes could save taxpayers tens or hundreds of millions of dollars.

But here again, there has been a distinct lack of leadership from the federal government. With federal guidance, coordination, and pilot programs, new video applications could be tested and put into place in a relatively short period of time. If the current silence from Washington continues, however, the potential impact of video on criminal justice— and its cost saving potential—may remain untapped.

In addition to technology, our approach to the criminal justice system requires innovative thinking about some age-old practices. One area that needs attention is deterring criminal behavior before it reaches serious levels. Too often, the response to minor offenses has been to ignore them, sending a message to young, first time offenders that they can commit crimes with impunity, and leading them to move on to major offenses.

For this reason my office crested a community service sentencing program. In 1982, we began the first program in New York City for individuals who committed minor offenses on the subway system. In the past, these offenders, usually fare beaters, vandals, or graffiti writers, received no punishment for their actions. I believed that punishment was necessary, so my office began sentencing them to scrub subway cars. Since the inception of the program, over 3,000 offenders have cleaned almost as many cars. The program has been remarkably effective: The attendance rate of over 92 percent is higher than that of many public high schools, and recidivism is virtually nonexistent.

In 1983 we expanded this program to include other nonviolent offenders in community service sentencing. Sentences require anywhere from eight to 300 hours of hard work. Offenders clean parks and benches, do maintenance work in hospitals, help prepare meals for senior citizens, and work in community centers. Almost 3,500 offenders have performed over 27,000 hours of community service. For many, it is their first encounter with real work.

What we have seen since the inception of these programs is that contrary to conservative myths about criminals, these offenders—usually teenagers—want to work. They achieve a sense of accomplishment from the work, even though it is administered as punishment. Many ask for jobs when the program is over; some have even been hired. Plainly, many of them are getting into trouble because they have nothing to do.

The obvious solution is to get these young people off the street and onto a path that is responsible and productive. That means jobs. A recent study found that half of black males between 16 and 24 in this country have never held a job. As our program shows, when young people are given the opportunity to be gainfully occupied—even in the context of a sentence—thousands willingly respond.

A serious problem is that many of these young people do not have the basic skills necessary for the work place. Almost 30% of the offenders in our transit crime program could not read the contract for the program. Similar rates of illiteracy are found in jails and prisons throughout the nation. Without being able to read, few can get and hold productive jobs. My office has begun to request that some offenders be sentenced to basic literacy programs. But it borders on the absurd that a prosecutor's office should have to provide services where the schools have failed. Plainly, a systemmatic effort to upgrade the quality of American schools, particularly in inner city areas, would help reduce the number of idle young people who become ready converts to crime.

The alienation and despair that often leads youths to commit crimes also contribute to the growing problem of drug abuse in this country. Recently, my office has seen astounding increases in the numbers of narcotics cases, including a 100 percent increase in a single year. Nationwide, the use of cocaine and crack has tripled over the last few years. While drug abuse cuts across all levels of the society, the hardest hit are the poor and minority communities.

Drug abuse exacts a terrible physical and psychological toll; also it exacerbates the cycle of crime. Crack use in particular has led to an upswing in crimes of grotesque and horrible violence, including attacks on family members and loved ones. Government must concentrate on permanent solutions to drug abuse, rather than "quick fixes." Unfortunately, the Reagan Administration has failed to wage an effective, consistent fight against drug abuse, or even it seems, to understand the scope of the problem. The Administration concentrated drug enforcement resources on ineffective interdiction strategies, undermining even these strategies with cutbacks in personnel. After heated rhetoric about the evils of drug abuse, the Administration cut nearly a billion dollars from the 1986 drug bill. And it took years before the Administration acknowledged that drug trafficking was a foreign policy issue.

The federal government must make a real effort to cut off the flow of drugs from abroad, either through crop eradication or by convincing foreign growers to reduce the drug supply. There must also be substantial increases in government funding for treatment programs, so that drug abusers can break their dependencies. Currently, treatment programs are overcrowded and woefully underfunded. Finally, there must be a continuing effort in the nation's schools and elsewhere to inform children about the dangers of drugs and discourage their use. Curbing the widespread use of drugs is a vital step in the reduction of crime.

In short, there are many steps that can and ought to be taken to make the criminal justice system more effective. Better technology and victim services will help police and prosecutors to fight crime. But there must be a broader approach to crime that understands, and attempts to eradicate, the environment of youth unemployment, drug abuse, and illiteracy in which crime flourishes.

CHAPTER 36

Bridging the Wage Gap: Pay Equity and Job Evaluations

The Honorable Geraldine A. Ferraro

DOCUMENTATION OF THE GROWING trend called the feminization of poverty has raised alarm among policymakers, psychologists, and others concerned with the economic and emotional stability of families. There are only 23 women in the 435-member House of Representatives. While in Congress and as a member of the Budget Committee, I made the needs of women and children a top legislative priority. Despite the phenomenal increase in women's participation in the labor force, women and children are the fastest-growing segment of our nation's poor, simply because most women's wages are barely above the poverty level.[1] It is estimated that if women were paid the wages that similarly qualified men earn, the number of families living in poverty would be cut in half. Clearly, the issue of pay equity for women must receive our highest priority if we are determined to reverse this trend.

In 1983, I cochaired extensive hearings on pay equity with my former colleagues Representatives Pat Schroeder and Mary Rose Oakar. During the course of those hearings, we

Note: This article is reprinted with permission of *The American Psychologist.*

learned of the persistence of the "wage gap"—women's earnings now hover at just 68 percent of men's—despite decades of social, legislative, and demographic change. We were told repeatedly of the two pervasive, yet often subtle, forms of employment bias that depress women's wages: occupational segregation and sex-based wage discrimination. Most of all, we were convinced that pay equity is more than a "women's issue." It is a poverty issue, a race issue, a family issue, and an aging issue. And to every woman who endures the degradation and self-doubt resulting from being paid less than she is worth, it is an issue of human dignity.

I appreciate the opportunity to share my insights into the importance of pay equity to the economic and emotional well-being of women and their families. I also welcome the chance to dispel many of the myths and misconceptions put forward by opponents of pay equity, as well as to discuss the ongoing and proposed solutions to bridge the wage gap.

IMPORTANCE OF PAY EQUITY

Since 1960, the number of women in the labor force has more than doubled; 55 percent of women now participate in the labor force. Women comprise 43 percent of the total labor force. With recent figures showing that 62 percent of married couples are dual-earner families and that 16 percent of all families are maintained by women, it is becoming increasingly clear that women are bearing a major responsibility for the economic support of their families. Yet, whether they are the sole support of themselves and their children or are contributing a portion of the family income, most women do not earn a living wage. In 1982, the majority of women working outside the home—60 percent of them—earned less than $10,000 a year.

A lifetime of low wages has implications for nearly every other issue relating to women's economic well-being. Pensions, Social Security, and disability insurance are all directly tied to a person's income. The inequity caused by the wage gap during a woman's working years becomes translated into economic insecurity in her retirement years.

A common argument against pay equity is that discrimination is not to blame for the wage gap, but that it is an inevitable consequence of women's lower skill level, lack of work-force attachment, and experience. Even intuitively, this does not explain why a secretary with 18 years of experience, whose "only" skills are typing, letter composition, office management, and the ability to deal with the public, is paid less than a parking lot attendant, whose required education is the ability to drive an automobile. Nor does it explain why, in 1984, the average male high school graduate earned considerably more than a female college graduate. But if these situations are not proof enough, study after study statistically demonstrates that even after adjustments are made for differences in education, skill level, motivation, experience, and other factors, about half of the wage gap between men and women remains unexplained by any factor other than sex discrimination.

One of the primary manifestations of this discrimination is the occupational segregation of women and men.

OCCUPATIONAL SEGREGATION

Job segregation creates economic ghettos. Women are first channeled into certain sectors of the economy, then clustered into the lowest-paying occupations within those sectors, and, finally, confined to jobs that, by virtue of being female-dominated, are undervalued and underpaid.

The U.S. Department of Labor's *Dictionary of Occupational Titles* lists 420 jobs; 80 percent of all employed women work in only 25 of them. Over half of all employed women work in two of the 12 major occupations—clerical workers and service workers (excluding private household workers).

There is growing evidence that the chief cause of this job segregation is initial assignment segregation, whereby men and women with equal skills, often unskilled entry-level applicants, are channeled into different jobs on the basis of sex. A study by Anne Kahl, of the Bureau of Labor Statistics, documented the differential placement of men and women entering the labor market in 1980–1981.[2]

Three out of five women went into white-collar jobs, compared with only one-third of male job entrants. Men were four times as likely to enter the well-paying blue-collar occupations as women: Over 48 percent of male entrants, but just 12 percent of female entrants, were placed in these jobs. Twenty-six percent of women job entrants, compared with 15 percent of men, found employment in the service sector.

The true extent of the disparities are apparent only when the segregation within the three broad sectors of the labor market are examined. Kahl concluded that "for men, white-collar employment means a professional, administrative, or scientific position, whereas for women, white-collar is often synonymous with clerical." In other words, for women, white-collar jobs are translated into "pink-collar" jobs— which are dominated by women and underpaid. These jobs include secretaries (99 percent are female); registered nurses (98 percent are female); clerks (86 percent are female); elementary school teachers (85 percent are female); and librarians (82 percent are female).

In the blue-collar sector, female entrants were concentrated in operative occupations (74 percent), whereas male entrants were more evenly distributed among craft, laborer, and operative jobs. And even within the operative jobs, women were likely to be working in low-paying textile, laundry, and stitching jobs, whereas men found more lucrative work in mining, precision machines, and welding.

Service occupations are typically low-skill, dead-end jobs in food, cleaning, health, protective, and private household service. Although young men and women share a high propensity for entering these jobs, men typically come in with more than minimal entry requirements and, therefore, can take advantage of additional education and training opportunities, and advance out of this sector, to occupations with higher pay and mobility. In contrast, many adult women enter these marginal jobs with minimal entry requirements.

The jobs into which women are directed have quite a lot in common. "Women's jobs" frequently are similar to work that is done in the home—housework, nursing, teaching, child care, organization and record keeping, and correspondence. The same discrimination that does not adequately value work done in the home by women is active when similar skills utilized outside the home are undervalued. The result is that dog-pound attendants (mostly men) are paid more than child care workers (mostly women), with whom we entrust responsibility for the future of our society.

Underlying this wage gap are two implicit, and conflicting, sets of values prevalent in American society. On the one hand, it is accepted that jobs be compensated on the basis of skill, effort, and responsibility—not on the basis of race, sex, or the age of the individual who holds the job. In fact, since the passage of the Civil Rights Act of 1964, discrimination in employment on the basis of sex has been legal. On the other hand, however, American society seems to accept that women's jobs are not valued by the same standards as those held predominantly by men.

In an article entitled "Prehistory and the Woman," Margaret Mead described this situation clearly and succinctly: "Whatever men do—even if it is dressing dolls for religious ceremonies—it is more prestigious than what women do and is treated as a higher achievement."

The National Academy of Sciences (NAS) came to the same conclusion, in a comprehensive study of pay inequity entitled *Women, Work, and Wages.*[3] The investigators found, "Not only do women do different work than men, but also the work women do is paid less, and the more an occupation is dominated by women, the less it pays."

This fundamental form of inequality cannot be excused in a society based on the idea of "justice for all." However, there is yet another argument: that discrimination is not responsible for the wage gap, but that an "invisible hand" moves the labor market so that the value of jobs to society is freely determined.

One of the most telling arguments against those who say the wage gap is the result of the free market is the examination of what occurs when an occupation changes from male to female, or vice versa. After the First World War, the job of bank teller, which had been held almost exclusively by white males, became a female job. Since that time, tellers' pay relative to that for predominantly male jobs in banking has decreased dramatically. A teller's job is no longer a step toward becoming a bank officer, but rather has become a dead-end, low-paying job.

The real problem with the free market theory is that we are not really operating in a free market, in which all individuals have equal access to employment opportunities and persons are compensated on the basis of their productivity or the value of their work. Instead, we are operating in a system that systematically excludes women from certain segments of the market and confines them to a narrow range of jobs that as a class, are undervalued and underpaid.

Other opponents of pay equity argue that women choose jobs that pay more poorly than average employment. There are two fundamental flaws to this argument. First, as noted above, women do not have the choice to enter most high-paying men's jobs. Whether through socialization or overt discrimination, women are trained, educated, and led to believe that only certain jobs are appropriate to their role in society.

This fact strikes me personally as I look back on my own career path. I went to college and became an elementary school teacher, an occupation that today is about 85 percent female. Although almost all schoolteachers have had four years of college and are required to continuously update their education, they earn, on the average, less than bus drivers. Did I and others choose teaching because of socialization? Yes, probably. But the fact is, there were very few alternatives open to me or other women at that time.

The second, and more important, flaw of this argument is that it misses the point. The jobs women perform—nursing, teaching, clerical work—are essential to society. Why should women who are highly skilled, who have invested a great deal in their careers in critically needed occupations, be forced to make different occupational choices because their jobs are undervalued and underpaid? Winn Newman, a prominent attorney in pay equity litigation, has offered this analogy: "Telling women whose jobs are illegally underpaid that they can work elsewhere is like telling a mugging victim to move to another neighborhood."[4]

This is not to say that job segregation is acceptable. We must continue to break down the barriers to women's access to male-dominated fields. But the bottom line is that sex-based wage discrimination is wrong. It is not only inequitable and unfair, it is illegal.

WHAT DOES PAY EQUITY REALLY MEAN?

There has been a great deal of discussion over just what the terms "pay equity" and "comparable worth" mean. We are all familiar with the concept of equal pay for equal work, which was mandated by the Equal Pay Act. Although this concept has gained almost universal acceptance, it does not go far enough. Since the passage of the Equal Pay Act, in 1963, employers have found creative ways to circumvent its mandate, by altering job duties slightly for women, thereby keeping them outside the scope of the law. The concept of pay equity emerged in response to the recognition that since most women and men do not perform equal work, the Equal Pay Act was of limited utility in closing the wage gap.

Pay equity simply takes the logical next step to equal pay for equal work: It calls for equal pay for work of comparable value. That is, men and women should receive comparable salaries for jobs that, although they are not the same, require equivalent overall effort, skill, responsibility, and working conditions.

Most of the controversy, it seems, swirls around the word "worth" in the phrase "comparable worth." How do we know what a job is worth? Most of us have always accepted that a job is worth what it is paid. But when we see that the jobs women perform have artificially depressed wages, it becomes difficult to accept this measure of job worth. The real issue is sex-based wage discrimination. According to attorney Newman, "It really doesn't matter what a job is 'worth,' or what an employer chooses to pay. What does matter is that an employer may not discriminate against its female employees who perform work of equal skill, effort, and responsibility by paying them less than it chooses to pay the occupants of traditional male jobs.''

Does this mean revolutionizing the workplace, as critics of pay equity contend? Will we be legislating the wages to be paid for specific jobs and imposing uniform job evaluation techniques on all employers? Not at all. First of all, pay equity advocates are not suggesting that nurses in Peoria be paid the same as electricians in Buffalo, even if the work they do is comparable. Rather, the effort is directed at individual employers to pay their own nurses, electricians, carpenters, and secretaries on a fair and comparable basis.

Second, the hue and cry over instituting job evaluations is unjustified. Job evaluations have been a basic tool in developing pay plans in the public and private sectors for more than 40 years, since long before pay equity became the issue it is today. In fact, many employers used their job evaluation systems in defense of Equal Pay Act claims to show that the jobs women were performing were not equal to men's.

JOB EVALUATIONS AND PAY EQUITY

In 1981, the Supreme Court handed down a landmark decision on pay equity in the case of *Gunther v. County of Washington*. The Court declared that women were no longer confined to bringing claims of sex-based wage discrimination under the Equal Pay Act, but could pursue such claims under Title VII of the Civil Rights Act, which prohibits sex discrimination in employment practices, including compensation. In *Gunther*, female jail matrons charged that the county paid them disproportionately less than it paid male prison guards. The women did not assert that their jobs were equal to the men's; they agreed that whereas the men spent most of their time guarding prisoners, they guarded fewer prisoners and spent a large portion of their time doing clerical work. However, they presented as evidence a county-conducted evaluation of male and female jobs that, while it ranked the matron and guard jobs differently, showed that the county paid the women only 70 percent of the evaluated worth of their jobs, but paid the men 100 percent of the evaluated worth of theirs.

This case raised two important points. The first is that the Court did not impose a job evaluation scheme on the county, nor did it independently judge the worth of the matrons' jobs in relation to that of the guards' jobs. Rather, it simply took as evidence an existing evaluation showing that the county artificially depressed the matrons' wages to a level 30 percent below what the county itself had determined that job to be worth.

The second point is that job evaluations probably offer women the best hope of achieving pay equity in the workplace. If employers are unwilling to institute them (as they may be now, for fear of implicating themselves in lawsuits), female employees and their unions may increasingly seek outside consultants to study their employer's wage-setting practices, using job evaluation techniques. However, it is important that industrial and organizational psychologists, personnel specialists, and others involved with designing job evaluations keep in mind that job evaluations will further the cause of pay equity only to the extent that they themselves are free of sex bias.

The NAS report identified several major problems with many job evaluation plans, particularly those designed before antidiscrimination laws were enacted. Many existing plans simply incorporate the sex bias already present in an employer's pay structure. For example, many employers developed their job evaluation systems by analyzing what characteristics of jobs best predict prevailing pay rates. Using this method, one knows in advance that the highest-paid job will receive the highest score, and the existing wage differentials will be perpetuated.

Another problem arises when job evaluators bring outdated or stereotyped assumptions into their analysis. For example, the job evaluator for the Government Printing Office awarded no points to female bindery workers for training or experience in hand sewing, "because the sewing was of the variety most women know how to perform"; the women's work was thus undervalued as compared with men's.

In addition, the way a job factor is measured may substantially affect the outcome of an analysis. For example, if effort is measured by the degree of physical strength required in a job, many male-dominated jobs will receive higher scores than female-dominated jobs that are equally demanding, but whose effort is better measured by concentration, manual dexterity, and strain on the eyes or back.

Another potential source of bias is the use of multiple job evaluation plans by an employer. Many organizations use one system for executive jobs, another for clerical jobs, and another for blue-collar jobs. This lack of uniformity makes it difficult to compare jobs across occupational sectors. Since the segregation of women into different job sectors from men is a major source of the wage gap, the inability to compare jobs across sectors renders such job evaluations useless in analyzing and eliminating wage discrimination.

There are, I am sure, other potential sources of discrimination to be found in the design and implementation of job evaluations. Most are not intentional, but are the result of outmoded assumptions and practices that have failed to adapt to social and legal change. Instead of women's waiting for these practices to be challenged in a pay equity lawsuit, it would be far better if job evaluation professionals, sensitized to the concept of pay equity, instigated change from within.

THE FUTURE OF PAY EQUITY

The issue of pay equity holds great promise and challenge for the working women of our country. It promises women fair and decent wages based not on their sex, but on the value of their work. But the challenge is that achieving pay equity is a slow and expensive process.

However, we do not need major new federal legislation on the scale of the Equal Pay Act to achieve pay equity. What we do need is vigorous enforcement of the laws, such as Title VII, that provide for the elimination of discrimination in employment. Unfortunately, in the Reagan administration, the very agency charged with securing equality in employment for women and minorities—the Equal Employment Opportunity Commission (EEOC)—has turned a deaf ear to women's appeals for pay equity. Proponents of pay equity in Congress have introduced several initiatives that would require the government to reassume a leadership role in the pay equity movement.

Fortunately, the lack of support on the part of the EEOC has not stopped the drive for pay equity from going forward. Thanks to the commitment of individual women and supportive unions, major strides have been made in remedying wage discrimination through negotiation, collective bargaining, and litigation. The use of job evaluation studies has figured prominently in these pay equity success stories. I hope that there will be increased activity and research to perfect the use of such studies as a pay equity tool, so that we may move closer to bridging the wage gap—and ultimately the poverty gap—between men and women.

1. D. Pearce, and H. McAdoo, *Women and Children, Alone and in Poverty.* National Advisory Council on Economic Opportunity, Washington, D.C., 1981.
2. A. Kahl, "Characteristics of Job Entrants in 1980–81," *Occupational Outlook Quarterly,* 1983.
3. H.I. Hartmann and D.J. Treiman, eds., *Women, Work and Wages,* National Academy Press, Washington, D.C., 1981.
4. W. Newman, testimony before the Manpower and Housing Subcommittee of the House Committee on Government Operations on Pay Equity, Washington, D.C., 1984.

PART FOUR

Nonpartisan Agendas for America

Get action, do things; be sane, don't fritter away your time; create, act, take a place wherever you are and be somebody; get action.

—President Theodore Roosevelt

CHAPTER 37

On the Road Again . . . A Six-Point Agenda Toward A Full-Employment Economy

Coretta Scott King, Murray H. Finley, and Calvin H. George

AMERICAN ECONOMIC THOUGHT HAS gone through recurring cycles. The preeminence of free enterprise and reliance on market forces to determine the path of growth are emphasized during some periods; at other points, what is stressed is an activist government that defines a common good and promotes the general welfare. The reality is that we have and always have had a "mixed economy," with varying, but nonetheless undeniable, roles for government, business, labor, and a uniquely American nonprofit voluntary sector.

America's job creation machine and the labor-market processes that make it run are no exception. From the earliest days of canal building to the massive investments in highway construction and space exploration two and three decades ago, and in military hardware during the first half of the 1980s, government has stimulated job growth. Similarly, the advent of free public education, land grant colleges, child labor laws, the eight-hour workday, the public employment service, the right to organize unions, the minimum wage, unemployment insurance, equal employment

409

opportunity laws, occupational health and safety regulations, retraining to meet the changing demands of automation, and summer jobs coupled with remedial education for poor teenagers are all examples of the advances (some modest) made in shaping the machinery of labor markets.

Americans, like people around the world, define themselves in large measure by the work they do or want to do. For most, their job is the source of their family income. It is how and where they spend the majority of their waking hours as adults. It is their path to economic prosperity and security, to more leisure time and retirement, to fulfilling their roles as parents and members of the community. For too many, it is also the source of failed expectations, lost hope, broken families, debilitating injuries and illness, a falling standard of living, and uncertainty—even fear—about the future. This has always been especially true during periods of economic recession. The last two decades, however, have seen rapid technological transformations, globalization of market forces, and demographic changes that have led to stagnant or falling income and substantial unemployment during the upswing, even at the peak of a recovery period.

Economic recovery, it would seem, no longer means high-quality job growth, a rising standard of living, and a more equal distribution of economic opportunity. The 1981–1982 recession was the deepest and most shattering downturn since the 1930s. Some regions of the country and some urban and rural areas have yet to recover. Some industries perhaps never will. Some population groups simply languish, barely surviving.

Instead of hope, which usually accompanies an economic recovery period, there is uncertainty, at best, and a lowering of expectations. Fifteen years ago, today's level of unemployment and underemployment would have been regarded as intolerable. Through a series of peaks and valleys in the business cycle, decreases in unemployment rates have fallen short of previous lows, and the nation's threshold of economic pain has crept tragically upward.

As inflation rose in the 1970s, higher unemployment became the chief economic tool used to lower it. High unemployment in the 1980s has been credited, in part, with reducing inflation. But are we better off? American workers have been suffering declines in real wages, because wage gains have not kept pace with even these recent low rates of inflation. Real compensation per hour has fallen one percent since the late 1970s. During the same time, productivity has risen by more than seven percent. Thus, low inflation rates have not led to income gains for workers even though there have been productivity gains. Some major economists express concern that falling unemployment rates and the possibility of rising inflation signal a renewed inflationary trend. Their priorities are skewed, however; generating employment and income growth commensurate with productivity growth ought to be the primary concern.

Nine of the 10 highest annual unemployment rates since World War II have been reached in the last decade. Too many now wonder if 6–7 percent unemployment is not the best that our economy can achieve. The overall unemployment rate, however, is only part of the story. The rate and quality of job growth are on the decline. Duration of unemployment is longer. And our position in the world economy is more tenuous. Analysis of these and other trends yields the following findings.

• The rate of job growth is down by more than a third. Between 1975 and 1980, a period affected by both the 1973–1975 and the 1980 recessions, the American economy grew by some 13.5 million net new jobs, or an average of 2.7 million per year. In contrast, from 1980 to 1986, America's job creation machine generated only 10.3 million jobs, or 1.7 million annually, representing a rate of growth some 37 percent lower than in the last half of the 1970s. (If the nation's population growth rate in the 20-to-30-year-old age bracket had not slowed by 20 percent during the 1980s, today's unemployment rates would be even higher.)

• The proportion of low-wage full-time employment is on the rise. Numerous studies, including work done by economists at the government's Bureau of Labor Statistics (BLS), point to increases in low-wage jobs. For example, the number of new full-time, year-round workers earning half the median wage for all workers fell by 10 percent between 1963 and 1973; but by 1978, the numbers of such workers rose by 12 percent, and since 1978, it has shot up by nearly a third.

BLS economists have found that full-time employment rose 25 percent between 1975 and 1985, and net new jobs in the bottom third of the income distribution accounted for 51 percent of the increase. This research also documented long-term employment shifts into high-paying occupational categories (a widely reported trend since the 1981–1982 recession), but found a shift toward lower pay levels in each category. Further, it should be noted that high-paying occupations employ fewer workers, and high rates of growth in these occupations are thus a misleading barometer of economic progress.

• Involuntary part-time employment is increasing. The number of people working part-time who wanted full-time jobs but could not find them or who had been reduced to part-time schedules, accounted for 3.2 percent of the labor force, or 3.4 million workers in 1979, four years into the recovery period. By 1986, at a similar point in the recovery from the 1981–1982 recession, nearly 5.6 million, or 4.8 percent of the labor force (a 50 percent proportional increase over 1979), were involuntarily in part-time jobs.

• Unemployment is lasting longer. The average duration of unemployment in 1986 stood at 15 weeks, up about 36 percent from the 11-week average in 1979. Similarly, while 20 percent of the unemployed were jobless more than 15 weeks in 1979, by 1986, more than 27 percent were without work for more than three months. Men in the prime age categories and at the peaks of their earning power had the longest periods of joblessness in 1986: Those 35-44 years old averaged 21 weeks, 45–54-year-olds averaged 24 weeks, and those 53–64 years old averaged 27 weeks.

• Profound structural shifts in the economy, rather than ups and downs in the business cycle, better explain much of today's joblessness. Between 1979 and 1986, the goods-producing sector of our economy, which accounts for the vast majority of our trade balances in global markets, suffered a net loss of nearly two million jobs. During this same period, BLS data reveal, more than 12 million workers (half of whom had held their previous jobs for over three years) were displaced because of plant closings or permanent layoffs. In a study of the 1984 labor-force status of workers dislocated between 1979 and 1983, it was found that only 62 percent were employed, while 14 percent had left the labor force, and 25 percent were officially unemployed—more than three times the overall eight percent unemployment rate for 1984. Moreover, two-thirds of dislocated workers had below-average earnings on their previous jobs. Manufacturing accounts for 42 percent of dislocated workers, and support industries, including transportation and wholesale trade, make up the balance. The highest rates of dislocation are in the South, the Plains states, and the Upper Midwest.

• Minority and female workers experience the greatest hardship from business closures and layoffs. While rates of economic dislocation are somewhat higher for minority workers (14 percent for Hispanics and 13 percent for blacks, in contrast to 12 percent for whites), the disproportionate impact on minority and female workers is seen in the duration of their joblessness and the subsequent fall in their wages. While the average male blue-collar worker was unemployed after dislocation for 25 weeks, female blue-collar workers averaged 45 weeks, black male blue-collar workers were jobless for 55 weeks, and black female blue-collar workers averaged an incredible 97 weeks. Earnings losses for both male and female blue-collar workers averaged 16 percent, but women who lost white-collar or service jobs suffered nearly double the losses of their male counterparts in these occupations.

• Joblessness and lack of preparation for the labor market among young people is getting worse, even though the youth population is declining. While the number of 16–19-year-olds fell by 14 percent between 1979 and 1986, the number of employed teens dropped by nearly 20 percent. For blacks and Hispanics, the situation is worse. On average, in 1986, only 25 percent of black and 33 percent of Hispanic teens were at work, in contrast to 49 percent of whites. Similarly, black and Hispanic teen unemployment rates (which mask lower labor-force participation rates) continued to be disproportionately higher in 1986: 39 percent and 25 percent respectively, compared with 16 percent for white youths. Education levels, moreover, do not offer a satisfactory explanation for these differences, as the unemployment rate for black high school graduates is 20 percent higher than that for white high school dropouts. This ongoing disparity may in some ways contribute to both lower labor-force participation rates for black teens, as they question the value of education, and dramatically higher dropout rates for both Hispanic and black high school students.

These problems, however pervasive and sometimes disheartening, are not without their solutions. In point of fact, many of them would be much more severe if it were not for current efforts in the public, private and voluntary sectors. The policy recommendations outlined below acknowledge the importance of current efforts. The last decade, however, has been one of massive retrenchment, where national leadership on the domestic social and economic front has been penny-wise and pound-foolish. The Six Point Agenda Toward a Full Employment Economy developed by the National Committee for Full Employment (NCFE) can put the nation "on the road again" to a more just, fair, and equal society.

SHORT-TERM GOALS: INVESTING IN HUMAN RESOURCES AND STRENGTHENING LABOR-MARKET INSTITUTIONS

1. Preparing the Future Generation

America's economic future depends on how well we prepare future generations for the world of work. The NCFE recommends policies that reaffirm the nation's commitment to equal education opportunity and promote the acquisition of basic skills (reading, math, and oral communication) that make advanced training possible.

• Federal funds should be restored for education programs of proven effectiveness, including Chapter 1 in elementary schools, handicapped and bilingual education, Head Start, Job Corps, and magnet schools.

• Additional federal funds should be provided for remedial education programs in middle schools and high schools, and for dropout prevention and recovery programs.

• Community-based organizations (CBOs) of demonstrated effectiveness provide a unique and critical linkage between economically disadvantaged individuals and opportunities for employment preparation and work experience. The federal government should therefore make greater efforts to utilize CBOs in service delivery systems.

• A nationwide Stay-in-School program to reduce high school dropout rates should be established, providing jobs (part-time during the school year and full-time in the summer) to disadvantaged teenagers contingent on school attendance and acquisition of basic skills. Particular attention should be focused on young people who are already parents; those who have had multiple foster care placements; those who have special needs because of disability, neglect, or abuse; and those who are at risk of dropping out because they are performing below grade level.

• The federal government should commit itself to guaranteeing access to postsecondary education by restoring and expanding student assistance, particularly TRIO programs (Upward Bound, Educational Opportunity Centers, and Talent Search), grants, and services to older and returning students.

• The federal government, with the states, should begin to explore alternative ways to increase black and Hispanic enrollment and retention, and to contain student indebtedness and college costs at public institutions (for example, targeted revenue sharing, incentives to institutions or states, and loan forgiveness).

• Additional funding should be allocated for cooperative education programs that help young people make the transition from secondary and postsecondary education to work by integrating part-time work experience into related academic curricula.

2. Strengthening Labor-Market Institutions and Easing Economic Transition

Job Training and Retraining

Broad education policies and investments must be supplemented by targeted programs to assist groups that bear a disproportionate burden of unemployment, are discriminated against, or for other reasons cannot compete successfully for jobs. These programs should be locally designed and managed, with appropriate federal oversight and provision of technical assistance to assure that model programs of demonstrated effectiveness are adapted and replicated across the nation. Current programs serve 3–5 percent of the populations in need of assistance.

• Federal funding with matching state, local, and private financing for job training should be expanded to provide the unemployed and underemployed with education and job-readiness skills necessary to meet the requirements of new technical, professional, and skilled occupations. Special attention should be given to occupations in our basic manufacturing, agricultural, mining, and construction industries, with emphasis on strengthening our vocational and technical schools, land grant colleges and extension services, and schools of engineering and science. Income supports should be provided to students and trainees on the basis of need and contingent on performance.

• Federal support with matching state, local, and private financing should also be provided to strengthen in-plant and agricultural on-the-job training to help current workers upgrade skills or adjust to anticipated changes in technology.

Business and Facility Closures

With over two million jobs lost each year to plant closings, permanent layoffs, and farm foreclosures, federal action is urgently needed. The NCFE recommends policies to avert such massive dislocation wherever possible, and to reduce the burden on displaced workers.

• Firms should be required to consult in good faith with workers and the community to explore alternatives to permanent layoffs or facility closings.

• Large and medium-sized firms should be required to give employees and affected communities advance notice of a business closing or mass layoff.

• Federally funded rapid response teams in each state should develop the capability to provide assistance to displaced workers. Services to displaced workers should include job counseling, training, and income support during retraining.

Equal Access to Employment

Existing equal employment opportunity laws and executive orders, including affirmative action plans and federal contract compliance efforts, need to be vigorously enforced, with adherence to goals and timetables for minorities, women, older workers, the disabled, and others who have historically been excluded.

3. Protecting Family Income and the Ability to Adapt to Changing Labor Markets

Federal policies have long played a significant role in raising the incomes of American workers and improving the quality of their lives. In recent years, however, as federal protections have eroded, incomes have fallen and inequities have grown.

At the same time, as the number of women participating in the labor force has been growing and their participation has become vital to the economic stability of the family and American consumption patterns. Areas like child care, parental leave and wage discrimination have been virtually ignored or mired in controversy. The results are both hardship for families and rising numbers of children at risk of growing up in poverty, their personal development stunted.

NCFE recommendations seek to address these family issues and also assure a more equitable shouldering of the burden of hard times and fairer sharing of the abundance of economic prosperity to come.

Unemployment Insurance

The unemployment insurance system should be restored and strengthened; it is the laid-off worker's first line of defense. The taxable wage base should be raised to 65 percent of the average annual wage to assure adequate funding. Benefit levels should be raised to two-thirds of the beneficiary's previous wages, with a cap of 75 percent of the state's average wage. In states and areas undergoing massive economic change and excess unemployment, benefits coupled with retraining and adjustment services should be available for up to two years.

Minimum Wage

The sharp drop in real minimum wage over the last decade should be reversed by raising the minimum wage to 50 percent of the average hourly wage in private industry. The increase should be accomplished in three steps to minimize any disruptive effects. Thereafter, the minimum wage should be indexed to inflation to prevent it from slipping in the future.

Equal Opportunity on the Job

A renewed commitment to equal opportunity is necessary to end all forms of economic discrimination, including wage discrimination, job segregation, and systematic undervaluation of work performed primarily by women and minorities. Existing laws should be vigorously enforced, including adherence to goals and timetables. New legislation should expand the principle of equal pay to include equal pay for work requiring comparable output, skill, effort, and responsibility.

Child Care

A national child care and parental leave policy must be forged. Only significant federal support can assure the adequate, affordable child care needed to support working families, especially single-parent families. Only federal standards for parental leave will assure their existence and mitigate against the whims of the marketplace. Funds should be increased for the Title XX Social Services Block Grant program; its scope should be broadened to include middle-income families; a portion of Title XX funds should be set aside specifically for children. Federal funding should be expanded for after-school care, child care for adolescent mothers, training and certification for caregivers, and information, referral and resource programs development. Incentive funds should be provided for community institutions, ranging from public housing authorities to school systems, to provide child care at reasonable cost and convenient locations. In like manner, incentive funds should be made available for the start-up of employer-based child care facilities.

4. Direct Federal Job Creation: Meeting Community Needs and Providing Transitional Relief

Community Service Jobs
Persistent high unemployment rates require reinstatement of a direct federal job creation program to provide transitional jobs. Employees working at entry-level wages for up to one year could perform needed community services at the state and local levels in areas such as public safety, health care, libraries, child care, education, social services, and energy conservation. Sufficient federal funds should be available to employ up to 20 percent of those who have lost jobs or are seeking reentry or initial entry into the labor force. Further, these jobs should provide at least one day per week for structured remedial education, occupational skills training, and job search activities.

Stimulating the Private Sector
The widespread deterioration of many public facilities— such as bridges, water and sewer systems, transit systems, ports, and libraries and other public buildings—calls for extensive restoration work. In addition, needed public works projects in many areas should be created. Here, primarily private contractors would perform the work under the guidance of appropriate government agencies. Because of the start-up time involved in many such projects, a "shelf" of public works should be developed at all levels of government to facilitate the implementation of an infrastruc-

ture repair and rebuilding effort. A combined federal-state-local funding approach (similar to the federal highway trust fund) should be developed and consolidated.

LONG-TERM GOALS: THE MACROECONOMY, TRADE, AND HIGH-QUALITY JOB GROWTH

5. The Federal Reserve, Responsible Monetary Policy, and Inflation

The existing economic policy-making system leaves monetary decisions in the hands of the Federal Reserve Board (FRB). Without any structural accountability, the FRB's actions are frequently in conflict with policy and have consistently sacrificed employment to the fight against inflation. The NCFE recommends that the FRB's membership more evenly reflect major sectors of the economy, and that its fiscal and monetary policies work in harmony with Congress and the goal of a full-employment economy.

The NCFE rejects the use of unemployment and recession or restricted growth as the chief weapons against inflation on both moral and economic grounds. Anti-inflation strategies should be directed at root causes: the specific sectors of the economy that account for the bulk of the inflationary pressures.

- Key elements of an anti-inflation program should include sound energy policies to foster independence from foreign oil and its manipulated pricing, vigorous efforts to expand and upgrade the housing supply in order to relieve the inflationary pressure created by housing shortages, and a firm commitment to health care cost containment.
- Adequate funding should be allocated to the Federal Trade Commission, the Securities Exchange Commission, and other responsible federal agencies so they can effectively guard against abuses of market power, such as price-fixing, in sectors of the economy with highly concentrated ownership.

Further, corporate mergers and acquisitions, coupled with largely unregulated multinational corporations, represent an enormous wastage of potential productive capital, wreak havoc in the lives of millions of Americans, and result in unwarranted price structures. The concepts of individual responsibility and accountability must also be extended and applied to corporate America.

6. Planning for the Future and Maximizing Our Resources: Competitiveness in Our Global Economy

Compared with our economic rivals, American investors, managers, workers, and government officials have been woefully shortsighted. The sorry results are evident in our deteriorated international competitive position and our declining living standards. The predatory practices of some established and newly industrialized countries can no longer be tolerated in the name of "free markets" that are anything but free, let alone fair. The NCFE recommends cooperative strategies toward a revitalized economy.

Planning

A broadly representative Council for Economic Progress—representing the labor, business, government, and public-interest sectors—should develop coordinated, long-run economic plans, balancing the needs and interests of each group. The council and its subgroups should assess trends in specific sectors of the economy, how public policy affects these trends, and their impact on individuals and communities. Its economic plans should guide federal budget priorities, identifying strategic investments in physical infrastructure and human capital needed to advance long-range objectives. Such a council would also provide the business sector with better information so that it could more effectively plan for future markets and production demands.

In view of depressed farm prices and purchasing power, the collapse of farmland values, a 50-year high in farm foreclosures and liquidations, the decline in agricultural export earnings, and the record treasury outlays, our nation's agricultural policy needs special attention by such a council.

The NCFE proposes a policy of managed abundance that would assure the production of sufficient goods to meet the needs of the nation, but would avoid the production of surpluses that have no visible markets and that bankrupt producers and endanger needed farm productive capacity.

Such a new policy would retain and sustain the family farm structure of American agriculture, benefiting consumers and U.S. industries as well.

An overall farm and food policy also needs to concern itself with demand expansion, since a significant cause of the farm economic crisis is related to widespread poverty and high unemployment.

Trade

Our national goal remains to maintain and enhance our standard of living—a goal that has been made infinitely more complex and difficult by the challenges of global competition. First, we must realize that achieving a greater capability to compete is not an end in itself, but a means to preserve and improve our standard of living while creating opportunities for less-developed countries to expand their own.

Second, we must be aware that achieving competitiveness involves improving our international economic arrangements. Specifically, we must encourage technological innovation, and we must develop a strong, modernized system of international trade law that is capable of meeting our needs in an increasingly challenging world. We must assure ourselves of the ability to deal with unfair trade, and with the disruptions caused by sectoral surges. Where bilateral trade deficits are too high, we must have the means to deal with them directly. And we have a right and obligation to require our trading partners to observe internationally accepted labor standards.

CHAPTER 38

Jobs for a Healthy Economy

Lane Kirkland

JOBS—JOBS PAYING A decent living wage—are the key to a healthy economy and a healthy society.

And the income from jobs is the biggest item determining the quality of family life.

Therefore, in considering candidates for public office, America's unions give high priority to those whose economic policies would increase the quantity and raise the quality of jobs.

If private business does not create enough jobs for our growing work force and jobs for the millions of unemployed workers, then government action is necessary to make sure that there are enough jobs for all Americans who want to work.

Capital and technology are important, but the fact remains that the way to increase production and raise living standards is to increase employment, hours of work, and income for America's workers and their families.

FULL EMPLOYMENT

America's economic system and our economic policies should aim at full employment. General economic stimulus can reduce unemployment to 3.5–4 percent without inflationary problems.

In our work-oriented society, the job defines the person. If you don't have a job, you have a serious problem—yet, in mid-1987, there were about 14 million Americans with no job or with loss of income.

This total was made up of 7.5 million people reported as jobless by official unemployment statistics, another 1.2 million discouraged workers who had stopped looking for jobs, and another 5.3 million part-time workers who wanted full-time jobs and full-time paychecks.

If there were a flood or some other natural disaster that wiped out the economic livelihood of millions of people, the nation would rush to meet the human needs and to restore lost economic activity.

But when 14 million workers with lost jobs and lost income are spread across the United States of America, they seem to disappear among the 120 million civilian labor force. They seldom demonstrate in front of TV cameras. They don't fill our newspapers with protests against misguided economic policies that wrongly create unemployment to fight inflation.

These jobless workers become less visible, less demanding of our attention, less a challenge to the nation's conscience. They are easier to forget, easier to ignore.

JOBLESS UNDERCLASS

There is a persistent shortage of jobs in the U.S. economy—a shortage that will persist into the 1990s.

Excessive and persistently high unemployment means job loss and income loss for more than 20 million workers a year. For many of these, employment and unemployment are intermittent, and there is some hope that job loss will be followed by finding a job.

But America has a substantial unemployed underclass of 4–6 million. Their lack of a constructive economic role threatens the stability of America's economic, social, and political institutions.

Here are some of the key factors causing the job shortage:

- Massive changes in the structure of the U.S. economy are under way. This industrial evolution will continue.
- Technology is displacing workers and overturning traditional work patterns. Industries and occupations are changing.
- Imports threaten more and more jobs. Reducing the high-value dollar that discouraged foreigners from buying U.S. exports is not enough by itself, to stem this job loss.
- More women and minority workers are looking for jobs. And young people face special problems in a labor-surplus society.
- Recession-depression and slow economic growth have raised the number of jobless Americans to levels that would have been considered unthinkable less than 15 years ago.

Such high levels of unemployment are intolerable today because they injure and destroy individuals and families, and weaken and disrupt society.

Even for workers fortunate enough to have a job, good wages and good working conditions are too often lacking in the new service-oriented economy.

The American standard of living is threatened by these shifts.

What will be the result if the shortage continues into the 1990s? What will excessively high unemployment do in America?

- Human and material resources are wasted when millions of Americans cannot find jobs.
- The nation loses at least $100 billion in goods and services and in income for every one million jobless workers.
- Human suffering, dependency, frustration, and alienation increase among the unemployed.

- Crime, social unrest, and family breakdowns occur more often when unemployment is high.
- Living standards fall, or rise very slowly, when economic growth and job creation slow down and unemployment rises.
- The U.S. competitive position in the world economy is weakened when continuing job shortage, lost income, lost buying power, and lost production reduce U.S. output and productivity.
- Serious consequences of a continuing job shortage are a loss of sense of national purpose and national will; a loss of confidence in the nation's economic, social, and political institutions; a loss of nerve; a loss of belief in the capacity of a democratic society to meet and solve the nation's problems in the last years of the twentieth century.

The American Federation of Labor and Congress of Industrial Organizations (AFL-CIO) insists that there are solutions to the job shortage, and that these solutions must be put into effect promptly and decisively.

We do not accept the dole as a realistic or desirable alternative to gainful employment in productive jobs.

Without successful solutions, America in the 1990s will be more and more polarized, more and more unstable—and will be operating far below its full potential in an increasingly competitive world economy.

AFL-CIO PROGRAM

New economic policies are needed to lay the foundation for economic and social progress.

The basic principles behind the economic policies supported by the AFL-CIO are simple. We believe that full employment is the key to a healthy economy and a healthy society, and that economic progress and social justice go together.

There are no simple solutions to the nation's economic and social problems. Both the private sector and the public sector have essential roles in America's economic and social life. Collective bargaining has a key role. And the federal government also has a key role.

The AFL-CIO is calling for programs to strengthen the American economy and American society. These include the following:

- National economic policies aimed at full employment
- Tax reforms that lead to a fair and productive tax system
- Lower interest rates to stimulate housing, small business, farming, and public investment
- Trade and industrial policies to achieve job-creating economic growth with balance and diversity, international competitiveness, national security, and rising living standards.

JOBS AND TRAINING

Full employment is a moral, social, political, and economic imperative. Economic efficiency and productivity improve at higher levels of employment and output. And a healthy, full-employment economy contributes to strong, stable family life. The commitment to full employment set forth in the Humphrey-Hawkins Full Employment and Balanced Economic Growth Act of 1978 must be fulfilled.

For America to move faster toward full employment and balanced economic growth, jobs must be created in the private sector and in the public sector for the millions of men and women who cannot find employment. It is clearly in the economic and social interest of the nation to put Americans who are able and willing—particularly those in communities with especially high unemployment—to work in jobs that produce useful goods and services, generate tax revenues, and stimulate the economy.

Throughout American history, organized labor has been in the forefront of movements to promote policies and programs to meet the needs of, and raise the quality of live for, American workers and their families. Labor support will continue for economic and social programs to improve conditions for the American family.

Direct, targeted, and adequately funded public job programs are needed to make up for the private-sector failure to create enough jobs, expand needed community services, construct planned community facilities, and build and rehabilitate low and moderate-income housing.

Low-wage jobs are not the solution to this nation's economic problems. In a competitive world economy, America will meet and beat the competition—not with low wages and high unemployment, but with educated, skilled, trained, experienced, fully employed, and highly paid workers. Effective minimum wage legislation is essential to a healthy U.S. economy.

To help women, blacks, Hispanics, and other minorities, antidiscrimination protections must be vigorously enforced. Day care opportunities should be expanded for working parents.

Jobless workers should have the opportunity for training in skills that lead directly to jobs. There should be better job placement through the Employment Service and better matching of workers and jobs. Job and training programs for displaced workers and youths should be greatly expanded. There should be more targeted job training opportunities for adult workers, including women, minorities, and other groups with special needs. Private- and public-sector training, including on-the-job training and upgrading and apprenticeship programs, needs to be broadened and strengthened. Training allowances and income support should be available for workers in training programs.

Human resource and productivity development should be achieved through opportunities for better education, training, upgrading, and upward mobility for all workers, both employed and unemployed. To prepare displaced workers and young people for jobs, national job training programs, Job Corps centers, and other employment programs should be retained and strengthened. Wage subsidies to private employers—direct payments of public funds, backdoor tax credits, and voucher systems—are the wrong way to produce jobs and training for jobless workers, because an exploiting, revolving door to layoffs is opened when the subsidy runs out.

To protect jobless workers and their families, Congress should initiate a permanent unemployment insurance program for long-term unemployed workers. There is no excuse for a system which leaves 7 out of every 10 jobless with no benefits whatsoever, as was the case in late 1987.

INTERNATIONAL TRADE

The trade policy of the United States must be aimed at achieving drastic cuts in our trade deficit, realistic exchange rates, and a fair trading environment that allows this nation to have an advanced and diversified economy that promotes full employment and rising living standards.

Some of our major trading partners have refused to open their markets and abolish their unfair trading practices as a step toward reducing their huge trade surpluses. Their focus on mercantilistic policies that depend on export-led growth must be changed to policies that increase the purchasing power of their own people and that allow fair access to their markets with products from the United States of America.

In many nations, workers are denied basic rights—the right to organize and bargain collectively, the right to a safe and healthy workplace, and other basic human rights. The denial of internationally recognized worker rights must be an actionable practice under U.S. trade law. This nation should use its trade policies to encourage basic worker rights.

CORPORATE MERGERS AND TAKEOVERS

Corporate mergers and takeovers continue to steal available credit from productive investment and threaten the nation's economic health. A broad array of government actions is needed to limit abuses of corporate power, close tax loopholes, strengthen securities laws, regulate bank lending practices, direct credit to productive uses, and protect workers, consumers, and local communities.

The power of big corporations and big financial institutions has become bigger and bigger through mergers, takeovers, and expansion of foreign operations, as well as through the pro-big business policies of the Reagan administration. Corporate power and corporate misconduct must be brought under control.

A wide range of corporate reforms is necessary, including effective enforcement of antitrust laws and adequate protections for workers and the public before corporate takeovers or mergers take place.

INDUSTRIAL POLICY

America needs a coherent and comprehensive industrial policy to rebuild its economy, to speed up healthy, balanced economic growth, and to strengthen the nation's response to international economic competition. To maintain economic and national security and to meet international challenges, America needs its basic industries as well as new technology industries.

Such a national industrial policy should:

- Provide a foundation for a long overdue full-employment policy, through which economic opportunities for all Americans would be expanded, not cut back
- Operate on the assumption that labor, industry, and government work together with concerned public interests in an industrial strategy council to strengthen the industrial sector both overall and in individual industries
- Be built upon an economic and social contract with the firms benefiting from direct industrial policy assistance including company commitments to respect workers' rights and to meet equal opportunity, occupational safety and health, and environmental standards
- Seek to make each American industry as strong as possible, with specific complementary contributions from

management, government, and labor, rather than engage in any futile effort to "pick winners and losers"
or to promote one kind of industry at the expense of
others

- Marshal adequate public investment resources through
a bank for national industrial development to provide
the financing needed for loans, loan guarantees, and
equity positions to support agreed-upon industrial investment and modernization programs

- Establish a priority program of public investment in
our eroding public infrastructure—the roads, rails,
bridges, ports, public buildings, and water systems,
without which no industries can be competitive

- Provide a framework for overhauling and coordinating
tax, trade, interest rate, job training, and other policies
that today often lead to the undermining of American
industry and jobs. Tax policies must support productive investment in the United States rather than abroad.
Trade policies must be oriented to supporting a diversified industrial base and preventing injury to domestic producers. Interest rates must be brought down,
especially for productive investments and needed consumer purchases. Education and job training policies
must be geared to strengthening access to decent economic opportunities for all Americans. A national industrial policy can help coordinate these critical
policies for the benefit of all Americans.

COLLECTIVE BARGAINING

The rights of workers to organize and to bargain collectively
are fundamental in a democratic society. The basic purpose
of unions is to help workers meet their needs for better
wages and working conditions, job security, dignity, and
self-respect, and to ensure their participation in the decisions that govern life on the job and life in American society.

Our basic labor laws guarantee to workers the right to
organize and to bargain collectively; but too often, this guarantee is an empty promise. Too often, anti-union employers
engage in coercion, intimidation, and illegal discharge of
workers for union activity.

Let me assure you that unions are not going to fade away

from the American scene. Unions are here to stay. America's trade unions are going to look very carefully at political candidates and support those whose views are most consistent with the interests of the workers we represent.

The American labor movement will continue to support a broad range of policies and programs that will improve the health and diversity of the American economy, assure expanding job opportunities, and strengthen social justice for all Americans.

CHAPTER 39

Cashing in the Commonweal for the Common*wheel* of Fortune

Norman Lear

I'M PLEASED AND HONORED to have been invited to be with you in this haven of serious thinkers, the Kennedy School of Government. I must also confess to feeling somewhat awed at being here.

People for the American Way began with my desire to write and direct a film I tentatively called *Religion*. It was to be a comedic look at the way religion is currently being used by tens of thousands of citizens who assume the mantle of preacher in order to save on their taxes. In the course of researching the subject, however, I watched dozens of hours of television ministers and became concerned about their mixture of religion and politics, and their insistence that viewers who did not agree with them on matters of public policy were poor Christians and bad Americans. Had I spoken here at the top of this decade, that would have been my topic.

Note: The text of this essay is based on remarks by Mr. Lear at the Institute of Politics, John F. Kennedy School of Government, Harvard University, February 17, 1987.

Understand this: The Religious Right is still of deep concern to me and 270,000 other Americans who are now members of People for the American Way. In fact, the problem is greater today than it was before. But some time ago, another problem in American life began to vie for my attention—a problem that is chronic and more elusive, and that, in its own way, makes possible the religious—political crusades of the Religious Right. I'm talking about the desolation of spirit, the loss of faith in leaders and institutions, the hunger for connectedness that stalks our nation today.

The societal disease of our time, I am convinced, is America's obsession with short-term success, its fixation with the proverbial bottom line. "Give me a profit statement this quarter that's larger than the last, and everything else be damned!" That is today's predominant business ethic. It took root in the business community, but has since spread beyond business and insinuated itself into the rest of our culture. In this climate, a quiet revolution in values has occurred, and it has not been for the better.

Short-term thinking, corrosive individualism, fixating on "economic man" at the expense of the human spirit—all have taken an alarming toll. I focus on the business community for starters not to scapegoat it—but because I believe business has become a fountainhead of values in our society. If the church was the focal point for personal values and public mores in medieval times, that role in our time has been assumed, unwittingly perhaps, by the modern corporation.

For better or worse, traditional institutions, such as the family, churches, and schools, are no longer as influential as they once were in molding moral-cultural values. There are, I suppose, dozens of reasons one could find: the disruptions of urbanization; the alarming increase of single-parent households; the rise of the mass media, especially television; the dizzy mobility of our car culture; the telecommunications revolution and the altered sense of time and distance it has created. At the same time, our nation has learned to acknowledge its actual diversity: the many racial groups, ethnic cultures, and religious heritages that increasingly make up this nation. The myth of a conformist white surburban American way of life has been shattered. I mention these many factors to underscore my point—that as traditional families have come under stress and splintered, as education has come under siege, and as churches and synagogues have become less influential in daily life, the modern corporation, with the help of the media, has stepped into the breach.

Mythologist Joseph Campbell has said that in medieval times, when one approached a city, one saw the cathedral and the castle. Now, one sees the soaring towers of commerce. People build their lives around these towers. Communities take shape. Work skills are learned. Social relationships are formed. Attitudes and aspirations are molded. A dense matrix of values develop around the towers of commerce and spread beyond.

Never before has the business of business been such a cultural preoccupation. If media attention is any indication of popular interest—and it is—today there is an unprecedented interest in business affairs. In recent years, a dozen new business programs have burst forth on commercial television, public television, and cable. There are business news updates, talk shows, panel discussions, news magazines, and even a business news quiz show—not to mention a flurry of new regional business magazines. Americans once found their heroes, for the most part, in Congress, in the entertainment world, or in sports. Now, more and more people find them in business: Lee Iacocca; T. Boone Pickens; H. Ross Perot; Carl Icahn; until 10 minutes ago, Ivan Boesky; and until a moment ago, Martin A. Siegel.

If American business is the preeminent force in shaping our culture and its values, what example are its leaders setting? What attitudes and behavior do they endorse and foster?

The *Wall Street Journal*, in an overview of the American corporation, concluded: "Gone is talk of balanced, long-term growth; impatient shareholders and well-heeled corporate raiders have seen to that. Now anxious executives, fearing for their jobs or their companies, are focusing their efforts on trimming operations and shuffling assets to improve near-term profits, often at the expense of both balance and growth."

Not much later, the *New York Times* wrote of corporate leaders pursuing the bottom line: "They eschew loyalty to workers, products, corporate structure, businesses, factories, communities, even the nation. All such allegiances are viewed as expendable under the new rules. With survival at stake, only market leadership, strong profits, and a high stock price can be allowed to matter."

There are no two-legged villains in this get-while-the-getting-is-good atmosphere. Only two-legged victims. The villain is the climate, which, like a house with a leaking gas pipe, is certain to see us all dead in our sleep one day, never knowing what hit us.

Daniel Bell has argued that in promoting an ethic of "materialistic hedonism," the free enterprise system tends to subvert the very values that help to sustain it. If American business insists upon defining itself solely in terms of its market share, profitability, and stock price—if its short-term material goals are allowed to prevail over all else—then it tends to subvert the moral-cultural values that undergird the entire system. What are these values? Social conscience, pride in one's work, commitment to one's community, loyalty to one's company—in short, a sense of the commonweal.

When we speak of the decline of public morality and personal values, of the "me generation" and "the culture of narcissism," of impulsive marriages and facile divorces, of a hundred social ills, I think we are talking about a trickle-down value system, originating with this short-term mentality that has come to consume everyone.

This ethic breeds in a climate where leadership everywhere—in business, Congress, federal agencies, state legislatures, organized labor, the universities—refuses, through greed or myopia or weakness, to make provisions for the future. And in this climate, with this kind of shortsighted leadership, we have been raising generations of children to believe that there is nothing between winning and losing. The notion that life has anything to do with succeeding at the level of doing one's best or that some of life's richest rewards are not monetary, is lost to these kids in this short-term, bottom-line climate.

America has become a game show. Winning is all that matters. Cash prizes. Get rich quick. We are the captives of a culture that celebrates instant gratification and individual success, no matter the larger costs. George Will, in his book *Statecraft as Soulcraft*, argues that the country's future is imperiled unless our leaders can cultivate in citizens a deeper commitment to the commonweal. Yet, rather than heed that admonition, we are turning the commonweal into the Common*wheel* of Fortune.

Take a look at the Common*wheel* of Fortune game board. It's not unlike the Monopoly board—but instead of real estate, just about every major American corporation is up for grabs. For you latecomers to the game, Owens Corning, NBC, Texaco, and TWA are off the board now—but Goodyear, USX Corporation, Union Carbide, and many more are still on the way. With a little roll of the dice and the junk bonds the game is played with, just watch the raids and mergers and acquisitions! What fun!

The game produced 14 new billionaires in 1986—not to mention what it's done for foreign investors who, with their yen and deutsche marks, have caught on to our national lack of concern for the future. We are now selling them America as cheaply, under the circumstances, as the Indians sold us Manhattan. Now turn the game board over. What does it say on the back? I thought so—"Made in Japan."

On the surface, we seem to have accepted the selling of America, just as we seem to have accepted the fact that we no longer make the best automobiles, radios, stereos, television sets, and compact discs. The fact is, we hardly make any of these products by ourselves today, where we once were responsible for most of them. We've accepted that without a whimper.

With numbers and charts, economists and policymakers can write scenarios to explain all of this in every direction. But there is a psychic, spiritual dimension to these changes that cannot be ignored. There is an open wound, a gash, on the American psyche that must be attended to.

Take the American motor car. Through all the years I was growing up, it was the standard of the world. "Keeping up with the Joneses" in those years meant only one thing: You were trading up either the General Motors line, the Ford line, or the Chrysler line. My Dad was a GM man. He got as far as the Oldsmobile; one year, he almost made it to the Buick.

Caring for our American motor car was the universal family vocation. On weekends, anywhere in America, families could be seen washing, waxing, polishing their American motor cars. And any time we went to the movies, in every Fox Movietone newsreel where an international dignitary was seen getting out of an automobile, that dignitary was in a Cadillac limousine! The American motor car was the national nonmilitary symbol of America's macho—and one does not have to be a social scientist to know that when we lost that symbol, sometime in the past 25 years, it left a big dent in the American dream.

There are too many dents in the American dream today. And for too many Americans, the dream has already been consigned to the scrap heap. I know it can be reclaimed, pounded into shape, and, with a lot of political spit and polish, made as good as new. But that won't happen, as I see it, until we face up to the underlying cause of the embattled American dream: a culture that celebrates short-term success achieved at any cost; a culture that no longer takes pride in products and the people who make them, but that prizes instead the paper profits of the people who shuffle paper.

It's easy to follow the escalation of this obsession in recent years by looking at my industry, television, which happens to have the highest profile of all American businesses. What other American business has its performance rated half-hour by half-hour, seven days a week? Look at network television and you can see how a once strong, once vital industry succumbed to the siren of short-term thinking and degraded its product—and, finally, its profits.

When I first got into television, in the 1950s, the networks used to order 39 segments of a new program—and once, they were ordered, the show was rarely cancelled. A new entertainment series had nine full months to attract an audience—and during the 13 weeks of summer, the networks would run summer replacement shows in order to experiment with new talent and innovative program ideas.

Slowly, over the years, as a way to increase profit margins, the networks began to pare back their commitment to investments in innovation. First they axed the summer replacements, the try-out shows—and ran reruns instead. So, for a time, the new orders were 39 episodes and 13 repeats. As the need for short-term success intensified, the networks cut back even further on their investment in innovative programming. Soon they ordered only 26 segments of new shows, and filled the gap with 26 repeats. When we went on the air in January of 1971 with "All in the Family," our order was for 13 weeks, and 13 repeats. It wasn't until the 16th week, the third repeat, that "All in the Family" began to find its audience.

In 1984, when we went on the air with a new show, 'aka Pablo," which, as the first show to feature a large Hispanic family, certainly needed time to become an acquired taste, we were given four weeks to succeed. All four episodes were taped before the first one aired, and after two airings, we got work that the show had been cancelled.

Over the years, I saw firsthand how more and more, the name of the game for the networks became "How do I win Tuesday night at eight o'clock?" The actual substance of a program became almost incidental. At some point, the networks stopped asking themselves how to program responsibly; what the effects of sex, smarm, and violence might be on children in their audience; how to innovate, to keep network television consistently changing and maturing so it would stay ahead of the competition that was clearly on the way.

But despite the encroachment of cable TV, syndication, videocassettes, backyard satellite dishes, and other technologies, the networks frittered away their franchise by puttering around the same tired formats, adding more sex here and more violence there—more mindlessness—in an effort to grab the jaded viewer's attention quickly. In 1978, many of us were saying that if the network chiefs were standing in a circle with razors to their own throats, they could not be committing suicide more effectively.

We know the result now. The networks' share of prime-time audience has slipped from 92 percent in 1978 to less than 78 percent today. ABC has been acquired by Cap Cities and is still in trouble. NBC has been acquired by General Electric, and the once preeminent CBS, even after laying off hundreds, is struggling to keep its head above water.

I would suggest that a similar fate befell another Big Three many years before—the Big Three auto makers. As has been documented, they failed to heed the handwriting on the wall and refused to innovate, to build small, fuel-efficient cars; they refused to sacrifice a current quarterly profit statement to invest in the future and meet the threat of imports from abroad. Likewise, the ailing steel industry refused to modernize and invest in its future. The labor unions in both industries, which fought only for added wages and benefits, declined to fight to modernize and to protect their members' jobs in the long term. And the U.S. consumer electronics industry surrendered the compact disc technology to Japan and Holland, which were willing to make long-term investments in the fledgling technology.

In playing the Commonwheel of Fortune, what matters most are the numbers. Who can amass the highest sum? Who can become number one? We worship at the altar of the numerical bitch goddesses: the Nielsen ratings; the Dow-Jones index; opinion polls; and cost-benefit analyses. Politicians give more credence to opinion polls than to their own gut instincts. Students surrender their self-image to SAT scores. And on and on.

Despite our reliance on this imperium of numbers, we too easily forget that no numerical scale can truly represent the values that are most important: the spirit that makes a worker want to give his or her best; the determination that helps a less-endowed competitor prevail; the altruism that yearns to be used; the artistic impulse that creates a film or novel or TV show that becomes a cherished cultural symbol. As Robert Bellah has suggested, our individualism and our utilitarianism are no longer balanced by such values as concern for the common good.

These values have little place in the Commonwheel of Fortune, where numerical valuations are all that matter.

And, so, the TV executive need only point to the high Niel-sen ratings to justify the violent and the salacious. The col-lege coach need only point out how much a winning football team earns for the university to look the other way at academic cheating among his players. The company presi-dent can rationalize not curbing chlorofluorocarbons, which are destroying the earth's ozone layer, because to do so would hurt the company's bottom line in the fourth quar-ter—and that wouldn't be fair to the shareholders, whose well-being apparently doesn't require the protective ozone.

The consequences of all this are not theoretical. They af-fect real people and real communities. If the role of business in modern society is comparable in scope and influence to that of the church in medieval times, what kind of spiritual, cultural "home" is it providing?

There is a hurt, an emptiness, confusion in this nation to which attention must be paid. Fear, resentment, and anxiety among our fellow citizens vulnerable to extremists who offer promises of easy salvation. These feelings can also exacer-bate social tensions and result in an escalation of the kind of racism we have witnessed around the country recently.

Our values are askew: We are lacking symbols of whole-some pride. The mass of Americans are losing, or have lost, faith in institutions and in their leaders. There is little in the culture to satisfy the needs of the soul. As a society, we seem to have lost our spiritual bearings.

Robert Louis Stevenson said, "To travel hopefully is a bet-ter thing than to arrive." We think we arrive with each mo-ment of success—the high Nielsen rating, the latest political poll, the improved profit statement—and we ignore the hu-man values, the meaning of traveling hopefully.

To me, the cause seems to lie in the influence of a busi-ness-oriented society run amok. Conservative columnist Mi-chael Novak, an avid defender of the system, has said, "A commercial system needs taming and correction by a moral-cultural system independent of commerce."

I believe that. But what we have in America today is a commercial system that is, itself, the most dominant force in society—a commercial system whose influence is largely responsible for the moral cultural system!

If we agree that our culture has been weaned from a re-spect for other values to the worshiping of money and suc-cess and the fruits of instant gratification—and that this is resulting in a spiritual and cultural crisis—what do we do about it? How can we reclaim the commonweal from the mindless game show it has become?

We can start by recognizing that government has a major responsibility here. I am a product of the free enterprise system, and I cherish it. I am also a human being, and I cherish my humanity. But everything I know about human nature tells me we are innately selfish. We look out for our-selves first, and then our family, our loved ones. Some of us—not enough—reach out beyond that. But when we, the people, talk about caring for things that are ours—our water, our air, our safety, our protection from the myriad harmful things we reasonable, good people are capable of doing to each other—we have to know we can rely on our govern-ment! It is we, through government, who provide for the common welfare.

Business nurtures the conceit that its behavior is purely private. But take one look at the largess it receives from the government: It once accounted for 29 percent of federal tax revenues; now it accounts for six percent. Take a look, too, at the role of corporate political action committees in the polit-ical process; the public repercussions of private investment decisions; and the cultural values that business fosters. Then it is clear why government must play a more influen-tial role in protecting the commonweal from the Com-monwheel of Fortune.

This, again, is a climate we are seeking to change—and there are thermostats that address that climate in every home, in every school, in every church, in every business in this country. We can start, perhaps, by establishing a new set of symbols and heroes. We have had Rambo and Oliver North and Ivan Boesky; corporate raiders and arbitrageurs; the yuppie generation and the culture of conspicuous con-sumption; religious zealots who would abridge the First Amendment in the name of God and political extremists who would censor books and condone racism.

But we have also had people like the following, and more attention must be paid to them:

- Robert Hayes, an attorney with a top-flight New York law firm, who quit his lucrative job several years ago to start a new branch of legal practice: defending the rights of the homeless. His initiative inspired dozens of other such legal practices around the country.
- Eugene Lang, a New York millionaire, who while speaking at an inner-city elementary school graduation, spontaneously offered to pay for the college expenses of some 50 sixth-graders if they would study hard and not drop out of school. His example has caught on in other cities, where individuals and businesses "adopt" students to help them succeed.
- Warren Buffett, the down home Nebraska chairman of Berkshire-Hathaway, who has seen to it that a part of every single dollar among the millions of dollars returned to shareholders goes to a charity or a cause selected by that shareholder in advance.

These are people who have already launched a recommitment to enduring values and the commonweal. Let's more of us join them. We need to rehabilitate the idea of public service; to set new ethical standards for business; to harness the natural idealism of young people; and to encourage leadership everywhere to assume a greater burden of the responsibility to lead. As I said, the villain here is the climate. It needs changing.

We humans are as influenced by climate as by anything else in nature. Our values are shaped by the context in which we grow. The more we seek to understand that context, the better we understand ourselves.

Plant in your mind, if you will, the close-up actions of a man, as in a film. Savagely, he is cutting off the hands of another man. We are horrified; this action defies our understanding. Now, pull back to examine the context, and learn that we are in a different culture—perhaps, but not necessarily, in an earlier time. Eyes can be gouged out here. Men are drawn and quartered—sometimes for sheer entertainment.

We don't accept, but we understand better now, that first, savage act. The act and its perpetrator were behaving in the context of their time and culture.

Now look at Martin A. Siegel and gang, arrested for insider trading—thieves, broken trust. We don't understand. Siegel was making $2 million. Why did he need another $7 million? But let's pull back and see Siegel in the context of the culture I have been describing, and we must ask: In some perverse way, doesn't his story speak for the eighties?

Isn't Siegel's story an example in microcosm of the perverted values of our culture, where the making of money—not working hard, producing well, leaving something lasting behind, but the making of money—has become the sole value?

The problem isn't Martin Siegel's alone. It is ours. We have found the holy grail, and it is the bottom line.

Do we want it?

Must we continue cashing in the commonweal for the Common*wheel* of Fortune?

CHAPTER 40

Search for the Common Ground

Robert Redford

"NATIONAL SECURITY" IS A phrase we're hearing a lot these days. I propose that we think of the environment and our concern for the air, land, water, and resources as national security. I am amazed when I hear that national security is across the ocean or up there somewhere in another realm. To me, our domestic security, in terms of our own resources, our human resources, is just as much a part of our national security as Star Wars.

I sense in this country a strong anxiety about approaching the year 2000. I think it has something to do with the fact that we have had such accelerated growth and unlimited reach for so long, we are at a point where we're not so much reaping the benefits of what we've done, but becoming the victims of it.

How we as a nation develop and use our natural resources has become an issue of such critical proportions, it may well be the largest problem before us as we move toward the next millennium. Our leaders of government, business, and environmental organizations need to recognize that although strong measures and extreme points of view are sometimes necessary to create action, real advances cannot be made if all sides stubbornly hold on to those extremes.

We should take a National Natural Resource Inventory to evaluate our clean air technology, alternative fuels, timber, wilderness, oil and gas, and coal. We should look at this country as a whole, rather than examining individual issues, such as Chesapeake Bay, the Bering Sea, the Arctic National Wildlife Refuge, or where to establish nuclear waste dumps. We should inventory all sensitive areas, and then we would be in a position to make trade-offs. The way it is now, we lose a little bit of wilderness here or there, but the cumulative effects never register. We should think strategically about our nation's resources and no longer treat them as regional issues.

Strong positions can be used as bargaining tools by each side to get the other to move toward the center and create a workable blend—but most people don't recognize them as such. They cling to them with childish notions, hoping desperately to be right—so they can be better, bigger, and, hence, more powerful. But the battles we have been fighting for years can't be won. When we are all in the ring and can't get out, there are no winners or losers. And if we pull our perspective back far enough, we will see that we are all standing on the same small piece of common ground. That common ground is a concern for the quality of life.

Over the years, I have been labeled an environmentalist, a radical. This has not been entirely untrue. I do have radical feelings about preservation and conservation of our natural resources. I have very strong feelings about the need to preserve portions of land for our spiritual selves. What we pass on to our children should be of major concern to us all. If we don't give future generations some space to be alone, to be at one with nature, "to invite our soul," as Whitman said, then we will have robbed them of their heritage. But if we recognize ourselves as a development-oriented society, we will see that our task is a matter of finding the balance between what we preserve for our survival and what we develop for our survival.

The fact is that environmentally, we're not in great shape. Most of the propaganda that we have been hearing for the last few years about our strength and our progress is beginning to sound like a myth, if not a downright fraud. Take, for instance, Bhopal. The view that the single-minded quest for profit can thrive at the expense of humanistic and environmental values is backing up on us. For example, the rush to develop pesticides, without an understanding of the side effects or an exploration of the alternatives, led to the toxic waste dilemma. When environmentalists warned this might happen, they were called extremists. The fact is, they were correct in their concerns and their warnings. The safe disposal of toxic hazardous wastes is now a problem nearly too great to handle.

On the other hand, environmentalists are often more intransigent than businesspeople. Most environmental organizations are trying to either restore or maintain the natural balance of life. But sometimes we have to take down trees, drill for oil, and mine for coal. Sometimes we have to control the population of certain animals, a task the predator-prey cycle should naturally take care of. Humankind has been the greatest erosion source in modern geological history, and we have to accept some responsibility for this.

In this country, we tend to like things clear and simple—good guys, bad guys. It is easier to stereotype than to tackle the subtleties of tough issues. Corporations are for development; therefore, they are only for profit. Environmentalists are for wilderness; therefore, they are only for privilege. Both views are wrong. We live in a time when complex questions cannot be answered with simplistic notions.

Over the years, I have heard boneheaded arguments from both sides that were so inflammatory, it was hard to accept that people actually believed their own words. But when the spotlights went down, the microphones were turned off, I'd find that they felt quite differently. They were posturing, because they felt they had to.

I believe we must reach a balance between economic development and environmental protection, two interests that were considered irreconcilable 15 years ago. This belief is what led me to form the Institute for Resource Management (IRM). The purpose of the IRM is to bring industry and environmental leaders together to discuss areas of conflict before the conflicts take them into battle.

In August 1985, the IRM sponsored a conference to discuss the conflict that arose when oil companies wanted to procure leases to drill oil in the Bering Sea in areas that environmentalists felt were important to ocean ecology. The conference was held in Morro Bay, California. Members of the oil industry arrived full of suspicion and doubt. They were 90 percent convinced that talking about the issues wasn't going to do any good and that there was no point in attending. But they were also 10 percent convinced that there was nothing to lose, so they came. Environmental groups came prepared just to see what business would say and to rebut it.

To avoid polarization, we eliminated the long tables and sterile rooms, and mixed people and viewpoints. We began with an informal get-together on a boat that soon ran into nine-foot seas. People began clutching and grabbing each other and getting seasick. By the time they returned to shore, they were so grateful, they would have hugged anybody. Through human contact, a barrier had been broken.

Upon returning to the business of the conference, the participants were more willing to express their frustrations and were, therefore, able to quickly establish their priorities and a process for resolving their conflicts. After several tense meetings and months of negotiations, the oil companies and the environmentalists agreed on which areas should be drilled and which should not. This agreement and a map of proposed lease areas went to Secretary of the Interior Donald Hodel. The parties also established the Bering Sea Advisory Committee to continue the process in Alaska. With committee guidance, the sides can work to resolve future leasing conflicts and develop policies for further off-shore oil developments.

The IRM has also sponsored conferences on electric utility issues and has brought Indian tribal leaders and industry representatives to Canyon de Chelly, Arizona, to discuss resource development on Indian lands. Industry executives had their eyes opened when they heard the people who live on the land talk about their inner needs and fears. When an Indian talks about his religious beliefs, and why he feels the way he does about the earth—that it's sacred, that he worships it—he can alter someone's view about going in and developing the hell out of a piece of land. It makes one stop and think. We can all learn from the Indians' humility.

What has become clear as a result of these conferences is that industry can't cloak its intentions with smoke anymore. People will see through it. Industry makes it easier on itself and makes better economic gains in the long run by working with people at the outset. In the past, people have asked only one question: How much money can be made from a project in relation to the cost? Now, we have to realize that the cost includes the social and environmental aspects, as well as the economic.

Southern California Edison is a great example. In 1976 that company and I were fighting with each other over whether the company should build a 3,000-megawatt power plant, the largest in southern Utah, the largest in the whole Southwest; we aired our cases on "60 Minutes." I studied the issue for a year and came to the conclusion that it was a bad deal, a boondoggle. The cost of the plant was far greater than its benefits. Industry leaders challenged environmentalists in a typical all-or-nothing battle, and no one was addressing the true cost of the project.

But then, the head of the company, Howard Allen, took a hard look at the project and reassessed it from many different angles. After examining new problems the utility was having with its nuclear plants, he changed his point of view, cleverly blamed his pullout on me, and took a hike. Now, believe me, he didn't become an environmentalist. But he had enough flexibility to look at the additional costs. There are many industry people who think like that now; but, mind you, many don't.

We can't reach the future successfully by taking shutoff positions. The planet is too small, too fragile. If the people who have the power to make choices don't start working together, the only place they'll end up is in the courts on a devastated planet.

We need more national initiatives like Proposition 13 in California. This would get people involved with and thinking about these issues on a national level. When the three states chosen for sites of high-level nuclear waste dumps say they don't want them, or the forest service begins raping the national forest with below-cost timber sales, or the National Park Service ignores the fact that certain animal habitats are in danger, then a national referendum should be initiated so the people can do something about it. Congress's plate is so full, they're not dealing with it. If the president doesn't reflect the people's wishes, the people should have the opportunity to organize a national initiative to do something about it. For example, President Reagan appointed his own Republican commission to study the needs of the national parks. The commission recommended spending $1 billion a year, to be earned from the sales of nonrenewable resources, for parkland and wilderness acquisition. This recommendation was to address the fact that the land and water conservation fund expires in 1989. President Reagan rejected the findings of his own commission because they didn't say what he wanted to hear. This is an example of supreme arrogance in terms of our nation's resources, and the people should have some recourse.

We can't let the New Right seize the word "patriotism" and turn it into something simplistic. What is patriotism but love of country, love of land? We all have strong ties and vested interest in our land and our environment. In that sense, we are all environmentalists.

The world has become too small to allow us to maintain old stances, old-fashioned notions that there is all that space out there—the days of manifest destiny are over. It's antiquated thinking to assume that we have limitless resources and we don't have to worry, that technology will somehow solve all our problems. We can't afford that attitude any longer. We have to be more thoughtful about our actions. If we're not, we will be stealing from future generations rather than giving to them. To begin, we must search for the common ground.

CHAPTER 41

Leadership and America's Future in Space

Dr. Sally K. Ride

LEADERSHIP IN SPACE

FOR TWO DECADES, THE United States was the undisputed leader in nearly all civilian space endeavors. However, over the last decade the United States has relinquished, or is relinquishing, its leadership in certain critical areas; one such area is the exploration of Mars. With the *Mariner* and *Viking* missions in the 1960s and 1970s, this country pioneered exploration of Mars—but no American spacecraft has visited that planet since 1976. Our current plans for future exploration of Mars include only the *Mars Observer* mission, to be launched in 1992. In contrast, the Soviets have announced a program of extensive robotic exploration of the Martian surface, beginning in 1988 and extending through the 1990s.

The Soviets are now the sole long-term inhabitants of low-Earth orbit. The first, and only, U.S. space station, *Skylab*, was visited by three crews of astronauts before it was vacated in 1974; the U.S. has had no space station since. The Soviets have had eight space stations in orbit since the mid-1970s. The latest, *Mir*, was launched in 1986 and could accommodate cosmonauts and scientific experiments for nearly a dec-

451

ade before the U.S. Space Station can accommodate astronauts in 1995.

The United States has clearly lost leadership in these two areas, and is in danger of being surpassed in many others during the next several years.

The National Space Policy of 1982, which "establishes the basic goals of United States policy," includes the directive to "maintain United States space leadership." It further specifies that "the United States is fully committed to maintaining world leadership in space transportation," and that the civilian space program "shall be conducted . . . to preserve the United States leadership in critical aspects of space science, applications, and technology."

Leadership does not require that the U.S. be preeminent in all areas and disciplines of space enterprise. In fact, the broad spectrum of space activities and the increasing number of spacefaring nations make it virtually impossible for any nation to dominate in this way. Being an effective leader does mandate, however, that this country have capabilities which enable it to act independently and impressively when and where it chooses, and that its goals be capable of inspiring others—at home and abroad—to support them. It is essential for this country to move promptly to determine its priorities and to make conscious choices to pursue a set of objectives which will restore its leadership status.

To this end, NASA embarked last fall on a review of its goals and objectives. As NASA Administrator Dr. James Fletcher stated, "It is our intent that this process produce a blueprint to guide the United States to a position of leadership among the spacefaring nations of Earth."

The first step is this necessarily lengthy process was taken by NASA Senior Management's Strategic Planning Council when it adopted the statement in the box on the next page.

The next step in this process should be to articulate specific objectives and to identify the programs required to achieve these objectives. Of course, in some areas of study the programs have already been identified and are well under way. For example, the Hubble Space Telescope, a general-purpose astronomical observatory in space, is an element of NASA's program to increase our understanding of the universe in which we live; the redesign and requalification of the Space Shuttle's solid rocket booster joint is part of NASA's program to return the Space Shuttle to flight status. However, in other areas, such as piloted exploration, our objectives have not been clearly identified. Does this country intend to establish a lunar outpost? To send an expedition to Mars? What are NASA's major objectives for the late 20th and early 21st Centuries? The Space Shuttle and Space Station will clearly support the objectives, but what will be supporting?

These questions cannot, of course, be answered by NASA alone. But NASA should lead the discussion, propose technically feasible options, and make thoughtful recommendations. The choice of objectives will shape, among other things, NASA's technology program, the evolution of the Space Station, and the character of Earth-to-orbit transportation.

MEETING THE CHALLENGE IN AERONAUTICS AND SPACE

NASA's vision is to be at the forefront of advancements in aeronautics, space science, and exploration. To set our course into the 21st Century and bring this vision to reality, NASA will pursue major goals which represent its aspirations in aviation and space. These goals are:

- Advance scientific knowledge of the planet Earth, the solar system, and the universe beyond.
- Expand human presence beyond the Earth into the solar system.
- Strengthen aeronautics research and develop technology toward promoting U.S. leadership in civil and military aviation.

Successful pursuit of these major goals requires commitment to the following supporting goals:

- Return the Space Shuttle to flight status and develop advanced space transportation capabilities.
- Develop facilities and pursue science and technology needed for the nation's space program.

As NASA pursues these goals, we will:

- Promote domestic application of aerospace technologies to improve the quality of life on Earth and to extend human enterprise beyond Earth.
- Conduct cooperative activities with other countries when such cooperation is consistent with our national space goals.

LEADERSHIP INITIATIVES

To energize a discussion of long-range goals and strategies for the civilian space program, four bold initiatives were selected for definition, study, and evaluation:

1. **Mission to Planet Earth:** a program that would use the perspective afforded from space to study and characterize our home planet on a global scale.
2. **Exploration of the Solar System:** a program to retain U.S. leadership in exploration of the outer solar system, and regain U.S. leadership in exploration of comets, asteroids, and Mars.
3. **Outpost on the Moon:** a program that would build on and extend the legacy of the Apollo Program, returning Americans to the Moon to continue exploration, to establish a permanent scientific outpost, and to begin prospecting the Moon's resources.
4. **Humans to Mars:** a program to send astronauts on a series of round trips to land on the surface of Mars, leading to eventual establishment of a permanent base.

The intent is not to choose one initiative and discard the other three, but rather to use the four candidate initiatives as a basis for discussion. For this reason, it was important to choose a set of initiatives which spanned a broad spectrum of content and complexity.

PROGRAMMATIC ASSESSMENT

Each of the initiatives is a worthwhile program. Although each has something different to offer, each falls within the framework of NASA's vision, each builds on and extends existing capabilities, and each elicits the reaction, "America ought to be doing this." In the absence of fiscal and resource constraints, the United States would undoubtedly adopt all four. In the presence of those very real constraints, and the additional constraints imposed by the current state of our civilian space program, this course of action is not possible.

In its desire to revitalize the civilian space program, NASA must avoid the trap identified by the Rogers Commission during its investigation of the *Challenger* accident: "The attitude that enabled the agency to put men on the moon and to build the Space Shuttle will not allow it to pass up an exciting challenge—even though accepting the challenge may drain resources from the more mundane (but necessary) aspects of the program." The Commission further observed (in reference to the Shuttle flight rates): "NASA must establish a realistic level of expectation, then approach it carefully."

To establish a realistic level of expectation, NASA must consider the current condition of the space program, its strengths and limitations, and its capabilities for growth. Any bold initiative has to begin with and then build on today's space program, which unfortunately lacks some fundamental capabilities. For example, our most critical commodity, Earth-to-orbit transportation, is essential to each of the initiatives. But the Space Shuttle is grounded until at least June of

1988, and when it does return to flight status, the flight rate will be considerably lower than that projected before the *Challenger* accident (a four-Shuttle fleet is estimated to be capable of 12 to 14 flights per year).

In hindsight, it is easy to recognize that it was a crippling mistake to decree that the Space Shuttle would be this country's only launch vehicle. Several studies since the *Challenger* accident have recommended that the civilian space program include expendables in its fleet of launch vehicles. This strategy relieves some of the burden from the Shuttle, gives the country a broader, more flexible launch capability, and makes the space program less vulnerable in the event of an accident.

The problem of limited launch capability or availability will be magnified during the assembly and operation of the Space Station. Currently, NASA plans to use only the Space Shuttle to transport cargo and people to and from the Space Station. This places a heavy demand on the Shuttle (six to eight flights per year), but more important, it makes the Space Station absolutely dependent on the Shuttle. If Shuttle launches should be interrupted again in the mid-1990s, this nation must still have access to space and the means to transport cargo and people to and from the Space Station. The importance of this capability was emphasized by the National Commission on Space in its report, *Pioneering the Space Frontier:* "Above all, it is imperative that the U.S. maintain a continuous ability to put both humans and cargo into orbit."

From now until the mid-1990s, Earth-to-orbit transportation is NASA's most pressing problem. A space program that can't get to orbit has all the effectiveness of a navy that can't get to the sea. America must develop a cadre of launch vehicles that can first meet the near-term commitments of the civilian space program and then grow to support projected programs or initiatives.

Expendable launch vehicles should be provided for payloads which are not unique to the Space Shuttle—

this is required just to implement current plans and to satisfy fundamental requirements.

A Shuttle-derived cargo vehicle should be developed immediately. A Shuttle-derived vehicle is attractive because of its lift capacity, its synergism with the Space Transportation System, and its potential to be available for service in the early 1990s. This cargo vehicle would reduce the payload requirements on the Shuttle for Space Station support and would accelerate the Space Station assembly sequence.

The United States should also seriously consider the advisability of a crew-rated expendable to lift a crew capsule or a logistics capsule to the Space Station. The logistics vehicle, for Space Station resupply and/or instrument return, would be developed with autodocking and precision reentry capabilities. The crew capsule would carry only crew members and supplies, would launch (with or without a crew) on the expendable vehicle, would have autodocking capability, and might also be used for crew rescue.

These transportation capabilities are required just to launch, assemble, operate, and safely inhabit the Space Station, and to have some prospect of being able to support future initiatives.

Without sound, reliable Earth-to-orbit transportation available to lift sensors, spacecraft, scientists, and explorers to orbit, we will not be in a position to aggressively pursue either science or exploration. We have stated that transportation is not our goal—but it is essential to the successful pursuit of whatever goals we choose. If we do not make a commitment now to rebuild and broaden our launch capability, we will not have the option of pursuing any of the four initiatives described in the previous section.

The same can be said for advanced technology. The National Commission on Space observed that "NASA is still living on the investment made [during the *Apollo* era], but cannot continue to do so if we are to maintain United States leadership in space." Several recent studies concur, concluding that our technology base has eroded and technological research and development are underfunded. The technology required for bold ventures beyond Earth's orbit has not yet been developed, and until it is, human exploration of the inner solar system will have to wait.

Life sciences research is also critical to any programs involving relatively long periods of human habitation in space. Because the focus of our life sciences research for the last several years has been on Space Shuttle flights, which only last for five to ten days, there has been no immediate need for a program to study the physiological problems associated with longer flights. Without an understanding of the long-term effects of weightlessness on the human body, our goal of human exploration of the solar system is severely constrained.

Before astronauts are sent into space for long periods, research must be done to understand the physiological effects of the microgravity and radiation environments, to develop measures to counteract any adverse effects, and to develop medical techniques to perform routine and emergency health care aboard spacecraft.

EVALUATION OF INITIATIVES

A process to define and evaluate candidate strategies for the civilian space program is being developed at NASA. This process will seek to identify possible strategies, then assess the likelihood of success and possible implications of each. They will be evaluated in relation to the existing and projected environment, and to the various conditions which may influence their success, such as:

- NASA's strengths, its weaknesses, and its culture
- External threats to U.S. leadership
- Opportunities to exercise leadership
- Optimistic and pessimistic scenarios of uncontrollable factors which influence NASA and its ability to carry out its charter
- The existing U.S. space policy

CONCLUSION

It would not be good strategy, good science, or good policy for the U.S. to select a single initiative, then pursue it single-mindedly. The pursuit of a single initiative to the exclusion of all others results in leadership in only a limited range of space endeavor.

A strategy for the U.S. space program must be carefully selected to be consistent with our national aspirations and consistent with NASA's capabilities. It is not NASA's role to determine the strategy for the civilian space program. But it is NASA's role to lead the debate, to propose technically feasible options, and to make thoughtful recommendations.

It is in this spirit that we suggest the outline of one strategy—a strategy of evolution and natural progression. The strategy would begin by increasing our capabilities in transportation and technology—not as goals in themselves, but as the necessary means to achieve our goals in science and exploration. The most critical and immediate needs are related to advanced transportation systems to supplement and complement the Space Shuttle, and advanced technology to enable the bold missions of the next century. Until we can get people and cargo to and from orbit reliably and efficiently, our reach will exceed our grasp; proposed by Project Pathfinder, the realization of our aspirations will remain over a decade away.

The strategy emphasizes evolving our capabilities in low-Earth orbit, and using those capabilities to study our own world and explore others. With these capabilities, we would position ourselves to lead in characterizing and understanding planet Earth; we would also position ourselves to continue leading the way in human exploration.

According to NASA Advisory Council's Task Force on Goals, "Recognized leadership absolutely requires the expansion of human life beyond the Earth, since human exploration is one of the most challenging and compelling displays of our spacefaring abilities."

We should explore the Moon for what it can tell us, and what it can give us—as a scientific laboratory and observing platform, as a research and technology test bed, and as a potential source of important resources. While exploring the Moon, we would learn to live and work on a hostile world beyond Earth. This should be done in an evolutionary manner, and on a time scale that is consistent with our developing capabilities.

The natural progression of human exploration then leads to Mars. There is no doubt that exploring, prospecting, and settling Mars should be the ultimate objectives of human exploration. But America should not rush headlong toward Mars; we should adopt a strategy to continue an orderly expansion outward from Earth.

The National Commission on Space urges 21st Century America "To lead the exploration and development of the space frontier, advancing science, technology, and enterprise, and building institutions and systems that make accessible vast new resources and support human settlements beyond Earth orbit, from the highlands of the Moon to the plains of Mars." The United States space program needs to define a course to make this vision a reality.

CHAPTER 42

AIDS Prevention: Views on the Administration's Proposed Budget for FY 1988

Michael Zimmerman

SUMMARY

AS OF SEPTEMBER 1987, over 40,000 AIDS cases had been reported to the Centers for Disease Control (CDC), up from about 300 in 1981. In 1981, the federal budget included $200,000 for the Centers for Disease Control to study AIDS. For fiscal year 1988, the proposed federal Public Health Service budget had increased to more than $790 million, with about one-third ($247 million) for prevention activities.

Since researchers believe a vaccine will probably not be available for general use in the near future, federal, state, and local health department officials and other experts agree that prevention activities, such as education and voluntary counseling and testing, are the most powerful tools available to reduce the potential impact of the AIDS epidemic. GAO obtained the views of over 20 experts from the research and health professional communities, advocacy groups, and state and local health departments in New York, California, Florida, Massachusetts, Illinois, and Washington, D.C., on the adequacy of the funding levels and appropriateness of the funding priorities in the administration's AIDS prevention budget.

Overall, the experts GAO interviewed generally concurred with the priorities reflected in the administration's AIDS prevention budget but suggested that the proposed budget be increased by at least

- $50 million for methadone treatment to contain the spread of the AIDS virus among intravenous drug users,
- $65 million for educational campaigns targeted at high-risk groups and the general population, and
- $250 million for expanded capacity at voluntary testing and counseling centers.

These estimates reflect the views of the experts, not GAO, and were made without regard to competing health priorities or federal budgetary constraints. GAO identified some options that could minimize the need for increased federal funding.

Investing in prevention now could help contain the costs of AIDS. Treating AIDS victims may, according to CDC, cost $8.5 billion in 1991. Including productivity losses associated with deaths of persons in their prime working years, the total social costs of AIDS may reach $64 billion in 1991. A recent estimate of the total costs of treating AIDS predicted that cumulative medical treatment costs might reach $38 billion by 1991. Estimates of lifetime hospital costs ranged from $24,500 to $147,000. Most of the current studies on the costs of AIDS probably understate the total costs of treatment because they exclude the costs of services received outside the hospital, such as drugs, hospice care, and community volunteer support services.

Mr. Chairman and Members of the Subcommittee:

I am pleased to be here today to discuss issues related to federal efforts to limit the spread of Acquired Immunodeficiency Syndrome, commonly known as AIDS. My comments will primarily relate to the report[1] we issued last month on the adequacy of the administration's proposed fiscal year 1988 funding levels for AIDS prevention activities in the U.S. Public Health Service (PHS). I will also discuss the cost of caring for AIDS patients and the possible implications of alternative treatments on those costs.

My comments are based on our review of the literature and the views of over 20 experts from the research and health professional communities, advocacy groups, and state and local health departments in New York, California, Florida, Massachusetts, Illinois, and Washington, D.C. While the experts generally concurred with the prevention priorities as reflected in the budget, they told us that additional funds were needed for education, testing, and counseling services. These views are those of the individuals wo contacted and not necessarily those of their affiliated organizations.

GROWTH IN AIDS CASES AND FEDERAL EXPENDITURES

As of September 1987, over 40,000 AIDS cases had been reported to the Centers for Disease Control (CDC), up from about 300 in 1981. Most of the cases were clustered in high-incidence areas, such as New York City, San Francisco, Los Angeles, Miami, and Houston. The Public Health Service predicts that there will be a total of 270,000 cases by 1991. While San Francisco and New York currently account for over half the cases, by 1991, 80 percent of the cases are predicted to be in other areas.

The Public Health Service's budget for AIDS prevention and research has increased from $200,000 in fiscal year 1981 to over $790 million proposed by the administration for fiscal year 1988. Of this budget, about two-thirds ($519 million) would be spent on biomedical research to find a vaccine and cure. The remaining one-third ($247 million) would be used for prevention and education activities— $155 million for education ($55 targeted at IV drug users) and $92 million for testing and counseling ($15 million targeted at IV drug users). The budget request also includes $24 million for maintaining the safety of the blood supply and other activities.

EXPERTS' VIEWS ON THE FISCAL YEAR 1988 BUDGET

Since development of a vaccine is at least five years away and probably longer, federal, state, and local health department officials and experts in the research community agree that education and prevention activities are the most powerful tools available to reduce the potential impact of the AIDS epidemic.

Overall, the experts we interviewed concurred with the priorities reflected in the administration's AIDS prevention budget for fiscal year 1988—limiting the spread of AIDS among intravenous drug users, targeting education at high-risk groups and at the general population, and expanding voluntary counseling and testing. The experts did not, however, agree with the proposed funding levels and, as I will discuss, suggested that the administration's proposed budget be substantially increased.

The experts made their funding suggestions without regard to competing health priorities or federal budgetary constraints. Although GAO did not develop its own funding recommendations, we offer comments that may reduce the need for federal cost increases suggested by the experts.

LIMITING THE SPREAD OF AIDS IN INTRAVENOUS DRUG USERS

The experts cited the sharing of contaminated hypodermic needles by intravenous drug users as a dangerous and alarming problem because it represents the primary means of spreading the AIDS virus among the heterosexual population. Nationwide, 60 percent of heterosexual cases and 73 percent of cases in newborns were transmitted as a result of intravenous drug use.

Methadone treatment can, the experts believe, reduce the

spread of AIDS by reducing the number of addicts who inject heroin. Public health officials in New York suggested an additional $50 to $150 million to expand methadone treatment in New York City, where about one-third of the nation's intravenous drug users live. Officials in Boston and San Francisco also indicated that they need additional federal funds to expand methadone treatment, but did not cite a dollar amount.

Many social, political, and financial barriers preclude expansion of drug treatment programs and other means aimed at intravenous drug users. For example, communities often resist expansion of methadone clinics in their neighborhoods. While drug treatment may be the preferred option, rapid expansion over the next few years will be expensive. In the interim, less costly but also controversial methods of reducing the spread of AIDS that do not involve changing drug users' basic behavior, such as teaching drug users how to disinfect needles, can be implemented.

EDUCATING THE PUBLIC ABOUT AIDS

The experts told us that AIDS education for high-risk groups and the general population should be pursued with a sense of urgency and a level of funding that is appropriate for a life-or-death situation. Moreover, to limit the spread of AIDS infection, education must start or be expanded immediately in all geographic areas, including those where there are as yet few cases. In particular, because the virus can be spread through unprotected heterosexual intercourse, the experts believe that clear and direct messages about safer sexual practices, such as using condoms, can help prevent the spread of AIDS in the general public.

According to the experts we contacted, the administration's budget request of $155 million does not provide sufficient funding for education of the general public and targeted groups. Experts from the Institute of Medicine (IOM) Committee on a National Strategy for AIDS estimated that at least $100 million—in contrast to the $29 million in the budget request—is needed to launch a massive public education campaign on how AIDS is spread. They suggested that CDC use paid commercial advertising in prime viewing hours instead of relying on public service announcements, which are generally not aired during prime viewing hours. American Medical Association (AMA) experts suggested increasing funding for AIDS education by 3 to 5 times over the fiscal year 1987 spending level—$65 to $215 million more than the fiscal year 1988 budget request.

Many experts expect the federal government to underwrite a major portion of funding for educational AIDS efforts. We believe, however, that private sector organizations, such as insurance companies, have strong financial incentives to become involved in AIDS educational efforts because they will also have large outlays in the next few years if the AIDS epidemic goes unchecked. Also, the costs of the mass media campaign envisioned by the Institute of Medicine may be reduced if television and radio stations were encouraged to broadcast public service announcements during prime viewing hours as an alternative to paid advertising. Other relatively inexpensive measures, such as posting notices on public transportation, would provide a constant reminder of the threat of AIDS.

PROVIDING TESTING AND COUNSELING SERVICES

The experts expressed concern that individuals requesting testing and counseling typically had to wait several weeks to be tested. Citing unacceptable waiting periods at test sites in Chicago, for instance, the AMA recommended that testing capacity be increased by 3 to 5 times.

The populations at high risk of contracting AIDS, such as homosexual/bisexual men, IV drug users, and their sexual partners, number nearly 10 million persons, according to recent CDC estimates. At an average cost of $45 per person, potential resources needed if these individuals request testing would approach $450 million. Assuming the states match the administration's budget of about $90 million, about $250 million more in funding would be needed to meet this demand.

Experts we contacted at CDC and IOM were unable to predict, however, the potential demand for testing from either high-risk individuals or the general public. Additional costs also would be incurred for heterosexuals who perceived themselves to be at risk for whatever reason; persons who received multiple blood transfusions in high-incidence areas before 1985; and prostitutes. Moreover, intensive educational campaigns may increase demand for testing in relatively low-risk populations. Precise budgetary needs are, therefore, difficult to estimate.

THE TOTAL COSTS OF TREATING AIDS

Investing in prevention now can help contain the future direct medical costs of treating AIDS. A study prepared for the Centers for Disease Control projected that treating AIDS may cost $8.5 billion in 1991 (or 1.4 percent of total personal health expenditures, up from 0.2 percent in 1985). Including the indirect costs of losses in productivity associated with premature death, these researchers predicted the total social costs of AIDS may reach $64 billion by 1991.[2] A more recent estimate of the total costs of treating AIDS predicted that cumulative medical treatment costs might reach $38 billion by 1991.[3] This study based its projections on recent research indicating that the future caseload may be greater than the Public Health Service originally predicted.

These studies probably understate the total costs of treatment because they exclude the costs of services received outside the hospital, such as drugs, institutional or home-based long-term care, hospice care, ambulatory physician and ancillary services, and community support services. In fact, despite widespread concern about the financial repercussions of AIDS on the health care system, data on the costs for medical care of persons with AIDS are surprisingly scarce. Furthermore, no estimates are available of the costs associated with AIDS-related complex—AIDS-virus infections that do not meet the CDC definition of AIDS.

Other factors, however, may raise or lower total costs. First, the distribution of cases of AIDS and AIDS-related complex by diagnosis may change over time. For example, according to CDC, the proportion of AIDS patients with certain cancers, such as Kaposi's sarcoma, may decrease while severe lung infections, such as pneumocystis carinii pneumonia, may increase. Since the latter is more expensive to treat, direct personal medical costs would be expected to rise. Other changes in case-mix may also raise or lower total treatment costs.

Second, numerous drugs are being tested and are under development. Drugs like AZT (azidothymidine) affect treatment costs in two ways—by raising pharmaceutical costs and by changing the clinical course of the disease. Patients on this drug may live longer but require different health care services, which may in turn raise or lower costs. Moreover, drugs like AZT may improve the quality of life and decrease productivity losses if AIDS patients can continue to work longer than would have been possible without the drug. Obviously, development of a cure or vaccine will change the cost of situation.

COSTS PER CASE OF TREATING AIDS

A review of cost studies done between 1985 and 1987 shows that the costs per case of treating AIDS vary significantly.[4] Meaningful cost comparisons are difficult, however, because the studies varied in their definitions of AIDS, the types of costs included, the time periods analyzed, and the geographic areas. The studies were conducted using data from New York, California, Florida, Massachusetts, Maryland, Minnesota, Alabama, and New Mexico.

Estimates of lifetime hospital costs ranged from $24,500 to $147,000. The variation is due largely to differences in lengths of hospital stays for AIDS treatment, for which there is no standard medical model. There is also some evidence suggesting that AIDS patients are now less likely to be admitted to intensive care units than they were when less was known about the disease. According to two recent articles in the *Journal of the American Medical Association*,[5] the use of inpatient hospital treatment for AIDS appears to have decreased over time. As a result, lifetime treatment costs for AIDS patients seem to have fallen. Specifically, days in the hospital from diagnosis to death fell from 168 for the first 10,000 cases[6] to 35 days (based on San Francisco data) and to 62 days (based on Massachusetts data) in 1984 and 1985.

The average length of stay is also shorter in areas where alternatives to hospitalization exist, such as outpatient diagnosis and therapy and home- and community-based services. In San Francisco, the mean length of hospital stay for all AIDS diagnoses was 11.7 days in 1984. Voluntary organizations in San Francisco provide support services to AIDS patients that allow them to leave the hospital sooner or avoid hospitalization completely. Providers in Florida also have been able to cut hospital costs by setting up outpatient treatment services for AIDS patients.

While it may be possible to increase home-based services in other communities where the caseloads are comprised of mostly homosexual men, it is more problematic in areas where intravenous drug users account for a greater percent of cases. For example, the average length of stay for AIDS patients in New York City was 50 days in 1984. This may reflect, in addition to differences in severity of illness, a lack of outpatient or home-based care for AIDS patients in New York City, of whom 30 percent are intravenous drug users.

In summary, although it is difficult to predict how the costs of treating AIDS may change over time, there is evidence that the costs per case can be minimized by delivering care outside the hospital setting. This appears to be occurring in several areas of the country.

1. *AIDS Prevention: Views on the Administration's Fiscal Year 1988 Budget Proposals.* (GAO/HRD-87-126BR, August 12, 1987).
2. Scitovsky, Anne and Dorothy Rice. "Estimates of the Direct and Indirect Costs of Acquired Immunodeficiency Syndrome in the United States, 1985, 1986, and 1991," *Public Health Reports*, Vol. 102, No. 1, Jan.–Feb. 1987, pp. 5–16.
3. Pascal, Anthony. *The Costs of Treating AIDS Under Medicaid, 1986–1991.* Rand Corporation, Santa Monica, Calif., May 1987.
4. Sisk, Jane. "The Costs of AIDS: A Review of the Estimates." *Health Affairs*, Vol. 6, No. 2, Summer 1987, pp. 5–21.

5. Scitovsky, Anne, Mary Cline, and Philip Lee. "Medical Care Costs of Patients with AIDS in San Francisco," *Journal of The American Medical Association*, Vol. 256, No. 22, Dec. 12, 1986, pp. 3103–3106, and George Seage, *et al*, "Medical Care Costs of AIDS in Massachusetts," *Journal of The American Medical Association*, Vol. 256, No. 22, Dec. 12, 1986, pp. 3107–3109.
6. Hardy, Ann *et al*. "The Economic Impact of the First 10,000 Cases of Acquired Immunodeficiency Syndrome in the United States." *Journal of The American Medical Association*, Vol. 255, No. 2, 1986, pp. 209-215.

CHAPTER 43

Education and Economic Progress Toward a National Education Policy: The Federal Role

The Carnegie Commission on Excellence in Education

INTRODUCTION

ON FEBRUARY 2, 1983, 50 national leaders in government, business, labor, foundations, science, and education met in New York to discuss the education needs of a new American economy based heavily on science and technology. The first purpose was to review the extraordinary number of initiatives under way across the country. There are commissions, task forces, projects, and legislative proposals at all levels of government, and many private-sector initiatives as well. Many of these efforts are aimed at improving mathematics and science in secondary schools; others, at increasing the output of scientists and engineers in higher education; still others, at retraining adult workers dislocated by structural changes in the economy. The common denominator is the need for dramatic improvement in the quality of education to meet the demands of a technological economy that is highly dependent on educated men and women.

471

The conference's second purpose was to explore the desirability and feasibility of taking advantage of the current momentum to develop a coherent national policy linked to economic progress. What steps might be taken to mobilize the nation at the local, state, and federal levels, as well as within the private sector?

American education has always responded to the needs of society. In 1957, Sputnik and national defense issues drew forth massive public interest and support. In the 1960s, the Great Society and social justice became the incentive for reform and support. Today, the needs of the economy are paramount. The economic challenge from Japan and other countries is the modern Sputnik, a powerful lever for the reform and support of education. Indeed, the conferences concluded that the present economic challenge is more profound than Sputnik and as fundamental as the change from an agrarian to an industrial economy after the Civil War.

The conference participants further concluded that national leadership for a sustained period of time is essential to keep the nation's feet to the fire with respect to the need for improving education. Though the present emphasis should be upon mathematics, science, engineering, and foreign language skills, the conferees cited the need for qualitative improvement across the full spectrum of the humanities and social sciences as well. These areas not only develop critical thinking and problem-solving skills, but also address the essential value questions posed by science and technology that are linked to economic growth. Education must move to the top of the national agenda if the nation is to prosper. Without improvement, our future may be bleak. One speaker put the case more forcefully: Failure to attend to our education system is the equivalent of unilateral disarmament.

Governor James B. Hunt, Jr., of North Carolina, and David Hamburg, president of the Carnegie Corporation of New York, conveners of the conference, were asked to put together a working group from the broad coalition of people present at the conference to plan an ongoing mechanism that would provide such national leadership. They were also asked to address the immediate issue of federal legislation.

After an analysis of the current legislative proposals, the working group drafted this statement about the federal role, in the hope that it might be useful to policymakers over the short term.

THE FEDERAL ROLE

Better education for economic growth requires action at all levels of government—local, state, federal—and in the private sector. The argument for federal action is that there is a pressing national need that the states and the private sector cannot meet alone. Moreover, with a mobile population and an increasingly specialized economy, the benefits of education accrue to the nation as a whole and not to just any one state or locality. We think that federal legislation ought to reflect the following general guidelines.

1. Serve two major purposes: improvement in mathematical and scientific literacy for the general population and development of high-level skills, including foreign language proficiency, among the most talented.

A crash program to produce more scientists and engineers without attention to the general population is shortsighted. General scientific literacy among our citizens is just as important to the future of the nation as is the production of high-level experts. But concentration on the former to the neglect of the latter would also be a mistake. The nation badly needs highly trained and talented scientists, engineers, technical personnel, and persons proficient in foreign languages; having members of our society skilled in these areas is essential for economic growth, diplomacy, and world understanding.

2. Include three levels of education in a comprehensive approach: schools, colleges, and adult retraining.

Education for the new economy requires attention to both today's and tomorrow's workers in a systematic approach to improvement. The most immediate payoff comes with the retraining of adult workers. Midterm effects come with changes in higher education. School improvement shows results over the long term. Concentration on any segment alone is insufficient.

3. Build on state and local initiatives.

Many states have clearly taken the lead in the arena of education and economic growth. Federal legislation should recognize state and local leadership, and should encourage a bottom-up approach to program priorities. Local and regional needs vary. Federal accountability requirements should emphasize clear statements of goals, targets, and easily documented results.

4. Encourage partnerships among business/labor, education, and government.

In many states, this tripartite collaboration is already taking place. Business has a stake in education, and its active participation in improving education is heartening evidence of a new era. Partnerships hold great promise and should be encouraged.

5. Support both good programs already in operation and new programs aimed at reform.

Much of what goes on in American schools and colleges is good and needs strengthening, yet reform is needed as well. Encouraging innovation and disseminating the results of evaluation is a special federal responsibility. The use of computers as a tool for instruction is an example of an exciting innovation with enormous potential that needs to be developed.

6. Emphasize talent development among minorities and women.

A smaller group of young people will be required to carry a heavier work burden in a more complex, technological society in the years ahead. Within 10 years, 20 percent fewer college-age students will be entering the work force. And by the year 2000, upward of 30 percent of these young people will be black or Hispanic, the very groups now at the bottom of the education and economic ladder. The nation will need all the black, Hispanic, and female doctors, engineers, and scientists that we can educate. We can't afford education casualties between now and the year 2000.

7. Enlist the best scientific minds of the nation to work on school and college curriculum projects, as well as on teacher training.

There is evidence, for example, that major revision is necessary in school mathematics curricula to adjust to the advent of calculators and computers. Old topics may not be necessary; new ones become possible and desirable. The top scientific minds from industry, universities, and schools should be brought to bear on these issues on a sustained basis. Much was accomplished after Sputnik. Major new efforts are now necessary, especially to build lasting bridges between schools and colleges for mutual benefit.

8. Recognize the dignity and worth of teachers in schools and colleges.

Top-down reform on a large scale will not work. For change to take place, teachers must be involved at the beginning and feel committed to change. Improvement of the status of teachers is a long-term objective that is absolutely essential to the nation's future, as is the development of enhanced opportunities for teachers to refurbish their skills and knowledge.

9. Provide incentives to leverage and encourage state, local, and private investment in education.

A national approach to reform and support implies partnerships and multiple funding sources: federal, state, local, and private. An important federal role is to provide incentives for such widespread support and to build upon it. Matching funds, tax incentives, and loan programs are examples of appropriate mechanisms. On the other hand, targeted federal funds may also be necessary to ensure that underserved areas and populations have their needs met in the absence of funds from other sources.

Leveraging money is clearly a means to keep the federal price tag down while increasing the national impact. In addition, federal departments and agencies should be encouraged to look at their present activities in order to maximize their impact. For example, new uses for vocational education money may be appropriate, and there may be Defense Department funds that could properly be used for mathematics, science, and engineering training outside the military to assure an adequate supply of trained manpower.

10. Build in a sustained federal role.

This is a long-term problem that will not be solved by a quick fix. Only through sustained efforts over a period of time will significant results occur. An initial 3–5-year program is only a beginning. First-year funding should be modest to allow for adequate planning. Increased funding in subsequent years should follow. The precedents of the 120-year-old Land Grant Act argue strongly for the merits of a long-term program to build and sustain our education capacity and, through that capacity, our national economy.

We encourage congressional leaders, the president and others to help generate a nationwide dialogue on these issues. The current situation demands a sense of urgency and calls for bold and creative action. All major sectors are ready to pitch in behind leadership that is willing to put the highest priority on building our nation's human resources. Our economic vitality and national security depend on it.

CHAPTER 44

The Decline of the American Empire

Raymond Dalio

As an economist with a keen interest in history, who services clients in over 21 countries, I can't but view the U.S. economy within a long-term context and in relation to other countries. From this perspective, it appears that Americans are living in a rarefied environment, which they are jeopardizing through undisciplined debt accumulation and over-consumption.

A CYCLICAL EXPANSION IN A SECULAR DOWNWAVE

As shown in Figure 1, the long-term growth rate of real gross national product (GNP) has been a shade less than two percent since the year 1900. This trend has occurred because, over time, we have increased our knowledge and, thereby, raised our productivity and living standards.

However, major swings around this trend have not been due primarily to expansions and contractions in knowledge. For example, the Great Depression didn't occur because we forgot how to produce efficiently, and it wasn't set off by war or drought. All the elements needed to make the economy buzz were present, and yet it stagnated. Why didn't the idle

Figure 1
REAL
GROSS NATIONAL PRODUCT, 1900-1986

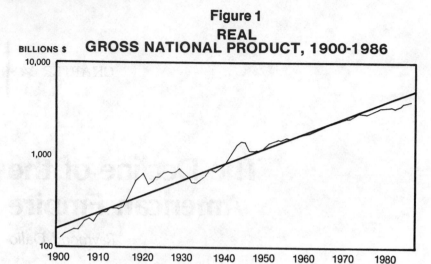

Figure 2
NET INTEREST
AS A PERCENTAGE OF GNP, 1900-1986

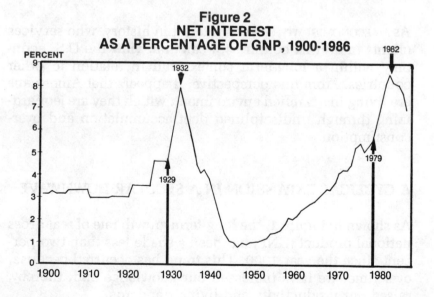

Figure 3
PERCENTAGE CHANGE
IN REAL TOTAL DEBT, 1900-1986

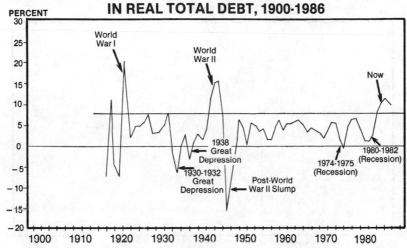

Figure 4
PERSONAL SAVINGS
DIVIDED BY GNP, 1900-1986

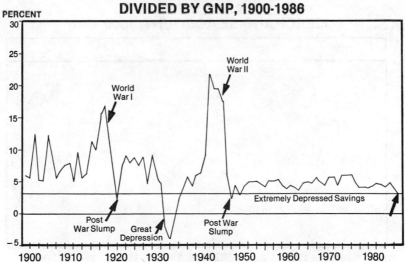

Figure 5
TOTAL DEBT
DIVIDED BY GNP, 1900-1986

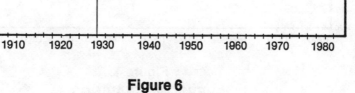

Figure 6
BALANCE OF TRADE
MERCHANDISE ACCOUNT, 1900-1986

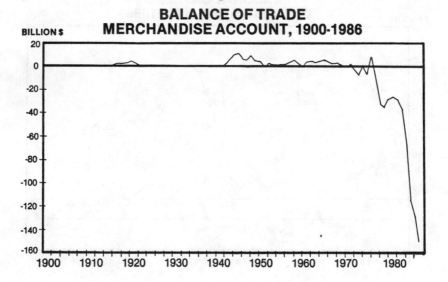

factories simply hire the unemployed to utilize the abundant resources in order to produce prosperity?

The reason is that major swings around the trend have been due primarily to expansions and contractions in credit. Very simply, when debt service represents a low percentage of GNP, demand can easily be stimulated through credit growth. However, when debt service rises to a high percentage of GNP, it chokes off economic growth and eventually leads to an economic contraction based on debt liquidation, a condition we call a depression. This "long wave cycle," as it has operated through this century, is clearly reflected in Figure 2, which shows net interest as a percentage of GNP.

Since 1980, debt has accelerated at a frightening pace. As shown in Figure 3, the only other times during this century that real (i.e., inflation-adjusted) debt growth was as fast as it has been recently was during World Wars I and II.

However, whereas savings rates were high to finance this debt growth during the two World Wars, they are now at their lowest since the Great Depression (see Figure 4).

As is shown in Figure 5, the rate of debt growth has raised the ratio of debt-to-GNP to levels previously reached only during the Great Depression.

Just as it is true for individuals and families, it is also true for countries that borrowing raises living standards over the short run and lowers them over the long run. Thus, this rapid debt growth is creating the illusion that Americans are getting richer, when they are really getting poorer. This illusion is encouraged because Americans tend to judge their well-being in terms of their consumption and to measure their wealth in dollars, paying too little attention to their debts or the impact of the falling dollar on their worth. However, to one who follows global economic statistics, recent trends are shocking. For example, consider that in 1987, the United States will borrow more money from the rest of the world than was borrowed by all less-developed countries combined in their year of largest borrowings, and that since 1985, the U.S. share of world GNP shrank from about 26 percent to 18 percent.

The extraordinary rate of deterioration in the trade balances, shown in Figure 6, reflects just how fast and severely we have become uncompetitive in world markets. While we like to blame others, particularly the Japanese, for our deficits, the truth is that our poor performance is more the result of our own failings than the inequities of others. Why aren't other industrialized countries having similar trade problems and why is it that the U.S. is running deficits with all other sectors of the world economy? Rather than being global, the problem is particular to the United States.

THE PROBLEM IS OUR ATTITUDES

Americans are now on an undisciplined buying spree financed by borrowing. Why is this?

We economists tend to think and talk almost exclusively in terms of statistics and equations. As a result, there is a tendency to ignore important economic influences simply because they cannot be quantified. For example, I don't know how many studies have taken hundreds of pages to conclude that we really don't know what affects productivity. Not one of these studies considered the impact of changing worker attitudes, because this influence can't be quantified. Since the economist cannot make such a statement as "In February 1988, workers' attitudes were 17.4 percent lower than they were 10 years earlier," he chooses to ignore this influence. Since most psychological influences on the economy are not quantifiable, they tend to be overlooked. Yet, readers of history might observe that the descendancy of civilization can be traced to attitudes about work and debt, which in turn are reflected in numerous deteriorating economic circumstances such as those shown earlier.

On the basis of my reading of history and my contact with other countries, I believe that the long-term cyclicity, as reflected in the debt service charts closely tracks an attitudinal cycle. Developments in the U.S. economy are more easily understood when put in the context of what I call the life cycle of a country.

At the earliest stages of a country's life cycle, its people are poor and think of themselves as poor. They work hard to subsist. There isn't enough money left over for saving and capital formation. As a result, work is done in the most primitive manner and economic growth is slow. Only when an individual's income exceeds his subsistence expenditures can he save and make capital expenditures. Saving is motivated principally by the fear that the future may not be as good as the present, and the feeling that resources are better off kept for necessities than spent on luxuries. Borrowers of these savings, also insecure about the future, use these funds to improve productivity, rather than to increase their consumption. For example, a borrower might replace his plow and oxen with a tractor, thereby producing substantial productivity gains. While we tend to think that productivity gains result almost exclusively from having shiny new equipment, it's important to realize that having a labor force that is willing to work harder for less compensation than the competition's is at least as important. This attitude is currently reflected in the ability of the Chinese to buy "obsolete" factories from the United States and use them to produce goods that undercut us in our own markets.

In the next stage of a country's life cycle, its people become rich, but still think of themselves as poor. They work and save just as hard as they did when they were poor and plow their wealth back into capital formation. While production costs rise, they don't rise enough to make them uncompetitive, particularly since the accelerated rate of capital spending in turn gives businesses the new equipment that further supports their competitiveness. During this stage, countries run large trade surpluses and build enormous foreign exchange reserves. The United States was in this position at the end of World War II. It then accounted for half the world economy and owned 80 percent of the world gold stock. Yet, nervous Americans reflecting on two decades of depression and war ran large trade surpluses and actively saved. Japan was in this stage until recently, and the newly industrialized countries in the Far East (Hong Kong, Korea, Taiwan, and Singapore) are currently in it.

Next, people become rich and think of themselves as rich. As a result, they increasingly want to enjoy "the good life," and they work and save less. A classic symptom of the transition from the last stage to this one is the shortening of the work week from six days to five. They divert more money to consumption at the expense of capital formation. The savings rate begins to decline, and the real debt growth rate picks up. Debt is increasingly used for consumption rather than for building for the future, and labor costs rise in comparison with those in competing countries. The United States entered this stage in the 1960s, when it was popularly believed that we were rich enough to raise our living standards, wipe out poverty, conquer outer space, and wage war at the same time. Japan is entering this stage now.

Eventually, people become poor and continue to think they are rich. During this stage, consumption is financed at the expense of capital formation; real debt growth accelerates and real savings fall even further; labor is priced uncompetitively; and plants and equipment become obsolete. As a result, trade and current account balances deteriorate, and foreign exchange rates decline. The United States is currently in this stage; the United Kingdom has been there since World War II. Though Americans haven't felt the consequences yet, principally because their debt finance overconsumption is continuing, they will during the next presidency. While the early eighties was a period of extraordinary debt accumulation, I believe that the late eighties and early nineties will be a period of paying back.

THE NEW PRESIDENCY

Whoever succeeds Ronald Reagan as president will probably preside over the worst economic contraction since the Great Depression. His temptation will be to try to legislate the problems away. Pressures to close our doors to the rest of the world will increase. Legislators will propose programs to subsidize our declining living standards. However, all such moves combined will not have the impact of even a modest change in America's attitude toward working, spending, and saving.

As I travel around the world, I am regularly asked whether Americans have yet realized the seriousness of their situation and if they are ready to start competing. It is widely believed that the United States can achieve enormous productivity gains if the American people get behind such an effort, just as they did during World War II.

Frankly, I believe that it is possible, though unlikely, that Americans will reverse this trend. On the one hand, I observe the discipline which has practically overnight changed the profile of the typical American from an overweight, cigarette smoking, sedentary beef eater to a fit, preservative-free, cholesterol-conscious jogger. And I think that it should not be much more difficult for Americans to work harder and cut their personal consumption in order to increase capital formation than it is for them to wake up early to go jogging or eliminate tasty though unhealthy foods from their diets. However, I also observe that one of the symptomatic differences between economics in ascendancy and those in decline is the length of the work week, and I can't imagine Americans moving from a five-day work week to a six-day work week. I believe that the greatest contribution that the new president could make to our economic health would be to favorably alter Americans' attitudes about working, borrowing, and saving by inspiring their commitment to fiscal health.

CHAPTER 45

The Need for a Better-Regulated Financial System

Henry Kaufman

AMERICA'S FINANCIAL SYSTEM IS going astray: Many deposit institutions are weak, and businesses and households have assumed massive debt burdens. This state of affairs poses serious risks for our economy, in light of which, the current system of financial regulation is inadequate to deal with changes in financial markets. Congress should abandon the system and pass comprehensive legislation to install a better one, developed in cooperation with the financial community.

In designing a better regulatory environment, we must ask ourselves what kind of a financial system we really want. What should the financial institutions and markets try to achieve? How can they accomplish their goals effectively, while safeguarding the public trust? Are there important distinguishing aspects between financial institutions and other private enterprises in the economy? In other words, we should set forth a rationale for our financial system, and then establish some of the tenets that will move us closer to an improved regulatory structure.

It would be impossible to run our complex and advanced economy effectively without integrated supportive activity from financial institutions and markets, whose role is to intermediate the savings and investment process. Financial institutions and markets reconcile the needs of both the demanders and the suppliers of funds. If we did not have an efficient financial system, the behavior of spending units and of savers would be severely limited, and our economic performance would be sharply curtailed. Among other responsibilities, a well-functioning financial system should facilitate stable economic growth. In a broader sense, it should promote reasonable financial practices and curb excesses.

Some members of the financial and academic community make an important distinction among the underlying functions of the financial system, dividing them into two groups: those that provide a mechanism through which flow all payments, and those that provide the framework through which credit is allocated efficiently. The reason for this distinction is that whereas there is a clear need to safeguard the payments mechanism, it is less clear that our system of credit allocation requires such safeguards.

I believe, however, that in today's financial world, these functions are intertwined. The differences between money and credit are blurred. In an attitude that has changed markedly over the past few decades, borrowings are considered by many to be a source of liquidity and, therefore, a substitute for money or highly liquid assets. Short-term assets, like Treasury bills and commercial paper, are considered substitutes for money. Thus, the greater risks that may be inherent in today's credit structure are not reduced by safeguarding the payments mechanism, which once upon a time was a cash-only function.

Moreover, other important financial changes have taken place that have affected the functioning of our financial system and that have often induced regulatory responses without full thought to the ultimate consequences. The following five developments need to be incorporated into plans to improve our financial system.

First, financial institutions today acquire funds primarily

by bidding in the open market. This bidding for funds has been partly responsible for blurring the differences among financial institutions. A broad menu of obligations is available to temporary holders of funds and to savers, many of whom are highly knowledgeable about these instruments and markets. Few institutions hold much in the way of captive funds at below-market yields.

Second, institutions and other participants in the financial markets now actively engage in "spread banking"—an effort through which institutions try to lock in a rate of return that exceeds the cost of their liabilities. This practice began years ago as a commercial banking technique, but other institutions and businesses have followed suit with the creation of many new credit instruments, ranging from floating-rate obligations to interest rate and currency swaps.

Third, spread banking and related opportunities were greatly enhanced through "securitization"—the process by which a nonmarketable asset is turned into a marketable instrument. Today, many credit instruments have been securitized, including consumer credit obligations, mortgages, high-yield corporate bonds, and many derivative instruments, such as options and futures. They have enhanced the growth of the open market and inhibited the growth of the traditional banking market. Yet, many of these instruments, new as they are, are not completely understood and have yet to be tested in both bull and bear markets.

Fourth, financial institutions and markets are much more international in their activities than was once the case. Funds flow electronically from one country to another with extraordinary speed and in large volume, sometimes moving counter to underlying trade developments. Facilitating these international flows, large U.S. commercial banks and investment banks have built up great operations in key foreign money centers, and concurrently, foreign financial institutions are enjoying an increased presence in the United States. Today, many U.S. borrowers participate in both domestic and foreign financial markets, and U.S. institutional investors are becoming more familiar with international opportunities. Again, the opportunity for reward has carried risk. Our money-center banks' experience in lending to developing countries is one example; managing the risk of floating exchange rates in a world of 24-hour-a-day trading is another.

Fifth, vast improvements in computer and communications technology are rendering many traditional institutional arrangements obsolete. Technological breakthroughs have a significant impact on the location of physical facilities, the communications linkages with clients, and the magnitude and speed of market decision making.

These changes, to a large extent, reflect the influence of deregulated interest rates unaccompanied by prudential safeguards. In view of these developments, a number of issues need to be raised and resolved. One is whether financial institutions should be subject to special regulatory treatment. My answer is yes, because of these institutions' extraordinary public responsibility. They have a fiduciary role as the holders of the public's temporary funds and savings. They generally have large liabilities (other people's money) and a small capital base, and are involved in allocating the proceeds from these liabilities to numerous activities that are critical to the functioning of our economy.

If the role of the financial system carries a public or fiduciary responsibility, as I believe it does, then a government role in guiding the system is valid. No highly developed society has treated financial institutions and markets as strictly private activity, and the Congress itself has long since recognized the role of central banking in guiding our financial system.

The characteristics that make the financial system distinctive also demand that its ownership remain separate from that of business and commercial activity. To combine the two would surely lead to economic and financial concentration, to major conflicts of interest, and to a compromise of the public responsibility of financial institutions. Equally important is that a marriage of business and the financial system would substantially widen the official financial safety net that is now extended only selectively to businesses and institutions when financial difficulties erupt. A mix of commerce and finance would spread the safety net to cover many large private enterprises. This, in turn, could lead to economic inefficiencies at the expense of small and medium-sized enterprises, which would suffer proportionately more in periods of economic distress. The result would be more economic and financial concentration.

Another question that needs to be addressed is whether financial institutions should experience the benefits and discomforts of monetary policy or be mere conduits that pass the full impact of policy on to households and businesses. In the past two decades, financial institutions have increasingly become conduits. Through spread banking and other techniques, for example, they have quickly passed on the higher cost of funds to local government, business, and household borrowers in order to protect their own profit margins. As a result, much higher interest rates have been required to achieve effective monetary restraint.

The final demanders of credit—such as consumers, businesses, and governments—have been encumbered with a higher interest cost structure. The ability of financial institutions to shift higher costs quickly has encouraged them to become more entrepreneurial and more aggressive as merchandisers of credit. Similarly, the securitization of credit obligations is probably loosening the traditional ties between creditor and debtor, adding to the entrepreneurial drive in the financial system.

The disquieting manifestations of this financial entrepreneurship abound today. Despite a sharp deterioration in the quality of credit reflected on the balance sheets of financial institutions, the drive to exploit growth through the continuing rapid creation of debt is very much alive. Banking institutions that are overloaded with the debt of financially weak developing countries are currently striving to extend credit to sectors in which debtors are still viable, such as households and businesses. The open credit market operates under the false assumption that marketability means high liquidity; it is exploiting the issuance of high-yield bonds and taking on activities that are akin to bank lending practices.

Financial market participants, however, will not escape from what has come about. The rapid growth of debt and its costs create a burden on households and businesses that is, in turn, reflected on the weaker and more marginal assets of our financial institutions; these institutions then become encumbered with inadequate capital and, consequently, experience pressures to improve profits by moving into other ventures. There is little solace when the deed has been done. By then, the financial system and its participants have been weakened.

In this context, the central bank operates precariously. It has to drive interest rates to hitherto unthinkably high levels when monetary policy restraint is required, because financial institutions have no vested interest in slowing credit availability early; it must also cut interest rates sharply, once restraint is effective, to avoid bankruptcies. The risk under this approach is that the central bank has increasingly to take on the role of lender of last resort to a widening range of financial and business participants. In essence, the recent changes in our financial system have facilitated the transfer of risk to the ultimate borrowers and investors. However, this has not eliminated risks from the system. Indeed, the process has contributed to a faster rate of debt creation, ultimately increasing the risks in the economy.

Financial institutions are not just the guardian of credit, but in a broader sense, they are also the mechanism that can either strengthen or weaken a market-based society. They should be part of a process that encourages moderate growth of debt and substantial growth of equity and ownership. To be sure, achievement of such objectives requires that a correct fiscal and tax structure be in place. Substantial risk taking and entrepreneurial zeal belongs properly in the world of commerce and trade, where large equity capital tends to reside, and not in financial institutions, which are heavily endowed with other people's money. Encouraging increased leveraging of financial institutions automatically induces greater leverage in the private sector, making this area more vulnerable and more marginal, and eventually inviting government intervention. The whole process thus undermines the essence of an economic democracy.

In this regard, there are a number of unalterable facts. First, when financial institutions act with excessive entrepreneurial zeal, the immediate outcome is a contribution to economic and financial exhilaration. Only later, when the loan cannot be repaid on time or the investment turns sour, are the debilitating and restrictive aspects of the excesses fully evident. In addition, official exhortation to limit the excesses of financial entrepreneurship are inadequate, if not futile.

To some extent, current regulations encourage risk taking, because large institutions are not allowed to fail, and it is virtually impossible for major financial participants to remain wholly uncompromised. As is clearly evident all about us today, the competitive pressure to be in the new mainstream of markets is intense. Growth aspirations are difficult to thwart once institutions set targets for profits, market penetration, and balance sheet size within a financial framework that prescribes no effective limits and that encourages, with great intensity, the application of financial ingenuity and liberal practices.

Thus, this issue comes down to whether or not financial institutions should be a vehicle for sheltering households and businesses from becoming highly exposed financially. I believe that a bias in this more prudent direction would be quite desirable. In addition to the vulnerabilities that I have already mentioned, a less-entrepreneurial financial system would reduce the wide gyrations in the financial markets, encourage longer-term investment decisions, and focus society's efforts on meeting economic goals. This shift in financial direction is not yet beyond our reach.

Much of the debate over the reregulation versus the deregulation of financial institutions rests on just these issues. Do financial institutions serve an important public role, and in this role, should financial institutions protect households and businesses from financial excesses? The debate should not be decided solely on the basis of the so-called inequities in the marketplace today or on the premise that U.S. financial institutions should have sufficient flexibility to compete with rapidly growing financial institutions and markets both at home and abroad. The resolution of the debate on these particular points will not necessarily strengthen our system. What others do may not be right. Indeed, if our banks had been inhibited in the past from competing so aggressively in the international arena, they would be stronger—not weaker—organizations.

However, if the Congress decides that a more deregulated financial system is preferred, at least two challenges will have to be met: How are institutions and markets to be disciplined? And how will institutions have to be structured to compete on a level playing field? The disciplines of a deregulated financial system are simple in concept; but, in reality, they are difficult—if not impossible— to accept, especially in a highly advanced economic society. Efficient institutions will amass profits and prosper, and inefficient ones will falter and then fail.

The difficulty in accepting such disciplines reflects the fact that the failure of financial institutions involves other people's savings, along with temporary funds from the institutions in question and from other organizations linked to the financial institutions through the intermediation process. Moreover, such a deregulated system will surely burden households and businesses with an even greater overload of debt and make the economy more marginal. I hope that the Congress will not move in this direction.

The obstacles to achieving a level playing field—a framework that would ensure competitive equality among the different types of institutions—are formidable. What kinds of standards, if any, should institutions be required to adhere to? Can there be true competitive equality if the liabilities of some institutions are federally insured, while others are not? I doubt that deposit insurance can be eliminated from our financial system. If it were, market participants would assume that the official safety net would cover an ever larger portion of the financial system until a major institution was allowed to fail, and then the risks of contraction in the financial system and economy would be extremely high. It is the type of risk that we, as a society, should avoid.

In formulating the groundwork for an improved financial system, we cannot and should not return to the compartmentalized structure that prevailed years ago. Financial life is evolving, and we should be able to retain the best and discard the undesirable aspects of this process of change. To ignore the developments of our financial world will invite the risk of substantial disarray.

Those who favor further substantial deregulation do so on the grounds that such a system, by being highly competitive, will provide services at the lowest cost. They ignore both the special fiduciary role of institutions and the fact that the costs of service delivery are only one aspect in judging the performance of the financial system. They also fail to recognize the consequences of allowing failures to be the sole disciplining force in this system.

Advocates of substantial deregulation, however, do not agree when it comes to deposit insurance. Large institutions often favor either the removal of insurance altogether or the setting of insurance fees according to the risks involved in the institution. The assumption here is that large institutions will have an advantage, because even in a fully deregulated environment, the government will be much more hesitant to allow such institutions to fail. The likely consequence would be increased financial concentration. Deposit insurance based on the associated risks would probably also not work well, because a higher fee would boost the cost to an already marginal institution, promote enlarged risk taking to offset this cost, and put depositors clearly on notice that they are maintaining accounts with a vulnerable institution, where deposit insurance may not hold.

Many advocates of regulation want to maintain the status quo. This position, I believe, is completely unrealistic. Adherents to this view fail to acknowledge some of the important changes that I mentioned earlier: the aggressive bidding for funds by institutions, the globalization and securitization of markets, and the quick passing along of costs by institutions to final demanders of credit.

Only a few voices have called for some sort of new regulation. For example, Gerald Corrigan, president of the Federal Reserve Bank of New York, has put forth a well-reasoned and articulate set of proposals for reforming the financial structure. On the whole, he emphasizes arranging the institutions in our system into three groupings: bank and thrift holding companies; financial holding companies; and commercial and financial conglomerates. I believe that this arrangement is influenced by his central banking responsibility: He wants to ensure that the central bank, as the lender of last resort, can function effectively in crisis periods.

Corrigan's analysis stresses having a well-functioning payments system, and he has argued persuasively for keeping commerce apart from banking. But, as I stated earlier, the blurring of the distinction between money and credit means that safeguarding the payments mechanism is only one step in improving financial regulatory structure.

What, then, should be done to establish a reformed financial system, which recognizes the changes that have occurred and provides the underpinnings to encourage stable economic growth and ensure the general well-being of an economic democracy? I suggest the following.

First, an official central authority should be established to oversee all major financial institutions and markets. We live in a highly integrated financial system in which, as I noted earlier, institutions bid for funds and, in some instances, carry on comparable activities in the allocation of these funds. The current system of diverse and overlapping official supervision lacks a coherent overview and fails to meet the realities of the financial world today. This new central authority should also establish minimum capital requirements and uniform reporting standards, and it should require much greater disclosure of the profitability and balance sheet data of our institutions.

When monetary restraint is required, this new centralized authority should increase the minimum capital of financial institutions. In this way, institutions would be restrained, and households and businesses would be less encumbered financially. The reverse, of course, would hold when monetary ease is needed. Basing capital requirements on the riskiness of assets is a step in the right direction. This authority should also require that at set intervals, all institutions report their assets, at the lower of cost or market value. Such a requirement would further inhibit the weakening of our financial institutions.

Second, an official international authority should be established to oversee major financial institutions and markets, regardless of their location. Its membership should consist of representatives from the major industrial nations. As noted earlier, global financial institutions and markets exist today—a fact that makes the supervision of institutions and markets by national authorities ineffective. Borrowers and institutions quickly arbitrage the regulatory, capital requirements and other differences between one financial center and another. At times, the agility of market participants limits the policy effectiveness of central banks. Consider, for example, how easy it is for participants who have access to international financial markets to circumvent the policy objectives of central banks, or how much more forcefully others have to be constrained in order for monetary policy restraint to achieve its objective in tightening markets. An official international authority should set minimum capital and reporting standards for all major institutions that operate internationally, and uniform trading practices and standards should be established for participants in open market activities.

Third, because conflicts of interest run the serious risk of undermining the efficient functioning of the financial system and the economy, they must be avoided. To avert conflicts of interest, the following principles should underlie new financial regulations.

• Commercial and financial institutions belong apart.

• Financial institutions should not be allowed to be both lenders and equity investors. The regulatory system should require financial institutions to choose whether to be an underwriter, a lender, or an equity investor in their dealings with the business sector.

• Deposit insurance should be used to strengthen the financial system—and not serve only as a guarantee of the safety of deposits. The proceeds from all insured deposits should be required to be invested in high-grade securities or loans that are deemed to be highly creditworthy by the official regulators. If deposit institutions prefer to make lower-quality loans and investments, these should be booked in another institution and financed with noninsured funds.

There are no quick fixes for the problems that now permeate our financial system. The comprehensive review that the Congress has undertaken is a welcome prerequisite for formulating a new and improved structure.

The investigation should focus not on how quickly the last vestiges of the Glass-Steagall Act can be removed, but, rather, on the question "If not Glass-Steagall, then what?" A fully deregulated financial system is not the solution. Financial institutions have a unique public responsibility. Consequently, a better-regulated financial system, incorporating the many changes that have taken place in the past few decades, is the correct way. Establishing such a system will position financial institutions and markets to facilitate economic growth instead of contributing to substantial economic turbulence in the future.

Dr. Kaufman's essay is reprinted with permission of Solomon Brothers, Inc.

CHAPTER 46

Oh, to Be a Glad-to-Be-Back Democrat

Michael W. Sonnenfeldt

I, LIKE MANY OTHER young, successful, and prospectively successful professionals supported President Reagan during the last two presidential elections. Many of us were not from Republican backgrounds, and many of my peer group had in fact been brought up in solid, if not conservative (if such a word retains any meaning in this context), Democratic traditions. The year 1980 presented choices between two sets of visions or leadership qualities. By 1984 we were faced with two candidates of immense personal integrity, yet the implications of their platforms left us with the choice between the lesser of two evils—and the one we knew seemed a lot better than the one about which we could only speculate.

My initial support of our president's programs revolved around my belief that the Reagan team had the political will necessary to stem the runaway growth of our government, while restoring some semblance of common sense to our government's operations. I believed that a businesslike, pragmatic approach to fiscal and monetary issues would be utilized to restore my confidence in the federal government's capacity to perform its legitimate functions. I fully believed that pork-barrel allocations of vast sums of money would come under close scrutiny, that the federal government would run on a more businesslike basis (expenditures, therefore, would relate to or not be greater than receipts), and that the military buildup, at the very least, would surely increase our national security.

On each count, almost the opposite occurred. Pork-barrel waste continues. The allocation of vast sums to questionable projects is not a practice created by the Republicans, but clearly is one that has always been conducted by many elected officials on both sides of the aisle. It was just a hope, in retrospect, that led us to believe that the shrinking of the government (or, at least, a shrinking of its growth rate) would force a greater scrutiny of our nation's priorities, and that these constraints would help tip the scale toward the reduction of such unnecessary waste. Issues and events ranging from the broad (the deficit) to the specific (contract overruns on the B-1 bomber) indicate a wanton disregard for sound business practice.

In all fairness, the Reagan team inherited a rather dismal situation; therefore, it is almost impossible to objectively determine, as in a controlled scientific experiment, which events—positive or negative—would have occurred under a different team. Many of the profligate practices I hoped that Mr. Reagan would end were surely not his or his party's doing. To the contrary, I believe much of the blame for large and wasteful allocations of limited national resources should be laid at the doorstep of the Democratic Party, often, the unintentioned result of its legitimate desire to promote a progressive social agenda. The problems they attempted to address were real, but the method of throwing money at the problem often didn't work, and even when it did, it often was at an unnecessarily huge cost.

With regard to Mr. Reagan's military buildup, I believe a far more accurate term for what occurred during the last seven years would be a "spend-up." To me, one of the most important facts to reflect this distinction is that our military readiness has increased very little, if at all, as a result of this spendup. Surely, there have been tremendous purchases of very expensive weapons. But were they needed? And if they truly are fulfilling the mission they were intended for, could the same effective defensive or offensive power have been achieved at a far smaller cost? In fact, I believe that the net effects of the Reagan administration fall somewhere between actually stimulating a decrease, rather than an increase, in our nation's security, and increasing our nation's security, but at a cost that has depleted our resources. And this has, in turn, potentially jeopardized our *long-term* security. Obviously, one's definition of national security will determine the outcome of the analysis, and I am inclined to include, beyond weapon counts or even readiness measures, indications of our economic strength and moral fiber. This last factor is critical in establishing the ability of our country to collectively make the necessary sacrifices to be secure.

So, now that the Reagan presidency is winding down, I find that I am a member of a growing group of young Americans who are beginning to question their previous acceptance of many of Mr. Reagan's principles, given that policies ostensibly based on those principles have apparently, at least in part, failed. Arguably, one could say that the policies have also, at least in part, succeeded—and in the public arena, this is tantamount to success. I believe that it is critical to remember the context in which many of us lent our support to the new economic agenda. There were real personal, emotional, and even ideological sacrifices that many of us felt we were making by lending our support to Mr. Reagan, which we justified by the anticipated results of his prospective policies. It is not enough to measure success or failure simply by what realistically might have been achieved; such results must be weighed against the sacrifices that were made in anticipation of the projected results.

Reflecting on the early Reagan years, we may recall a sense of being offered a chance to have our cake and eat it, too. The invisible hand of Adam Smith was once again propelling us to dive headfirst into seeking personal prosperity with almost reckless abandon, while at the same time, our tax and economic programs were being remodeled to stimulate these activities. We believed that this economic expansion would be great enough to lift the standard of living of *all* Americans. How many times I justified the new program by endorsing the commercial slogan of the eighties "All boats rise in a rising tide."

This belief, perhaps more than any other, justified supporting a Republican ideology that also paid homage to religious fundamentalism, flag waving, social regressiveness, and, ultimately, lip service to sound business practices. So it is not simply the success or lack thereof that was achieved by the Reagan programs (in comparison to what levels of success could have been achieved by other programs) that is relevant—it is also critical to remember what levels of sacrifices or subjugation of long-held principles would have been required to support these other programs. At the time, I didn't feel that I was "abandoning" anything, but that I was taking a measured approach to what events really affect a person's life the most. I truly felt that if the Reagan economic agenda was implemented with the anticipated results, more opportunity would be created for the poor of our country to move into the middle class.

Additionally, I was so concerned about our country's economic future that it was clear to me that if my choice of supporting Reagan was positioned as a choice between expanded job opportunity, real growth, and slightly diminished social freedoms on the one hand, and, on the other, expanded government programs unable to be funded without increased taxes that would put a drag on any real growth, I would choose real growth, even at the cost of temporarily halting expanded social development. The impetus for this article is my belief that the Democratic Party finds itself in the unique position of having a window of opportunity to capture the high ground on real growth, while retaining its traditional respect for the embodiment of social freedoms.

Ironically, the very tools that were developed in this new generation of success-oriented youth are the tools now being put to use to identify the shortcomings of the current program. The economic programs are not being measured along the old ranges of left to right or conservative to liberal. Rather, we are searching for new benchmarks that are non-ideological and pragmatic. Such benchmarks should enhance one's ability to measure the extent to which particular policies do or do not work. When supply-side economics is looked at from this new perspective, it is not important whether it relies on the intellectual underpinnings of the conservative movement or is antithetical to the liberal movement. Instead, can it be clearly demonstrated that federal deficits can be eliminated and real growth maintained through the reduction and flattening of taxes? Will this reduction and flattening of taxes result in increased demand, which might be so stimulative to our economy as to increase both its size and, accordingly, the tax revenues that could be generated from that increased economic activity? And would this increased tax revenue be sufficient to both balance the budget and maintain necessary government programs? Many of us pledged fealty to the program because it seemed better than any of the other options at the time and, frankly, it seemed to both support and justify our own personal missions. We felt that this was a time in which hard work was once again respectable and that through one's abundant work effort, society's goals and our goals would be brought into harmony. We felt that a unique opportunity existed for both the individual and society to benefit simultaneously from the implementation of this program.

Unfortunately, while we intuitively believed that supply-side economics had a lot to offer, we never had the chance to see it in action. What occurred was not the implementation of a concept, but the implementation of a platform. And that platform never was able to maintain any internal consistency. The unwillingness to control military expenditures, coupled with an absence of the backbone necessary to reign in domestic spending would bankrupt any sound policy initiative intended to increase the economy and the resultant tax revenues enough to achieve a balanced budget.

One can romanticize about the effectiveness of supply-side economics, but the inconceivable deficits that have been run on a continuous basis, essentially doubling the deficit that had been accumulated in the past 200 years, brings into question the entire fiscal sanity of the Republican platform. One could surely argue whether, in fact, the deficits were generated by Republican/supply-side economics, or whether, in fact, they would have been greater had Republican/supply-side economics not been implemented.

Claims of achievement by the current administration in terms of economic expansion, inflation, and interest rates do not appear to be credible. The numbers are just not good. The economy apparently has expanded little more (perhaps little less) than many economists say it should have been expected to, given the point in the economic cycle we find ourselves at. Compared with other postwar expansions, ours is not particularly distinguished.

While inflation has come down far faster than predicted, I have the feeling that we have only begun to pay the price— an even greater inflation in the future, triggered in part by the severe and still continuing decline in the dollar, which has yet to take its long-term toll. Our situation is a little like that of a desert town that has to watch its water supply carefully, although it has months of reserves. A new mayor promises prosperity and starts distributing greater quantities of water, in the hope that this will lead to greater crop formation, which will, in turn, change the weather pattern to increase the rainfall. At the end of the first year of this new practice, the town has only half of the reserves that it used to have, but the mayor is sure the increase in rainfall will soon begin, as the crops are now well grown and people have enjoyed the reduction of restrictions on water usage.

The numbers about interest rates are far less encouraging. Because of the swift decline in inflation, the lower interest rates have masked the fact that we are experiencing record real interest rates (the nominal, or stated, rate, less the rate of inflation). These have traditionally averaged about 1–3 percent, and recently have been running at twice that rate. Such high real interest rates have created a tremendous hidden drag on our economic performance at a time when we should arguably be at the top of our economic cycle. They are like two people in a roller coaster on the way down from a peak and just reaching the bottom before they start up the next one: One rider is telling the other how fast they are going, using relatively accurate terms that can be scientifically validated, but the other is more concerned about knowing if they are going fast enough to make it up to the top of the next peak.

Characteristically, though, as pragmatists with some intellectual capacity and a now well-developed skepticism (which should not be confused with cynicism) concerning a president's ability to effectively shape the events around him, we will not, in our disappointment with the current Republican agenda, be propelled automatically onto another bandwagon. However eager we are to return to a more comfortable place, we are waiting for some real signals from the Democrats as well. This particular moment in time affords an opportunity to the Democrats that has not been available to them in a very long time. Although there appears to be a vacuum of ideas in both parties, at least the Democrats have a cleaner slate from which to generate new initiatives. They are not burdened with a Republican agenda that, at the very least, is a root cause of the recent deficits.

We are searching for signals that a Democratic president would not be as blind to wanton pork-barrel domestic spending as Mr. Reagan would appear to be about wanton pork-barrel military spending. We are searching for a platform that does acknowledge that if you start increasing taxes again in concert with reducing expenditures as a means to reduce the budget deficit, that this should not be a mechanism for once again expanding the role of the government.

We are searching for a platform that can distinguish between taxes that will support real growth and taxes that will not. We are searching for a platform that vows to search for real solutions to our country's poverty and seeks to reform our education and justice systems to once again reflect the moral will of our people, who want and seek to demand the best in these severely eroded institutions. We are searching for a platform and a candidate that reflect our desire to have a church and state apart from one another.

While we respect the value of family life, and the role religion plays in it, we want religion out of the state. We want the right to have the freedom to choose, in the privacy of our own home, whether or not we want abortions. We don't want some preacher who can't exercise control over his own life-style or the finances of his own ministry trying to exercise control over our own intimate decisions. We don't want a president who is willing to mortgage our future because he is unwilling to lead us today.

We are searching for a platform that pays homage to the free market system of capitalism, which has made this country as great as it is, and that also acknowledges that we are living in a world that has never before existed. A world where international economic trends will affect the day-to-day lives of all Americans to a greater extent than ever before. A world where the complexity of the international economy demands a level of skill in our government that has yet to be demonstrated. "Standing tall" is hardly responsive to the need for a reasoned approach to our nation's agenda. And, finally, a world where our military allies have become our economic adversaries. This fact alone places a heavy burden on managing conflicting policy initiatives. We want policies that encourage initiative among individuals, but also stimulate our populace to understand that in virtually every facet of economic life, we have foreign economic adversaries who are every bit as qualified as we are, and sometimes are overqualified to compete with us.

And we want a platform that implicitly reflects that we are a people who will respond to a challenge that is honestly and properly framed. We are a dynamic people with plenty of reserve. So this platform must also strike that balance between the proper caution that flows from the knowledge of our problems and the optimism justified by our inherent strengths as a great nation. And, finally, what we seek is a platform that strikes a balance between the need for a strong defense and the need to allocate resources to ensure the achievement of our other goals as well.

Our challenge to the Democrats, then, is this: Prove to us that you know how to go about implementing these goals, and prove to us that we can be sure it will be done with honesty and integrity. If the Democrats show the will to shake off much of their old baggage and understand the new reality in which we live, the possibility exists to have this pragmatic core of movers and shakers in our society return to the fold. Only after we are convinced that the Democrats have taken the high ground will we have our banner emblazoned with the slogan "We are Glad-To-Be-Back-Demo-crats."

Bring me back, Democrats, and prove to me that you are prepared to respond to my hopes and desires in a responsible way that will ensure a policy of security through real growth. A policy that reflects the knowledge that security and real growth go hand in hand—and that over the long term neither can be achieved without the other. Then I, too, will be waving my banner as a Glad-to-Be-Back-Democrat.

Needed: A New Political Agenda for the 1990s

Wilbur J. Cohen

BOTH DEMOCRATS AND REPUBLICANS campaigning for the presidency in 1988 face serious handicaps in developing innovative policies to give the nation vigorous leadership for domestic progress on festering social problems. The continuing fiscal and trade deficits and President Reagan's opposition to a tax increase prevent enactment of any spectacular forward thrust on domestic needs until after 1991.

Recently a senator who knew of my support for welfare reform and Medicare expansion pre-empted our discussion of these proposals by admonishing me to discover attractive proposals that didn't cost money. If that is the probable agenda for 1988–89, it will be well into the 1990s before any new "quantum leaps" are proposed, accepted and enacted. Meanwhile, it is important to remember that American experience in major domestic areas of social reform indicates that it takes from 15 to 25 years for a controversial new idea to be transformed into legislative reality as an old idea whose time has come.

Wilbur J. Cohen was professor of public affairs at the Lyndon B. Johnson School of Public Affairs at the University of Texas at Austin. He was secretary of Health, Education and Welfare in 1968.

The first state unemployment insurance bill was introduced in Massachusetts in 1916 and the first such state law was enacted in Wisconsin in 1932, 16 years later. But even then with major federal incentives, the last state to enact a state law was Illinois, in 1937. The basic idea behind Medicare was first suggested around 1942; the first bill to incorporate the idea was introduced in 1951, but it took until 1965 for the concept to be enacted into federal law. The first state workers' accident compensation law was passed around 1910 in Wisconsin; the last state to put such a law into effect was Mississippi, in 1946.

It is not clear what the social reform agenda will be during the 1990s, but a reading of American history suggests that whatever it is going to be, its basic thrust very likely is being germinated right now. That some idea which is being processed now is vigorously opposed by an important group is not in itself an indication of later acceptability of the idea. Every major social reform on the law books was once vigorously opposed as being unwise, unnecessary, too expensive, impractical or un-American. But someone, some group, persisted in advocating the idea until the right historical moment occurred when a political leader welded together a working majority consisting of liberals and conservatives in a state legislature or in Congress to enact it. That is the way new ideas become old programs.

Insurance of bank deposits was strongly opposed by the banking industry in 1905 on the grounds that it would lead to the socialization of banking. But in recent years, when banks began to fail, it has become virtually impossible to find banks that oppose the principle of governmental deposit insurance. During the mid-1920s, many groups opposed the Sheppard-Towner Act providing for federal maternal and child health funds [1921–29] and the law was repealed. The opposition was formidable. Then the program was included as part of the Social Security Act and has been accepted by medical and other groups that opposed it during the 1920s. It was improved in 1986 in the midst of Gramm-Rudman budget reductions and is operative in every state.

It is likely that some renaissance of social reform will occur during the 1990s. Social reform in the United States in this century has seemed to go in cycles of 25 to 30 years. Arthur Schlesinger Jr. has explored this phenomenon in terms of generational swings between support for public purposes and private interests.

The first important reform efforts in the 20th Century occurred between 1905 and 1912 with adoption of the Food and Drug Act in 1906, Workers' Accident Compensation and mothers' benefits in 1910, and establishment of the Children's Bureau in 1912. The big splurge of social legislation embodying both a quantum leap and incremental improvements took place in 1935 with enactment of 10 programs—some old, some new—in the omnibus Social Security Act; 30 years later came passage of the far-reaching national health legislation of Medicare and Medicaid and aid to elementary and secondary education.

A future president committed to further social progress is likely to sign some new epic-making piece of social legislation into law in the mid-1990s. It might even be a she who approves such a quantum leap on Aug. 14, 1995—three decades after Medicare, Medicaid and education legislation, and the 60th anniversary of the landmark Social Security Act. Such a piece of social legislation is most likely to be in the field of health care—perhaps legislation that would result in every person in the U.S. being insured for comprehensive and catastrophic health care from the day they are born to the day they die. It probably would include long-term nursing care and alternatives to institutional care. Such action would eliminate most medical indigency and reduce the need for welfare.

It might also be some form of an income strategy—building on the ill-fated Truman, Nixon and Carter proposals—that will result in every child in every family receiving sufficient income to enable future generations to say that poverty had been abolished throughout the land by the year 2000. It might be publicly financed education and low-cost student financial aid for four years at the level of community college costs, and probably the nationwide adoption of the

Equal Rights Amendment either by all of the states or by a constitutional amendment.

There are many other possibilities, such as resolving the problems of the homeless. Someone may discover how to resolve the comparable worth issue, how to bring unemployment down to a "full employment" level and how to provide additional support for families.

While I might not be present when that next quantum leap comes, I believe there is someone in this country right now who is thinking up a new strategy, a revised priority, even an old scenario in new dress for 1992. That strategy will become part of the American way of life during 1993–1997— just as other social reforms enacted earlier in this century have been accepted and retained despite all the critical rhetoric invoked against them since 1980.

Future reforms will build on the experiences of the New Deal and the Great Society. But there will be new problems, new challenges and new programs. A wider and stronger "safety net" will become a reality, but only after the Reagan revolution has run its course and the electorate is willing to accept new leadership for a more just society.

Appendix

About the Contributors

GORDON ADAMS

Gordon Adams is the founder and director of the Defense Budget Project. He is the author of *The Politics of Defense Contracting: The Iron Triangle* and contributes regularly to defense, economic and international affairs journals. Dr. Adams is a regular advisor on the defense budget, national security and arms control issues to such groups as the League of Women Voters and the Coalition on Human Needs. Prior to founding the Project in 1983, he was director of military research at the Council on Economic Priorities in New York and taught political science at Columbia University, Rutgers University and the City University of New York.

BRUCE BABBITT

Bruce Babbitt is the former Governor of Arizona (1978–1987), a Democrat, and a third generation member of a pioneer family of ranchers and merchants who settled the land around the Grand Canyon.

Moved by the poverty he saw as an Acción volunteer in Latin America and changed by the events he witnessed in Selma, Alabama, during civil rights protests, Babbitt set out with degrees from Notre Dame and Harvard Law School to fight the war on poverty in the South during the 1960s.

Babbitt's election as Arizona Attorney General in 1974 resulted in prosecutions that helped clean up Arizona and led the underworld to put a murder contract on his life. He became governor suddenly in 1978 upon the death of his predecessor, was elected to his first full term in that same year, and re-elected in 1982 with 63% of the vote.

A tough negotiator and strong executive, he won passage of progressive laws from a Republican legislature—by showing that Democrats can balance budgets and lead the way to an explosion of economic productivity. He helped make his state's economy the nation's fastest growing. And he helped give Arizona a groundwater protection code, a health care program for the poor and initiatives for children—all now models for the rest of the nation.

511

MARY JO BANE

Mary Jo Bane is professor of public policy at the John F. Kennedy School of Government, Harvard University, and director of the school's Center for Health and Human Resources Policy. From 1984 to 1986, Ms. Bane was Executive Deputy Commissioner of the New York State Department of Social Services. Ms. Bane's experience has included service as deputy assistant secretary for program planning and budget analysis at the U.S. Department of Education, and at Harvard as associate professor of education and lecturer in sociology. Ms. Bane is the author of several books in the area of human services and public policy, including The State and the Poor in the 1980's, (1984) and Here to Stay: American Families in the Twentieth Century, (1981).

JOSEPH R. BIDEN

Joseph R. Biden, Jr., of Delaware, is one of the new generation of leaders in the U.S. Senate. Although he is only 45 years old, he has served longer in the Senate than three-fourths of its other 99 members—first elected to the Senate in 1972, he is now 18th in seniority and Chairman of the Senate Judiciary Committee.

He is also the second most senior Democrat on the Senate Foreign Relations Committee.

A former trial lawyer, the Senator has been active on the Judiciary Committee in developing legislation to deal with the nation's crime problems, particularly the problem of illegal drug trafficking. He is chairman of the Senate Democratic Task Force on Crime and was a chief architect of the major crime bill enacted in 1984 and the anti-drug abuse legislation enacted in 1986. He has also been a strong defender of civil rights legislation.

Senator Biden is widely recognized as one of the Senate's leading foreign policy experts and is generally in the forefront of debates on such critical areas as NATO, U.S.-Soviet relations and the Middle East. He has also been a leading advocate of arms control efforts.

Senator Biden is a graduate of the University of Delaware and the Syracuse University College of Law. Prior to his election to the Senate, he served for two years as a member of the New Castle County, Delaware, Council.

The Senator lives in Wilmington with his wife Jill, and three children and commutes four hours daily to Washington, D.C.

BILL BRADLEY

Bill Bradley (D-N.J.) was elected to the United States Senate in 1978 and reelected to a second term in 1984 by a record-breaking margin. He is a member of the Finance Committee, the Select Committee on Intelligence, the Energy and Natural Resources Committee, and the Special Committee on Aging. Widely regarded for his knowledge of finance and economics, Bradley was the only American and the only elected official to serve on a select seven person international panel to advise the General Agreement on Tariffs and Trade (the international trading system's organization). He first took an interest in the third world debt issue in the early 1980's, and in 1987 he assumed the chairmanship of the International Debt Subcommittee of the Finance Committee. Bradley is recognized as the "father" of the Tax Reform Act of 1986 and has been deeply involved in issues of education, health care for the elderly, and the environment.

Bradley, 44, was born in Crystal City, Missouri, and attended Princeton University. He graduated with honors in 1965 and was awarded a Rhodes Scholarship for study at Oxford University, where he earned a Masters Degree after studying politics, philosophy, and economics. An All-American basketball player, Bradley captained the U.S. basketball team that won a gold medal at the 1964 Olympic Games in Tokyo. He played professional basketball with the New York Knickerbockers from 1967 to 1977 and was inducted into the Basketball Hall of Fame in 1983.

RICHARD F. CELESTE

A native of Lakewood, Ohio, Richard F. Celeste graduated magna cum laude from Yale University and was selected as a Rhodes Scholar in 1960. In 1963, he was appointed Executive Assistant to the U.S. Ambassador to India. He returned to Cleveland and began his career in politics when he was elected in 1970 to the first of two terms to the Ohio House of Representatives. He later served for four years as Ohio's Lieutenant Governor, and was appointed Director of the Peace Corps in 1979 by President Jimmy Carter, a position he held until January, 1981. Celeste was elected Ohio's 64th Governor on November 2, 1982, and was re-elected in 1986. He currently chairs the Council of Great Lakes Governors and the Midwestern Governors' Conference. Governor Celeste and his wife, Dagmar, have six children: Eric, Christopher, Gabriella, Noelle, Natalie and Stephen.

PAT CHOATE

Pat Choate is Director of TRW's Office of Policy Analysis, where he studies long-term U.S. competitiveness. He received a Ph.D. in economics from the University of Oklahoma.

A specialist in economic development and public policy, Dr. Choate has been a Fellow at the Battelle Memorial Institute's public policy research arm, the Academy for Contemporary Problems. His wide experience in government includes service as a senior economist on the President's Reorganization Project in 1978–1979, several positions in the Economic Development Administration, where he served as director of the Office of Economic Research and as regional director for Appalachia and the Southern United States.

Dr. Choate is the author of numerous monographs, reports, papers and books on economic competitiveness, management and public administration. His books include *America in Ruins: The Deteriorating Infrastructure*; *Being Number One: Rebuilding the U.S. Economy*; *Thinking Strategically: A Primer for Public Leaders*; and *The High-Flex Society: Shaping America's Economic Future* (with J.K. Linger, Alfred A. Knopf, Inc., 1986).

HENRY CISNEROS

Henry Cisneros was first elected to public office in April of 1975. He served two more terms as a councilmember before he ran and was elected Mayor in 1981.

The Mayor of the nation's ninth largest city holds three advanced degrees, from Texas A & M, The JFK School at Harvard, and George Washington University. He was the nation's youngest White House Fellow, working for Secretary of HEW, Elliott Richardson in 1971.

As the immediate past president of the National League of Cities, Mayor Cisneros was invited by Vice President George Bush to meet with General Secretary Mikhail Gorbachev to describe the role which the nation's cities play in America.

Mayor Cisneros is married to Mary Alice Cisneros. They have two daughters and an infant son.

BILL CLINTON

Bill Clinton, 41, is the second person in Arkansas's history to be elected to four terms as governor. He received a bachelor's degree from Georgetown University and was a Rhodes Scholar at Oxford University. He earned his law degree from Yale University School of Law in 1973. He is married to Hillary Rodham Clinton, an attorney and chairman of the board of the Children's Defense Fund. They have a seven year old child, Chelsea.

In 1986 Clinton served as chairman of the Southern Growth Policies Board. During his tenure he appointed the third Commission on the Future of the South, and he actively participated in the development of its highly acclaimed report, "Halfway Home and A Long Way To Go." Clinton is the immediate past chairman of the National Governors' Association. As chairman, his major project was "Making America Work: Productive People, Productive Policies." He is also the immediate past chairman of the Education Commission of the States, which recently published his study on leadership and education, "Speaking of Leadership." He is the only governor ever to have chaired both ECS and NGA simultaneously. He currently serves as vice-chairman of the Democratic Governors' Association and is the leading spokesman for the governors in pushing national welfare reform legislation in Congress.

WILBER J. COHEN

Wilbur Joseph Cohen (1913–1987) was born in Milwaukee, Wisconsin, graduated in Economics at the University of Wisconsin, and married Eloise Bittel of Texas. He was father of three sons, Christopher, Bruce and Stuart, and had five grandchildren. His working life was devoted to government service and education and started at age 21 as research assistant to the Chairman of President Roosevelt's Committee on Economic Security which drafted the Social Security Act; it culminated in his serving as Secretary of HEW (1968–1969). His educational contributions also included a professorship in the School of Social Work and deanship of the School of Education, University of Michigan, and professorship in L.B.J. School of Public Affairs in Austin, Texas. He died in Seoul, South Korea, while attending an International Symposium on Cross-Cultural Aspects on Aging.

MARIO M. CUOMO

Mario M. Cuomo took the oath of office as New York's 52nd Governor in January 1983.

In 1986 he was elected to a second four-year term with the highest gubernatorial plurality in the history of New York, and with board support in the election from New York's diverse urban, suburban and rural citizens.

Under Governor Cuomo's leadership New York State has experienced a dynamic economic resurgence and significant progress in social and legal justice.

Governor Cuomo has balanced New York's budget and brought fiscal prudence to the management of the State. A series of record income tax cuts were enacted, reducing every New Yorker's tax burden and removing hundreds of thousands of working poor from the tax rolls. The ongoing tax reductions will bring the State's maximum tax rate to one-half its 1974 level.

An array of economic development incentives, including special tax and energy incentives exclusively for economically distressed areas, were created to attract job-creating businesses to New York and far-sighted investments were made to rebuild New York's infrastructure and secure the State's future economic well-being.

This comprehensive economic development effort helped produce a gain of over one million jobs in New York since 1983 and a significant drop in unemployment.

Determined to widen the circle of opportunity to include every citizen of his State, the Governor has made education a top priority. New York's annual aid to public education was increased by 58 percent and special efforts were launched to make teaching more attractive. The Governor's affirmative action efforts and his reorientation of public assistance toward meaningful employment furthered this basic goal.

To promote essential public confidence in the integrity and efficiency of government, the Governor fought for and won enactment of landmark ethics legislation aimed at deterring conflicts of interests and corruption.

Major legislation enacted during Governor Cuomo's tenure include the nation's first acid rain law and first seat belt law. A life-saving increase in the State's minimum purchase age for alcohol was also enacted at the Governor's urging. The Governor won voter approval of a billion-dollar environmental bond issue.

Governor Cuomo gained widespread recognition for his inspirational eloquence at the 1984 Democratic National Convention, where the Governor delivered the keynote address. Subsequent speeches by the Governor, including important statements on the First Amendment, Democratic Party principles, judicial selection and the teaching of values, have attracted broad attention and generated productive debate.

Mario Matthew Cuomo was born on June 15, 1932. An alumnus of New York City public schools, Governor Cuomo graduated summa cum laude from St. John's University in 1953. He graduated from St. John's Law School in 1956. He had a distinguished career as an attorney and law school faculty member prior to entering public service. The Governor is the author of two books, including *Diaries of Mario M. Cuomo: The Campaign for Governor*, an account of his 1982 gubernatorial race.

He was appointed New York's Secretary of State in 1975 and he was elected Lieutenant Governor in 1978.

He is married to Matilda Raffa Cuomo, and they have five children.

RAYMOND T. DALIO

Since receiving his MBA in finance from Harvard Business School in 1973, Mr. Dalio has been involved in judging the merits of the world's major markets by identifying the economic conditions that affect the directions of these markets. He began his career with Dominick as the Director of Commodities and later as Director of Institutional Futures Trading at Shearson. In 1975, he left Shearson to devote all his time and efforts to trading his own account and operating Bridgewater Associates.

THOMAS J. DOWNEY

Thomas J. Downey has represented the Second Congressional District of New York since 1975. He is a member of the Ways and Means Committee, where, as Acting Chairman of the Subcommittee on Public Assistance and Unemployment Compensation, he guided the Family Welfare Reform Act through the House. He also serves as the Acting Chairman of the Select Committee on Aging's Subcommittee on Human Services. Congressman Downey introduced the legislation which created the bipartisan National Economic Commission to deal with the politically thorny issues of the trade and budget deficits. As a member of the House Budget Committee from 1981 to 1986, he was a leader in the fight against the Reagan budget policies.

MICHAEL S. DUKAKIS

Michael Stanley Dukakis was born of Greek immigrant parents on November 3, 1933, in Brookline, Massachusetts, where he has resided ever since. He graduated from Swarthmore College in 1955, earning highest honors in political science. Following service in the U.S. Army in Korea, he returned to Massachusetts to study law at Harvard, graduating with honors in 1960.

As a member of the Massachusetts House of Representatives from 1963–71, Dukakis was the first legislator in America to introduce a no-fault automobile insurance bill. After a long four-year fight, the state enacted the nation's first no-fault system in 1971.

Michael Dukakis was inaugurated as the 65th Governor of the Commonwealth of Massachusetts on January 2, 1975. At the time, the state unemployment rate was nearly 12 percent, and the Commonwealth faced a deficit of over half a billion dollars. Under the Dukakis Administration the state's economic condition improved dramatically. Unemployment dropped to 4.3 percent by October, 1978. Two hundred fifty thousand new jobs were added to the state's economy. Crime, between 1975–78, dropped substantially. When Dukakis left office in 1979, Massachusetts state government had a budget surplus of $200 million.

On January 17, 1979, Dukakis was appointed lecturer and director of Intergovernmental Studies at Harvard University's John F. Kennedy School of Government. In the Democratic primary of 1982, Dukakis defeated incumbent Edward J. King, and on January 6, 1983, Michael S. Dukakis was again inaugurated as Governor of Massachusetts. Since taking office in 1983, Dukakis has made the economic future of the state a key priority of his administration.

For 1986, the Massachusetts annual unemployment rate was 3.8 percent, the lowest yearly unemployment rate of any of the nation's top industrial states. In all, more than 300,000 new jobs have been created and 54,000 new businesses started in Massachusetts since 1983. In addition, the state's Employment and Training Choices program (ET) has been successful in helping more than 30,000 welfare recipients find jobs with more than 8,000 of the state's businesses. This innovative program saved taxpayers an estimated $107 million in 1986 alone. Dukakis led the fight against drunk driving on Massachusetts highways; and, in October 1984, created the Governor's Alliance Against Drugs—a state-wide effort involving public and private leaders that has set as its goal drug-free schools by 1990.

His innovative Revenue Enforcement and Protection Program—by providing greatly improved services to taxpayers and aggressively pursuing tax evaders and delinquents—has allowed Massachusetts to not only balance its books but to cut taxes five times in the last four years.

Nationally, Dukakis serves as Chairman of the Committee on Economic Development and Technological Innovation of the National Governors' Association and is Chairman of the Committee on The Industrial and Entrepreneurial Economy for the Policy Commission of the Democratic National Committee. In 1984, Dukakis presented the platform to the Democratic Convention in San Francisco and in August, 1986, Dukakis was elected Chairman of the Democratic Governors' Association.

STUART E. EIZENSTAT

Stuart E. Eizenstat, at 45, has had an abundance of experience at the highest levels of government. He was President Carter's Assistant to the President for Domestic Affairs and Policy in the White House and Executive Director of the White House Domestic Policy Staff from 1977 to 1981.

As the chief domestic policy adviser to President Carter, he earned a reputation for his ability and integrity in coordinating the Administration's policies.

Mr. Eizenstat was a principal author of the 1976 and 1980 Democratic Party platforms. He has occupied a variety of positions for the Democratic Party at the national, State, and local levels.

He worked for President Johnson on the White House staff from 1967 to 1968 and was the research director for Vice President Humphrey's 1968 presidential campaign.

Mr. Eizenstat is a partner in the Washington office of one of the largest firms in Atlanta, Georgia, Powell, Goldstein, Frazer & Murphy. He is a lecturer on the faculty of the Kennedy School of Government at Harvard University. He is a Phi Beta Kappa graduate of the University of North Carolina and of Harvard Law School. He has authored numerous articles for legal periodicals, public policy journals, and leading newspapers.

DIANNE FEINSTEIN

Dianne Feinstein has served as Mayor of San Francisco since Dec. 4, 1978—just over nine years. She also served as the first woman president of the San Francisco Board of Supervisors and was a member of the Board for more than eight years. The Mayor has served as chair of the U.S. Conference of Mayors Executive Committee, as chair of its Urban Economic Policy Committee and as chair of its Task Force on AIDS. Mayor Feinstein has won numerous awards and was named by *City and State Magazine* as "Mayor of the Year for 1987."

GERALDINE A. FERRARO

Geraldine A. Ferraro, following her historic campaign as the first woman vice presidential candidate on a national party ticket, continues to be active in the United States and abroad as a lecturer, author, and policy expert.

Because Ms. Ferraro's candidacy generated tremendous interest during the 1984 presidential campaign, she has continued to speak out and tackle tough issues with candor and precision, at home and abroad.

Ms. Ferraro is an active participant in foreign policy debate as a board member of the National Democratic Institute of International Affairs and as a member of the Council On Foreign Relations.

Since the '84 election, she was traveled to many of the NATO countries as well as Japan, China, the Soviet Union and Israel, and has met with world leaders including Prime Ministers Margaret Thatcher, Shimon Peres, Bettino Craxi, Yashuhiro Nakasone and others.

Her vice-presidential candidacy highlighted a lifetime of achievement. Ms. Ferraro served three terms in the United States House of Representatives. She was elected to represent New York's Ninth Congressional District in 1978 and won re-election in 1980 and 1982 by increasing margins.

In Congress, she served on the Budget Committee which sets national spending priorities. She was also a member of the Committee on Public Works and Transportation, and Select Committee on Aging.

In January 1984, Ms. Ferraro was named Chair of the Democratic Platform Committee for its national party convention and was widely acclaimed for her success in skillfully steering through a consensus platform document.

MURRAY H. FINLEY

Murray H. Finley is the immediate past president of the Amalgamated Clothing and Textile Workers Union and a former vice-president of the

American Federation of Labor—Congress of Industrial Organizations. Retiring in 1987 after 38 years of service to his union, Mr. Finley continues public involvement as a director of the Amalgamated Bank of New York, a member of the board of the A. Philip Randolph Institute, the Council on Foreign Relations and as Co-Chairperson of the National Committee on Full Employment and the Full Employment Action Council. Mr. Finley received his A.B. from the University of Michigan and his J.D. from the Northwestern University Law School.

RAYMOND L. FLYNN

Raymond L. Flynn, mayor of Boston, is chairman of the U.S. Conference of Mayors Task Force on Hunger and Homelessness, a member of the National League of Cities' Election '88 Task Force, and a member of the Democratic Party Platform Committee. He was elected 46th mayor of Boston in November 1983 and overwhelmingly re-elected in November 1987 by a 67 percent majority, the largest in history. Prior to serving as Mayor, he served in the Massachusetts Legislature and the Boston City Council. He received his undergraduate degree in public administration from Providence College in 1963 and his masters degree in education from Harvard University in 1981. He and his wife Catherine have six children and live in South Boston. Mayor Flynn was born July 22, 1939.

CALVIN H. GEORGE

Calvin H. George is Executive Director of the National Committee for Full Employment and the Full Employment Action Council. Prior to his work with NCFE/FEAC, Mr. George served as a consultant to the Eleanor Roosevelt Institute, a youth employment and education organization. Before moving to Washington D.C., George was with the Social Development Coion for ten years, an intergovernmental social planning and community action agency for Milwaukee, Wisconsin. George holds a graduate degree in Urban Planning from the University of Wisconsin, Milwaukee.

RICHARD A. GEPHARDT

Congressman Richard A. Gephardt (D-Mo) was elected to Congress in 1976 to represent Missouri's third district, and has worked closely with the House Democratic leadership, especially in the area of economic policy.

Gephardt has been a member of the Ways and Means Committee since 1977, and served three terms on the House Budget Committee.

In December of 1984 and again in 1986, Gephardt was elected Chairman of the House Democratic Caucus.

Gephardt was the founding Chairman of the Democratic Leadership Council, which has involved elected officials in the development of policy initiatives for the Democratic Party.

Congressman Gephardt has been a leader in the House since his arrival. He first promised tax reform in his successful 1976 campaign, and he co-authored, with Senator Bill Bradley, the tax simplification plan which became the basis of the Tax Reform Act of 1985.

In 1985, then Speaker "Tip" O'Neill asked Gephardt to head the House Democratic Task Force charged with revising the Senate-passed Gramm-Rudman-Hollings amendment. As written, the amendment would have indiscriminately gutted all federal anti-poverty programs. Gephardt successfully fought to have these programs exempted from the amendment, making the deficit reduction measure much more progressive.

Gephardt has also been a leader on foreign affairs—especially arms control—in the House. The Schroeder Gephardt nuclear test ban passed the House in 1986 and is the national focus of arms control efforts. Additionally, Gephardt has been a leading opponent of contra aid.

Gephardt has been a key congressional leader on a multitude of other issues. The Harkin-Gephardt Family Farm Bill is the national rallying point to save the family farm.

Another Gephardt amendment demanded get-tough trade policies to open foreign markets. It passed the House in 1986 and is expected to be included in trade legislation soon to be considered by the House.

In addition to trade and other economic issues, Congressman Gephardt has taken a special interest in health policy and social security within the Ways and Means Committee.

AL GORE

Al Gore is a Democratic senator from Tennessee. He is currently serving his third year in the U.S. Senate, before which he served four terms in the U.S. House of Representatives. Gore is considered one of the leading experts in Congress on nuclear arms control. He is one of ten Senate observers to the Geneva arms control talks.

He serves on the Senate Armed Services; Commerce, Science and Transportation; and Rules committees.

Senator Gore has produced a broad list of substantive legislative achievements. He is Co-Chairman of the Environmental and Energy Study Conference and Vice-Chairman of the Biomedical Ethics Board. He is co-author of the Small Business Innovation Act of 1982, and was the principal sponsor of the Infant Formula Act of 1980 concerning nutrition and safety standards. Gore is co-author of the Superfund Act of 1980, creating the primary federal program to clean up hazardous waste sites and chemical spills. He is coauthor of the 1983 telephone legislation which resulted in reduced federal access charges for residential and small business rate-payers and increased support for rural, high-cost companies.

Senator Gore has proven to be one of the most effective leaders in reduction of oversight in the Congress over the past decade. He has ac-tively led investigations into cases of government waste and abuses of power, criminal activity in the hazardous waste dumping industry, inade-quate nutrition and labelling of food products, biotechnology, and many other issues.

Gore was born on March 31, 1948. The son of former U.S. Senator Albert Gore Sr. and his wife Pauline, he was raised in Carthage, Tennes-see, and Washington, D.C. He received his degree in government with honors from Harvard University in 1969. After graduating, he enlisted in the U.S. Army and served in Vietnam. Upon his return to civilian life, Gore became an investigative reporter with the Nashville *Tennessean*. He attended Vanderbilt University Divinity School and Vanderbilt Law School, and operated a small home-building business.

Gore is married to the former Mary Elizabeth "Tipper" Aitcheson. They have three daughters and a son: Karenna, born August 6, 1973; Kristin, born June 5, 1977; Sarah, born January 7, 1979; and Albert III, born October 19, 1982. Gore owns a small livestock farm near Carthage where he and his family reside when Congress is not in session. The family attends New Salem Missionary Baptist Church near Carthage.

WILLIAM H. GRAY, III

U.S. Rep. William H. Gray, III, of Philadelphia, who has represented Penn-sylvania's Second Congressional District since 1979, chairs the House Committee on the Budget. A member of the Appropriations Committee and the District of Columbia Committee, he also sits on the influential Democratic Steering and Policy Committee and is a co-chair of the Demo-cratic Leadership Council. In addition to his work on the budget, Gray has been a leading spokesman on African policy, and authored the House versions of the Anti-Apartheid Acts of 1985 and 1986. A graduate of Franklin and Marshall College, Gray has master degrees from Drew Theo-logical Seminary and Princeton Theological Seminary. Since 1972 he has been the senior minister at Bright Hope Baptist Church in North Philadel-phia.

TOM HARKIN

Tom Harkin is the leading congressional proponent of progressive farm policy reform. He was raised in the small Iowa town of Cumming, and later earned his B.S. at Iowa State University and his law degree at Catho-lic University of America in Washington D.C. Harkin represented Iowa's

Fifth District for 10 years beginning in 1974 and served as chairman of the House Agriculture Subcommittee on Livestock, Dairy and Poultry. Elected to the Senate from Iowa in 1984, Harkin is a member of the Agriculture, Appropriations, Labor and Human Resources, and Small Business Committees.

GARY HART

Since 1960—as a young activist in John F. Kennedy's presidential campaign, a lawyer in Robert Kennedy's Justice and Stewart Udall's Interior Departments, and as Senator George McGovern's campaign manager—Gary Hart has influenced the direction of the Democratic Party and the United States.

He was elected to the United States Senate from the State of Colorado in 1974. During his two terms in the Senate, Mr. Hart served on the Armed Services, Budget, Environment and Public Works, and Select Intelligence Committees.

Gary Hart was one of only seven Senators never to have cast a vote for "Reaganomics," opposing the 1981 budget and tax cuts, the Line Item Veto, and the proposed Constitutional amendment to balance the Federal budget. He led the fight against the Gramm-Rudman-Hollings budget law.

Hart believed the Democratic Party had to offer alternative policies—not simply oppose Reaganomics. As a member of the Senate Budget Committee, Hart offered several plans contemplating tax cuts matched dollar-for-dollar with specific spending reductions. In 1985–1986, he was co-chair of a Senate Democratic economic policy task force which ultimately drafted and sent to the Senate floor a "Growth and Investment Budget." The budget reflected numerous legislative proposals authored by Senator Hart in the areas of education, job training, scientific research, and infrastructure revitalization.

His commitment to proposing alternatives was highlighted when he opposed moves within the Democratic Party toward protectionist trade policies. Hart authored the first comprehensive Democratic bill, aimed at opening foreign markets and increasing domestic competitiveness, without proposing additional trade barriers.

Senator Gary Hart, who ran for president in 1984 and 1987, resumed the practice of law at the Denver firm of Davis, Graham, and Stubbs in January, 1987. He and his wife, Lee, reside in Kittridge, Colorado.

JIM HIGHTOWER

Jim Hightower is now serving in his second term as the elected Texas Commissioner of Agriculture. A founder of the New Populist Forum,

Hightower has worked closely with Sen. Tom Harkin and Rep. Richard Gephardt in developing the Family Farm Act, designed to re-establish the family farm at the heart of American agriculture. He has also created grassroots economic development and marketing programs to revive rural economies throughout Texas. In 1970, Hightower co-founded the Agribusiness Accountability Project and for the next five years investigated the impact of monopolies on farm and food policies. In the late 1970s he was editor of the *Texas Observer* and then president of the Texas Consumer Association prior to his election as agriculture commissioner in 1982. Jim Hightower was the subject of a 1987 profile on CBS' "60 Minutes" and has been listed by the *National Journal* as one of the people outside federal government who "make a difference" in Washington.

FRITZ HOLLINGS

It has been said that what a man will do in public life is best told by what he's done. Firtz Hollings has given a lifetime of public service.

Upon graduation from the Citadel in 1942, Hollings joined the U.S. Army. He was decorated with seven campaign stars for his service in Africa and Europe. After the war, Hollings earned his law degree at the University of South Carolina. In 1948 he was elected to the South Carolina House of Representatives, serving as the legislature's speaker pro tem from 1951 until 1954, when he was elected lieutenant governor. Four years later, he was elected governor, one of the youngest men in South Carolina history to hold that post. Since 1966 he has been a United States Senator, and he currently serves on the Commerce, Science and Transportation Committee as its chairman; on the Budget Committee as its senior member; on the Appropriations Committee and on the Select Committee on Intelligence.

ELIZABETH HOLTZMAN

Elizabeth Holtzman is District Attorney of Kings County (Brooklyn), New York, one of the largest district attorney's offices in the country, to which she was first elected in 1981. She is the first woman District Attorney in New York City. Before that, Holtzman served as a Congresswoman for eight years (from 1973–1981). She served on the House Judiciary Committee, chaired its Immigration and Naturalization sub-committee, and served on the House Budget Committee. She still holds the record as the youngest woman ever elected to the House of Representatives.

JESSE LOUIS JACKSON

Jesse Jackson was born October 8, 1941, in Greenville. SC. to Helen (Burns) Jackson; his adopted father, Charles Henry Jackson, died in 1980; his grandmother, Matilda Burns, 79 (February 21, 1908), is still living with his mother in Greenville.

Jackson graduated from Sterling High School in Greenville, SC (1957); attended the University of Illinois on a football scholarship for one year, then transferred to North Carolina A&T State University, where he was active in sports (baseball and football), student government, and the student sit-in movement, which began in Greensboro on February 1, 1960. He graduated with a B.A. in Sociology (1963); attended the Chicago Theological Seminary for two-and-one-half years before dropping out in 1965 to join Dr. King in the voting rights march in Selma, Alabama. The school later conferred on him an honorary doctorate degree.

He has served as Executive Director, Operation Breadbasket, the economic arm of the Southern Christian Leadership Conference, Dr. Martin Luther King Jr.'s organization (1966–1971). He was National President, Operation PUSH (People United to Serve Humanity), a Chicago-based national volunteer self-help human rights organization concerned with economic development, moral and academic excellence in education, health care, housing, justice and international peace issues (1971–1983).

Jackson was a Democratic presidential candidate in 1984. Jackson launched his candidacy on November 3, 1983; he won 3.5 million primary and caucus votes, 21 percent of total; 465.5 delegates in San Francisco, 11 percent of the total; won five states: District of Columbia, Virginia, South Carolina, Louisiana and Mississippi.

PAUL A. JARGOWSKY

Paul A. Jargowsky is a doctoral candidate in public policy at the John F. Kennedy School of Government, Harvard University. He served as project director for the New York State Task Force on Poverty and Welfare and was a principal author of the task force report, A New Social Contract: Rethinking the Nature and Purpose of Public Assistance. Mr. Jargowsky is the author of several articles and book reviews on domestic policy issues, and was executive editor of Governance: The Harvard Journal of Public Policy.

HENRY KAUFMAN

Dr. Henry Kaufman is currently president of Henry Kaufman & Company, Inc. Dr. Kaufman was formerly a managing director and member of the

Executive Committee of Salomon Brothers Inc. Before joining the firm in 1962, Dr. Kaufman was in commercial banking and served as an economist at the Federal Reserve Bank of New York. He was admitted as a general partner of Salomon Brothers in 1967 and was appointed to the Executive Committee in 1972.

Dr. Kaufman, who was born in 1927, received a B.A. in economics from New York University in 1948, an M.S. in finance from Columbia University in 1949, and a Ph.D in banking and finance from the New York University Graduate School of Business Administration in 1958. He also received an honorary Doctor of Laws degree from New York University in 1982 and an honorary Doctor of Humane Letters degree from Yeshiva University in 1986. In 1987, Dr. Kaufman was awarded the first George S. Eccles Prize for excellence in economic writing, from the Columbia Business School for his book *Interest Rates, the Markets, and the New Financial World.*

CORETTA SCOTT KING

Coretta Scott King has been co-chairperson of the National Committee for Full Employment and the Full Employment Action Council since 1974. She also serves as president of the Atlanta-based Martin Luther King Center for Non-Violent Social Change. A graduate of Antioch College and the New England Conservatory of Music, Mrs. King is a member of the board of directors of the Southern Christian Leadership Conference and the Robert F. Kennedy Foundation; an author, lecturer and writer, the mother of four children and a member of the choir of Ebenezer Baptist Church in Atlanta.

LANE KIRKLAND

Lane Kirkland was elected president of the AFL-CIO on November 19, 1979. He had served for ten years as secretary-treasurer, the labor federation's second-highest office.

Kirkland was born on March 12, 1922, in Camden, South Carolina. He graduated in 1942 from the U.S. Merchant Marine Academy in King's Point, Long Island, and served throughout World War II as a deck officer aboard merchant vessels carrying ammunition and other war materials to both Atlantic and Pacific combat zones.

Licensed as a master mariner near the end of the war, Kirkland entered the U.S. Navy's Hydrographic Office in Washington, D.C., as a nautical scientist while studying at night at Georgetown University's School of Foreign Service, from which he received a Bachelor of Science degree in 1948.

Shortly afterward, Kirkland joined the research staff of the AFL. Over a ten-year period in the AFL and AFL-CIO, he handled a wide range of assignments.

He joined the International Union of Operating Engineers as director of research and education in 1958 and two years later returned to the AFL-CIO as executive assistant to President Meany, a post he held until his election as secretary-treasurer in 1969. He was elected president without opposition at the 1979 convention.

Kirkland is a member of the International Organization of Masters, Mates and Pilots; president, Trade Union Advisory Committee, OECD; vice president, International Confederation of Free Trade Unions; and a fellow of the American Association for the Advancement of Science. He has served on fifteen presidential commissions and advisory bodies.

Kirland and his wife, Irena, living in Washington, D.C.

EDWARD I. KOCH

Born in the Bronx in 1924, Edward Irving Koch was the second of three children born to parents who had immigrated to the United States from Poland. Following service in Europe with the U.S. Army Infantry in World War II, he returned to New York and earned a Bachelor of Laws degree from New York University.

After establishing a private law practice in 1949, Mr. Koch moved to Greenwich Village in 1956 and became a charter member of the Village Independent Democrats. An unsuccessful 1962 run for the State Assembly was followed the next year by a successful race for Democratic district leader against Carmine DeSapio, "the boss of bosses." In 1966 he won a seat on the New York City Council and, two years later, was elected to the U.S. House of Representatives from Manhattan's "silk stocking district." During his five terms, he served on the House Committee on Banking and Currency and on Appropriations. In 1976, the city delegation voted him their "most effective Congressman."

In 1977, Mr. Koch led a Democratic primary field of seven candidates for Mayor with 20 percent of the vote. After winning a runoff against Mario Cuomo and receiving 50 percent of the vote in the general election, he was inaugurated as the 105th Mayor of New York City on January 1, 1978. He was reelected in 1981 with 75 percent of the vote, carrying every Assembly district in the city. In 1982 he was defeated by Mario Cuomo for the Democratic nomination for Governor, but three years later was re-elected to a third term with 78 percent of the vote, again carrying every Assembly district in the city. He intends to run again in 1989 and, if successful, will be the first Mayor in the city's history to have won four terms.

Mayor Koch, 63, is the author of two books: *Mayor*, on The New York

Times bestseller list for 21 weeks, and *Politics*. He is currently at work on a book with John Cardinal O'Connor to be entitled *His Eminence and Hizzoner*. He also is a regular weekly contributor to The Staten Island Advance, El Diario, The New York Voice, The New York City Tribune, Noticias del Mundo, and WINS Radio.

RICHARD D. LAMM

Richard D. Lamm served as Governor of the State of Colorado from January 14, 1975, until January 7, 1987. He was a member of the Colorado House of Representatives, 1966–74.

He has served as University Professor and Director of the Center for Public Policy and Contemporary Issues at University of Denver; partner, O'Connor and Hannan, Attornies at Law; Distinguished Professor of History, University of New Orleans, Innsbruck, Austria; and was Montgomery Fellow, Dartmouth College; and Visiting Professor, University of Colorado at Denver, Graduate School of Public Affairs, 1984–1985.

NORMAN LEAR

Norman Lear is one of the television industry's most prominent writers and producers. It has been estimated that over 120,000,000 Americans—more than half the nation's population—have watched his shows, which include such hits as "All in the Family;" "Sanford and Son;" "Maude;" "The Jeffersons;" "Good Times;" and "Mary Hartman, Mary Hartman." He is Chairman and Chief Executive Officer of ACT III Communications, Inc., a diversified media and entertainment company. Also known for political activism, Lear is the Founding Chairman of People for the American Way, the non-profit, non-partisan constitutional liberties organization.

MICKEY LELAND

Representative Mickey Leland, Democrat, Eighteenth Congressional District (Houston), Texas, was born November 27, 1944. He graduated from Texas Southern University, Houston, with a B.S. in pharmacy in 1970. He is a member of the Congressional Black Caucus, serves on the Energy and Commerce Committee, and is chairman of the Subcommittee on Postal Operations and Services, Post Office and Civil Service Committees. He is also chairman of the House Select Committee on Hunger, and has traveled extensively studying hunger in the United States and throughout the world, particularly in Africa.

ROBERT LEVIN

Robert Levin, editor of *Democratic Blueprints*, was born in Fresno, California on June 26, 1955. As a boy, he excelled in school and spent weekends with his family working and playing at their ranch in the Sierra Nevadas, and riding his horse, Gunsmoke. He is a graduate of the University of California at Berkeley and New York University Graduate School of Business Administration. In 1975, Robert studied in France for a year at l'Institut des Etudes Politiques at the University of Bordeaux and worked in Holland the following summer on the docks of Rotterdam. He moved to New York from California in 1979 and worked on Wall Street for an international commodities trading firm, Chilewich Corporation, as an analyst and trader. In 1987, he joined Salomon Brothers, Inc., a New York-based investment bank.

Robert Levin has been involved in Democratic politics since 1972. In 1977, as a student, he co-founded with several other students, a California Public Interest Research Group at Berkeley. In 1980, he founded a nonpartisan foreign policy foundation, The International Forum, and in 1983, an economic policy forum in the financial community, The Wall Street Democrats. Both forums have organized discussions with national leaders from government, business and academia around domestic and international policy issues facing the United States. He has also been involved in several Jewish causes, and in January 1986 participated in an ADL Congressional delegation to Israel. In December 1986, he traveled to the Phillipines with the American Jewish World Service, a humanitarian relief and development assistance organization. Mr. Levin lives in New York City.

SALLY K. RIDE

Sally Ride was born May 26, 1951, in Los Angeles, California. She graduated from Westlake High School, Los Angeles, California, in 1968; received from Stanford University a bachelor of science in Physics and a bachelor of arts in English in 1973, and master of science and doctorate degrees in Physics in 1975 and 1978, respectively. She enjoys tennis (having been an instructor and having achieved national ranking as a junior), running, rugby, volleyball, softball and stamp collecting.

Dr. Ride has held teaching assistant and research assignments while a graduate student in the Physics Department at Stanford University. Dr. Ride was selected as an astronaut candidate by NASA in January 1978. In August 1979, she completed a 1-year training and evaluation period, making her eligible for assignment as a mission specialist on future Space Shuttle flight crews. She subsequently performed as an on-orbit capsule communicator (CAPCOM) for the STS-2 and STS-3 missions.

Dr. Ride was a mission specialist on STS-7, which launched from Kennedy Space Center, Florida, on June 18, 1983. Mission duration was 147 hours before landing on a lakebed runway at Edwards Air Force Base, California, on June 24, 1983.

Dr. Ride served as a mission specialist on STS 41-G, which launched from Kennedy Space Center, Florida, on October 5, 1984. Their 8-day mission deployed the Earth Radiation Budget Satellite. Mission duration was 197 hours and concluded with a landing at Kennedy Space Center, Florida, on October 13, 1984.

In June 1985 Dr. Ride was assigned to serve as a mission specialist on STS 61-M. She terminated mission training in January 1986 in order to serve as a member of the Presidential Commission on the Space Shuttle Challenger Accident.

ROBERT B. REICH

Robert B. Reich is one of America's foremost political economists. His best-selling 1983 book, *The Next American Frontier*, launched a national debate about America's industrial strategy. A professor at Harvard's John F. Kennedy School of Government, he is the author of many other books on government, business, and the international economy, including *Minding America's Business* (1981), *New Deals: The Chrysler Revival and The American System* (1985) and, most recently, *Tales of a New America*. His articles appear regularly in the *Harvard Business Review*, and the *Atlantic*. He is also a leading advisor to politicians, government agencies, and firms; a contributing editor of *The New Republic* and of *World Policy*; a regular columnist for *Nihon Keizai Shimbun*, one of Japan's most influential newspapers; a regular contributor to the op-ed pages of the *New York Times*; and a frequent guest on ABC's *Night Line* and other television programs.

Before coming to Harvard, Mr. Reich had a distinguished government career. In the Ford Administration he served as Assistant to the Solicitor General; in the Carter Administration, as Director of Policy Planning for the Federal Trade Commission.

Mr. Reich holds degrees from Dartmouth College, Yale Law School, and Oxford University, where he was a Rhodes Scholar.

JOSEPH P. RILEY, JR.

Joseph P. Riley, Jr. is now in his fourth four-year term as Mayor of the City of Charleston, South Carolina, and has just concluded his term as President of the United States Conference of Mayors.

In 1968, Mayor Riley was elected to the South Carolina House of Representatives and was its youngest member at that time. During his six years in the House of Representatives, Mayor Riley was co-author and floor leader of numerous bills, including ethics legislation, legislature reform, creation of the South Carolina Commission on Human Affairs, election law reform, Tidelands legislation and state support of the College of Charleston. He was active in the field of Mental Health, Mental Retardation and Alcohol and Drug Abuse reform. In 1974, he received the South Carolina Association for Retarded Children's Legislative Award for his service in behalf of retarded children.

On December 9, 1975, Mayor Riley was first elected Mayor of the City of Charleston. As Chief Executive Officer of the City, he presides over a twelve-member Council, elected from single-member districts. Under his leadership, the City Government has undergone an extensive reorganization. In 1978, the City was named an All-American City by the National Municipal League.

His administration has been marked by his aggressive leadership in rebuilding the Old and Historic City of Charleston.

Mayor Riley was born in Charleston in 1943. He was graduated from Bishop England High School, The Citadel and the University of South Carolina School of Law.

CHARLES S. ROBB

Governor Charles S. Robb served as 64th chief executive of the Commonwealth of Virginia from 1982–1986. During his term in office he also served as Chairman of the Southern Governors' Association, the Democratic Governors' Association, the Education Commission of the States and president of the Council of State Governments. Since leaving office he has been a partner in the Richmond-based law firm of Hunton & Williams working primarily out of their offices in Fairfax, Virginia, and Washington, D.C. He is currently chairman of the Democratic Leadership Council and Jobs for America's Graduates and serves as a member of the Board of Directors of Crestar Financial Corporation, The Carnegie Foundation for the Advancement of Teaching, the National Commission on the Public Service. He chaired The Twentieth Century Fund's Task Force on the Senior Executive Service, and is a member of the Council on Foreign Relations, Inc.

PATRICIA SCHROEDER

Patricia Scott Schroeder, Democrat, represents the First Congressional District of Colorado. Schroeder was first elected to Congress in 1972 and reelected seven times. Schroeder is a member of the House Armed Services Committee, the House Judiciary Committee, the House Post Office and Civil Service Committee, and the House Select Committee on Children, Youth and Families.

In the House Armed Services Committee, Schroeder sits on the Subcommittee on Research and Development, the Defense Policy Panel, and the Subcommittee on Military Personnel and Compensation. Schroeder has focused on cutting wasteful defense spending, promoting arms control, increasing our allies' share of mutual defense burdens, and improving the quality of life for military personnel and their families.

In 1985, Schroeder introduced historic legislation calling for a mutual nuclear testing moratorium. On three different occasions, the House passed Schroeder's amendment prohibiting the use of funds for nuclear testing.

In the House Judiciary Committee, Schroeder sits on the Subcommittee on Civil and Constitutional Rights and the Subcommittee on Courts, Civil Liberties, and the Administration of Justice. Schroeder played a major role in the passage of the Voting Rights Act and the 1984 Civil Rights Act. She is also a primary sponsor of the Equal Rights Amendment.

Schroeder was born in Portland, Oregon, in 1940. She attended public elementary and high schools in Texas, Ohio, and Iowa. Schroeder graduated magna cum laude from the University of Minnesota in 1961, where she was a member of Phi Beta Kappa honor society. She graduated from Harvard Law School and passed the Colorado bar in 1964.

Prior to her election to Congress, Schroeder lectured at Denver colleges and practiced law. Schroeder is married to attorney James Schroeder. They have a son Scott, 21, who attends Georgetown University, and a daughter Jamie, 16, who attends a public school.

CHARLES E. SCHUMER

Congressman Charles E. Schumer was born on November 23, 1950, in Brooklyn, New York, the neighborhood he now represents in Congress. After attending New York City public schools, he graduated with honors from Harvard College and Harvard Law School. Upon graduation, he was elected to the New York State Assembly, making him, at 23, one of that legislature's youngest members since Theodore Roosevelt.

In 1980, he won a seat in the United States House of Representatives, and now represents the 10th Congressional District in the heart of Brooklyn. He sits on the House Committee on Banking, Finance and Urban Affairs, Committee on the Judiciary, and Committee on the Budget. Congressman Schumer has been a leader on emerging issues related to the international economy and the problem of Third World Debt.

PAUL SIMON

Paul Simon believes that the Democrats can't regain the leadership of this country by being just like the Republicans, only less so. He is an alternative to the pack of candidates who believe America has moved to the right and the Democratic party must follow. He stands for an engaged and effective federal government, and he brings the caring and the courage of a Harry Truman or Franklin Roosevelt back into the Democratic party.

At 19, Paul Simon quit college to start a newspaper. He was the youngest editor and publisher in the country. His first paper (he eventually owned thirteen local weeklies) was instrumental in closing down syndicated gambling and exposing government corruption in Southern Illinois.

At 22, Simon enlisted as a private in the U.S. Army. He was assigned to counter-intelligence, and spent most of his two years as a special agent in countries bordering the Iron Curtain.

Paul Simon entered and won a race for the Illinois State House at the age of 25. During three terms in the Illinois House, and then two terms in the State Senate, he received the Independent Voters of Illinois "Best Legislator Award" more often than any other politician, before or since. He won passage of 46 major pieces of legislation. His battles for "pay-as-you-go" financing of state capital investments earned him a reputation for fiscal responsibility.

Simon was elected to the U.S. House of Representatives in 1974. Over the next ten years, he became a national leader in education, a key critic of the Reagan Administration's arms policies, and a sponsor of the Civil Rights Restoration Act.

Simon upset Charles Percy to win a seat in the U.S. Senate in 1984. His priorities there include his Guaranteed Job Opportunity Program, education, and balancing the budget. He has also written legislation to extend veteran's benefits, to make the insurance industry more competitive, to reform campaign financing, and to put an end to merger mania.

Simon's record on labor, civil rights, and social programs stand squarely in the Democratic Party tradition. But he is not one to merely follow a party line. His opposition to the recent tax bill, his fight for a balanced budget amendment, and his stand in favor of tough acid rain legislation were not calculated to make friends. They are just three instances of Paul Simon bucking the political tide to work for what he knows is right.

Paul Simon says if he were President, "I think I can change things." Anyone can say that, but Paul Simon can back it up with a forty year record of fighting effectively for change. Simon has already made America a better place to raise children. He has risen steadily through the democratic system by proving to his constituents and to his colleagues that he has a powerful vision for America. More than that, he has the intelligence, the experience, and the commitment to make that vision a reality.

MICHAEL W. SONNENFELDT

Michael, age 32, has an M.B.A. from M.I.T. where he graduated Phi Beta Kappa. He was with Goldman Sach Real Estate Department and subsequently became co-developer of the Harborside Financial Center, the nation's largest commercial redevelopment. In addition to his business activities, he is Resources Chairman of BENS, Business Executives for National Security, a non-partisan, non-ideological organization of over 5,000 business executives devoted to redefining and insuring our nation's security. He serves on the Board of Governors of the American Associates of Ben-Gurion University, an Israeli university located in the Negev desert. He lives with his wife, Katja Goldman, and his daughter, Joya Claire, in the New York Metropolitan Area.

TED WEISS

Ted Weiss has represented New York's 17th Congressional District since 1977. He chairs the Governmental Operations Subcommittee on Human Resources and Intergovernmental Relations and serves on the Select Committee on Children, Youth and Families as well as the Committee on Foreign Affairs. He authored the no first-use of nuclear arms resolution and is the prime sponsor of legislation to plan for conversion of defense industries to peace-time use. He has been at the forefront of efforts to increase funding in the fight against AIDS and for the homeless. A strong advocate of human rights, he has focused special attention on the plight of Soviet Jewry and the Jewish community in Ethiopia.

MICHAEL ZIMMERMAN

Since joining GAO in December 1968, Mr. Zimmerman has been involved with major social programs. In 1980, he became the Associate Director responsible for managing GAO's audits and evaluations of the Medicare and Medicaid Programs and related health policy issues. As a career civil servant, Mr. Zimmerman has received several GAO awards including the Distinguished Service Award for 1987.

Index

Acquired Immune Deficiency
Syndrome (AIDS), 306, 307,
309, 312, 322–323; and
Medicare, 307; and NAS, 322;
and AZT, 468; counseling,
462–463; prevention, 461–470;
testing, 462–463; the Reagan
administration and 461–470
Adams, Gordon, 256–268, 511; and
defense budget, 256–268; and
U.S. military policy, 259–265
agriculture, Harkin on, 347–358;
Hightower on, 359–367;
Jackson's program, 91, 100–
101; trade, 54, 349–350, 422
Aid to Families with Dependent
Children (AFDC), 38, 131, 155,
156, 375, 378, 386; and ET,
38, 197; and job training, 155;
and Omnibus Budget Reconcil-
iation Act of 1981, 386
Alternative Use Committee, 251–253
American Conservation Corps, 128–
129
American dream, 165, 289, 290, 299,
438
American Federation of Labor and
Congress of Industrial
Organizations (AFL-CIO), 426–
427
American Investment Bank, 92, 93–94
American Medical Association
(AMA), and AIDS, 466;
Journal of the, 468–469
Argentina, 211, 212, 224, 227
Atlantic Alliance, 241, 246
automobile, industry, 73, 145–146,
170, 232, 249; workers, 73,
145–146, 170

Babbitt, Bruce, 3–12, 511; and
Democratic Workplace, 5, 7–
12; and Progressive National
Consumption Tax, 7, 310
Baker Plan, 29, 217, 221
balanced budget, 19, 80; amendment,
153, 199; Gore on, 68–69;

Hollings on, 198–208
Balanced Budget and Emergency
Deficit Control Act of 1985 *see*
Gramm-Rudman-Hollings Act
Bane, Mary Jo, 368–379, 512; on
diversity of poverty, 368–376;
on poverty policy, 368–379
Biden, Joseph, 13–30, 512; and
American Economic Renais-
sance, 13–28
Boston Housing Partnership, 293–294,
298, 301
Bradley, Bill, 58, 209–217, 512–513;
and Bradley-Gephardt Fair Tax
Bill, 58–59; and debtor country
reforms, 214–215; and foreign
debt, 209–217, 221–222; and
Marshall Plan, 209–217
Bradley-Gephardt Fair Tax Bill, 58–59
Brazil, 359, 361; and foreign trade,
227, 229, 230, 233, 239
Britain, and foreign trade, 205, 235;
economy of, 216, 484
Broder, David, 184–185
budget deficit, 6, 13–14, 18, 45, 52,
53, 77, 85–86, 97, 110–111,
114, 141, 184, 248, 316–317,
341, 349; and defense
spending, 242–243, 245, 259,
499–500, 502, 504; and
Strategic Investment Initiative,
85–86; and VAT, 202; Choate
and Linger on, 236–239; Dalio
on, 477–485; Gray on, 189–
197; Hollings on, 198–208;
Reagan administration and,
13–14, 52–54, 64, 68–69, 76–
77, 89–90, 149–156, 189–197,
198–208, 498–506; reduction,
18–19, 80, 114, 149–156, 157,
193–195, 257, 258; Rivlin on,
175–180; Sonnenfeldt on, 498–
506
Bureau of Labor Statistics, 204, 249,
398–399, 411–413
Business and Technology Center, 339
Buy America Act, 232

535

Carter, James, 151, 167–168, 176, 509
Carter administration, 50, 151, 167
catastrophic health care, 159–160
Celeste, Richard, 275–280, 513; on
    Edison Seed Development
    Fund, 276–280; on Ohio's
    economic competitiveness,
    275–280
Centers on Advanced Technology, 49
Centers for Disease Control (CDC), and
    AIDS, 307, 322, 461–462, 463,
    466–468
Centers of Excellence, 39–40, 49
China, 235, 483
Cisneros, Henry, 333–346, 514; on
    diversification, 336–341; on
    education in Texas, 334, 339–
    342, 344; on Texas economy,
    336–341, 344; on Texas ethnic
    relations, 342–344; on Texas
    politics, 341–342
civilian research and development,
    25–26, 48, 49, 70, 92, 94, 104,
    115–116
civil rights, 184, 185, 324–325, 400
Civil Rights Act of 1964, 400; Title VII
    of, 403, 405
Challenger, 455–456
child care, 20–21, 147, 155, 321, 373,
    387; and Title XX Social
    Service Block Grant, 418–419;
    tax credits for corporations,
    20–21; vouchers, 11
Choate, Pat, 226–239, 513–514; on
    trade policies, 226–239; on
    trade strategies, 226–239
Clean Water Act, 46, 181, 183
Clinton, Bill, 269–274, 514–515; and
    Bringing Down the Barriers,
    272; and Making America
    Work project, 272–274; and
    Task Force on Jobs, Growth,
    and Competitiveness, 271
Cohen, Wilbur, 507–510, 515; on
    Reagan administration, 507–
    510
Community Development Block Grant,
    181, 301, 326–327
competitive trade, 15, 23–24, 25, 29,
    55–56, 58, 82–83, 94–100,
    171–172, 191–192, 269, 344,
    429; Choate and Linger on,
    226–239; Hollings on, 203–207
Comprehensive Employment and
    Training Act (CETA), 127, 132–
    133, 151
Conference of Mayors Task Force on

Hunger and Homelessness,
    290, 292, 314–315, 326; and
    National Urban Investment
    Policy, 315–332
Congress, 6, 7, 68, 69, 80, 184, 186,
    194–195, 199–201, 206, 220,
    222, 273, 314, 355, 386, 429,
    508; and debt relief, 222–223;
    and defense spending, 250–
    251, 257; and Federal Technol-
    ogy Transfer Act, 279; and
    Food Security Act of 1981,
    386; and homelessness, 296;
    and housing, 296–299, 302;
    and JPTA, 386; and Omnibus
    Budget Reconciliation Act of
    1981, 386; and Omnibus Drug
    Bill, 306; and pay equity, 406;
    and U.S. financial system, 486,
    489, 493, 497; First, 205; Joint
    Economic Committee of, 222;
    Ninety-ninth, 223; One
    Hundredth, 218, 223, 295–296
Constitution, 110–111, 153, 183, 184
Corrigan, Gerald, 494–495
Council of Economic Advisors, 251
Council for Economic Progress, 421–
    422
crime, and criminal justice system,
    389–395; and illiteracy, 394,
    395; and unemployment, 121,
    426; see also criminal justice
    system
criminal justice system, and commu-
    nity service, 393; and crime,
    389–395; and illiteracy, 394,
    395; and literacy programs,
    394; and video technology,
    391–392; Holtzman on, 389–
    395
Cuomo, Mario, 115, 515–516

Dalio, Raymond, 477–485, 516; on the
    economy, 477–485
Declaration of Independence, 135–136
defense budget, 19, 60, 80–81, 90,
    110, 179, 191, 199, 242, 248–
    255, 256–268, 270, 333, 388;
    Adams on, 256–268; and
    budget deficit, 242–243, 248–
    255, 259, 499–500; and
    Congress, 250; and employ-
    ment, 249; and Pentagon, 242;
    and U.S. allies, 114–115;
    Reagan administration and,
    80–81, 115, 499–500, 502,
    504; reductions, 252, 256–268;

Schroeder on, 240–247;
Sonnenfeldt on, 499–500, 502,
504; *see also* national defense
Defense Department, 95, 252, 258,
265, 302, 324; and economic
conversion, 253–254
Defense Economic Adjustment Act,
251–254; and Alternative Use
Committees, 251–253; and
Defense Economic Adjustment
Council, 251–252
Defense Economic Adjustment
Council, 251–252
deinstitutionalization, 295
Democratic Workplace, 5, 7–12
Democrats, liberal, and social justice
and prosperity, 165–174
Department of Agriculture, Texas,
363–365, 367; U.S., 353, 383
Department of Health and Human
Services, 383
Department of Housing and Urban
Development (HUD), 291, 297–
298, 301; and federal funding,
291–293, 297–298
Department of Labor, and Guaranteed
Job Opportunity Program, 126;
*Dictionary of Occupational
Titles*, 398
Disraeli, Benjamin, 54–55
Downey, Thomas, 181–186, 517; and
federalism, 181–186
Drew, Daniel, 232; and "little unfair
advantage," 232, 234–235
drug abuse, 90, 270, 309, 323–324,
395; and AIDS, 462, 463–466;
and Anti-Drug Abuse Act of
1986, 323; and Omnibus Drug
Bill, 306, 394; and Reagan
administration, 394
Dukakis, Michael, 31–51, 293, 517–
518; and the "Massachusetts
Miracle," 33–44; national
challenge of 44–51

earned income tax credit (EITC), 373
economic conversion, 248–255
economic growth, and social justice,
165–174; Biden on, 13–30;
Choate and Linger on, 236–
239; Dukakis on Massachu-
setts, 31–51; Gephardt on,
52–63; Gore on, 64–74; Gray
on, 193–197; Hart on, 75–88;
Jackson on, 89–105; Reich on,
165–174; Rivlin on, 175–180;
Robb on, 139–148; Schroeder

on, 106–117; Simon on, 118–
136
economy, and education, 286, 471–
476; and employment, 423–
432; and housing, 292–293;
and poverty, 369, 372, 376–
377; Biden on, 13–30; Celeste
on Ohio, 275–280; Cisneros on
Texas, 336–341, 344; Dalio on,
477–485; Dukakis on Massachusetts, 33–51; global, 5,
106–117, 178–179, 226–239,
315, 320, 421–422; Harkin on
farm, 347–358; Hart on world,
79–87; Hightower on farm,
359–367; Jackson on 89–105;
Keynesian, 165–166, 167, 169,
199; Kirkland on, 423–432;
Robb on, 139–148; Schroeder
on global, 106–117; trickle-
down, 111; Weiss on, 248–255
Edison Seed Development Fund, 276–
280
education, 14, 15, 38, 56–58, 68, 71–
74, 80, 84–85, 88, 90, 147,
196, 249, 320–321, 326, 383,
385, 409, 414–416, 471–476;
AIDS, 322, 462, 463, 465–466;
and Guaranteed Job Opportunity Program, 125; and IDEA,
58; and poverty, 369, 374, 375;
and Strategic Investment
Initiative, 84–85; and student
loan programs, 22, 110, 155,
273; and the economy, 256,
471–476; and the work ethic,
283–288; budget, 288;
Feinstein on, 281–288; for the
handicapped, 183; high school
equivalency, 125, 127;
illiteracy and, 57–58, 71–72,
163, 196, 271, 283, 287;
maternal, 384–385; national,
policy, 471–476; reform, 21–
23, 38, 57–58, 71–74, 84–85,
115, 155–156, 163, 196, 274;
Reform Act, 38; Texas, 334,
339–342, 344
Eizenstat, Stuart, 149–156, 518; on
Democratic and Republican
programs, 149–156; on
inflation, 152–156; on the
Great Society, 152–153; on the
New Deal, 153; on the Reagan
administration, 149–156
Employee Stock Ownership Plan, 11,
12, 19–20, 87, 173

employment, and AFL-CIO, 426–427;
    and NCFE, 414–422; and Six
    Point Agenda Toward a Full
    Employment Economy, 414–
    422; and the economy, 423–
    432; Ferraro on, 398–405; full,
    423–424, 427–429, 510; full,
    economy, 409–422; Kirkland
    on 423–432; programs, 73,
    154–155, 326; programs and
    Reagan administration, 150;
    see also job training
Equal Employment Opportunity
    Commission (EEOC), 406
Equal Pay Act, 402–403, 405
Equal Rights Amendment (ERA), 324,
    510
equity, individual, accounts, 11; pay,
    396–406; sharing, 10
European Community (EC), 351–352
Evans, Daniel, 156, 185

Family Farm Act, 351–352, 355–356
farmers, 100–101, 161–162, 177, 226,
    347–358, 359–367; see also
    farm policy
Farmer's Home Administration, 100,
    353
farm policy, 161–162, 422; Harkin on,
    347–358; Reagan administra-
    tion, 347–348, 351, 354, 359–
    361
Federal Aviation Administration
    (FAA), 150
federal budget, 6, 7, 64, 68–69, 114–
    115, 149–156, 319; Hollings
    on, 198–208; Rivlin on, 165–
    170
Federal Bureau of Investigation (FBI),
    80, 389
Federal Reserve Board, 18, 77, 167,
    217, 222, 420
Federal Highway Aid, 181, 183
federalism, 305; Downey on, 181–186
Feinstein, Dianne, 281–288, 334, 519;
    on education, 281–288
Ferraro, Geraldine, 396–406, 519; on
    pay equity, 396–406
Finley, Murray, 409–422, 519–520; on
    full-employment economy,
    409–422
Flynn, Raymond, 289–303, 520; on
    housing, 289–303
Food and Agricultural Policy Research
    Institute (FAPRI), 350, 355
Food Security Act of 1981, 349, 386
food stamps, 122, 371, 378, 386, 388,

    and Guaranteed Job Opportu-
    nity Program, 125
foreign debt, 14, 29–30, 60–61, 64,
    179, 209–217; American, 14,
    24, 52, 54, 60, 69, 77; Bradley
    on, 209–217; Latin American,
    80, 103, 210, 211–212, 218–
    225; relief, 29–30, 218–225;
    Schumer on, 218–225; Third
    World, 53, 60, 68, 78, 116,
    209–217, 218–225; U.S.
    response to, 220–225; World
    Bank and, 30, 60
foreign policy, 79–83
foreign trade, see trade
France, 230, 233–236, 285
free trade, 31–32, 55, 81, 97, 198;
    Gore on, 67–68; Hollings on,
    203–207

gain sharing, 10, 87, 173
General Accounting Office, 7, 298;
    and AIDS, 461–462
General Agreement on Tariffs and
    Trade (GATT), 67, 75, 98, 231–
    232, 351
George, Calvin, 409–422, 520; on full-
    employment economy, 409–422
Gephardt, Richard, 52–63, 520–521;
    and Advanced Technology
    Institute, 61; and Bradley-
    Gephardt Fair Tax Bill, 58–59;
    and Family Farm Act, 351–352,
    354, 355; on foreign debt, 60–
    61; and IDEA, 58; on National
    Literacy Project, 57; on trade
    policies, 53–56
global economy, 5, 106–117, 178–179,
    226–239, 315, 320, 421–422;
    Choate and Linger on, 226–239
Gore, Albert, 64–74, 296, 521–522;
    and Readfare, 72; on educa-
    tion, 71–74
Gramm-Rudman-Hollings Act, 80,
    114, 153, 195, 257, 508;
    Hollings on, 198–208
Gray, William, 189–197, 522; on
    economic growth, 193–197; on
    the budget deficit, 189–197; on
    the Reagan administration,
    189–197
Great Depression, 33, 134, 141, 308,
    313, 477, 481, 484
Great Society, 84, 152–153, 311, 312,
    510
Guaranteed Job Opportunity Program,
    123–136; and education, 125;

and food stamps, 125; and infrastructure, 127–129; and job training, 125; and Social Security, 126; and welfare, 124, 125

Harkin, Tom, 347–358, 522–523; and Alternative Agricultural Product Research Act of 1987, 356; and Family Farm Act, 351–352, 354–355; on farm economy, 347–358; on the family farm, 352–357
Harkin-Gephardt Bill see Family Farm Act
Hart, Gary, 75–88, 523; and Industrial Modernization Agreements, 82–83; and Strategic Investment Initiative, 84–86; on economic policies, 83–87; on world economy, 79–83
Head Start, 183, 196, 378, 380, 383, 415
health, benefits, 252; care, 323, 381, 382–383; insurance, 373
Hightower, Jim, 359–367, 523–524; and Texas Department of Agriculture, 363–365, 367; on agriculture, 359–367
Hollings, Ernest, 198–208, 524; and competitive trade, 203–208; and deficit reduction, 201–208; and Gramm-Rudman-Hollings Act, 198–208; and Trade Enforcement Act, 205–207; on taxes, 201–203
Holtzman, Elizabeth, 389–395, 524; on criminal justice system, 389–395
homeless see homelessness
homelessness, 270, 282, 292, 294–295, 325–326; and Conference of Mayors Task Force on Hunger and Homelessness, 290; and Homeless Person's Survival Act, 291; and the Reagan administration, 290; Congress and, 296; Flynn on, 289–303; in New York City, 307–312
Homeless Person's Survival Act, 296
Hong Kong, 226, 228, 239, 483
H.R. 813 see Defense Economic Adjustment Act
House Select Committee on Hunger, 382, 385
housing, 49–50, 92, 149–150, 314, 316, 326; and community-based partnerships, 297–303; and CDBG, 181, 301, 326–327; and home ownership rates, 291–292; and National Partnership for Affordable Housing, 50; and National Urban Investment Policy, 318; and Nehemiah Project, 300, 309; and Tax Reform Act (1988), 292; crisis, and economy, 292–293; federal, programs, 140; Flynn on, 289–303; in New York, 307–312; Reagan administration and, 291–293, 297
Humphrey-Hawkins Full Employment and Balanced Economic Growth Act of 1978, 427
hunger, and IMR, 382–383; and poverty, 380–388; Leland on, 380–388
Hunt, Jim, 156; on national education policy, 471–476

illiteracy, 57–58, 71–72, 163, 196, 271, 283, 287; and criminals, 394, 395; and National Literacy Project, 57
Individual Development and Education Account (IDEA), 58
industry, Biden on, 13–28; Choate and Linger on, 236–239; Dukakis on Massachusetts, 33–51; Kirkland on, policy, 430–431; Reagan administration and, 52–54; Reich on, 165–174, Robb on, 139–148
infant mortality rate (IMR), 382–383
inflation, 18, 77, 110, 151, 153–156, 176, 373, 410–411, 503; and salaries, 154–155; anti-, program, 420; Eizenstat on, 152–156
infrastructure, 36–37, 183–184; and Guaranteed Job Opportunity Program, 127–129; and WPA, 130–131; Massachusetts, 36–37, 41–44, 45–46; urban, 327–329
Institute of Medicine (IOM), Committee on a National Strategy for AIDS, 465, 467
insurance, 27–28; deposit, 494, 496; federal flood, 56; wage, 26–27
interest rates, 18, 190–193, 503

International Monetary Fund, 60, 75, 217, 219, 220–221
International Trade Commission (ITC), 206, 235

Jackson, Jesse, 89–105, 525; and Agricultural Program, 91, 100–101; and American Investment Bank, 92, 93–94; and Energy Program, 91, 101–104; and National Investment Program, 91–94; and Pan American Energy and Environmental Security Alliance, 91, 102, 103–104; and Trade and Competitiveness Program, 91, 94–100
Japan, 5, 67, 69, 81, 101, 179, 199, 275, 281–282, 351, 384; American defense of, 241, 245, 246; and foreign trade, 67, 176, 207, 228–229, 230, 233, 234, 235, 239; economy of, 78, 79–80, 108, 119, 216, 226; education in, 285, 287; employes in, 281–282; literacy rate in, 72; management in, 144, 145; productivity of, 204
Jargowsky, Paul, 368–379, 525; and diversity of poverty, 368–376; and poverty policy, 368–379
Job Corps, 415, 428
jobs see employment
job training, 427–429, 431; and AFDC, 155; and full employment, 427–429, 431; and Guaranteed Job Opportunity Program, 125; assistance, 22–23; programs, 37–38, 73, 83, 98, 127, 147, 294, 316, 326, 375, 416–417; Reagan administration and, 150; see also Job Training Partnership Act
Job Training Partnership Act, 37, 46–47, 85, 132–133, 386; Private Industrial Council of the, 123; Title IV of, 73–74
Johnson, Lyndon, 151, 152
Joint Economic Committee of Congress, 134, 222

Kahl, Anne, 398–399
Kaufman, Henry, 486–497, 525–526; and deregulation, 492–497; on the financial system, 486–497
Kennedy, John F., 88, 151, 153, 190, 269, 355, 357

Keynes (Lord), 78; (-ian) economics, 165–166, 167, 169, 199
King, Coretta Scott, 409–422, 526; on full-employment economy, 409–422
King, Jr., Martin Luther, 120, 388
Kirkland Lane, 423–432, 526–527; on collective bargaining, 431–432; on employment, 423–432; on industrial policy, 430–431; on international trade, 429; on the economy, 423–432
Koch, Edward, 305–312, 527–528; urban agenda of, 305–312

Lamm, Richard, 157–164, 528; and farm policy, 161–162; and Medicare, 159–160; and Social Security, 160–161; and the Democratic party, 157–164; on public policy, 157–164; on catastrophic health care program, 159–160
Lear, Norman, 433–444, 528
Leland, Mickey, 296, 380–388, 528; on hunger and poverty, 380–388
Levin, Robert, 529
liberal Democrats, and social justice and prosperity, 165–174
Linger, Juyne, 226–239; on trade policies and strategies, 226–239
"little unfair advantage," 232, 234–235
Local Initiative Support Corporation (LISC), 300, 301

Madison, James, 136, 185, 205; and The Federalist Papers, 190
Making America Work, 272–274
management, 112–113; Gephardt on, 61–63; Japanese, 144; Robb on, 143–146
Marshall Plan, 79–80, 116, 242; Bradley on, 209–217
Massachusetts Housing Partnership, 42; and Boston Housing Partnership, 293–294
"Massachusetts Miracle," 33–51
Medicaid, 80, 122, 156, 185, 323, 373, 378, 381, 509
Medicare, 86, 159, 160, 191, 322, 323, 377, 507–508; and AIDS, 307, 509
Melman, Seymour, 249, 253–254; and Profits Without Production, 253

Mexico, 210, 212, 227, 337; and debt restructuring, 219, 221; and foreign trade, 229–230, 233, 239; foreign debt of, 210, 212, 218–220, 222
military research and development, 25–26, 48, 49, 95, 104, 115–116, 279–280
military spending see defense budget
Moynihan, Patrick, 112, 119, 296
multinationals, 95, 361–362

National Academy of Sciences (NAS), and AIDS, 322; and Women, Work, and Wages, 400, 404
National Aeronautics and Space Administration (NASA), 451–460; future objectives of, 452–460; Ride on, 451–460
National Commission on Space, 456–457, 460; and Pioneering the Space Frontier, 456
National Committee for Full Employment (NCFE), 414–422
National Community Housing Partnership, 301, 302
national debt see budget deficit
national defense, and nuclear weapons, 240, 245, 246, 259–263; and U.S. allies, 29, 240–247; expenditures, and allies, 240–247; Schroeder on, 240–247
National Governor's Association, 271; and A Time for Results, 271; and welfare reform proposal, 272–274
National Science Foundation, 279; Engineering Research Centers, 49, 279
Nehemiah Project, 300, 309
New Deal, 84, 116, 139–141, 142, 153, 182, 312, 510
Newman, Winn, 401–403
North Atlantic Treaty Organization (NATO), 241, 243–244, 262–263
nuclear, arms, 248–251, 259–263; arms control, 260, 262–263; arms expenditures, 387–388; arms reductions, 261; war, 257

Office of Technology Assessment (OTA), 352–353
oil import fee, 60, 86, 102, 202
OPEC, 77, 310, 352

Pan American Energy and Environmental Security Alliance, 91, 102, 103–104
pay equity, 396–406
pensions, 252, 397; funds, 92, 93; portable, 12, 26, 147
Pentagon, 302; and defense budget, 242, 257, 258; and Defense Guidance, 256–257; management, 265
People for the American Way, 433–434
performance pay, 10, 11, 12, 145
Philippines, 210, 213, 215, 224
poverty, 90, 112, 119, 152, 159, 185, 270, 368–379; and children, 294, 370; and education, 369, 374, 375; and hunger, 380–388; and IMR, 382–383; and the economy, 369, 372; and transportation, 387; and unemployment, 119, 371; and welfare, 371–372, 375; diversity of, 368–376; feminization of, 374, 396–397; Jargowsky and Bane on, policy, 368–379; Leland on, 380–388; myths of, 370–371; Reagan administration and, 112, 150, 294
profit sharing, 10, 19, 173
Progressive National Consumption Tax, 7, 310
prosperity, 195, 269–270; Republican and Democratic views on, 165–174
protectionism, 31–32, 55, 67, 81–82, 144, 204–205, 216, 228, 232–233, 236, 246
Public Health Service, and AIDS, 461, 463, 467

Railroad Retirement, 126
Readfare, 72
Reagan administration, 30, 76–77, 80–81, 89–90, 97, 107, 109, 110–112, 122, 135, 184, 189–197, 498–506; and AIDS, 461–470; and defense spending, 80–81, 115, 499–500, 502, 504; and deficit reduction, 80–81; and drug abuse, 394; and education, 150; and EEOC, 406; and EPA, 150; and employment programs, 150; and farm policy, 347–348, 351, 354, 359–361; and FAA, 150; and free trade, 97; and Gramm-Rudman-Hollings Act, 198–

208; and homelessness, 290; and housing programs, 291–293, 297; and industry, 52–54; and job training programs, 150, 294; and nutrition programs, 150; and poverty, 112, 150, 294; and social justice, 168; and taxes, 191, 199, 502; and the budget deficit, 13–14, 52–54, 64, 68–69, 76–77, 89–90, 149–156, 189–197, 198–208, 498–506; and trade, 225; and TAA, 74; and unemployment, 122; Cohen on, 507–510; economic policies of, 89–90, 107, 110–112, 114–115, 198–208, 498–506; energy policies of, 101–102

Reagan, Ronald, 52, 54, 56, 68, 89–90, 97, 100, 110–111, 122, 153, 168, 176, 189, 194–195, 198–208, 256, 257, 259, 305, 306, 307, 348, 351, 450, 484, 498–506, 507–510

Redford, Robert, and IRM, 447–448; on environmental resources, 445–450

Reemployment Assistance Program (REAP), 35, 38, 45

Reich, Robert, 165–174, 530; on prosperity, 165–174; on social justice, 165–166; on the economy, 165–174

Reingold, Edwin, 281–282

Religious Right, 433–434

Republicans, conservative, and social justice and prosperity, 165–174

research and development, 40, 48, 49, 53, 61, 76, 104, 337, 340; civilian, 25–26, 48, 49, 70, 92, 94, 115–116; military, 25–26, 95, 104, 115–116

Ride, Sally, 451–460, 529–530; on NASA space program, 451–460

Riley, Jr., Joseph, 313–332, 530–531; on urban investment policy, 313–332

Rivlin, Alice, 175–180; on the federal budget, 175–180

Robb, Charles, 139–148, 156, 531; on democratic capitalism, 144–147; on economics, 139–148

Roosevelt, Franklin, 1, 3, 78, 116–117, 130, 136, 140

Schroeder, Patricia, 106–117, 240–247, 396, 531–532; on global economy, 106–117; on national defense, 240–247

Schumer, Charles, 218–225, 532; and Schumer Options Plan, 223–224; on the debt crisis, 218–225

Schumer Options Plan, 223–224

Senate, 223, 356; Budget Committee, 314

Simon, Paul, 118–136, 533; and Guaranteed Job Opportunity Program, 123–136; on unemployment, 118–136

Singapore, 226, 228, 239, 483

Six Point Agenda Toward a Full Employment Economy, 414–422

Smith, Adam, 111, 500

social justice, 97, 190, 194, 195, 342; and economic growth, 165–174; Republican and Democratic views on, 165–174

Social Security, 6, 80, 140, 154, 160–161, 191, 199, 322, 377, 397; Act, 508, 509; and Guaranteed Job Opportunity Program, 126, 130; tax payments, 373

Sonnenfeldt, Michael, 498–506, 534; on the defense budget, 499–500, 502, 504; on the Reagan administration, 498–506

South Korea, 5, 95–96, 98, 207, 214, 234; and foreign trade, 226, 228, 230, 239, 483; and U.S. defense, 241–242

Soviet Union, 211; and ABM Treaty, 257; and arms control, 257, 260–263; and nuclear war, 257; economy of, 226; education in the, 283, 285; expansionism, 242, 264; military, 244, 246, 247, 259; space program of the, 451–452

Special Supplementary Food Program for Women, Infants and Children, 378, 383

Star Wars see Strategic Defense Initiative

Strategic Defense Initiative (SDI), 61, 84, 85, 112, 179, 257, 262, 280, 445

Strategic Investment Initiative, 84–86

student loans, 22, 110, 155, 273

sunset legislation, 59–60

Supplementary Security Income, 377

supply-side economics, 52, 176, 502–503

Supreme Court, 182, 183, 200, 403

Taiwan, 204, 207, 226, 228, 229, 230, 234, 239, 483
tax(es), 11, 18, 45, 80–81, 122, 179, 182, 189–197, 318, 431; Babbitt on, 6–7; compliance, 45, 311; Gephardt on, 58–59; Hollings on, 201–203; Progressive National Consumption, 7, 310; Reagan administration and, 191, 199, 502; real estate, and unemployment, 120; Republicans and, reduction, 167; revenue, 80, 179, 184, 310–311; Social Security, payments, 373; telephone, 202; value-added, 202, 233
Tax Bill of 1981, 184, 191
Tax Reform Act (1988), 18, 58, 154; and Bradley-Gephardt Fair Tax Bill, 58; and housing, 292
Third World, 53, 60, 68, 78, 80, 81, 96, 114, 116, 349, 356–357; and UNICEF, 384; debt, 53, 60, 68, 78, 116, 209–217, 218–225; defense of, 260, 266; political stability of, 263–264
Thomas Edison Program, 49, 275–280
Title XX Social Services Block Grant, 418–419
trade, 14, 67, 226–239, 420–422, 431; Choate and Linger on, 226–239; free, 31–32, 55, 81, 97, 198; Gephardt on, 53–56; Gore on, 67–68; Hart on, 79–88; Hollings on, 203–207; Jackson on, 94–100; laws, 207–208, 319; protectionist, 31–32, 55, 67, 81–82, 144, 204–205; unfair, practices, 28, 319; U.S., policies, 226–239, 366, 429; see also trade deficit
Trade Act of 1934, Section 201 of, 155, 205–206
Trade Adjustment Assistance (TAA), 27, 74, 85, 155
trade deficit, 14, 24, 52, 53–54, 64, 65, 67, 77, 79, 80, 81, 108, 111, 193, 216, 221, 287, 507; reduction, 193–194
Trade Enforcement Act, 205–207
Treasure Department, 222, 224, 225

unemployment, 76, 89, 118–136, 250, 270, 295, 317, 395, 410–413, 419, 420, 423–432; abroad, 78; and crime, 121, 426; and federal expenditures, 122; and foreign imports, 72; and poverty, 119, 371, 375; benefits, 26–27, 155, 252; compensation, 119, 122; insurance, 26–27, 140, 294, 409, 418, 429; Massachusetts, rates, 33–35, 41; Simon on, 118–136
unemployment compensation, 119, 122; and Guaranteed Job Opportunity Program, 124, 127
unemployment insurance, 27, 140, 294, 409, 418, 429, 508
United Nations, Children's Fund (UNICEF), 380, 384; Food and Agriculture Organization of the, 381
United Nations Children's Fund (UNICEF), 380, 384, 388; Child Survival Initiative of, 384
U.S. Air Force, 243, 388
U.S. Army, 243, 258; National Guard, 243; Reserves, 243
U.S. Navy, 243, 258, 263, 284
Universal Needs Test, 6
urban policy, Koch on, 305–312; Riley on, 313–332

value-added tax (VAT), 202, 233
Volcker, Paul, 167–168
voodoo economics, 110–111, 199

wage, 411, 431; gap, 396–406; insurance, 26–27; minimum, 124, 154, 373, 385–386, 409, 418, 428; two-tier, 171
War on Poverty, 151, 152, 311
Warsaw Pact, 244, 245, 262–263
Washington, George, 111, 205
Weinberger, Caspar, 256–257, 258, 266
Weiss, Ted, 248–255, 534; and Defense Economic Adjustment Act, 251–254; and Economic Adjustment Fund, 252; on economic conversion, 248–255
Weitzman, Martin, 154–155
welfare, 119, 122, 183, 185, 270, 271, 272, 369, 371–372, 374–375, 378; and Guaranteed Job Opportunity Program, 124, 125, 127; and poverty, 371–372, 375; and work performance, 155; reform, 196–197, 272–274, 320, 371–372, 375, 507; state, 152–153, 156; -to-work program, 185
Western Alliance, 244, 247

West Germany, American defense of,
    241, 245; and foreign trade,
    230, 233, 234, 235; education
    in, 285; military, 263
Will, George, and *Statecraft as
    Soulcraft*, 427
Wilson, Woodrow, 181–182, 183, 185
Workfare, 125, 127, 371, 378

Works Progress Administration (WPA),
    130–131
World Bank, 75, 93, 215; and foreign
    debt, 30, 60–61, 217, 221; and
    hunger, 381–382

Zimmerman, Michael, 461–470, 534;
    on AIDS and the Reagan
    administration, 461–470